Authors
K.M. VICKERS
M.J. TIPLER
H.L. van HIELE

Copyright ©
K.M. VICKERS
H.L. van HIELE

First Published January 1993
Reprinted three times in 1993
Reprinted January 1994
Reprinted May 1994

ISBN 1-873941-06-4

Published by
Canterbury Educational Ltd
Canterbury House
1 Sheffield Road
Southborough
Tunbridge Wells
Kent TN4 0PD

Printed at
The Alden Press
Oxford

1

PREFACE

"National Curriculum Mathematics" by K.M. Vickers, M.J. Tipler and H.L. van Hiele is a complete course of seven books for pupils aged from 11 to 16. This is the sixth of the seven books. It covers all the material in Level 8 of the National Curriculum. This book is arranged in four separate sections: Number, Algebra, Shape and Space, Data Handling. Using and Applying Mathematics is integrated throughout each chapter of these sections. The material is presented in this order to enable a pupil, or a group of pupils, to work across different areas of mathematics at different levels, as required by the National Curriculum.

Each section begins with revision from Levels 1 to 7, printed on pink paper for ease of identification and to distinguish it from Level 8 material. Each section ends with a review chapter which contains revision questions on the Level 8 material. In each of the other chapters, every skill developing exercise finishes with review questions.

This book does not replace the teacher. Rather, it is a resource for both the pupil and the teacher. The teacher can be flexible about what is taught and when.

Throughout the book there is a variety of activities: skill developing exercises, investigations, practical work, problem solving activities, discussion exercises and games. All the activities are related to the topic being studied. Whenever possible, activities and exercises have been written as open rather than closed tasks.

There is a good balance between tasks which develop knowledge, skills and understanding, and those which develop the ability to tackle and solve problems. Many activities do both. There is a thorough and careful development of each topic. Questions within each exercise or activity are carefully graded to build pupil confidence.

This book takes into consideration:
- pupils' needs
- pupils' interests
- pupils' experiences

- the need for pupils to explore mathematics
- the use of technology
- both independent and co-operative work habits

This book encourages pupils to:
- use a wide range of mathematics
- discuss mathematical ideas
- undertake investigations
- participate in practical activities
- use reference material

- relate mathematics to everyday life
- select appropriate methods for a task
- analyse and communicate information
- discuss difficulties
- ask questions

2

It is hoped that the pupil who uses this book will:
  develop a real interest in mathematics
  become well motivated
  gain much enjoyment from mathematics
  develop a fascination with mathematics
  develop an ability to use mathematics in other subjects
  become confident in the use of the calculator and computer
  gain a firm foundation for further study
  become proficient at applying mathematics to everyday life
  develop both independent and co-operative work habits
  become aware of the power and purpose of mathematics
  develop an ability to communicate mathematics
  develop an appreciation of the relevance of mathematics
  develop an ability to think precisely, logically and creatively
  become confident at mathematics
  gain a sense of satisfaction

Calculator keying sequences are for the Casio FX82C and FX82D calculators. Some slight variation may be needed for other makes and models.
The programming language used is BBC BASIC.

K.M. Vickers

Acknowledgements

The author wishes to thank all those firms and enterprises who have so kindly given permission to reproduce tables and other material. A special thanks to S.P.R. Coxon, I. Kelderman, S.C. Lees-Jeffries, J.A. Ogilvie and S. Napier for their valuable contributions and to F. Tunnicliffe for the illustrations.

Every effort has been made to trace all the copyright holders. If any have been inadvertently overlooked the publishers will be pleased to make the necessary arrangement at the first opportunity.

Contents

ALGEBRA

SHAPE and SPACE

DATA HANDLING

LEVEL 8

Programme of Study

Statements of Attainment

AT1 ● devising and extending a mathematical task, making a detailed plan of the work; working methodically; checking information; considering whether results are of the right order.

a) Give logical accounts of work with reasons for choice made.

● making statements of conjecture using 'if ... then ...'; defining, reasoning, proving and disproving, using counter-examples.

b) Understand the role of counter-examples in disproving generalisations or hypotheses.

● construct an extended chain or argument using 'if ... then ...' appropriately.

AT2 ● expressing and using numbers in standard index form, with positive and negative integer powers of 10.

a) Calculate with numbers expressed in standard form.

● using index notations to represent powers and roots.

● substituting negative numbers into formulae involving addition, subtraction, multiplication and division.

b) Evaluate formulae, including the use of fractions or negative numbers.

● calculating with fractions.

● estimating and approximating to check that the results of calculations are of the right order.

c) Solve numerical problems, checking that the results are of the right order of magnitude.

AT3 ● manipulating algebraic expressions.

a) Manipulate algebraic formulae, equations or expressions.

● understanding and using a range of formulae and functions.

● understanding the relationship between powers and roots.

● understanding direct and inverse proportions.

● interpreting and using m and c in
$y = mx + c$

- solving a variety of linear and other inequalities.

b) Solve inequalities.

- using straight-line graphs to locate regions given by linear inequalities.

- knowing the form of graphs of simple functions, eg quadratic, cubic, reciprocal.

c) Interpret graphs which represent particular relationships.

- interpreting graphs which describe real-life situations and contexts.

AT4
- understanding and using mathematical similarity; knowing that angles remain unchanged and corresponding sides are in the same ratio.

a) Use mathematical similarity to solve problems.

- using sine, cosine and tangent in right-angled triangles, in 2-D.

b) Use sine, cosine or tangent in right-angled triangles.

- distinguishing between formulae for perimeter, area and volume by considering dimensions.

c) Distinguish between formulae by considering dimensions.

- understanding and using vector notation, including its use in describing translations.

AT5
- designing and using a questionnaire with multiple responses or an experiment with several variables, collating and analysing results to test a hypothesis.

a) Design and use a questionnaire or experiment to test a hypothesis.

- constructing a cumulative frequency table.

b) Construct and interpret a cumulative frequency curve.

- constructing a cumulative frequency curve using the upper boundary of the class interval, finding the median, upper quartile, lower quartile and inter-quartile range, and interpreting the results.

- calculating the probability of a combined event given the probability of two independent events, and illustrating the combined probabilities of several events using tabulation or tree diagrams.

c) Calculate the probability of a combined event given the probabilities of independent events.

- understanding that when dealing with two independent events, the probability of them both happening is less than the probability of either of them happening (unless the probability is 0 or 1).

9

NUMBER

Number from Previous Levels

Calculation with the Calculator

The scientific calculator does operations in the correct order. An expression such as 14 – 2 (5 + 1) is keyed in as ⌷14⌷ ⌷–⌷ ⌷2⌷ ⌷×⌷ ⌷[⌷ ⌷5⌷ ⌷+⌷ ⌷1⌷ ⌷]⌷ ⌷=⌷ to get the correct answer of 2. (Some calculators do not need the × pressed before the [sign.)

We sometimes need to insert brackets or use the memory function.

For instance, $\dfrac{29 + 6}{4 + 3}$ can be worked out in one of the following ways.

Either **Key** ⌷[⌷ ⌷29⌷ ⌷+⌷ ⌷6⌷ ⌷]⌷ ⌷÷⌷ ⌷[⌷ ⌷4⌷ ⌷+⌷ ⌷3⌷ ⌷]⌷ ⌷=⌷

or **Key** ⌷29⌷ ⌷+⌷ ⌷6⌷ ⌷=⌷ ⌷Min⌷ ⌷4⌷ ⌷+⌷ ⌷3⌷ ⌷=⌷ ⌷INV⌷ ⌷X ↔ M⌷ ⌷÷⌷ ⌷MR⌷ ⌷=⌷

Calculation without the Calculator

If an expression such as 14 – 2 (5 + 1) is worked out without the calculator we must
1. work out the brackets first
2. then do × and ÷
3. finally do + and –

For instance, 14 – 2 (5 + 1) $= 14 - 2 \times 6$
$$= 14 - 12$$
$$= 2$$

The word "of", used in calculation, means "multiply".

For instance, $\frac{5}{6}$ of 42 means $\frac{5}{6} \times 42$. That is, $\frac{5}{6}$ of 42 = 35.

3^4 is read as "three to the power of four" and means $3 \times 3 \times 3 \times 3$. That is, $3^4 = 81$.

To multiply 23 × 90, without using the calculator, first multiply 23 by 10 to get 230; then multiply 230 by 9 to get 2070.

To divide 3600 by 400, without using the calculator, first divide 3600 by 100 to get 36; then divide 36 by 4 to get 9.

Methods for **long multiplication** and **long division**, without using the calculator, follow.

continued . . .

. . . *from previous page*

895 × 41

	800	90	5
40	32000	3600	200
1	800	90	5

$$895 \times 41 = 32000 + 3600 + 200$$
$$+ 800 + 90 + 5$$
$$= 36695$$

895 ÷ 41

	41		
			895
10	410	−	410
			485
10	410	−	410
			75
1	41	−	41
21			34
↑			↑
answer			remainder

Writing a Number as a Product of Prime Factors. HCF, LCM.

This "factor tree" can be used to rewrite 90 as 2 × 3 × 3 × 5.

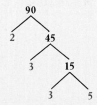

The **highest common factor (HCF)** of two numbers is the greatest number that is a factor of both of the given numbers.
For instance, since 36 = 2 × 2 × 3 × 3 and 90 = 2 × 3 × 3 × 5, the HCF of 36 and 90 is 2 × 3 × 3 i.e. 18.

The **lowest common multiple (LCM)** of two numbers is the smallest number that is a multiple of both of the given numbers. The lowest common multiple is sometimes called the **least common multiple.**
For instance, since 36 = 2 × 2 × 3 × 3 and 90 = 2 × 3 × 3 × 5, the LCM of 36 and 90 is 2 × 2 × 3 × 3 × 5 i.e. 180.

Decimals

Place value is given by the following.

100000	10000	1000	100	10	1 •	$\frac{1}{10}$	$\frac{1}{100}$	$\frac{1}{1000}$

For instance, the number 4809·203 consists of   four thousands
     eight hundreds
     nine ones (or units)
     two tenths
and three thousandths

continued . . .

. . . *from previous page*

A decimal such as 0·166666..., in which the digit 6 repeats, is called a **recurring decimal**; it is written as 0·1̇6̇. Recurring decimals are sometimes called **repeating decimals.**

Multiplying a given number by a number greater than 1 will increase the given number. Multiplying by a number smaller than 1 will decrease the given number.
For instance, 12·8 × 2·4 has an answer larger than 12·8; 12·8 × 0·4 has an answer smaller than 12·8.

Dividing a given number by a number larger than 1 will decrease the given number. Dividing by a number smaller than 1 will increase the given number.
For instance, 12·8 ÷ 2·4 has an answer smaller than 12·8; 12·8 ÷ 0·4 has an answer larger than 12·8.

Approximation and Estimation

To approximate (round) to d.p. (**decimal places**), decide how many figures are wanted after the decimal point. Omit all the following figures with the proviso that, if the first figure omitted is 5 or larger, increase the last figure kept by 1.
For instance, 34·548 rounded to 1 d.p. is 34·5; 34·548 rounded to 2 d.p. is 34·55.

To approximate to s.f. (**significant figures**), count from the first non-zero figure. Zeros may need to be inserted so the size of the number is unchanged.
For instance, 34·548 rounded to 3 s.f. is 34·5; 34·548 rounded to 1 s.f. is 30; 0·03458 rounded to 2 s.f. is 0·035.

Finding a rough answer to a calculation is called **estimating** an answer. To estimate an answer proceed as follows.

Step 1   Round each number in the calculation to one (or perhaps two) significant figures.

Step 2   Use these rounded figures in the calculation to get an estimate of the answer.

For instance, an estimate of the answer to 212 × 48 is 200 × 50 = 10000.

Always estimate the answer when using the calculator for a calculation.

Problem Solving

The **"trial and improvement"** method of finding an answer to a problem consists of the following steps.

Step 1   Guess a likely answer.

Step 2   Check to see if this answer fits the given facts (the trial).

Step 3   Make a better guess (the improvement).

Repeat from Step 2 until the actual answer is found.

continued . . .

. . . *from previous page*

Number Lines. Negative Numbers

$<$ means "is less than" $>$ means "is greater than".
On a number line, the smaller a number the further to the left it is placed.
For instance, since $2 \cdot 1 < 2 \cdot 8$, $2 \cdot 1$ is to the left of $2 \cdot 8$ on a number line;
since $\frac{4}{5} > \frac{2}{5}$, $\frac{4}{5}$ is to the right of $\frac{2}{5}$ on a number line.

The $\boxed{+/-}$ key on the calculator is pressed to display a negative number.
Positive numbers, such as +2, may be written without any sign.
Negative numbers, such as –2, are always written with the negative sign.
The negative numbers are shown on a number line, or scale, as numbers that are less than zero.

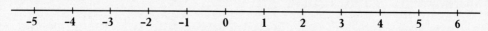

Fractions and Ratio

In the fraction $\frac{4}{9}$, 4 is called the **numerator**; 9 is called the **denominator**.
The numerator is the number on top; the denominator is the number on the bottom.

$\frac{4}{9}$ is read as "four-ninths" and means 4 divided by 9. It also means 4 parts out of every 9.
$\frac{4}{9}$ may also be written as the **ratio** 4 : 9.

The ratio of two quantities x and y is written as x : y and is read as "the ratio of x to y".
A ratio compares quantities of the same kind.
For instance, if A = 3cm and B = 7mm then the ratio A : B is 3cm : 7mm which is 30mm : 7mm or simply 30 : 7.

Equivalent fractions (equal fractions) may be formed by multiplying (or dividing) both the numerator and denominator by the same number.

For instance, since $\frac{16}{24} = \frac{32}{48}$ (multiplying top and bottom by 2)

and $\frac{16}{24} = \frac{2}{3}$ (dividing top and bottom by 8)

then $\frac{2}{3}, \frac{16}{24}, \frac{32}{48}$ are equivalent fractions.

continued . . .

. . . from previous page

Equivalent ratios (equal ratios) may be formed by multiplying (or dividing) both parts of a ratio by the same number.

For instance, the ratios 2 : 3, 16 : 24 and 32 : 48 are equivalent ratios.

A fraction (or ratio) is written as the **simplest fraction** (or **simplest ratio**) if the numbers in the fraction (or ratio) are the smallest possible whole numbers. A fraction written in its simplest form is said to be written in its **lowest terms**.

For instance, since $\frac{16}{24} = \frac{2}{3}$ we say that, in its lowest terms the fraction $\frac{16}{24}$ is $\frac{2}{3}$.

For instance, since $1{\cdot}2 : 3 = 12 : 30 = 2 : 5$, we say that $1{\cdot}2 : 3$ written as the simplest ratio is 2 : 5.

All decimals may be written as fractions.

It is useful to remember the following: $0{\cdot}1 = \frac{1}{10}$, $0{\cdot}2 = \frac{1}{5}$, $0{\cdot}3 = \frac{3}{10}$, $0{\cdot}4 = \frac{2}{5}$, $0{\cdot}5 = \frac{1}{2}$, $0{\cdot}6 = \frac{3}{5}$, $0{\cdot}7 = \frac{7}{10}$, $0{\cdot}8 = \frac{4}{5}$, $0{\cdot}9 = \frac{9}{10}$, $0{\cdot}25 = \frac{1}{4}$, $0{\cdot}75 = \frac{3}{4}$.

To **increase** (or decrease) a quantity **by a given fraction** firstly work out the actual increase (or decrease).

For instance, to decrease 720cm by $\frac{1}{3}$ proceed as follows:

> *Step 1* $\frac{1}{3}$ of 720cm = 240cm
>
> *Step 2* Decrease 720cm by 240cm to get the answer of 480cm.

To **increase** (or decrease) a quantity **in a given ratio** firstly rewrite the ratio as a fraction.

For instance, to increase 100g in the ratio 5 : 4 proceed as follows:

> *Step 1* Rewrite 5 : 4 as $\frac{5}{4}$.
>
> *Step 2* Find $\frac{5}{4} \times 100g = 125g$.

To **share in a given ratio** proceed as shown in the following example.

Example To share £600 between two people in the ratio 2 : 3 take the following steps:

> *Step 1* For every £2 that the first person gets, the second person gets £3. That is, from every £5, the first person gets £2 and the second person gets £3.
>
> Hence the first person gets $\frac{2}{5}$ of the money; the second person gets $\frac{3}{5}$.
>
> *Step 2* $\frac{2}{5}$ of £600 = £240; $\frac{3}{5}$ of £600 = £360.
>
> Hence one person gets £240 and the other gets £360.

continued . . .

. . . *from previous page*

Percentages

7% means 7 parts in every 100. That is, 7% means $\frac{7}{100}$.

Any percentage, decimal, fraction or ratio may be written in one of the other forms.

For instance, 7% may be rewritten as $\frac{7}{100}$ or 0·07 or 7 : 100.

For instance, $\frac{2}{5}$ may be rewritten as 0·4 or 40% or 2 : 5.

For instance, 0·61 may be rewritten as $\frac{61}{100}$ or 61% or 61 : 100.

For instance, 3 : 4 may be rewritten as $\frac{3}{4}$ or 0·75 or 75%.

In **percentage calculations** we usually rewrite the percentage as either a fraction or a decimal.

For instance, to find 15% of £5 we may begin with $\frac{15}{100} \times £5$ or 0·15 × £5 to get answer of 75p.

To **write a given quantity as a percentage of another quantity** proceed as follows:

Step 1   Write the given quantity as a fraction of the other quantity.

Step 2   Rewrite this fraction as a percentage.

For instance, £5 as a fraction of £8 is $\frac{5}{8} = \frac{5}{8} \times 100\%$
$$= 62\cdot5\%$$

Time Measure

$$1 \text{ minute} = 60 \text{ seconds}$$
$$1 \text{ hour} = 60 \text{ minutes}$$
$$1 \text{ day} = 24 \text{ hours}$$
$$1 \text{ year} = 365 \text{ days (or 366 days in a leap year)}$$

April, June, September, November have 30 days.

January, March, May, July, August, October, December have 31 days.

February has 28 days except in a leap year when it has 29 days.

All years that are divisible by 4 are **leap years** except centuries which are leap years only if they are divisible by 400. For instance, 1600 and 1988 were leap years; 1900 and 1986 were not.

a.m. time is from midnight until noon; p.m. time is from noon until midnight. For instance, 1100 hours is 11a.m., 2300 hours is 11p.m.

continued . . .

. . . *from previous page*

Metric Measures

length	km	hm	Dm	**m**	dm	cm	mm
capacity	k*l*	h*l*	D*l*	***l***	d*l*	c*l*	m*l*
mass	kg	hg	Dg	**g**	dg	cg	mg

Each unit on the table is 10 times as large as the unit immediately to its right. The relationships between the metric units in common use are as follows.

Length
1km = 1000m
1m = 1000mm
1m = 100cm
1cm = 10mm

Capacity
1*l* = 1000m*l*
1m*l* = 1cm^3 (1c.c.)

Mass
1kg   = 1000g
1g   = 1000mg
1 tonne = 1000kg

Imperial Measure and Metric Measure

Some **imperial units** still in common use and the relationships between these units are as follows.

Length
1 mile = 1760 yards
1 yard = 3 feet
1 foot = 12 inches

Capacity
1 gallon = 8 pints

Mass
1 ton   = 160 stone
1 stone = 14lb
1 lb   = 16oz

Rough approximations between imperial and metric units are:

1kg is about $2\frac{1}{4}$ lb, 1 litre is about $1\frac{3}{4}$ pints, 1 inch is about $2\frac{1}{2}$ cm,

5 miles is about 8km,   1m is a little longer than 3 feet.

Compound Measures

average speed = $\dfrac{\text{distance travelled}}{\text{time taken}}$ $\left(v = \dfrac{s}{t}\right)$ Units for speed are km/h, m/s, mph.

density = $\dfrac{\text{mass}}{\text{volume}}$ $\left(d = \dfrac{m}{v}\right)$ Units for density are g/cm^3, kg/m^3.

continued . . .

. . . from previous page

Possible Error in a Measurement

The maximum possible error in a measurement is half a unit. That is, a measurement given to the nearest mm has a possible error of 0·5mm, a measurement given to the nearest tenth of a second has a possible error of half of one-tenth of a second i.e. 0·05sec.

For instance, a distance given as 289km could be between 288·5km and 289·5km.

REVISION EXERCISE

1. How much larger is the 9 than the 5 in **(a)** 6925 **(b)** 19·035?

2.

   At both of these shops a CD usually costs £8·80.
   Shadia buys a CD in the sale at the Stereo Market. Lucy buys a CD in the sale at the Audio Discount Store.
   Who pays more, Shadia or Lucy? How much more?

3. Without doing any calculation, state which of these will have an answer greater than 269·7.

   (a) 269·7 × 0·34   (b) 269·7 ÷ 0·34   (c) 269·7 × 3·4   (d) 269·7 ÷ 3·4

4. Write the following as the simplest possible fraction.

   (a) $\frac{4}{50}$ (b) 0·24   (c) 5 : 30   (d) 30%   (e) 0·007

5. During each week day, Mrs Allen's central heating is set as shown.
   How long is the heating on during each of these days?

On	Off
0630	0915
1600	2130

6. Which of the following years were (or will be) leap years?

   1896   1900   1902   1975   1990   2000   2020   2034

7.

km   m   mm   t   kg   g   mg   *l*   m*l*

Which of the units of measurement in the box would most likely be used for

(a) the width of a postage stamp   (b) the mass of an apple
(c) the weight of a ship's cargo   (d) the height of a flagpole
(e) the distance of a marathon   (f) the mass of a postage stamp
(g) the capacity of a teacup?

8. Without using the calculator find

(a) $11 + 3 \times 7$ (b) $27 - 2(4 + 3)$ (c) 248×34 (d) $868 \div 28$

(e) 7^2 (f) 600×0.3 (g) $\dfrac{600}{0.3}$ (h) $\frac{5}{6}$ of 54.

9. Elizabeth made a scale drawing of the floor plan of one of the school buildings. She used the scale 1 : 50.
   (a) On the drawing, one of the rooms was 160mm long. What was the actual length of this room?
   (b) The building was 12 metres wide. What was the width of the building on the drawing?

10.

County	Primary Schools	Primary Pupils	Secondary Schools	Secondary Pupils
Cheshire	473	80037	72	65801
Durham	299	48929	45	36489
Devon	433	69529	73	55116
Gwent	229	39895	34	28359

This table gives the number of primary and secondary schools in four counties and the number of pupils in these schools.

(a) **Estimate** the total number of primary and secondary schools in these counties. Calculate this number.
(b) Find the average number of pupils in the secondary schools in these counties.

11. Write these ratios in their simplest form.

(a) £2 : 90p   (b) 1·6m : 480cm   (c) 45sec : 2min

12. Find the missing numbers.

(a) 384mm = . . . cm   (b) 2·4km = . . . m   (c) 1·74*l* = . . . m*l*
(d) 194m = . . . km   (e) 0·7t = . . . kg   (f) 2825g = . . . kg

13.

⑫	74 miles	⑬	51 miles	⑭	45 miles	⑮

The distances between motorway service areas 12, 13, 14 and 15 are shown.

(a) Roger stops at service area 13 and again at service area 15. About how many kilometres does he travel between these two stops?

(b) Anne took 36 minutes to travel between service areas 14 and 15.
In mph, what was Anne's average speed?

(c) The capacity of the petrol tank of Sandhya's car is 60 litres. The petrol consumption rate of this car is 17km/*l*. Petrol costs 51p per litre.
Sandhya fills her tank at service area 12 and again at service area 15.
How much does it cost her for the petrol she buys at service area 15?

14. In Winchester, at 5p.m., the temperature was 2°C. The expected temperature at midnight was –3°C.

(a) How many degrees was the temperature expected to fall between 5p.m. and midnight?

(b) If the temperature at midnight was 1°C lower than expected, what was the midnight temperature?

15. (a) How much, in German money, will it cost Amanda to have one of these tape recorders sent to her?

(b) When Amanda bought marks, the exchange rate was £1 = 2·73 marks.
How much British money does Amanda need to exchange to buy one of these tape recorders?

> **Tape Recorders**
> TOP QUALITY
> **Special Price: 80 marks**
>
> **Packing & Postage:
> 15 marks**
> (worldwide)

16. Melanie is doing a survey on oak trees. She measures the circumference of the trunk of one tree as 66·2cm. If Melanie's measurement is correct to the nearest tenth of a centimetre find (a) the greatest possible circumference
(b) the least possible circumference of this tree.

17. For a coursework task, Ben gained $\frac{5}{8}$ of the available marks while Natasha gained $\frac{2}{3}$.

(a) Who got the better mark, Ben or Natasha?

(b) If a : b gives the ratio of Ben's mark to Natasha's, find possible values for a and b.

18. 0·1$\dot{6}$ Write this (a) as a decimal, rounded to 2 decimal places
(b) as a percentage, rounded to 3 significant figures.

19. In manufacturing today, the average number of hours worked per week is 43·4. Fifty years ago, this average was 47·8 hours.
What percentage decrease is this? (Answer to 1 decimal place.)

20. (a) Find the volume of this fish tank, in cm³.
    (b) Jerry pours water into this tank at the rate of 120 m*l* per second.
    How long does it take Jerry to completely fill the tank?

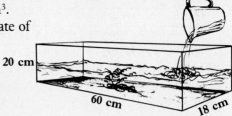

20 cm   60 cm   18 cm

21. Use your calculator for the following. Give the answers to three significant figures.

    (a) $\dfrac{13{\cdot}7 - 8{\cdot}08}{5{\cdot}61 + 1{\cdot}35}$

    (b) $\dfrac{\sqrt{687}}{3\,(14{\cdot}7 + 7{\cdot}24)}$

22. The ratio of British coins to foreign coins in Samantha's coin collection is 2 : 5.
    Samantha has 28 British coins.
    How many foreign coins does she have?

23.

European Communities Population Comparisons		
Country	**Population** (thousands)	**Percentage of Population**
		Under 15 · **65 and over**
Belgium	9,901·7	19·0 · 13·9
Denmark	5,129·5	17·9 · 15·3
France	55,883·7	20·8 · 13·3
Germany	61,444·7	14·7 · 15·2
Greece	10,004·4	20·3 · 13·5
Ireland	3,538·0	28·7 · 10·9
Italy	57,451·9	18·4 · 13·4
Luxembourg	373·3	16·9 · 13·3
Netherlands	14,758·6	18·8 · 12·3
Portugal	10,286·2	22·7 · 12·4
Spain	38,809·0	22·3 · 12·3
United Kingdom	57,065·6	18·9 · 15·5

Source: Key Data 1991/92

(a) What percentage of the Spanish population is aged between 15 and 65?
(b) Which country has the greatest number of people aged under 15?
(c) Which country has the smallest percentage of people aged between 15 and 65?

24. (a) Written as a product of prime factors $180 = 2 \times 2 \times 3 \times 3 \times 5$.
    Write 84 in a similar way.
    (b) Find the LCM of 84 and 180.
    (c) Find the HCF of 84, 108, and 180.

25. Mariette's family were refunded the £26·25 VAT paid on photographic equipment they had bought while on holiday in England.

    What price (including $17\frac{1}{2}$% VAT) had they paid for this equipment?

Visitors

Claim back $17\frac{1}{2}$% VAT here.

26.

PRICES PER PERSON in £s Minimum two persons	THREE-NIGHT WEEKEND Friday–Monday		SEVEN-NIGHT HOLIDAY		EXTRA NIGHTS (Add to 7 night stays only)	
	BY CAR-FERRY SHORT SEA-CROSSING	FLY-DRIVE, BY AIR HEATHROW-PARIS	BY CAR-FERRY SHORT SEA-CROSSING	FLY-DRIVE, BY AIR HEATHROW-PARIS	BY CAR-FERRY	FLY-DRIVE
NORMANDY HOTEL DE DIEPPE, Rouen. Room & breakfast in twin/double	123	199	239	352	23	36
CHAMPAGNE ALTEA, Rheims Room & breakfast in twin/double	132	208	276	289	Fri/Sat/Sun 26 Mon-Thur 30	Fri/Sat/Sun 39 Mon-Thur 43
LOIRE VALLEY DOMAINE DE SEILLAC, Onzain HALFBOARD: in Chateaux: in twin/double	189	265	393	506	45	58
in 'Pavillon': each of two	162	238	330	443	36	49
each of three	133	215	278	377	31	40
each of four	120	201	256	348	29	36

HOTEL SUPPLEMENTS, Domaine de Seillac — per person per night.
Jul 6 - Aug 25; in Chateau, twin room £3.00; in 'Pavillon' — each of two £6.00; each of three £4.00; each of four £3.00

FERRY SUPPLEMENT, ON WEEKEND/3 NIGHT HOLIDAYS: £22.00 per car July 13 – Sep 2

SUPPLEMENTS FOR DEPARTURES FROM PROVINCIAL AIRPORTS ON DIRECT AIR FRANCE FLIGHTS TO PARIS:-
GATWICK deduct £23; STANSTED/SOUTHAMPTON deduct £7; BRISTOL add £8; BIRMINGHAM add £10 — Except Jul 14 - Sep 13
deduct £16; MANCHESTER add £24; NEWCASTLE add £2; EDINBURGH/GLASGOW add £44; ABERDEEN add £59; BELFAST add £36

(i) Find the cost of a holiday for 2 people for a three-night weekend
   (a) during April, staying in the Hotel de Dieppe, flying from Heathrow
   (b) during May, staying in the Chateaux, flying from Aberdeen
   (c) at the end of July, staying in the Pavillon, taking a car on the ferry.

(ii) Find the cost of a 12-day holiday for 2 people, beginning on a Thursday, staying at the Altea and flying from Gatwick.

27. The density of this paint is 1·4 g/cm³.
    What is the weight of the paint? (Answer in kg.)

28. Aaron's average speed for a road race was 15 km/h. Peter's average speed for this race was 5 m/sec.
    Who finished first; Aaron or Peter?

29. 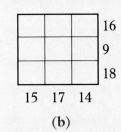 Is it possible to place numbers in the squares which add across and down to the given numbers? If so, find possible answers. If it is not possible, explain why not.

    (a)   (b)

30. Before a meeting of the Governors of Nayworth School, each Governor had one telephone conversation with every other Governor. Altogether there were 45 telephone conversations.
How many Governors did Nayworth School have?

31. $371 = 3^3 + 7^3 + 1^3$ Find another three-digit number that is equal to the sum of the cubes of its digits.

32. An explorer, who can carry supplies for a maximum of 5 days, sets out from base camp. The next camp where supplies will be waiting is 8 days from base camp.
The explorer can reach the next camp by building up supply depots along the way.
For instance, at the end of the first day, 3 days supplies could be left at the first supply depot and the explorer could return to the base camp for more supplies.
Find the minimum number of times the explorer needs to return to base camp for supplies.

Charles Babbage

Charles Babbage was born at Teignmouth, Devon in 1792 and died at London in 1871. He is known as "The Father of Computers."

From 1828 until 1839 he was a professor of mathematics at Cambridge University. He resigned to concentrate on building elaborate calculating machines. He assisted in founding The Royal Astronomical Society, The British Association for the Advancement of Science, The Statistical Society of London and The Analytical Society. The aim of the Analytical Society was to introduce into England methods and notations then used in mathematics in Europe. He produced the first life insurance tables and wrote a book on analysing efficiency in manufacturing.

Babbage's Difference Engine

Babbage is usually best remembered not for these successes but for his failure to complete either his "Difference Engine" or his "Analytical Engine". It has been claimed that the technology at the time was the major cause of the failure but this has been disputed recently. The Difference Engine was to calculate and print, to 26 significant figures, various mathematical tables. Not only did he have government funding for this but he also invested, and lost, most of his own fortune. When this venture failed, he designed the "Analytical Engine" which was to perform many different calculations automatically. Babbage's Difference Engine was built in the 1980s and is in the Science Museum in London. Although Babbage's meticulous drawings for the machine were in existence, they had to be redrawn for modern manufacturing techniques.

It is said that Babbage wrote to the famous poet, Alfred Lord Tennyson, to complain about a couplet in the poem "The Vision of Sin." He is supposed to have written as follows:

> *Every minute dies a man*
> *Every minute one is born.*

I need hardly point out to you that this calculation would tend to keep the population of the world at a standstill, whereas it is a well-known fact that the said sum total is constantly on the increase. I would therefore take the liberty of suggesting that in the next edition of your excellent poem the erroneous calculation to which I refer should be corrected to have it read:

> *Every moment dies a man*
> *And one and a sixteenth is born.*

Strictly speaking this is not correct, the actual figure being so long that I cannot get it into a line, but something must, of course, be conceded to the laws of poetry.

INTRODUCTION

DISCUSSION EXERCISE 1:1

Discuss how to find the answers to the following problems. Find the answers.

1. Jamilah spent one third of her savings on her plane fare and one quarter of the remainder on her accommodation. She then had £120 left for spending money. What was Jamilah's plane fare?

2. To escape, a spy has to cross three borders.
   The spy agrees to pay one half of her money to someone at each border in order to be escorted to the next border.
   The spy needs to have at least £200 left after crossing the last border.
   What is the least amount of money this spy needs in order to escape?

PROPER and IMPROPER FRACTIONS. MIXED NUMBERS

A fraction such as $\frac{7}{8}$ is called a **proper fraction**. In a proper fraction the numerator (top) is smaller than the denominator (bottom).

A fraction such as $\frac{23}{4}$ is called an **improper fraction**. In an improper fraction the numerator is larger than the denominator. Improper fractions can be thought of as being "top heavy".

A number such as $3\frac{2}{5}$ is called a **mixed number.** A mixed number consists of a whole number and a fraction.

DISCUSSION EXERCISE 1:2

Each section of this diagram has been divided into fifths. The shading represents 13 fifths; that is $\frac{13}{5}$. Which mixed number does the shading represent?

Discuss how improper fractions can be rewritten as mixed numbers. Make and test statements as part of your discussion.

● **Discuss** how mixed numbers can be rewritten as improper fractions. Make and test statements as part of your discussion.

Worked Example (a) Rewrite $\frac{25}{6}$ as a mixed number.

(b) Rewrite $3\frac{4}{5}$ as an improper fraction.

Answer (a) $1 = \frac{6}{6}$, $2 = \frac{12}{6}$, $3 = \frac{18}{6}$, $4 = \frac{24}{6}$. (b) 3 can be rewritten as $\frac{15}{5}$.

Hence $\frac{25}{6} = 4\frac{1}{6}$. Hence $3\frac{4}{5} = \frac{19}{5}$.

EXERCISE 1:3

1.

| $\frac{7}{5}$ | $\frac{5}{7}$ | $\frac{2}{5}$ | $\frac{3}{4}$ | $\frac{4}{3}$ | $\frac{17}{4}$ | $\frac{8}{9}$ | $\frac{5}{6}$ | $\frac{6}{5}$ | $\frac{9}{8}$ | $\frac{10}{3}$ | $\frac{3}{10}$ |

(a) Which of these are proper fractions? (b) Which are improper fractions?

2. Write these as mixed numbers.
   (a) $\frac{13}{5}$ (b) $\frac{17}{4}$ (c) $\frac{5}{3}$ (d) $\frac{9}{2}$ (e) $\frac{11}{5}$
   (f) $\frac{19}{6}$ (g) $\frac{25}{2}$ (h) $\frac{25}{3}$ (i) $\frac{36}{7}$ (j) $\frac{14}{9}$

3. Write these as improper fractions.
   (a) $2\frac{3}{4}$ (b) $3\frac{1}{2}$ (c) $2\frac{2}{5}$ (d) $1\frac{5}{8}$ (e) $5\frac{1}{4}$
   (f) $2\frac{5}{6}$ (g) $5\frac{3}{8}$ (h) $7\frac{1}{6}$ (i) $3\frac{4}{9}$ (j) $5\frac{3}{10}$

Review (i) Write as mixed numbers. (a) $\frac{28}{5}$ (b) $\frac{19}{7}$

(ii) Write as improper fractions. (a) $3\frac{1}{4}$ (b) $5\frac{2}{3}$

MULTIPLYING FRACTIONS

DISCUSSION EXERCISE 1:4

- Since $4 \times 5 = 4 + 4 + 4 + 4 + 4$, then $\frac{1}{2} \times 5 = \frac{1}{2} + \frac{1}{2} + \frac{1}{2} + \frac{1}{2} + \frac{1}{2}$. **Discuss** this statement. As part of your discussion, refer to the following diagrams.

$\frac{1}{2} \times 5$

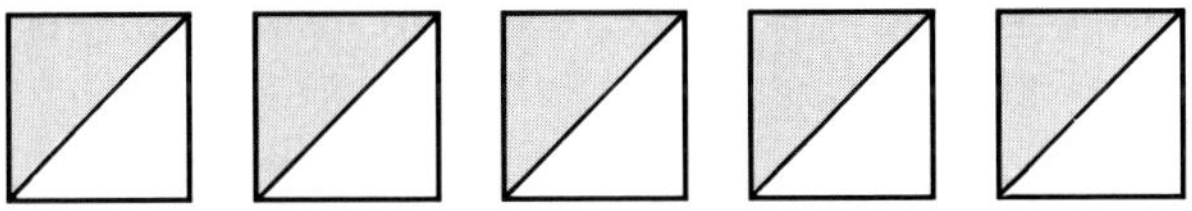

$2\frac{1}{2}$

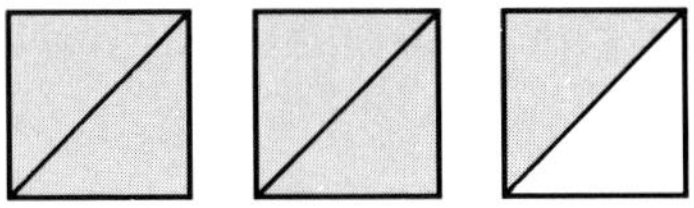

$\frac{1}{2}$ of 5

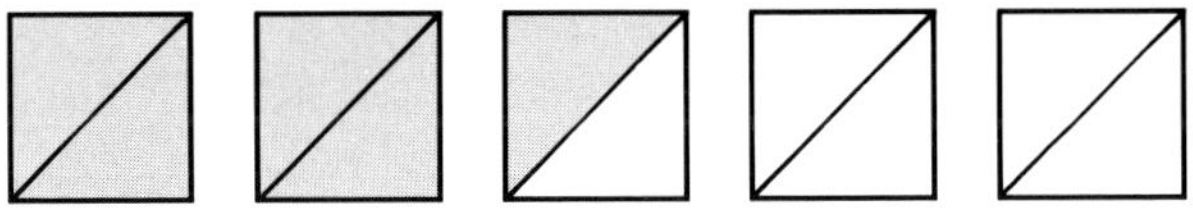

- Use diagrams to find the answers to $\frac{1}{4} \times 6$, $\frac{3}{5} \times 10$, $\frac{2}{3} \times 5$.

  Discuss how the answers could be found without using diagrams.

- 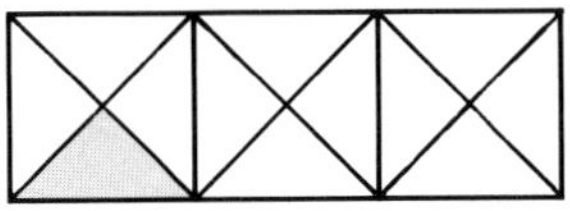 This diagram can be used to find the answer to $\frac{1}{4} \times \frac{1}{3}$. **Discuss.**

- Draw diagrams to find the answers to $\frac{1}{2} \times \frac{1}{5}$, $\frac{3}{4} \times \frac{1}{3}$, $\frac{1}{4} \times \frac{2}{3}$, $\frac{5}{8} \times \frac{3}{4}$, $\frac{3}{8} \times \frac{4}{5}$, $\frac{3}{4} \times \frac{2}{3}$.

  Discuss how the answers could be found without using diagrams.

- 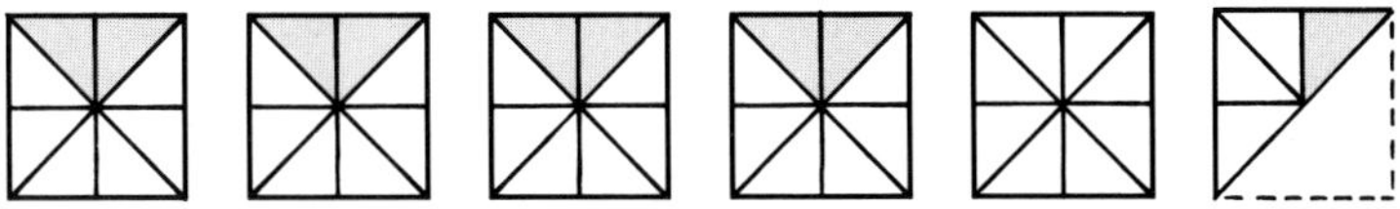 This diagram shows that the answer to $\frac{1}{4} \times 5\frac{1}{2}$ is $\frac{11}{8}$ or $1\frac{3}{8}$.

  Discuss how to draw diagrams to find the answers to $\frac{1}{2} \times 3\frac{1}{4}$, $\frac{3}{4} \times 2\frac{1}{2}$, $\frac{2}{3} \times 3\frac{3}{4}$, $\frac{3}{5} \times 4\frac{1}{3}$.

  Discuss how to find the answers without drawing diagrams.

- **Discuss** how the following diagrams could be used to show that the answer to $2\frac{1}{2} \times 3\frac{2}{5}$ is $8\frac{1}{2}$.

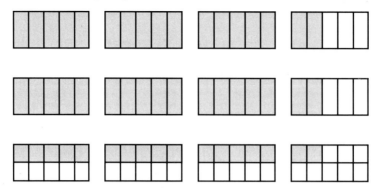

Discuss how the answer to $2\frac{1}{2} \times 3\frac{2}{5}$ could be found without using a diagram. As part of your discussion, you may like to find the answer to other multiplications involving mixed numbers.

- Make and test statements about how to multiply fractions. **Discuss.**

Fraction calculations can be simplified by **cancelling.**

Consider the calculation $\frac{3}{4} \times \frac{6}{5}$.

This may be rewritten as $\frac{3 \times 6}{4 \times 5}$ or as $\frac{3 \times 6}{5 \times 4}$ or as $\frac{3}{5} \times \frac{6}{4}$.

$\frac{6}{4}$ may be replaced by the equivalent fraction $\frac{3}{2}$.

Then $\frac{3}{4} \times \frac{6}{5} = \frac{3}{5} \times \frac{6}{4}$

$= \frac{3}{5} \times \frac{3}{2}$

$= \frac{9}{10}$

The working may be shortened as follows: $\frac{3}{2\cancel{4}} \times \frac{\cancel{6}^3}{5} = \frac{9}{10}$

Rewriting $\frac{3}{4} \times \frac{6}{5}$ as $\frac{3}{2\cancel{4}} \times \frac{\cancel{6}^3}{5}$ is called cancelling.

Example $\frac{\cancel{6}^2}{7} \times \frac{4}{\cancel{9}_3} = \frac{8}{21}$

To multiply fractions:

Step 1   Write any whole numbers or mixed numbers as improper fractions.
Step 2   Cancel if possible.
Step 3   Multiply the numerators; multiply the denominators.
Step 4   If the answer is an improper fraction, write it as a mixed number.

Example $\dfrac{1}{\cancel{2}}_{3} \times \dfrac{7}{\cancel{10}_5} = \dfrac{7}{15}$

Example $4 \times \dfrac{3}{5} = \dfrac{4}{1} \times \dfrac{3}{5}$

$= \dfrac{12}{5}$

$= 2\dfrac{2}{5}$

Example $3\dfrac{3}{4} \times 1\dfrac{1}{5} = \dfrac{^3\cancel{15}}{\cancel{4}_2} \times \dfrac{^3\cancel{6}}{\cancel{5}_1}$

$= \dfrac{9}{2}$

$= 4\dfrac{1}{2}$

EXERCISE 1:5

1. Find the answer to these.

   (a) $\dfrac{2}{5} \times \dfrac{2}{7}$ (b) $\dfrac{2}{3} \times \dfrac{3}{5}$ (c) $\dfrac{5}{12} \times \dfrac{8}{9}$ (d) $\dfrac{2}{3} \times \dfrac{4}{5}$ (e) $\dfrac{5}{6} \times \dfrac{9}{11}$

   (f) $6 \times \dfrac{2}{5}$ (g) $3 \times \dfrac{4}{7}$ (h) $8 \times \dfrac{5}{6}$ (i) $\dfrac{2}{3}$ of $\dfrac{3}{4}$ (j) $\dfrac{3}{8}$ of 6

2. Calculate.

   (a) $2\dfrac{1}{4} \times 3\dfrac{1}{3}$ (b) $2\dfrac{3}{5} \times 1\dfrac{2}{3}$ (c) $3\dfrac{3}{4} \times 1\dfrac{3}{5}$ (d) $3\dfrac{1}{3} \times 1\dfrac{2}{5}$

   (e) $4\dfrac{1}{6} \times 2\dfrac{4}{5}$ (f) $4\dfrac{2}{7} \times 2\dfrac{1}{3}$ (g) $2 \times 1\dfrac{5}{8}$ (h) $4 \times 3\dfrac{1}{3}$

3. Find the answer to these.

   (a) $\left(1\dfrac{1}{2}\right)^2$ (b) $\left(2\dfrac{2}{3}\right)^2$ (c) $\dfrac{2}{3} \times 1\dfrac{2}{5} \times 2\dfrac{1}{7}$ (d) $2\dfrac{1}{2} \times 3\dfrac{3}{10} \times 1\dfrac{2}{3}$

4. Susan claims that three-fifths of one-quarter is the same as three-quarters of one-fifth. Is she correct?

5. Two-fifths of a garden is used to grow vegetables. One-quarter of this is planted in potatoes.
   What fraction of the garden is planted in potatoes?

6. A train travels at an average speed of 96mph.
   How far does it travel in $2\dfrac{1}{4}$ hours?

7. David's bedroom floor measures $3\dfrac{1}{4}$ metres by $3\dfrac{1}{2}$ metres.
   What is the area of this floor?

8. (a) Find three different pairs of fractions which multiply to $\frac{25}{32}$.

(b) $\frac{a}{3} \times \frac{2}{b} = \frac{8}{15}$ What values could **a** and **b** have?
Is there more than one answer?

Review 1   Find the answer to these.

(a) $\frac{2}{3}$ of 8   (b) $\frac{5}{8} \times \frac{4}{15}$ (c) $6 \times 2\frac{2}{3}$ (d) $3\frac{1}{4} \times 1\frac{3}{5}$

Review 2   Find the area of the top of this square table.

DIVIDING FRACTIONS

DISCUSSION EXERCISE 1:6

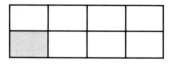

$\frac{1}{4}$ of $\frac{1}{2}$ shaded $\frac{1}{8}$ shaded $\frac{1}{4} \div 2$ shaded

or $\frac{1}{4} \times \frac{1}{2}$ shaded   or $\frac{1}{4} \div \frac{2}{1}$ shaded

Use these diagrams to compare $\frac{1}{4} \times \frac{1}{2}$ with $\frac{1}{4} \div \frac{2}{1}$. **Discuss.**

• Draw diagrams to compare   (a) $\frac{1}{2} \times \frac{1}{3}$ with $\frac{1}{2} \div \frac{3}{1}$ (b) $\frac{2}{5} \times \frac{1}{4}$ with $\frac{2}{5} \div \frac{4}{1}$.

Discuss. As part of your discussion make and test statements about how to divide fractions.

To **divide** by a fraction, multiply by the reciprocal.
Remember: to find the reciprocal of a fraction, invert the fraction. That is, turn the fraction "upside down".

Example $\frac{3}{4} \div 6 = \frac{3}{4} \div \frac{6}{1}$

$$= \frac{\cancel{3}^1}{4} \times \frac{1}{\cancel{6}_2}$$

$$= \frac{1}{8}$$

Example $6 \div \frac{3}{4} = \frac{6}{1} \div \frac{3}{4}$

$$= \frac{2\cancel{6}}{1} \times \frac{4}{\cancel{3}_1}$$

$$= 8$$

Example $\frac{3}{4} \div \frac{5}{12} = \frac{3}{\cancel{4}_1} \times \frac{\cancel{12}^3}{5}$

$$= \frac{9}{5}$$

$$= 1\frac{4}{5}$$

Example $1\frac{2}{3} \div 4\frac{1}{6} = \frac{5}{3} \div \frac{25}{6}$

$$= \frac{1\cancel{5}}{\cancel{3}_1} \times \frac{2\cancel{6}}{\cancel{25}_5}$$

$$= \frac{2}{5}$$

EXERCISE 1:7

---

1. Find the answer to these.

   (a) $\frac{3}{4} \div 3$ (b) $\frac{4}{5} \div 4$ (c) $\frac{9}{10} \div 5$ (d) $\frac{5}{8} \div 4$ (e) $\frac{7}{10} \div 3$

   (f) $3 \div \frac{3}{4}$ (g) $2 \div \frac{4}{5}$ (h) $9 \div \frac{3}{10}$ (i) $8 \div \frac{2}{3}$ (j) $4 \div \frac{1}{5}$

   (k) $\frac{2}{3} \div \frac{1}{2}$ (l) $\frac{7}{10} \div \frac{4}{5}$ (m) $\frac{9}{10} \div \frac{3}{4}$ (n) $\frac{5}{6} \div \frac{2}{3}$

2. Calculate.

   (a) $3\frac{1}{2} \div 2\frac{1}{2}$ (b) $2\frac{3}{4} \div 1\frac{1}{4}$ (c) $1\frac{2}{3} \div 2\frac{2}{3}$ (d) $1\frac{1}{3} \div 2\frac{2}{5}$ (e) $2\frac{3}{8} \div 1\frac{1}{4}$

   (f) $10 \div 1\frac{2}{3}$ (g) $8 \div 2\frac{2}{3}$ (h) $4\frac{1}{2} \div 3$ (i) $2\frac{1}{4} \div \frac{3}{8}$ (j) $3\frac{2}{5} \div \frac{3}{10}$

3. A recipe for a Christmas cake needs $\frac{1}{4}$ lb of flour.
   How many of these cakes can be made from a $2\frac{1}{2}$ lb bag of flour?

4. 1 gallon (8 pints) is about $4\frac{1}{2}$ litres.
   About how many pints is 1 litre?

5. A yacht is sailing at an average speed of $7\frac{1}{2}$ km/h.
   How long will this yacht take to travel 60 km?

6. If $2\frac{1}{2}$kg of fruit costs £3, what is the cost per kg?

7. A hovercraft completes one crossing in three-quarters of an hour.
   What is the greatest number of crossings that it could make in 18 hours?

8. (a) Find three different pairs of fractions which give the answer $\frac{4}{9}$ when they are
       divided.

   (b) $\frac{4}{a} \div \frac{b}{3} = \frac{6}{7}$ What values could **a** and **b** have?
                                       Is there more than one answer?

Review 1   Calculate (a) $\frac{3}{5} \div \frac{9}{10}$ (b) $6 \div \frac{2}{3}$ (c) $3\frac{1}{8} \div 1\frac{2}{3}$.

Review 2   It takes Saad $1\frac{1}{2}$ minutes to make a milkshake?
                 How many could he make in 12 minutes?

Review 3   A short skirt can be made from $\frac{3}{4}$ m of fabric.
                 How many of these skirts could be made from $10\frac{1}{2}$m of this fabric?

INVESTIGATION 1:8

ALL THE DIGITS

$\frac{1}{5} = \frac{2697}{13485}$ Each of the digits 1, 2, 3, 4, 5, 6, 7, 8, 9 has been used once to form
                 the fraction $\frac{1}{5}$.

Can other fractions such as $\frac{1}{2}$, $\frac{1}{3}$, $\frac{1}{4}$ etc. be formed in a similar way? **Investigate.**

$\frac{1}{9} = \frac{10638}{95742}$ Each of the ten digits 0 to 9 has been used once to form the fraction $\frac{1}{9}$.

Can these ten digits be rearranged in other ways to form the fraction $\frac{1}{9}$? **Investigate.**

ADDING and SUBTRACTING FRACTIONS

We can add 10 pence + 14 pence to get answer of 24 pence.
We can add 2a + 5a to get answer of 7a.

We cannot add 3x + 2a; neither can we add 5cm + 6kg.

To add two quantities they must be the same type of quantity.
This statement is also true for fractions.

To **add** (or **subtract**) **fractions** the fractions must be the same type.
Fifths may be added to fifths, quarters may be added to quarters but to add fifths to quarters we must first rewrite as the same type. That is, we must find equivalent fractions which have the same denominator.

Examples $\frac{2}{5} + \frac{1}{5} = \frac{3}{5}$ $\frac{5}{8} - \frac{3}{8} = \frac{2}{8}$

$= \frac{1}{4}$

Example   To find $\frac{4}{5} + \frac{3}{4}$ first find fractions equivalent to $\frac{4}{5}$ and $\frac{3}{4}$ which have the same denominator.

$$\frac{4}{5} = \frac{8}{10} = \frac{12}{15} = \frac{16}{20} \qquad\qquad \frac{3}{4} = \frac{6}{8} = \frac{9}{12} = \frac{12}{16} = \frac{15}{20}$$

$$\text{Then } \frac{4}{5} + \frac{3}{4} = \frac{16}{20} + \frac{15}{20}$$

$$= \frac{31}{20}$$

$$= 1\frac{11}{20}$$

Worked Example   In Baysdown, $\frac{3}{8}$ of the population is under 5 while $\frac{1}{3}$ is aged between 5 and 16. What fraction of the population is over 16?

Answer   Fraction aged 16 or under $= \frac{3}{8} + \frac{1}{3}$

$$= \frac{9}{24} + \frac{8}{24}$$

$$= \frac{17}{24}$$

Fraction aged 16 or over $= 1 - \frac{17}{24}$

$$= \frac{24}{24} - \frac{17}{24}$$

$$= \frac{7}{24}$$

33

EXERCISE 1:9

1. Find the answer to these.

   (a) $\frac{1}{3} + \frac{1}{3}$ (b) $\frac{7}{12} + \frac{1}{12}$ (c) $\frac{7}{9} - \frac{2}{9}$ (d) $\frac{5}{9} - \frac{2}{9}$

   (e) $\frac{7}{10} + \frac{3}{10}$ (f) $\frac{5}{8} + \frac{7}{8}$ (g) $\frac{11}{12} + \frac{5}{12} - \frac{1}{12}$ (h) $\frac{7}{8} - \frac{1}{8} - \frac{3}{8}$

2. Calculate.

   (a) $\frac{3}{10} + \frac{2}{5}$ (b) $\frac{7}{8} - \frac{1}{4}$ (c) $\frac{5}{12} - \frac{1}{3}$ (d) $\frac{1}{4} + \frac{1}{3}$

   (e) $\frac{3}{4} + \frac{5}{6}$ (f) $\frac{5}{6} - \frac{1}{8}$ (g) $\frac{7}{10} - \frac{1}{12}$

3. Find the answer to these.

   (a) $\frac{1}{3} + \frac{3}{4} + \frac{5}{12}$ (b) $\frac{2}{3} + \frac{1}{8} + \frac{3}{4}$ (c) $\frac{7}{10} + \frac{1}{2} - \frac{2}{3}$ (d) $\frac{9}{10} - \frac{2}{5} - \frac{1}{4}$

4. In a horse race, there was $\frac{1}{3}$ of a length between the first and second horses and $\frac{1}{2}$ of a length between the first and third horses.
   What fraction of a length was there between the second and third horses?

5. The glass is filled from the thermos flask.
   Which now contains more, the glass or the
   thermos flask?

6. Three children share their parents' estate as follows: the eldest gets $\frac{1}{2}$, the youngest gets $\frac{1}{3}$. What fraction of the estate does the other child get?

7.

   Jenny estimated that her first golf shot reached $\frac{2}{5}$ of the way to the hole while her third (and last) shot covered $\frac{1}{8}$ of the distance.
   What fraction, of the distance to the hole, did Jenny's second shot cover?

8. Find the next term in the sequence $\frac{1}{2}, \frac{2}{3}, \frac{5}{6}, 1, \ldots$

Review 1 Find the answer to these.

(a) $\frac{5}{9} + \frac{3}{9}$ (b) $\frac{5}{6} - \frac{2}{3}$ (c) $\frac{2}{3} + \frac{3}{4}$ (d) $\frac{1}{4} + \frac{7}{12} - \frac{2}{3}$

Review 2 The earth consists of three main layers; crust, mantle and core. The mantle is about $\frac{4}{5}$ of the earth and the core is about $\frac{1}{6}$.
What fraction of the earth is crust?

To **add** (or **subtract**) **mixed numbers** we can begin by writing each mixed number as an improper fraction.

Examples

$$3\frac{2}{3} + 1\frac{3}{4} = \frac{11}{3} + \frac{7}{4}$$
$$= \frac{44}{12} + \frac{21}{12}$$
$$= \frac{65}{12}$$
$$= 5\frac{5}{12}$$

$$3\frac{1}{6} - 1\frac{1}{2} = \frac{19}{6} - \frac{3}{2}$$
$$= \frac{19}{6} - \frac{9}{6}$$
$$= \frac{10}{6}$$
$$= \frac{5}{3}$$
$$= 1\frac{2}{3}$$

Another method of adding (or subtracting) mixed numbers is to add (or subtract) the whole numbers, then add or subtract the fractions.

Example

$$3\frac{2}{3} + 1\frac{3}{4} = 3\frac{8}{12} + 1\frac{9}{12}$$
$$= 4\frac{17}{12}$$
$$= 5\frac{5}{12}$$

DISCUSSION EXERCISE 1:10

Discuss the advantages and disadvantages of both of the above methods. As part of your discussion use calculations such as: $\quad 3\frac{2}{3} + 1\frac{3}{4} \quad 15\frac{1}{2} + 23\frac{3}{8} \quad 14\frac{3}{5} - 7\frac{3}{10} \quad 3\frac{1}{6} - 1\frac{1}{2}.$

EXERCISE 1:11

1. Find the answer to these.

   (a) $1\frac{1}{2} + 2\frac{3}{4}$ (b) $3\frac{2}{3} + 1\frac{1}{4}$ (c) $2\frac{4}{5} - 1\frac{1}{2}$ (d) $5\frac{1}{2} + \frac{7}{10}$

   (e) $4\frac{5}{8} - 2\frac{3}{4}$ (f) $2\frac{1}{3} - \frac{4}{5}$ (g) $2\frac{1}{3} - 1\frac{1}{2}$

2. Sam works in a restaurant for $3\frac{1}{2}$ hours each Saturday and $2\frac{3}{4}$ hours each Sunday. How long does Sam work each weekend?

3. The last 8 pages of a magazine are for advertisements.

   Two days before publication, $6\frac{7}{8}$ pages of advertising had been sold, then $2\frac{1}{4}$ pages were cancelled. How much still has to be sold?

4. Find the next term in the sequence $\frac{2}{3}$, $2\frac{1}{2}$, $4\frac{1}{3}$, $6\frac{1}{6}$, . . .

5. What might ■ and ● be in each of the following?

   (a) ■ + ● = $3\frac{5}{6}$ (b) ■ − $2\frac{1}{2}$ = ●

6. Copy and complete these magic squares.
   Remember: the numbers on each row, column and diagonal must add to the same total.

$\frac{1}{2}$		
$1\frac{2}{3}$	1	
$\frac{5}{6}$		

(a)

		$1\frac{2}{5}$
$2\frac{1}{10}$	$2\frac{9}{20}$	$\frac{7}{10}$

(b)

		$4\frac{3}{4}$
	$3\frac{23}{24}$	
$3\frac{1}{6}$		$6\frac{1}{3}$

(c)

Review 1   Find the answer to these.

   (a) $3\frac{1}{4} + 1\frac{7}{10}$ (b) $2\frac{2}{3} - 1\frac{1}{4}$ (c) $2\frac{3}{8} - 1\frac{2}{3}$

Review 2   Beth made plum sauce. She filled these two bottles to the top.

   (a) How much plum sauce did Beth make altogether?

   (b) How much more did Beth pour into the large bottle than into the small bottle?

CALCULATIONS with ×, ÷, +, −

In the next exercise some questions involve just one of +, −, ×, ÷ and some involve more than one of these.

EXERCISE 1:12

---

1. Which operation, +, −, × or ÷, does the ⋆ stand for?

   (a) $4 \star \frac{1}{5} = 20$ (b) $4 \star \frac{1}{5} = 4\frac{1}{5}$ (c) $4 \star \frac{1}{5} = \frac{4}{5}$ (d) $4 \star \frac{1}{5} = 3\frac{4}{5}$

2. Andrea delivers papers 6 days a week. Each day her paper round takes $1\frac{1}{4}$ hours.
   How many hours a week does Andrea work on this paper round?

3. One-third of a cake has been eaten. Michael and his 4 friends share the rest of this cake.
   What fraction of the cake does each get, if they each get the same size piece?

4. Najma travels from Birmingham to Edinburgh, a distance of 485km.
   If $\frac{2}{5}$ of Najma's journey is by motorway, how many km does she travel on other roads?

5. Copy these. Complete by finding the missing fractions.

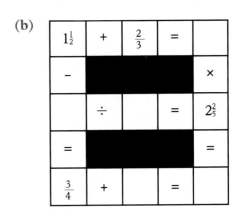

6. Theatre tickets cost £5, £8 and £15. Of the 600 tickets sold for one performance, $\frac{1}{3}$ sold for £15 and $\frac{2}{5}$ sold for £8.

   (a)   What fraction of the tickets sold for £5?
   (b)   What total revenue from ticket sales did the theatre get for this performance?

7. Every $\frac{1}{4}$ of an hour a street cleaning machine cleans $1\frac{1}{3}$ km of road.
   How many km does it clean in 3 hours?

8.

This diagram is enlarged on a photocopier by a scale factor of $1\frac{1}{3}$.

(a) How long is the enlarged design?
(b) The enlarged design is then reduced back to its original size. What is the scale factor of this reduction?

9. Aaron spent $\frac{5}{8}$ of his savings, then half the remainder.
What fraction of his savings did Aaron have left?

10. A tank, when three-quarters full, contains 45*l* of petrol.
How much petrol does a full tank hold?

11. Three-fifths of a class are boys. Three-fifths of the girls play netball. Four girls do not play netball.
How many boys are in this class?

Review 1 There were three candidates in an election; A.J. Beatie, T. Davison and I.M. Mahon.

Candidate	Fraction of Votes
A. J. Beatie	$\frac{1}{3}$
T. Davison	$\frac{1}{4}$
I. M. Mahon	

(a) What fraction of the votes did I. M. Mahon poll?
(b) Who won the election?
(c) If 6756 people voted, how many votes did T. Davison get?

Review 2 On holiday, Beth spent one-third of her money on travel and two-fifths of the remainder on food and accommodation. She then had £60 for other expenses.
How much did Beth spend on travel?

INVESTIGATION 1:13

FRACTION PATTERNS

$\frac{1}{2} + \frac{1}{4} + \frac{1}{8} + \frac{1}{16} + \frac{1}{32} + \ldots$ **Investigate** this fraction pattern.

You could begin by finding the sums $\frac{1}{2} + \frac{1}{4}$, $\frac{1}{2} + \frac{1}{4} + \frac{1}{8}$, $\frac{1}{2} + \frac{1}{4} + \frac{1}{8} + \frac{1}{16}$ etc.

You could use the fraction functions on a calculator to help in your investigation or you could use the following program. This will print the first 6 sums. To print more than 6 rewrite line 40.

```
10    MODE 3
20    DENOM = 2
30    SNUM = 1 : SDENOM = 2
40    FOR I = 1 TO 6
50    DENOM = 2 * DENOM
60    NEWSNUM = 2 * SNUM + 1
70    NEWSDENOM = 2 * SDENOM
80    PRINT SNUM , 1 , NEWSNUM
90    PRINT SPC (7) ;   "_ _ _" ; SPC (3) ;   " + " ; SPC (3) ;
         "_ _ _" ; SPC (3) ;  " = " ; SPC (3) ;  "_ _ _"
100   PRINT SDENOM , DENOM , NEWSDENOM
110   PRINT
120   SNUM = NEWSNUM : SDENOM = NEWSDENOM
130   NEXT
140   END
```

You could draw a sequence of diagrams such as the following.

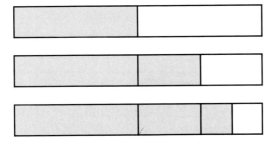

Investigate the fraction pattern: $\frac{1}{3} + \frac{1}{9} + \frac{1}{27} + \frac{1}{81} + \ldots$ You could use the above program. You will need to replace every 2 with 3.

Investigate other fraction patterns such as $\frac{1}{2} + \frac{1}{3} + \frac{1}{4} + \frac{1}{5} + \ldots$

$\frac{1}{2} - \frac{1}{4} + \frac{1}{8} - \frac{1}{16} + \ldots$

continued . . .

. . . *from previous page*

What fraction patterns occur in this diagram?
Investigate.

If more than one operation is involved in the same calculation, the operations must be done in the following order. Brackets, then × and ÷ , then + and −.

Example $4\frac{1}{3} + 2\frac{2}{3} \div 2\frac{2}{5}$

$$= 4\frac{1}{3} + \frac{8}{3} \div \frac{12}{5}$$

$$= 4\frac{1}{3} + \frac{\overset{2}{\cancel{8}}}{3} \times \frac{5}{\cancel{12}_3}$$

$$= 4\frac{1}{3} + \frac{10}{9}$$

$$= 4\frac{1}{3} + 1\frac{1}{9}$$

$$= 5 + \frac{1}{3} + \frac{1}{9}$$

$$= 5 + \frac{3}{9} + \frac{1}{9}$$

$$= 5\frac{4}{9}$$

Example $4\frac{1}{3} \div 2\frac{2}{3} + 2\frac{2}{5}$

$$= \frac{13}{3} \div \frac{8}{3} + 2\frac{2}{5}$$

$$= \frac{13}{\cancel{3}} \times \frac{\overset{1}{\cancel{3}}}{8} + 2\frac{2}{5}$$

$$= \frac{13}{8} + 2\frac{2}{5}$$

$$= 1\frac{5}{8} + 2\frac{2}{5}$$

$$= 3 + \frac{5}{8} + \frac{2}{5}$$

$$= 3 + \frac{25}{40} + \frac{16}{40}$$

$$= 3\frac{41}{40}$$

$$= 4\frac{1}{40}$$

Example $(1\frac{3}{4} + 2\frac{1}{3}) \times 1\frac{3}{7}$

$$= (3 + \frac{3}{4} + \frac{1}{3}) \times 1\frac{3}{7}$$

$$= (3 + \frac{9}{12} + \frac{4}{12}) \times 1\frac{3}{7}$$

$$= 3\frac{13}{12} \times 1\frac{3}{7}$$

$$= 4\frac{1}{12} \times 1\frac{3}{7}$$

$$= \frac{\overset{7}{\cancel{49}}}{\cancel{12}_6} \times \frac{\overset{5}{\cancel{10}}}{\cancel{7}_1}$$

$$= \frac{35}{6}$$

$$= 5\frac{5}{6}$$

EXERCISE 1:14

Find the answer to these.

1. $3\frac{1}{3} + \frac{2}{5} \times 4\frac{1}{6}$

2. $\frac{3}{4} \div \frac{1}{2} + 3\frac{1}{2}$

3. $6 - 1\frac{7}{9} \times 3\frac{3}{8}$

4. $\frac{3}{4}$ of $1\frac{1}{7} + 2\frac{1}{2}$

5. $\frac{2}{3}$ of $(1\frac{1}{2} + \frac{3}{4})$

6. $(2\frac{1}{2} - 1\frac{5}{8}) \div \frac{3}{4}$

7. $\frac{4}{5}(1\frac{5}{12} + \frac{7}{8})$

8. $\frac{5}{8} + \frac{7}{10} \div 1\frac{2}{5}$

9. $3\frac{2}{5} \div (8\frac{3}{7} - 7\frac{7}{10})$

10. $(4\frac{1}{5} - \frac{3}{10}) \div 3\frac{1}{4}$

Review 1 $5\frac{1}{4} \times (\frac{3}{4} - \frac{2}{3})$

Review 2 $2\frac{7}{10} + 3\frac{1}{5} \div 1\frac{1}{3}$

EVALUATING FORMULAE

Worked Example   The total resistance R in this circuit
is given by $R = \dfrac{R_1\,R_2}{R_1 + R_2}$.

Find R if $R_1 = 7\frac{1}{2}$, $R_2 = 11\frac{1}{4}$.

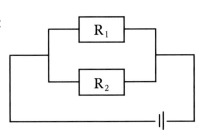

Answer $R = \dfrac{7\frac{1}{2} \times 11\frac{1}{4}}{7\frac{1}{2} + 11\frac{1}{4}}$

$= \dfrac{\frac{15}{2} \times \frac{45}{4}}{18\frac{3}{4}}$

$= \dfrac{15}{2} \times \dfrac{45}{4} \div \dfrac{75}{4}$

$= \dfrac{{}^{1}\cancel{15}}{2} \times \dfrac{{}^{9}\cancel{45}}{\cancel{4}_{\,1}} \times \dfrac{{}^{1}\cancel{4}}{\cancel{75}\cancel{8}_{\,1}}$

$= \dfrac{9}{2}$

$= 4\frac{1}{2}$

EXERCISE 1:15

1. $\text{Area} = \frac{1}{2}\,bh$

   Find the area if   (a) $b = 2\frac{1}{2}$, $h = 4\frac{2}{5}$

   (b) $b = 13\frac{1}{3}$, $h = 8\frac{1}{4}$.

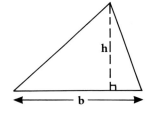

2. $I = \frac{PRT}{100}$ Find I if   (a) $P = 200$, $R = 6\frac{1}{4}$, $T = 8$

(b) $P = 100$, $R = 8\frac{1}{2}$, $T = \frac{1}{2}$.

3. The volume of a pyramid is given by the formula
   $V = \frac{1}{3}(\text{base area}) \times \text{height}$.
   Use this formula to find the volume of the sketched pyramid.

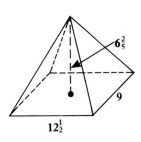

4. The marks from two tests are combined using the formula $M = \frac{2}{5}X + \frac{3}{5}Y$. M is the combined mark, X is the mark from the first test, Y is the mark from the second test.

   Use the formula to find M for the following students.
   Alison: Test 1 - 40,   Test 2 - 55
   Brenda: Test 1 - 36,   Test 2 - 60
   Ben: Test 1 - 42,   Test 2 - 54

5.   Area = length × width   Perimeter = 2 (length + width)
   These formulae can be used to find the area and perimeter of a rectangle.
   Find the area and perimeter of the following rectangles.
   (a)   length = $2\frac{1}{4}$m, width = $1\frac{1}{3}$m
                                             (b)   length = $3\frac{1}{3}$m, width = $2\frac{1}{4}$m

6. The mean of three numbers a, b, c is given by $m = \frac{1}{3}(a + b + c)$.
   Use this formula to find the mean of: (a)   2, 3, 6
                                            (b) $2\frac{1}{2}$, $3\frac{1}{4}$, 5.

7. $A = \frac{h}{2}(a + b)$ gives the area of a trapezium.
   Find the area of a trapezium for which:
   (a)   a = 4, b = $5\frac{1}{3}$, h = 3
   (b)   h = $4\frac{1}{6}$, a = $5\frac{1}{2}$, b = $4\frac{1}{10}$.

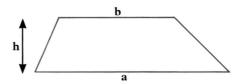

8. The sum of the first n terms of the sequence 1, $2\frac{1}{4}$, $3\frac{1}{2}$, . . . can be found by using the formula $S = \frac{n}{2}[2 + (n - 1) \times 1\frac{1}{4}]$.
   Use this formula to find the sum of (a) 5 terms   (b)   17 terms

9. The formula $t = \dfrac{hc}{h + c}$ gives the time, **t** minutes, taken for a bath to fill if both the hot and cold taps are turned on. **h** minutes is the time it takes to fill the bath if just the hot tap is turned on, **c** minutes is the time taken if just the cold tap is turned on.
   Find t if   (a)   h = 5, c = $3\frac{1}{3}$ (b)   h = $4\frac{4}{5}$, c = $2\frac{2}{5}$.

10. $s = ut + \frac{1}{2}at^2$.   Find s if   (a)   u = $12\frac{1}{2}$, a = $7\frac{1}{2}$, t = 4
                                                      (b)   u = $5\frac{1}{2}$, a = $7\frac{1}{5}$, t = 10
                                                      (c)   u = 10, a = 6, t = 0·5.

11. $\dfrac{1}{f} = \dfrac{1}{v} + \dfrac{1}{u}$.   Find f if u = $7\frac{1}{2}$, v = 6.

Review 1   Overtime Wage $=$ $\dfrac{\text{Basic Wage}}{37\frac{1}{2}} \times 1\frac{1}{2} \times h$

Find the overtime wage if   **(a)**   h = 3, basic wage = £150

(b)   h = $2\frac{1}{2}$, basic wage = £120.

Review 2 $s = \frac{1}{2}(u + v)\, t$.   Find s if t = $5\frac{3}{5}$, u = $8\frac{1}{4}$, v = $10\frac{1}{2}$.

PUZZLE 1:16

? ?

A coin collection was to be divided amongst three children so that the eldest was to get half of the coins, the youngest was to get a ninth of them and the other child was to get a third. There were 17 coins in this collection.
The oldest child decided the collection could be shared in this way as follows:

Borrow one coin from a friend to make a total of 18 coins.

The eldest takes $\frac{1}{2}$ of 18 = 9 coins.

The youngest takes $\frac{1}{9}$ of 18 = 2 coins.

The other child takes $\frac{1}{3}$ of 18 = 6 coins.

Now that the 17 coins have been taken, the borrowed coin is returned to the friend.

The youngest child saw that there was a catch and explained this catch to the other children. What explanation might the youngest child have given?

? ?

Ada Lovelace

Ada Lovelace was born in England in 1815 and died at the age of 36 in 1852. She was the daughter of the famous poet, Lord Byron. A month after Ada was born, her father left England never to return. Neither Ada nor her mother saw him again. Lord Byron wrote about Ada in some of his poems.

Ada's mother was known for her mathematical ability. She had many influential friends, some of whom were mathematicians. Her friends nick-named her "The Princess of Parallelograms".

Ada did not attend school or any university. Her family was wealthy and she was taught by governesses and tutors. Ada's mother insisted that she receive instruction in mathematics which was not the custom for girls in those days. When Ada was five her daily lessons included grammar, spelling, reading, French, arithmetic, music, drawing and geography. Ada was tutored by mathematicians when she was older.

When she was 18, she met Charles Babbage. Some claim they met at a party; others claim they met when Ada went to his workshop. He tutored her for a time and they corresponded frequently. They became close friends.

Babbage was impressed with her understanding of his "Analytical Engine", an early computer. Ada wrote an analysis of the mathematics involved and described techniques which became important in computing. Her work was forgotten for many years. She is now viewed as the person who laid the groundwork for the development of computer language and computer programming. In the late 1970s she was honoured by the American Department of Defence who named the computer language ADA after her.

Ada did not publish her work using her own name as women mathematicians were not thought highly of in those times. She published using her initials A.A.L. Her husband, Lord Lovelace, whom she married when she was 19, encouraged her in her work. Although it was not the custom then, he took responsibility for running their household and bringing up their children.

Ada had a passion for horse racing. She and Charles Babbage worked out a betting system which Ada put into practice. It failed! It is claimed that she fell into debt and pawned the family jewels, creating a scandal.

Throughout her life, Ada suffered from poor health and in later years lived in London to be close to her doctors. She was an asthmatic and was manic-depressive. It is believed that she suffered from anorexia. She died from cancer.

based on an article from the book "Women Sum It Up" — Hazard Press

Estimating Answers to Calculations

ROUNDING ANSWERS SENSIBLY

The calculator gives the answer to the calculation $\frac{17 \cdot 3}{0 \cdot 24}$ as 72·083333.

We would not give all of these 8 digits in the answer we write down.

We can choose whether to use decimal places (d.p.) or significant figures (s.f.) when we round an answer. The following guidelines can be used to decide how accurate the answer should be given.

1. Count how many d.p. (or s.f.) there are in the number with the fewest d.p. (or s.f.).
2. Round the answer to this many d.p. (or s.f.).

Using these guidelines, an acceptable answer to $\frac{17 \cdot 3}{0 \cdot 24}$ is 72 to 2 s.f. (17·3 has 3 s.f. while 0·24 has just 2 s.f.).

Using these guidelines, another acceptable answer to $\frac{17 \cdot 3}{0 \cdot 24}$ is 72·1 to 1 d.p. (17·3 has 1 d.p. while 0·24 has 2 d.p.).

These guidelines are not rules.

It sometimes seems sensible to give an answer to one more s.f. than these guidelines suggest.

For instance, it seems more sensible to give the answer to $\frac{1}{7}$ as 0·14 (2 s.f.) rather than 0·1 (1 s.f.).

These guidelines do not apply to a calculation, such as 6340 × 17, which has an exact answer. The calculator gives the answer to 6340 × 17 as 107780 and we usually write the answer to 6340 × 17 as 107780. The calculator gives the answer to $\frac{3}{8}$ as 0·375 and we usually write the answer as 0·375.

DISCUSSION EXERCISE 2:1

● How would you write down the answers to the following calculations? **Discuss.**

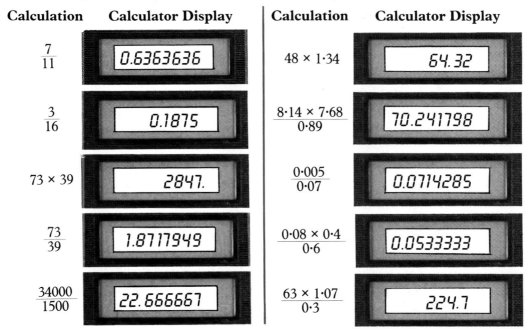

Calculation	Calculator Display	Calculation	Calculator Display
$\frac{7}{11}$	0.6363636	48 × 1·34	64.32
$\frac{3}{16}$	0.1875	$\frac{8·14 × 7·68}{0·89}$	70.241798
73 × 39	2847.	$\frac{0·005}{0·07}$	0.0714285
$\frac{73}{39}$	1.8717949	$\frac{0·08 × 0·4}{0·6}$	0.0533333
$\frac{34000}{1500}$	22.666667	$\frac{63 × 1·07}{0·3}$	224.7

● Never round until the final answer is found.

Suppose A = $\frac{3·4}{26·1}$ and B = 5·9A. We are to find the answer to B to 1 decimal place.

What answer do we get for B if we round the answer for A?

What answer do we get for B if we do not round the answer for A? **Discuss.**

ESTIMATING ANSWERS

When finding the answer to a calculation using the calculator, it is very easy to press an incorrect key. It is most important to have some idea of the size of the answer. You will then know if the answer shown on the calculator screen is reasonable.

Always **estimate** the answer when using the calculator for a calculation. The estimate does not have to be very accurate.

We estimate by approximating each number in the calculation; then we use these approximations in the calculation.

For instance, to estimate the answer for 34·72 ÷ 6·8 we could use the approximation 35 ÷ 7 to get an estimate of 5.

Each number in the calculation should be made as simple as possible so the estimate is easy to work out mentally. Some guidelines follow.

Chapter 2

Guidelines:

- Remember it is an estimate. The approximations don't need to be very accurate.

  For instance, approximate $20 \div 5 \cdot 7$ as $20 \div 5$ rather than $20 \div 6$.

- Wherever possible, approximate to numbers such as 1, 2, 5, 10, 50, 100 etc. that are easy to work with mentally.

  For instance, $\dfrac{72 \cdot 6 \times 347 \cdot 05}{0 \cdot 89}$ may be approximated as $\dfrac{100 \times 350}{1}$

  to give an estimate of 35000.

- Look for numbers that will cancel.

  For instance, $\dfrac{12 \cdot 48 \times 487 \cdot 31}{3 \cdot 69}$ may be approximated as $\dfrac{\overset{3}{\cancel{12}} \times 500}{\underset{1}{\cancel{4}}}$

  to give an estimate of 1500.

- Decimals, between 0 and 1, are often best approximated with fractions.

  For instance, $\dfrac{82 \cdot 61}{0 \cdot 27}$ may be approximated as $80 \div \frac{1}{4}$ to give an

  estimate of 320.

- When multiplying or dividing, never approximate a number with 0. Rather, use $0 \cdot 1$ or $0 \cdot 01$ or $0 \cdot 001$ etc.

  For instance, $205 \cdot 7 \times 0 \cdot 012$ should not be approximated as 200×0.

  Rather, approximate as $200 \times 0 \cdot 01$ or $200 \times \frac{1}{100}$ to get an estimate of 2.

It is often convenient to use the symbol $\simeq$ which means "is approximately equal to".

Worked Example   Estimate the answer to   (a) $8 \cdot 98 \times 24 \cdot 6$

(b) $(6 \cdot 35)^2$

(c) $\dfrac{198 \times 71 \cdot 6}{11 \cdot 3 \times 0 \cdot 83}$

(d) $0 \cdot 09 \times 59 \cdot 6$

Answer

(a) $8 \cdot 98 \simeq 10$, $24 \cdot 6 \simeq 25$. An estimate is $10 \times 25 = 250$.

(b) $(6 \cdot 35)^2$ is more than 6^2 but less than 7^2.

An estimate for $(6 \cdot 35)^2$ is: between 36 and 49.

(c) $198 \simeq 200$, $71 \cdot 6 \simeq 70$, $11 \cdot 3 \simeq 10$, $0 \cdot 83 \simeq 1$.

An estimate is $\dfrac{200 \times \overset{7}{\cancel{70}}}{\underset{1}{\cancel{10}} \times 1} = 1400$.

(d) $0 \cdot 09 \simeq 0 \cdot 1 = \frac{1}{10}$, $59 \cdot 6 \simeq 60$.

An estimate is $\frac{1}{10} \times 60 = 6$.

EXERCISE 2:2

1. Estimate the answer to these.

   (a) $7 \cdot 6 \times 4 \cdot 123$ (b) $67 \cdot 34 \div 9 \cdot 3$ (c) $7 \cdot 24 \times 18 \cdot 07$ (d) $(10 \cdot 14)^2$

   (e) $\dfrac{19 \cdot 6 \times 34 \cdot 7}{4 \cdot 35}$ (f) $\dfrac{7 \cdot 62 + 2 \cdot 21}{5 \cdot 23}$ (g) $81 \cdot 2 \times 0 \cdot 27$ (h) $\dfrac{27 \cdot 8 \times 3 \cdot 67}{7 \cdot 64}$

   (i) $\dfrac{28 \cdot 6 \times 24 \cdot 4}{5 \cdot 67 \times 4 \cdot 02}$ (j) $\dfrac{18 \cdot 3 + 11 \cdot 1}{57 \cdot 03}$ (k) $\dfrac{8 \cdot 34 \times 96 \cdot 7}{0 \cdot 26}$

2. Use the calculator to find the answer to these. Round the answers sensibly. Check that the answer is reasonable by making an estimate.

   (a) $37 \cdot 64 \times 23 \cdot 1$ (b) $44 \cdot 9 \div 8 \cdot 76$ (c) $0 \cdot 47 \times 19 \cdot 1$ (d) $\dfrac{38 \cdot 4 + 22 \cdot 5}{18 \cdot 4}$

   (e) $\dfrac{274 \times 31 \cdot 4}{49 \cdot 3}$ (f) $\dfrac{31 \cdot 2}{0 \cdot 24}$ (g) $(3 \cdot 24)^2$ (h) $\dfrac{(7 \cdot 05)^2}{4 \cdot 68}$

   (i) $\dfrac{87 \cdot 9}{1 \cdot 3 + 5 \cdot 01}$ (j) $\dfrac{4 \cdot 7 \times 49 \cdot 2}{0 \cdot 18}$ (k) $\dfrac{51 \cdot 6 \times 0 \cdot 12}{9 \cdot 8}$ (l) $\dfrac{24 \cdot 4 \times 8 \cdot 2}{3 \cdot 9 \times 2 \cdot 1}$

3. 1 nautical mile is approximately 1·853km.
   Estimate how many km are in 214 nautical miles.

4. 1 ounce is about 28·35 grams.
   Estimate the number of ounces in 600 grams.

5. Estimate, then use the calculator to find the answer to the following. If rounding is required, round your answers sensibly.

   (a) Find the cost of 9·7m of material at £8·19 a metre.

   (b) Find the perimeter of this triangle.

   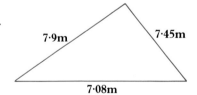

   (c) Shirts in a sale were priced at £8·85, £7·95, £11·15 and £5·45.
   During the first day of the sale, the following quantities were sold.
        27 at £8·85   15 at £7·95   24 at £11·15   47 at £5·45
   How much were all these shirts sold for?

   (d) Amanda has been visiting relatives in Australia.
   If the exchange rate is 1 Australian dollar for 37·02p, how much British money would Amanda get for the $48·65 she brought back to England with her?

(e) A formula for finding the area of a trapezium is
$A = \frac{1}{2}(a + b) \times h$.

a and **b** are the lengths of the parallel sides and **h** is the distance between these sides.
Find the area of this trapezium.

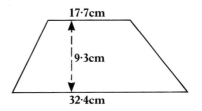

(f) A formula for finding the area of a circle is $A = \pi r^2$.
Using $\pi = 3 \cdot 142$, find the area of a circle with radius 26·7cm.

(g) A formula for the volume of a pyramid is $V = \frac{1}{3}$ (base area) × height.
Find the volume of a pyramid which has a rectangular base, measuring 81·2mm by 58·6mm, and height 19·7mm.

(h) Kareema is reading this book.
She takes an average of 2min. 5sec. to read a page.
How long will it take her to read the book?

(i) Jim bought 213 feet of decking timber.
This was in planks, each 5'11" long.
How many planks did Jim buy?

6. Write down 10 different calculations which could have an estimated answer of 15.
Use at least two of the operations +, −, ×, ÷ and squaring in each calculation.
Use decimals in all of the calculations.

Review 1   Estimate the answer for these.

(a) 38·2 × 4·67

(b) $\dfrac{28 \cdot 7}{0 \cdot 44}$

(c) $\dfrac{21 \cdot 4 \times 38 \cdot 7}{3 \cdot 68 \times 4 \cdot 71}$

(d) $\dfrac{7 \cdot 204 + 2 \cdot 63}{1 \cdot 934}$

(e) $4 \cdot 9 \times (3 \cdot 14)^2$

Review 2   Estimate, then use the calculator to find the answer to the following. Round your answers sensibly.

(a) $\dfrac{36 \cdot 7 \times 72 \cdot 6}{6 \cdot 94}$

(b) 48·6 × 0·098

(c) $\dfrac{7 \cdot 64 + 14 \cdot 1}{3 \cdot 84}$

(d) $\dfrac{(9 \cdot 63)^2}{4 \cdot 78}$

Review 3   A formula for the volume of a cylinder is
$V = \pi r^2 h$.
Using $\pi = 3 \cdot 142$, find the volume of this cylinder. Give the answer to 2 s.f.

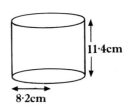

Leopold Kronecker

Leopold Kronecker was born in 1823 at Liegnitz, in what was then Prussia. He died at Berlin in 1891.

He insisted that all mathematics be based on the positive integers. He used to say "God made the positive integers and all else is the work of man".

Kronecker had wealthy Jewish parents but from an early age he was interested in Protestant Christianity. However, he was 67 years old before he actually converted from Judaism.

His early education was with a private tutor. Later he attended a preparatory school and then the University of Berlin where he gained a doctorate in mathematics. As was usual with German university students at that time, he did part of his studies at other universities. While Kronecker was at Bonn University, the authorities were trying to stop the students drinking, duelling and brawling. By secretly siding with the students, Kronecker made many lasting friendships that were to later prove useful in the advancement of his ideas.

The custom at the time Kronecker completed his Ph.D. was for the successful student to give a party for his examiners. Kronecker's party was a wild affair. The memory of this party was one of the happiest of his life.

He got along easily with people and instinctively formed lasting friendships with people who were successful or were to become successful.

From university, Kronecker went into business. He managed the family mercantile and land business until the age of 30 when he was wealthy enough to retire. While in business, he continued his mathematics as a hobby.

From 1861, he gave lectures at the University of Berlin for no payment. These lectures were usually on his own personal work and research. In 1883 he was appointed Professor of Mathematics. He then travelled a great deal to attend scientific meetings. One of the countries he visited was Great Britain. Kronecker openly criticized other mathematicians in lectures and in conversation and it is claimed that his criticisms were a factor in the nervous breakdown of another of Germany's famous mathematicians.

Kronecker had a critical and questioning approach to everything, including mathematics. He was a short man, about five feet tall. He talked enthusiastically, with his whole body. A story is told of this excited short man, waving his arms and hands around in the midst of a group of spellbound students while the traffic all around came to a standstill.

As an old man, Kronecker claimed that music is the finest of all the fine arts with the possible exception of mathematics which he likened to poetry.

Calculating with Negative Numbers

ADDING and SUBTRACTING

DISCUSSION EXERCISE 3:1

Using the calculator, the answer to $5 + (-2)$ is found by keying $\boxed{5}$ $\boxed{+}$ $\boxed{2}$ $\boxed{+/-}$ $\boxed{=}$.

Use your calculator to find the answers to many additions involving negative numbers. Consider additions in which both numbers are negative as well as those in which just one of the numbers is negative.

Discuss your answers. As part of your discussion, make and test statements about adding without using the calculator.

You may like to refer to movement along a number line.

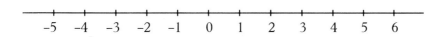

Use your calculator to find the answers to many subtractions involving negative numbers. How could you subtract without using the calculator? **Discuss.** Make and test statements as part of your discussion.

We may use a number line to **add** or **subtract**.

To add a positive number, move to the right.
To add a negative number, move to the left.

Examples

1 + 3   Begin at 1, move 3 to the right.   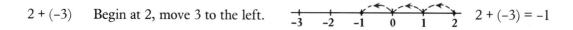   1 + 3 = 4

2 + (−3)   Begin at 2, move 3 to the left.   2 + (−3) = −1

−2 + 3   Begin at −2, move 3 to the right.   −2 + 3 = 1

−2 + (−1)   Begin at −2, move 1 to the left.   −2 + (−1) = −3

Addition and subtraction are inverse operations. To subtract, we must move in the opposite direction to that in which we move to add.

To subtract a positive number, move to the left.
To subtract a negative number, move to the right.

Examples

4 − 1   Begin at 4, move 1 to the left.   4 − 1 = 3

1 − 3   Begin at 1, move 3 to the left.   1 − 3 = −2

1 − (−3)   Begin at 1, move 3 to the right.   1 − (−3) = 4

−1 − (−3)   Begin at −1, move 3 to the right.   −1 − (−3) = 2

EXERCISE 3:2

1. Find the answer to these.

    (a)   2 + (−5)   (b)   −2 + (−5)   (c)   2 + 5   (d)   −2 + 5

    (e)   2 − (−5)   (f)   −2 − (−5)   (g)   2 − 5   (h)   −2 − 5

    (i)   −3 + (−4)   (j)   5 − (−3)   (k)   −8 − (−2)   (l)   4 + (−3)

    (m) −7 − 3   (n)   −8 + (−4)   (o)   −3 − (−7)

2. Calculate.

    (a)   −5 + 3 + (−4)   (b)   2 + (−4) + (−1)   (c)   3 − (−4) + 5

    (d)   −2 − (−1) + (−5)   (e)   3 + (−7) − (−2)   (f)   −5 − (−2) − 4

    (g)   7 − (−2) + 5   (h)   2 + (−1) − 4

3. Copy and complete these addition squares.

(a)
+	−4		−2
			2
	−10	−1	
2			

(b)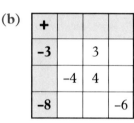

(c)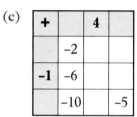

4. What are the next two terms in these sequences?   (a)   −14, −11, −8, −5, . . .

                                              (b)   7·7, 5·7, 3·7, 1·7, . . .

5. At 8 a.m. Sharon's temperature was 1·2° above normal.
By 11 a.m. it had dropped by 2·1°.
How far below normal was Sharon's temperature at 11 a.m.?

6.

The approximate altitude (height above sea level) of some places is shown in this table.

   (i)   What is the difference in altitude between
       (a) London and the Caspian Sea
       (b) The Dead Sea and Ayers Rock?
  (ii)   How much higher is Nairobi than Rotterdam?

Place	Altitude (m)
Ayers Rock	900
Caspian Sea	−30
London	30
Nairobi	1800
Rotterdam	−5
The Dead Sea	−400

7. McIver Manufacturing have two bank accounts.
   One of these accounts has a balance of £2349·20 while the other account is overdrawn by £3594·85. If these two accounts are combined, what will the balance be in the combined account?

8. Find the answer to these.
   (a) −3·4 + 1·8 (b) −6·8 − 2·3 (c) 2·4 + (−4·2) (d) −1·9 + (−2·3)
   (e) 6 + (−2·6) (f) 2·6 − (−4) (g) 6·1 + (−4)

9.

How might this addition square be completed?

+	3		
	−4		
		−5	
			4

Review 1 Calculate.

(a) −3 + (−5) (b) 2 − (−3) (c) −1·6 − 0·9 (d) 2·3 + (−1·4)
(e) −2 + (−5) − 4

Review 2

City	Local time difference (hrs)
Brussels	+1
London	0
Mexico City	−6
Peking	+8
Reykjavik	0
Santiago	−4

This table gives the time difference between local time and GMT (Greenwich Mean Time).

(i) If it is 6 a.m. in London, what time is it in (a) Santiago
   (b) Peking?

(ii) If it is midday in Mexico City, what time is it in (a) Brussels
   (b) Santiago
   (c) Reykjavik?

Review 3

Two counters are dropped onto this board. The score is found by adding together the numbers on the squares on which the counters land.
Write down all the possible scores.

−4	2
3	−1

MULTIPLYING and DIVIDING

DISCUSSION EXERCISE 3:3

- Using the calculator, the answer to $(-3) \times (-2)$ is found by keying

    $\boxed{3}\ \boxed{+/-}\ \boxed{\times}\ \boxed{2}\ \boxed{+/-}\ \boxed{=}$.

    Use your calculator to find the answers to many multiplications involving negative numbers.

    Discuss your answers. As part of your discussion, make and test statements about multiplying without using the calculator. You may like to copy and complete the following table using the calculator, then use the completed table in your discussion.

×	-6	-5	-4	-3	-2	-1	0	1	2	3	4	5	6
-6													
-5													
-4													
-3													
-2													
-1													
0							0	0	0	0	0	0	0
1							0	1	2	3	4	5	6
2							0	2	4	6	8	10	12
3							0	3	6	9	12	15	18
4							0	4	8	12	16	20	24
5							0	5	10	15	20	25	30
6							0	6	12	18	24	30	36

- Using the calculator, the answer to $\dfrac{-20}{5}$ is found by keying $\boxed{20}\ \boxed{+/-}\ \boxed{\div}\ \boxed{5}\ \boxed{=}$.

    Use your calculator to find the answers to many divisions involving negative numbers.

    Discuss your answers.

    What if more than two numbers are involved?

    For instance $(-3) \times 4 \times (-2)$, $\dfrac{(-4) \times (-6)}{-2}$ etc.

To **multiply or divide** proceed as follows:

Disregarding the signs, multiply (or divide) the numbers, then find the sign for the answer using:

  two like signs (both + or both −) give positive
  two unlike signs (one + and the other −) give negative.

Worked Example   Calculate   (a) $(-2) \times 3$ (b) $\dfrac{-16}{-8}$ (c) $2 \times (-8) \times (-3)$

Answer   (a)   2 multiplied by 3 is 6.
      Since the signs are different the answer is negative.
      i.e. $(-2) \times 3 = -6$

   (b)   16 divided by 8 is 2.
      Since the signs are the same the answer is positive.
      i.e. $\dfrac{-16}{-8} = 2$

   (c)   Disregarding the signs, the calculation is $2 \times 8 \times 3$ which has answer of 48.
      The signs are + − −. The first two of these (+, −) combine to give −.
      Then this − combines with the last sign (−) to give +. The answer is then positive.
      i.e. $2 \times (-8) \times (-3) = 48$.

EXERCISE 3:4

1. Find the answer to these.

   (a) $3 \times (-7)$ (b) $(-2) \times 5$ (c) $(-8) \times 2$ (d) $(-4) \times (-5)$ (e) $3 \times (-5)$

   (f) $8 \div (-2)$ (g) $(-24) \div (-4)$ (h) $(-12) \div 3$ (i) $(-18) \div (-6)$ (j) $20 \div (-5)$

   (k) $\dfrac{-16}{-4}$ (l) $\dfrac{-30}{-5}$

2. Calculate.

   (a) $(-2) \times (-3) \times 4$ (b) $(-3) \times 4 \times (-5)$ (c) $(-2) \times (-3) \times (-5)$ (d) $2 \times (-3) \times (-1)$

   (e) $\dfrac{(-6) \times (-3)}{2}$ (f) $\dfrac{8 \times (-5)}{4}$ (g) $\dfrac{(-2) \times (-6) \times 3}{9}$ (h) $\dfrac{-3 \times 8}{-2 \times (-6)}$

3. Calculate.

   (a) $2 \times (-1 \cdot 5)$ (b) $(-4) \times (-2 \cdot 2)$ (c) $2 \cdot 5 \times (-3)$ (d) $4 \cdot 8 \div (-3)$

   (e) $\dfrac{-8 \cdot 2}{-2}$ (f) $\dfrac{-16 \cdot 8}{8}$

4.

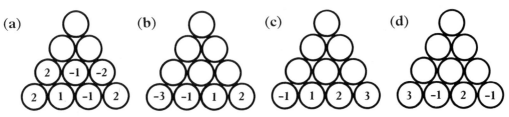

(a) (b) (c) (d)

The numbers in the circles are found by multiplying the two numbers immediately below. Find the number in the top circle of each "pyramid".

5.

How might this multiplication square be completed?

×				
	-10			
		2		
			-24	
				30

Review 1

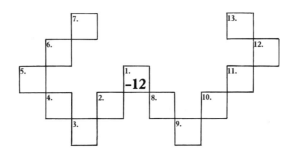

Copy this diagram.
Use the following clues to find the numbers in **square 7.** and **square 13.**

Clues

Square 2. The answer to **1.** divided by 2.
Square 3. The answer to **2.** divided by -2.
Square 4. The answer to **3.** multiplied by -1.
Square 5. The answer to **4.** multiplied by -5.
Square 6. The answer to **5.** divided by 3.
Square 7. The answer to **6.** multiplied by -4.

Square 8. The answer to **1.** multiplied by -2.
Square 9. The answer to **8.** divided by -6.
Square 10. The answer to **9.** divided by 4.
Square 11. The answer to **10.** multiplied by 3.
Square 12. The answer to **11.** multiplied by -4.
Square 13. The answer to **12.** divided by -3.

Review 2   Calculate.

(a) $7 \times (-3)$

(b) $(-5) \times (-8)$

(c) $(-4) \times (-2) \times (-3)$

(d) $(-40) \div 4$

(e) $\dfrac{30}{-6}$

(f) $\dfrac{2 \times (-5) \times 4}{-10}$.

CALCULATIONS with ×, ÷, +, −

Remember: When more than one operation is to be done do Brackets then Multiplication and Division, then Addition and Subtraction.

Remember: A fraction line acts as a bracket.

Examples

$$\frac{3 + (-4) \times 6}{3} = \frac{3 + (-24)}{3}$$
$$= \frac{-21}{3}$$
$$= -7$$

$$-8 + 2\,[(-3) - 2 \times 5] = -8 + 2\,[(-3) - 10]$$
$$= -8 + 2\,[-13]$$
$$= -8 + [-26]$$
$$= -34$$

EXERCISE 3:5

1. Calculate.

   (a) $2 \times (-4) + (-3)$ **(b)** $-3 - 4 \times (-2)$ **(c)** $-2\,[5 + (-4)]$

   (d) $3\,[(-2) - (-5)]$ **(e)** $(-2)^2 + 8$ **(f)** $-6 - (-3)^2$

   (g) $7 - (-4) \times 3^2$ **(h)** $2 \times (-3) - (-2) \times 5$ **(i)** $-4 + 3 \times (-4) + (-5)$

2. Evaluate.

   (a) $-1 + 3\,[2 - (-4)]$ **(b)** $(-4) \times 3 - 5 \times 2^2$ **(c)** $(-2)^2 - 3\,[4 - 3^2]$

   (d) $3 - (-2) \times [4 + (-2)]$ **(e)** $2 \times (-4) + (-6)^2$ **(f)** $-4 + (-5)^2 \times 2$

   (g) $\dfrac{3 \times (-2) + (-9)}{-3}$ **(h)** $\dfrac{5 \times (-4) + (-8)}{4}$ **(i)** $\dfrac{-4 + 2[3 - (-6)]}{-2}$

3. Insert $+$, $-$, $\times$, $\div$ signs to make these true. You may use the same sign more than once. You may use brackets.

   (a) -3 4 -1 $=$ 2

   (b)   2 -3 -4 $=$ -10

   (c)   1 -4 -2 3 $=$ 0

   (d) -2 -6 -3 5 $=$ 1

   (e)   6 -4 5   3 $=$ 2

4.   **−5**   **−3**   **−2**   **2**

Some of the ways these four numbers can be combined are:

$-5 \times (-3) - (-2) \times 2$, $\dfrac{-3 + 2 + (-5)}{-2}$, $-5\,[-3 + (-2)^2]$.

Combine the four numbers to give the greatest possible answer.

5.

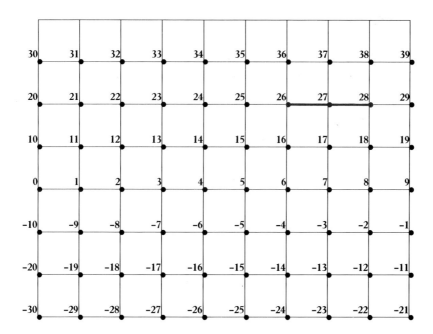

On grid paper, draw up a rectangle as shown.
Calculate each of the questions below; find the answers on the grid, connecting them in order.
For instance since **(a)** has answer 28 and **(b)** has answer 26 then 28 is connected to 26 as shown.

(a) $7[6 + (-2)]$

(b) $-2[(-14) + 1]$

(c) $(-4)^2$

(d) $10 - 5 - (-2)$

(e) $-8 + 5 + (-10)$

(f) $-2[4 - (-8)]$

(g) $-4 \times 8 + 5$

(h) $3[(-5) + 2] + 1$

(i) $-6 + 2[1 - (-3)]$

(j) $2 + -3(7 - 4)$

(k) $2 \times (-1) - 3 \times (-5)$

(l) $6 + (-6) + 5$

(m) $6 \times 2 + 4 \times (-4)$

(n) $\dfrac{3[6 - (-2)]}{4}$

(o) $10 + \dfrac{-30}{-6}$

(p) $(-4)^2 - (-9)$

(q) $40 - (-2)^2$

(r) $\dfrac{(-4) \times 9 - 1}{(-1)}$

(s) $\dfrac{24}{-8} \times \dfrac{-18}{2}$

Review   Calculate

(a) $(-3) \times 4 + 7$

(b) $-5 + 3 \times (-2)$

(c) $-5[1 + 2 \times (-4)]$

(d) $3^2 + (-4)^2$

(e) $-2 + 2(3 - 5^2)$

(f) $2 \times (-6) - 7 \times (-2)^2$

(g) $\dfrac{(-4)^2 - 5 \times (-4) + 6}{-2}$.

INVESTIGATION 3:6

NUMBER CHAINS

Number chains can be formed with positive numbers as follows:

If the number is even, divide it by 2.

If the number is odd, multiply it by 3 and add 1.

Repeat with the new number formed.

For instance, beginning with 20 the number chain formed is:

20, 10, 5, 16, 8, 4, 2, 1, 4, 2, 1, 4, 2, 1, . . .

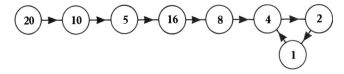

How is the following number chain formed? –5, –14, –7, –20, –10, –5, –14, . . .

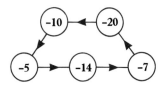

Investigate number chains formed in this way. You could use the following program to help in your investigation.

```
10    DIM  AN(1000)
20    LOOPFOUND = FALSE : I = 1
30    CLS
40    INPUT   "TYPE IN STARTING NUMBER :     "N
50    REPEAT
60    AN(I) = N
70    M = INT(N/2) * 2
80    IF  M = N  THEN  N = N/2  ELSE  N = 3 * N + 1
90    FOR  J = 1 TO I
100   IF  N = AN (J)  THEN  LOOPFOUND = TRUE : J = I
110   NEXT J
120   PRINT  N;
130   I = I + 1
140   UNTIL  LOOPFOUND  OR   I = 1000
150   PRINT
160   IF LOOPFOUND PRINT   "CHAIN NOW LOOPS"    ELSE  PRINT    "AFTER
      1000 NUMBERS THE CHAIN HAS NOT LINKED YET."
170   END
```

Investigate number chains formed in other ways. If you use the above program to help in your investigation you will need to change lines 70 and 80.

Chapter 3

EVALUATING FORMULAE

Worked Example $a = 2bc - d^2$ Find the value of a if $b = 3$, $c = -4$, $d = -2$.

Answer   Without using the calculator: Using the calculator:

$$a = 2bc - d^2$$
$$= 2 \times 3 \times (-4) - (-2)^2$$
$$= -24 - 4$$
$$= -28$$

$$a = 2bc - d^2$$
$$= 2 \times 3 \times (-4) - (-2)^2$$
$$= -28$$

Keying $\boxed{2}$ $\boxed{\times}$ $\boxed{3}$ $\boxed{\times}$ $\boxed{4}$ $\boxed{+/-}$
$\boxed{-}$ $\boxed{2}$ $\boxed{+/-}$ $\boxed{\text{INV}}$ $\boxed{x^2}$ $\boxed{=}$

Worked Example $s = ut + \frac{1}{2}at^2$ Find s if $t = 0.2$, $u = -20$, $a = 10$.

Answer   Without using the calculator: Using the calculator:

$$s = ut + \frac{1}{2}at^2$$
$$= -20 \times 0.2 + \frac{1}{2} \times 10 \times (0.2)^2$$
$$= -4 + 5 \times 0.04$$
$$= -4 + 0.2$$
$$= -3.8$$

$$s = ut + \frac{1}{2}at^2$$
$$= -20 \times 0.2 + \frac{1}{2} \times 10 \times (0.2)^2$$
$$= -3.8$$

Keying $\boxed{20}$ $\boxed{+/-}$ $\boxed{\times}$ $\boxed{0.2}$ $\boxed{+}$ $\boxed{0.5}$ $\boxed{\times}$
$\boxed{10}$ $\boxed{\times}$ $\boxed{0.2}$ $\boxed{\text{INV}}$ $\boxed{x^2}$ $\boxed{=}$

EXERCISE 3:7

1. $y = mx + c$ Find the value of y if:

   (a) $m = -2$, $x = 3$, $c = -1$ (b) $m = -1$, $x = -2$, $c = 3$ (c) $m = \frac{1}{2}$, $x = -2$, $c = 5$

   (d) $m = -\frac{1}{2}$, $x = 3$, $c = -2$ (e) $m = 0.5$, $x = -6$, $c = 2$.

2. If $a = -4$, $b = 0.5$, $c = 2$, $d = -\frac{1}{4}$ evaluate

   (a) $3a - 5c$ (b) $a^2 - c^2$ (c) $8d + a - b$ (d) $cd + a$

   (e) $(a + c)(a - c)$ (f) $2a + 3c^2$ (g) $b - a^2$ (h) $\frac{c - a}{2b + a}$

   (i) $4(a + b - c)$ (j) $3 + a(b - d)$.

3. The formula $S = \frac{59}{2}[8 + (-50)]$ can be used to work out the sum of all of the terms of the sequence 8, 7, 6, ... -50.
   Use this formula to find this sum, S.

61

4. The y coordinate of any point on this graph can be calculated using the formula $y = -\frac{1}{2}x + 4$.

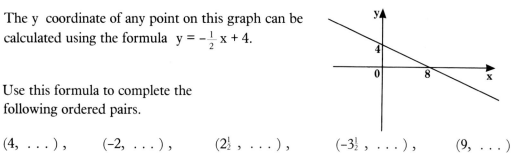

Use this formula to complete the following ordered pairs.

$(4, \ldots)$, $(-2, \ldots)$, $(2\frac{1}{2}, \ldots)$, $(-3\frac{1}{2}, \ldots)$, $(9, \ldots)$

5. To change a temperature from °C to °F we can use the formula $F = \frac{9}{5}C + 32$. Use this formula to write the following in °F.

(a) 100°C   (b) 0°C   (c) −10°C   (d) −15°C   (e) −40°C

6. Use the formula $s = ut + \frac{1}{2}at^2$ to find s if:

(a) $u = 25, t = 3, a = -5$ (b) $u = -10, t = \frac{1}{4}, a = 8$ (c) $u = -5, t = 0{\cdot}5, a = 10$

(d) $u = -15, t = 0{\cdot}5, a = -2$.

Review 1 $C = \frac{5}{9}(F - 32)$ is a formula that can be used to change a temperature from °F to °C. Write the following in °C.   (a) 14°F   (b) −4°F

Review 2 $y = m(x - 3) + 2$
Find y if   (a) $m = -3, x = 5$ (b) $m = 3, x = -5$ (c) $m = -1, x = -1$
            (d) $m = -2, x = 1\frac{1}{2}$ (e) $m = \frac{1}{2}, x = -0{\cdot}5$.

PUZZLES 3:8

? ?

1. The four numbers, along each side of this triangle, must add to the same total. What might these numbers be?

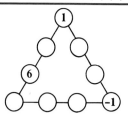

2. 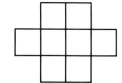 Place negative and positive numbers in these boxes so the total of each row and column is zero.

? ?

continued . . .

. . . from previous page

? ?? ?

3. Replace the letters with numbers
to give the totals shown.

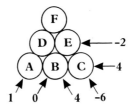

4.

		-2
	-5	
		-6

This is to be a magic square. Each row, each
column and each diagonal is to add to the same
number.
How might this magic square be completed?

5.
$$9 = \frac{-4}{-4} - [-4 + (-4)]$$

Can the other 1-digit whole numbers (0, 1, 2, 3, 4, 5, 6, 7, 8) also be
written using –4 *exactly* four times?

? ?? ?

Franciscus Vieta

François Viète, better known as Franciscus Vieta, was born in France in 1540 and died in 1603. He is known as "The Father of Modern Algebra". Interestingly, he disliked the Arabic name algebra.

Vieta was the most important mathematician of his time. He did not regard himself as a mathematician. Mathematics was what Vieta did as a leisure activity, not as a profession. He was a lawyer before becoming involved in politics. He became a member of a provincial government and later a King's adviser. He had important connections at the courts of Henry III and Henry IV.

Vieta is best known for using letters to represent numbers. He used consonants to represent known or given numbers and vowels to represent unknown numbers.

Vieta introduced a simplified notation for powers. For A, A^2, A^3 he used A, A quad., A cubus which clearly showed the relationship. His work on algebra established algebra as a separate study from arithmetic.

Apart from his work in algebra, he also made important contributions in other areas of mathematics.

He used decimal fractions and made a strong plea for these to be more widely used. In one of his books he wrote:

Sexagesimals and sixties are to be used sparingly or never in mathematics, and thousandths and thousands, hundredths and hundreds, tenths and tens, and similar progressions, ascending and descending, are to be used frequently or exclusively.

The notation he used for decimal fractions was to write the integer part of a number in boldface type. He separated the integer part from the fractional part with either a comma or a stroke. That is, he wrote 21,305·78 as either **21,305**,78 or **21,305**| 78. Although the decimal point was used by some mathematicians at this time, its use did not become common until shortly after Vieta's death when the scotsman, John Napier made it popular.

The work that Vieta did in geometry was further developed by the French mathematicians René Descartes and Pierre de Fermat. Sir Isaac Newton was later inspired by the work of these three.

Vieta was also interested in the reform of the calendar. He opposed Clavius' work on this. This lead to much criticism of him, mainly because of his unscientific approach.

It was for his work in deciphering codes that the French government valued Vieta. He deciphered a code used by the Spanish to send secret messages during a war between France and Spain. This gave the French a considerable advantage. The Spanish did not believe it was possible to decipher the code which contained more than 500 signs and symbols. They complained to the Pope that the French were using black magic and sorcery.

NEGATIVE and FRACTIONAL INDICES

DISCUSSION EXERCISE 4:1

Since $2^3 = 2 \times 2 \times 2$ then
$$\frac{1}{2^3} = \frac{1}{2 \times 2 \times 2}$$
$$= \frac{1}{8}$$
$$= 0 \cdot 125.$$

Use the following calculator keying sequence to find the value of 2^{-3}.

$\boxed{2}$ $\boxed{\text{INV}}$ $\boxed{x^y}$ $\boxed{3}$ $\boxed{+/-}$ $\boxed{=}$. Compare the answers for $\frac{1}{2^3}$ and 2^{-3}.

What if 3 was replaced with 1?
What if 3 was replaced with 2?
What if 3 was replaced with 4?
What if 3 was replaced with 5?
What if . . .

Make a statement about the value of $\frac{1}{2^n}$ and 2^{-n}. **Discuss.**

Consider again $\frac{1}{2^3}$ and 2^{-3}. **What if** 2 was replaced by 4?
What if 2 was replaced by 5?

Make a statement about the value of a^{-n} and $\frac{1}{a^n}$. Test your statement for many values of a and n.

EXERCISE 4:2

Find the missing index in each of the following.

1. $4^{-5} = \frac{1}{4 \cdots}$ 2. $7^{-2} = \frac{1}{7 \cdots}$ 3. $10^{-5} = \frac{1}{10 \cdots}$ 4. $1 \cdot 7^{-8} = \frac{1}{1 \cdot 7 \cdots}$ 5. $\frac{1}{2^7} = 2^{\cdots}$

6. $\frac{1}{3^6} = 3^{\cdots}$ 7. $\frac{1}{10^4} = 10^{\cdots}$ 8. $\frac{1}{3 \cdot 4^{10}} = 3 \cdot 4^{\cdots}$ 9. $5^{-4} = \frac{1}{5 \cdots}$ 10. $\frac{1}{6^9} = 6^{\cdots}$

11. $8^{-3} = \frac{1}{8 \cdots}$ 12. $\frac{1}{10^3} = 10^{\cdots}$ **Review 1** $7^{-4} = \frac{1}{7 \cdots}$ **Review 2** $\frac{1}{10^9} = 10^{\cdots}$

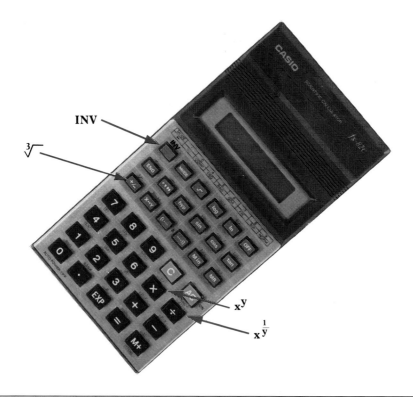

DISCUSSION EXERCISE 4:3

- What is the value of $\sqrt{16}$?

  Use this calculator keying sequence to find the value of $16^{\frac{1}{2}}$: 16 INV $x^{\frac{1}{y}}$ 2 = .
  Compare the answers for $\sqrt{16}$ and $16^{\frac{1}{2}}$.
  What if 16 was replaced with 49?
  What if 16 was replaced with 25?
  What if 16 was replaced with 7?
  What if ...

  Make a statement about the values of $a^{\frac{1}{2}}$ and $\sqrt{a}$. **Discuss.**

- Use the cube root key ($\sqrt[3]{}$) on your calculator to find the value of $\sqrt[3]{8}$.

  Use this calculator keying sequence to find the value of $8^{\frac{1}{3}}$: 8 INV $x^{\frac{1}{y}}$ 3 = .

  Compare the answers for $8^{\frac{1}{3}}$ and $\sqrt[3]{8}$.

  Make a statement about the values of $a^{\frac{1}{3}}$ and $\sqrt[3]{a}$. **Test your statement for many values of a. Discuss.**

- How could you use the $x^{\frac{1}{y}}$ key to find the values of the following: $\sqrt[4]{16}, \sqrt[4]{30}, \sqrt[5]{20}, \ldots$?
  Discuss.

EXERCISE 4:4

1. What is the missing index?

    (a) $\sqrt{36} = 36^{\cdots}$ **(b)** $\sqrt{28} = 28^{\cdots}$ **(c)** $\sqrt{100} = 100^{\cdots}$ **(d)** $\sqrt[3]{64} = 64^{\cdots}$

    (e) $\sqrt[3]{10} = 10^{\cdots}$ **(f)** $\sqrt[4]{18} = 18^{\cdots}$ **(g)** $\sqrt[7]{94} = 94^{\cdots}$

2. Evaluate

    (a) $4^{\frac{1}{2}}$ **(b)** $16^{\frac{1}{2}}$ **(c)** $9^{\frac{1}{2}}$ **(d)** $64^{\frac{1}{2}}$ **(e)** $100^{\frac{1}{2}}$ **(f)** $8^{\frac{1}{3}}$

    (g) $27^{\frac{1}{3}}$ **(h)** $125^{\frac{1}{3}}$ **(i)** $16^{\frac{1}{4}}$ **(j)** $81^{\frac{1}{4}}$ **(k)** $32^{\frac{1}{5}}$.

Review 1   Find the missing index.   **(a)** $\sqrt{72} = 72^{\cdots}$ **(b)** $\sqrt[3]{24} = 24^{\cdots}$

Review 2   Evaluate   **(a)** $25^{\frac{1}{2}}$ **(b)** $36^{\frac{1}{2}}$ **(c)** $64^{\frac{1}{3}}$ **(d)** $64^{\frac{1}{6}}$.

STANDARD FORM

DISCUSSION EXERCISE 4:5

- $254{\cdot}13 \times 10^3 = 254{\cdot}13 \times 1000$
  $= 254130$

  $254{\cdot}13 \times 10^{-3} = 254{\cdot}13 \times \dfrac{1}{10^3}$
  $= \dfrac{254{\cdot}13}{1000}$
  $= 0{\cdot}25413$

  Discuss the following statement in relation to these examples. "To multiply a decimal number by 10^n, where n is an integer, move the decimal point n places. If n is positive, move the decimal point in the positive direction; if n is negative, move the decimal point in the negative direction". As part of your discussion, rewrite other numbers such as $26{\cdot}2 \times 10^4$, $0{\cdot}7 \times 10^{-2}$, $7{\cdot}8 \times 10^2$, $8{\cdot}65 \times 10^{-1}$ etc. in decimal form.

- The answer to the calculation $50\,000 \times 800\,000$ is $40\,000\,000\,000$.
  How is this answer displayed on a calculator screen? **Discuss.**

  The answer to the calculation $2\,600\,000 \times 50\,000$ is $130\,000\,000\,000$.
  How is this displayed on the calculator screen? **Discuss.**

  The answer to a calculation is displayed on a calculator screen as 2.3 ^{05}. What is the answer to this calculation? **Discuss.**

  Discuss the answers the calculator displays for $\dfrac{5}{1000}$, $\dfrac{5}{10\,000}$, $\dfrac{5}{100\,000}$ etc.

The numbers 10, 100, 1000, 10000, . . . can be rewritten as 10^1, 10^2, 10^3, 10^4, . . .
The number 70000 can be rewritten as 7×10000 or as 7×10^4 or as $7{\cdot}0 \times 10^4$.
The number 736 can be rewritten as $7{\cdot}36 \times 100$ or as $7{\cdot}36 \times 10^2$.

The numbers $\frac{1}{10}$, $\frac{1}{100}$, $\frac{1}{1000}$, . . . can be rewritten as $\frac{1}{10^1}$, $\frac{1}{10^2}$, $\frac{1}{10^3}$, . . . or as 10^{-1}, 10^{-2}, 10^{-3}, . . .

The number 0·086 can be rewritten as $\frac{8{\cdot}6}{100}$ or $\frac{8{\cdot}6}{10^2}$ or $8{\cdot}6 \times 10^{-2}$.

The numbers $7{\cdot}0 \times 10^4$, $7{\cdot}36 \times 10^2$, $8{\cdot}6 \times 10^{-2}$ are written in a notation known as **Standard Index Notation**. Standard Index Notation is usually called **Standard Form**. It is also often called **Scientific Notation.**

Numbers written in **standard form** consist of two parts. They have a decimal number part in which there is always just one digit (not zero) before the decimal point and this part is multiplied by a power of 10.
For instance, the following numbers are in standard form: $6{\cdot}2 \times 10^{14}$, $7{\cdot}01 \times 10^{-1}$, $8{\cdot}3 \times 10^0$. The following numbers are *not* in standard form: $0{\cdot}6 \times 10^6$, $3{\cdot}4$, $78{\cdot}2 \times 10^{-3}$.

Another way of stating the standard form notation is:
Standard form is $a \times 10^n$ where $1 \le a < 10$ and n is an integer.

Standard form is a very useful way of writing very large or very small numbers.
On a calculator screen, the standard form notation is not written in full; the × and 10 are omitted.
For instance, a calculator displays $7{\cdot}3 \times 10^5$ as 7.3 ^{05}. (Some of the older Casio scientific calculators and some other scientific calculators display $7{\cdot}3 \times 10^5$ as 7.3   05.)

Take the following steps to rewrite a number given in standard form as a number in decimal form.
> **Step 1**   Move the decimal point. The index with the 10 gives the number of places and the direction in which the point is to be moved.
> **Step 2**   Omit the multiplication sign and the power of 10.

Examples   1. $2{\cdot}47 \times 10^4 = 24700$ (move the point 4 places in the positive direction)
2. $3{\cdot}0 \times 10^{-4} = 0{\cdot}0003$ (move the point 4 places in the negative direction)
3. $4{\cdot}5 \times 10^0 = 4{\cdot}5$ (move the point 0 places)

Take the following steps to rewrite a number given in decimal form as a number in standard form.
> **Step 1**   Write the decimal point after the first non-zero digit.
> **Step 2**   Insert a multiplication sign and a power of 10. The index with the 10 is found by considering the number of places, and the direction, the point would need to be moved to get back to the original number.

Examples

1. $36 \cdot 2 = 3 \cdot 62 \times 10^1$ (the point in $3 \cdot 62$ needs to be moved 1 place in the positive direction to get $36 \cdot 2$)

2. $8957 = 8 \cdot 957 \times 10^3$ (the point in $8 \cdot 957$ needs to moved 3 places in the positive direction to get 8957)

3. $5 = 5 \cdot 0 \times 10^0$ (the point in $5 \cdot 0$ needs to be moved zero places to get 5)

4. $0 \cdot 0903 = 9 \cdot 03 \times 10^{-2}$ (the point in $9 \cdot 03$ needs to be moved 2 places in the negative direction to get $0 \cdot 0903$)

5. $0 \cdot 004 = 4 \cdot 0 \times 10^{-3}$ (the point in $4 \cdot 0$ needs to be moved 3 places in the negative direction to get $0 \cdot 004$)

EXERCISE 4:6

1. Which of the following are in standard form?

   (a) $7 \cdot 3 \times 10^4$ (b) $62 \cdot 4 \times 10^2$ (c) $0 \cdot 3 \times 10^1$ (d) $2 \cdot 0 \times 10^0$

   (e) $3 \cdot 49$ (f) $8 \cdot 2 \times 10$ (g) $3 \cdot 05 \times 10^{-17}$ (h) $80 \cdot 1 \times 10^{-3}$

   (i) $7 \cdot 6824 \times 10^{92}$ (j) $0 \cdot 305 \times 10^4$

2. Write these in decimal form.

   (a) $3 \cdot 4 \times 10^2$ (b) $8 \cdot 12 \times 10^3$ (c) $6 \cdot 25 \times 10^{-2}$ (d) $8 \cdot 0 \times 10^{-3}$

   (e) $7 \cdot 03 \times 10^4$ (f) $2 \cdot 05 \times 10^0$ (g) $7 \cdot 8 \times 10^{-1}$ (h) $1 \cdot 01 \times 10^{-4}$

   (i) $3 \cdot 7 \times 10^5$ (j) $3 \cdot 7 \times 10^{-5}$ (k) $1 \cdot 52 \times 10^1$ (l) $3 \cdot 4 \times 10^0$

   (m) $4 \cdot 81 \times 10^{-3}$ (n) $8 \cdot 0 \times 10^1$ (o) $2 \cdot 61 \times 10^{-5}$ (p) $6 \cdot 0 \times 10^{10}$

   (q) $7 \cdot 05 \times 10^{-2}$ (r) $8 \cdot 154 \times 10^2$ (s) $8 \cdot 154 \times 10^{-3}$ (t) $9 \cdot 407 \times 10^1$

   (u) $9 \cdot 407 \times 10^{-1}$ (v) $6 \cdot 0 \times 10^4$ (w) $6 \cdot 0 \times 10^{-4}$

3. Find the missing index.

   (a) $36 \cdot 4 = 3 \cdot 64 \times 10^{\cdots}$ (b) $482 \cdot 5 = 4 \cdot 825 \times 10^{\cdots}$ (c) $7 = 7 \cdot 0 \times 10^{\cdots}$

   (d) $17 = 1 \cdot 7 \times 10^{\cdots}$ (e) $8478 = 8 \cdot 478 \times 10^{\cdots}$ (f) $0 \cdot 42 = 4 \cdot 2 \times 10^{\cdots}$

   (g) $0 \cdot 0591 = 5 \cdot 91 \times 10^{\cdots}$ (h) $0 \cdot 308 = 3 \cdot 08 \times 10^{\cdots}$ (i) $0 \cdot 008 = 8 \cdot 0 \times 10^{\cdots}$

   (j) $2 \cdot 6 = 2 \cdot 6 \times 10^{\cdots}$ (k) $89 = 8 \cdot 9 \times 10^{\cdots}$ (l) $0 \cdot 05 = 5 \cdot 0 \times 10^{\cdots}$

   (m) $0 \cdot 6 = 6 \cdot 0 \times 10^{\cdots}$ (n) $22 \cdot 71 = 2 \cdot 271 \times 10^{\cdots}$ (o) $0 \cdot 00092 = 9 \cdot 2 \times 10^{\cdots}$

4. Write these numbers in standard form.

   (a) 64   (b) 782   (c) 3640   (d) $55 \cdot 2$ (e) 7

   (f) 1000   (g) $34 \cdot 2$ (h) $555 \cdot 61$ (i) $72 \cdot 4$ (j) $0 \cdot 8$

   (k) $0 \cdot 91$ (l) $0 \cdot 0043$ (m) $0 \cdot 804$ (n) $0 \cdot 04$ (o) $2 \cdot 4$

   (p) $0 \cdot 24$ (q) 24   (r) $0 \cdot 0024$ (s) 240   (t) 9

   (u) 90   (v) $0 \cdot 09$ (w) $0 \cdot 9$

5. An estimate of the population in the UK in the year 2031 is 61·2 million.
   Write this in standard form.

6. In the early 1990s, the population of the South East of England was about $1·8 \times 10^7$.
   Write this in decimal form.

7. About $1·9 \times 10^6$ cars were registered in the UK in 1990.
   Write this in decimal form.

8. The velocity of light is 300 000 km/sec.
   Write this velocity in standard form.

9. In a year, light travels about $9·46 \times 10^{12}$ km.
   Write this distance in decimal form.

10. The most distant objects yet observed are 15 000 000 000 light-years distant from the earth. Write this in standard form.

11. The half-life of one of the polonium isotopes is about $3·0 \times 10^{-7}$ seconds.
    Write this in decimal form.

12. The wavelength of visible light is about $5·0 \times 10^{-5}$ cm.
    Write this in decimal form.

13. The diameter of an atom is about 0·000 000 000 1 mm.
    Write this in standard form.

Review 1 Write these in decimal form.

(a) $2·3 \times 10^4$ (b) $2·3 \times 10^0$ (c) $2·3 \times 10^{-4}$ (d) $3·0504 \times 10^{-1}$
(e) $9·01 \times 10^6$ (f) $6·4 \times 10^{-3}$ (g) $3·465 \times 10^2$

Review 2 Write these in standard form.

(a) 52·7   (b) 16005   (c) 6   (d) 0·83
(e) 0·1   (f) 0·0002

Review 3 In mid 1991, there were about $2·2 \times 10^6$ people unemployed in the UK.
Write this in decimal form.

Review 4 The sun is about 0·000016 light-years from the earth.
The centre of the Milky Way is about 26000 light-years from the earth.
Write these distances in standard form.

MULTIPLYING and DIVIDING numbers written in STANDARD FORM

We use the laws of indices when we multiply or divide numbers written in standard form.

We use $a^x \times a^y = a^{x+y}$ and $a^x \div a^y = a^{x-y}$.

Worked Example   Calculate the following, giving the answers in standard form.

$$\textbf{(a)} \quad (2 \cdot 4 \times 10^{-4}) \times (3 \cdot 1 \times 10^{7}) \qquad \textbf{(b)} \quad (2 \cdot 4 \times 10^{-4}) \div (3 \cdot 0 \times 10^{7})$$

Answer

(a)
$$\begin{aligned}
&(2 \cdot 4 \times 10^{-4}) \times (3 \cdot 1 \times 10^{7}) \\
&= 2 \cdot 4 \times 10^{-4} \times 3 \cdot 1 \times 10^{7} \\
&= 2 \cdot 4 \times 3 \cdot 1 \times 10^{-4} \times 10^{7} \\
&= (2 \cdot 4 \times 3 \cdot 1) \times (10^{-4} \times 10^{7}) \\
&= 7 \cdot 44 \times 10^{3}
\end{aligned}$$

(b)
$$\begin{aligned}
&(2 \cdot 4 \times 10^{-4}) \div (3 \cdot 0 \times 10^{7}) \\
&= \frac{2 \cdot 4 \times 10^{-4}}{3 \cdot 0 \times 10^{7}} \\
&= \frac{2 \cdot 4}{3 \cdot 0} \times \frac{10^{-4}}{10^{7}} \\
&= 0 \cdot 8 \times 10^{-11} \\
&= 8 \cdot 0 \times 10^{-1} \times 10^{-11} \\
&= 8 \cdot 0 \times 10^{-12}
\end{aligned}$$

EXERCISE 4:7

In this exercise, give all the answers in standard form.

1. Calculate.

   (a) $(3 \cdot 7 \times 10^{5}) \times (2 \cdot 0 \times 10^{4})$

   (b) $(5 \cdot 0 \times 10^{3}) \times (1 \cdot 7 \times 10^{6})$

   (c) $(1 \cdot 82 \times 10^{5}) \times (4 \cdot 0 \times 10^{2})$

   (d) $(2 \cdot 4 \times 10^{6}) \times (2 \cdot 0 \times 10^{-3})$

   (e) $(4 \cdot 12 \times 10^{-5}) \times (2 \cdot 0 \times 10^{-3})$

   (f) $(4 \cdot 24 \times 10^{7}) \div (2 \cdot 0 \times 10^{4})$

   (g) $(6 \cdot 9 \times 10^{4}) \div (3 \cdot 0 \times 10^{7})$

   (h) $(8 \cdot 4 \times 10^{6}) \div (4 \cdot 0 \times 10^{-2})$

   (i) $(7 \cdot 5 \times 10^{-3}) \div (5 \cdot 0 \times 10^{-5})$

2. Calculate.

   (a) $(4 \cdot 8 \times 10^{7}) \times (3 \cdot 0 \times 10^{5})$

   (b) $(1 \cdot 5 \times 10^{4}) \div (5 \cdot 0 \times 10^{1})$

   (c) $(4 \cdot 2 \times 10^{4}) \div (6 \cdot 0 \times 10^{-2})$

   (d) $(3 \cdot 2 \times 10^{-2}) \times (4 \cdot 0 \times 10^{-4})$

   (e) $(3 \cdot 2 \times 10^{-2}) \div (4 \cdot 0 \times 10^{-4})$

   (f) $(6 \cdot 0 \times 10^{-3}) \times (8 \cdot 1 \times 10^{7})$

   (g) $(1 \cdot 34 \times 10^{7}) \times (8 \cdot 76 \times 10^{3})$

   (h) $(2 \cdot 681 \times 10^{3}) \times (3 \cdot 4 \times 10^{-4})$

   (i) $(1 \cdot 44 \times 10^{7}) \div (1 \cdot 2 \times 10^{9})$

   (j) $(8 \cdot 23 \times 10^{-2}) \times (7 \cdot 6 \times 10^{-3})$

   (k) $(4 \cdot 75 \times 10^{-2}) \div (2 \cdot 5 \times 10^{3})$

3. A rectangle has length of $2 \cdot 6 \times 10^3$ mm and width of $1 \cdot 8 \times 10^2$ mm.
   What is the area of this rectangle?

4. One oxygen atom has a mass of about $2 \cdot 7 \times 10^{-23}$ grams.
   How heavy would 5000 oxygen atoms be?

5. The half-life of radium is about $1 \cdot 622 \times 10^3$ years.
   One year is about $8 \cdot 76 \times 10^3$ hours.
   How many hours is the half-life of radium?

6. The density of brass is $8 \cdot 5 \times 10^3$ kg/m³.
   What is the mass of $2 \cdot 4 \times 10^{-2}$ cubic metres of brass?

7. A large stone has a mass of $5 \cdot 5 \times 10^2$ kg. It is known that the density of this stone is $2 \cdot 2 \times 10^3$ kg/m³.
   What is the volume of this stone?

8. The mass of a hydrogen atom is about $1 \cdot 67 \times 10^{-24}$ g while that of a uranium atom is about $3 \cdot 95 \times 10^{-22}$ g.
   About how many times heavier is a uranium atom than a hydrogen atom? (Answer to 3 significant figures.)

9. The nearest star, Proxima Centauri, is about $4 \cdot 0 \times 10^{13}$ km from the earth.
   In a year, light travels about $9 \cdot 46 \times 10^{12}$ km.
   About how many light-years is Proxima Centauri from the earth?

10.

Planet	Diameter (km)
Mercury	$4 \cdot 9 \times 10^3$
Venus	$1 \cdot 2 \times 10^4$
Earth	$1 \cdot 3 \times 10^4$
Mars	$6 \cdot 8 \times 10^3$
Jupiter	$1 \cdot 4 \times 10^5$
Saturn	$1 \cdot 2 \times 10^5$
Uranus	$5 \cdot 2 \times 10^4$
Neptune	$4 \cdot 9 \times 10^4$
Pluto	$2 \cdot 4 \times 10^3$

   (a) Which planet is the smallest?
   (b) Which planet is the largest?
   (c) Which planet has diameter about 10 times that of Venus?
   (d) Which planet has diameter about half that of Mercury?
   (e) One of the planets has diameter about 20 times larger than that of Pluto. Which planet?
   (f) The diameter of Venus is larger than that of Pluto. About how many times larger?

The mass of the earth is about $5 \cdot 97 \times 10^{24}$ kg. How many tonnes is this?

12. A billion is a million million. A trillion is a million billion. A quadrillion is a million trillion.

Write, in standard form   **(a)**   one trillion
                         (b)   one quadrillion.

13. 1 micron is 10^{-4} centimetres.
  (a)   How many microns are there in 1mm?
  (b)   1 Angstrom is 10^{-8} centimetres. How many microns are there in 1 Angstrom?

Review 1   Calculate.
    (a) $(2 \cdot 4 \times 10^3) \times (4 \cdot 0 \times 10^2)$ **(b)** $(2 \cdot 0 \times 10^5) \times (5 \cdot 3 \times 10^0)$
    (c) $(8 \cdot 4 \times 10^3) \div (2 \cdot 0 \times 10^{-2})$ **(d)** $(6 \cdot 5 \times 10^{-1}) \times (7 \cdot 8 \times 10^{-3})$
    (e) $(2 \cdot 5 \times 10^{-3}) \div (5 \cdot 0 \times 10^{-2})$

Review 2   The U.K. value for one billion is $1 \cdot 0 \times 10^{12}$. The American value for one billion is $1 \cdot 0 \times 10^{9}$.
    How much larger is the U.K. value for one billion than the American value?

Review 3

City	Bombay	Cape Town	Darwin	London	Paris	Rome	Tokyo
Distance (in km) **from Berlin**	$6 \cdot 3 \times 10^3$	$9 \cdot 6 \times 10^3$	$1 \cdot 3 \times 10^4$	$9 \cdot 2 \times 10^2$	$8 \cdot 7 \times 10^2$	$1 \cdot 2 \times 10^3$	$8 \cdot 9 \times 10^3$

    Which city is   **(a)**   closest to Berlin
                      (b)   the greatest distance from Berlin
                      (c)   about twice as far from Berlin as Bombay
                      (d)   about 10 times closer to Berlin as Tokyo?

Review 4   1 hour = $3 \cdot 6 \times 10^3$ seconds.
    (a)   What is the velocity, in km/sec, of an object which is travelling at $7 \cdot 2 \times 10^2$ km/h?
    (b)   The velocity of light is about $3 \cdot 0 \times 10^5$ km/sec. Give this velocity in km/h.

USING the EXP key on the CALCULATOR

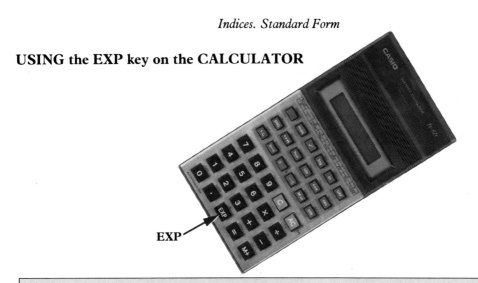

EXP

DISCUSSION EXERCISE 4:8

Look closely at what appears on the calculator screen after each of the following is keyed:
7·82 EXP 3. **Discuss.**

Discuss how to use the EXP key to find the answer to a calculation such as
$$(7{\cdot}82 \times 10^3) \times (2{\cdot}0 \times 10^4) \,.$$

What if the calculation was $(7{\cdot}82 \times 10^3) \times (2{\cdot}0 \times 10^{-4})$?

What if the calculation was $(7{\cdot}82 \times 10^{-3}) \times (2{\cdot}0 \times 10^{-4})$?

ADDING and SUBTRACTING NUMBERS written in STANDARD FORM

One way of calculating $3{\cdot}6 \times 10^6 + 2{\cdot}3 \times 10^4$ is by rewriting $3{\cdot}6 \times 10^6$ and $2{\cdot}3 \times 10^4$ in decimal form, then adding.
Another way is to use the EXP key on the calculator as follows.
Key $\boxed{3{\cdot}6}$ $\boxed{\text{EXP}}$ $\boxed{6}$ $\boxed{+}$ $\boxed{2{\cdot}3}$ $\boxed{\text{EXP}}$ $\boxed{4}$ $\boxed{=}$ to get a screen display of 3 623 000. If the answer is to be given in standard form, $3{\cdot}623 \times 10^6$ would be written down.

DISCUSSION EXERCISE 4:9

Another way of calculating $3{\cdot}6 \times 10^6 + 2{\cdot}3 \times 10^4$ is:

$$\begin{aligned}
3{\cdot}6 \times 10^6 + 2{\cdot}3 \times 10^4 &= 3{\cdot}6 \times 10^4 \times 10^2 + 2{\cdot}3 \times 10^4 \\
&= 10^4 \,(3{\cdot}6 \times 10^2 + 2{\cdot}3) \\
&= 10^4 \,(360 + 2{\cdot}3) \\
&= 10^4 \times (362{\cdot}3) \\
&= 10^4 \times (3{\cdot}623 \times 10^2) \\
&= 3{\cdot}623 \times 10^6
\end{aligned}$$

Discuss each step of this method. You may like to refer to **Chapter 6** for the step
$3{\cdot}6 \times 10^4 \times 10^2 + 2{\cdot}3 \times 10^4 = 10^4 \,(3{\cdot}6 \times 10^2 + 2{\cdot}3)$.

EXERCISE 4:10

Use a calculator or non-calculator method to find the answers to the questions in this exercise.   Give all the answers in standard form.

1. Calculate.

   (a) $6 \cdot 8 \times 10^3 + 1 \cdot 5 \times 10^2$ (b) $2 \cdot 7 \times 10^5 - 8 \cdot 2 \times 10^4$ (c) $6 \cdot 07 \times 10^2 + 3 \cdot 4 \times 10^0$

   (d) $4 \cdot 152 \times 10^7 + 6 \cdot 7 \times 10^3$ (e) $8 \cdot 9 \times 10^2 - 2 \cdot 81 \times 10^{-1}$ (f) $7 \cdot 6 \times 10^2 + 8 \cdot 541 \times 10^{-2}$

   (g) $7 \cdot 8 \times 10^{-3} - 4 \cdot 6 \times 10^{-4}$ (h) $3 \cdot 05 \times 10^{-2} + 1 \cdot 62 \times 10^{-4}$ (i) $6 \cdot 81 \times 10^9 - 3 \cdot 04 \times 10^8$

2. In 1990, Central Government spent about £$6 \cdot 7 \times 10^{10}$ while local authorities spent about £$4 \cdot 3 \times 10^{10}$.
   How much was spent by both?

3. There were about $1 \cdot 459 \times 10^5$ males and $6 \cdot 9 \times 10^3$ females in the army in 1990.
   About how many people were in the army?

4. In 1989, about $9 \cdot 13 \times 10^4$ tonne of shell fish and $5 \cdot 804 \times 10^5$ tonne of other fish was caught.
   What total weight of fish was caught in 1989?

5. In 1990, about $8 \cdot 416 \times 10^5$ people were on the NHS hospital waiting lists. Of these, about $4 \cdot 53 \times 10^4$ were waiting for plastic surgery.
   How many were waiting for surgery other than plastic surgery?

6. The cost of running NHS hospitals and community health services was about £$1 \cdot 6676 \times 10^{10}$ in 1990 and £$8 \cdot 162 \times 10^9$ in 1980.
   What was the increase in running costs?

7. In April 1990, about $1 \cdot 104 \times 10^6$ people flew on Domestic Services on UK airlines while in April 1989, about $9 \cdot 802 \times 10^5$ people flew.
   How many more flew in April 1990 than in April 1989?

8. Q1 : $1 \cdot 02 \times 10^8$ Q2 : $9 \cdot 2 \times 10^7$ Q3 : $9 \cdot 4 \times 10^7$ Q4 : $9 \cdot 8 \times 10^7$
   These figures give the number of British Rail journeys on which passengers used season tickets in 1990. Q1 is the first quarter of 1990, Q2 is the second quarter etc.
   What total number of journeys in 1990 were season tickets used on?

Review 1   Calculate   (a) $6 \cdot 1 \times 10^{-2} + 5 \cdot 01 \times 10^{-3}$ (b) $8 \cdot 7 \times 10^{-1} - 9 \cdot 6 \times 10^0$.

Review 2   The Pacific Ocean covers an area of about $1 \cdot 65 \times 10^8$ km² while the Atlantic Ocean covers about $8 \cdot 22 \times 10^7$ km².
        (a)   How much larger is the Pacific Ocean than the Atlantic Ocean?
        (b)   What total area do these two oceans cover?

USING the SCIENTIFIC MODE on the CALCULATOR

To get the calculator operating in **scientific mode, Key** [MODE] followed by [8] . You do not need to remember that MODE 8 is the scientific mode as the 8 is printed above SCI on the calculator.

To get the calculator out of scientific mode, **Key** [MODE] followed by [9] . You do not need to remember that MODE 9 is the normal mode as the 9 is printed above NORM on the calculator.

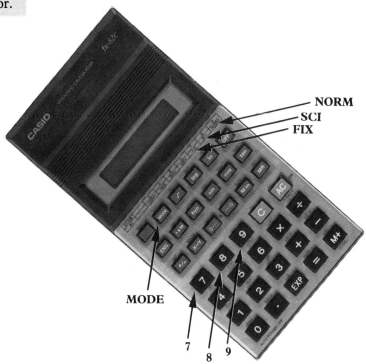

NORM
SCI
FIX

MODE

7
8 9

DISCUSSION EXERCISE 4:11

- Key the calculation 6·7821 × 3·488 as follows:

  [MODE] [8] [2] [6·7821] [×] [3·488] [=] .

  What is the effect of keying the 2? **Discuss.** As part of your discussion first replace the 2 with 1, then with 3, then with 4, then with 5 etc.

  When the calculator is operating in scientific mode, is the EXP key used in the normal way? **Discuss.** As part of your discussion key in some calculations such as
  $$(3\cdot4 \times 10^5) \times (1\cdot05 \times 10^4) .$$

- Key the calculation 6·7821 × 3·488 as follows:

  [MODE] [7] [2] [6·7821] [×] [3·488] [=] .

  What is MODE FIX? **Discuss.** As part of your discussion replace the 2 with 1, 3, 4, 5 etc.

CALCULATIONS with LARGE or SMALL NUMBERS not written in standard form

Very large numbers, such as 753 000 000, and very small numbers, such as 0·000 000 000 781, cannot be keyed directly into an 8-digit calculator.
If numbers such as these are part of a calculation, they may be keyed into the calculator in standard form.

Worked Example   Calculate   34 820 000 000 × 734 000 000.

Answer $34\,820\,000\,000 = 3·482 \times 10^{10}$
$734\,000\,000 = 7·34 \times 10^{8}$
Hence $34\,820\,000\,000 \times 734\,000\,000 = (3·482 \times 10^{10}) \times (7·34 \times 10^{8})$

Keying $\boxed{3·482}$ $\boxed{\text{EXP}}$ $\boxed{10}$ $\boxed{\times}$ $\boxed{7·34}$ $\boxed{\text{EXP}}$ $\boxed{8}$ $\boxed{=}$ gives a screen display of $2·555788^{19}$.
We will give the answer to 3 significant figures since there were just 3 s.f. in one of the numbers being multiplied.
Hence $34\,820\,000\,000 \times 734\,000\,000 = 2·56 \times 10^{19}$ to 3 s.f.

Note   An alternative keying sequence is:
$\boxed{\text{MODE}}$ $\boxed{8}$ $\boxed{3}$ $\boxed{3·482}$ $\boxed{\text{EXP}}$ $\boxed{10}$ $\boxed{\times}$ $\boxed{7·34}$ $\boxed{\text{EXP}}$ $\boxed{8}$ $\boxed{=}$ which gives a screen display of $2·56^{19}$.

EXERCISE 4:12

Use the calculator to find the answer to these. Round your answers sensibly.

1.   253 000 000 000 × 3 640 000 000

2.   1 300 000 000 000 × 28 200 000 000

3.   75 000 000 000 000 × 824 500 000 000

4.   71 598 000 000 × 8 143 000 000 000

5.   246 000 000 ÷ 134 000 000

6.   897 200 000 000 ÷ 9 982 000 000

7.   0·000 000 000 082 × 0·000 000 000 37

8.   0·000 000 007 89 ÷ 0·000 000 000 388

9.   0·000 000 000 73 × 0·000 000 000 834

10.   0·000 000 034 82 ÷ 0·0000 000 785

11. $\dfrac{347\,000\,000\,000 \times 2\,440\,000\,000\,000}{2\,374\,000\,000}$

12. $\dfrac{458\,900\,000\,000}{361\,000\,000 \times 783\,000\,000}$

Review 1   2 480 000 000 000 ÷ 17 800 000 000   **Review 2**   0·000 000 003 281 × 0·000 000 078 9

PROJECT

Choose one branch of Science such as astronomy, chemistry, ecology etc.

Research a topic from your chosen branch of Science. Use reference books in this research.

Make a summary of your research. In your summary, include calculations done in standard form.

1. Write in standard form.
   (a) 678   (b) 2   (c) 0·704   (d) 0·02   (e) 28·3

2. (a) Write $\frac{25}{6}$ as a mixed number.

   (b) Write $7\frac{3}{8}$ as an improper fraction.

3. Estimate the answer to   (a) $0·25 \times 83·4$ (b) $\dfrac{7·8 \times 21·4}{0·23}$

4. Copy and complete the addition and multiplication tables.

(a)

+		3	
			−1
	−7	−2	
−4			−8

(b)

×		−2	
		4	
−1	−7		
2			−6

5. Write these in decimal form.
   (a) $4·7 \times 10^{4}$ (b) $6·0 \times 10^{-2}$ (c) $1·8 \times 10^{0}$

6. In 1990, the population of Scotland was about 5·1 million.
   Write this in standard form.

7. The speedometer of a car registers just 6 digits.
   At the beginning of January, the reading on this speedometer was 98783·2 km. At the end of January the reading was 1249·1 km.
   How far did this car travel during January?

8. Calculate   (a) $\frac{3}{4} \times \frac{2}{15}$ (b) $8 \times 3\frac{3}{4}$ (c) $2\frac{2}{5} \times 3\frac{1}{8}$

   (d) $\frac{5}{9} \div \frac{2}{3}$ (e) $3\frac{3}{5} \div 2\frac{1}{10}$ (f) $\frac{5}{6} - \frac{1}{4}$ (g) $\frac{2}{5} + \frac{3}{4} + \frac{1}{2}$

   (h) $2\frac{2}{3} + 5\frac{3}{5}$ (i) $3\frac{1}{4} - 1\frac{5}{6}$ (j) $\frac{2}{5} + \frac{3}{4} \times 3\frac{1}{3}$ (k) $\frac{3}{5}\left(\frac{2}{3} + 2\frac{1}{4}\right)$.

9. Find the missing index.

    (a) $3^{-8} = \frac{1}{3^{\cdots}}$ (b) $\frac{1}{8^3} = 8^{\cdots}$ (c) $\sqrt{47} = 47^{\cdots}$ (d) $\sqrt[3]{96} = 96^{\cdots}$

10. 1 hour is about 0·000114 years. Write this in standard form.

11. In a survey, it was found that $\frac{1}{6}$ of families had 1 child, and $\frac{3}{10}$ had 2 children.
    What fraction of the families surveyed had 1 or 2 children?

12. Without using the calculator, evaluate:
    (a) –2 + (–7)   (b) 5 – (–4)   (c) (–2·8) – 1·1   (d) –3 + 4 – (–2)

    (e) 8 × (–7)   (f) (–6) × (–1)   (g) 30 ÷ (–5)   (h) –3 × 4 + (–6)

    (i) 6 + (–1) × 4   (j) $\frac{(-2)^2}{-1}$ (k) –2 – [3 + (–4)]   (l) 3 + 2 [–1 + (–5)]

13. Evaluate   (a) $49^{\frac{1}{2}}$ (b) $27^{\frac{1}{3}}$.

14. Use the calculator to find the following. Estimate as a check.

    (a) 44·7 (5·82 + 2·15)   (b) $\frac{0.59 \times 135.9}{6.8 \times 1.04}$

15. $s = \frac{1}{2}(u + v)t$ Find s if u = 5, v = –20, t = 0·5.

16. (a) Cleopatra poisoned herself in 30 B.C. She was then 39 years old. In what year
        was Cleopatra born?
    (b) Julius Caesar was born in 100 B.C. He was assassinated in 44 B.C. How old was
        Julius Caesar at his death?
    (c) How much older was Julius Caesar than Cleopatra?

17. Mince is packed in trays, each weighing $\frac{3}{5}$ kg.
    How many lasagne meals could be made from 10 trays if each meal needs $\frac{3}{4}$ kg of
    mince?

18. $y = \frac{1}{2}x - 3$ gives the equation of this line.
    Use this equation to complete the following ordered
    pairs.

    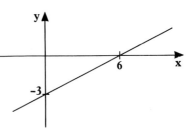

    $(4, \ldots)$, $(-2, \ldots)$, $(-1, \ldots)$, $(1\frac{1}{2}, \ldots)$,

    $(-1\frac{1}{2}, \ldots)$

19. Without using the calculator, find the answers to these in standard form.

    (a) $(7.8 \times 10^{-3}) \times (3.0 \times 10^5)$ (b) $(8.4 \times 10^{-2}) \div (2.0 \times 10^{-5})$

20. On their holiday, on the Norfolk Broads, the Petrie family travelled a total of 45 km on the canals.

    How many hours did they travel on these canals if they averaged $2\frac{1}{4}$ km per hour?

21. The diameter of an electron is about $4 \cdot 0 \times 10^{-13}$ cm.
    (a) How many mm is this?   (b) How many metres is this?

22. James weighs 60 kg. $\frac{1}{3}$ of Simon's mass is the same as $\frac{2}{5}$ of James'.

    How heavy is Simon?

23. Use the formula $a = \dfrac{t^2 - s^2}{2d}$ to find **a** when $t = 0, s = 16 \cdot 7, d = -7 \cdot 5$.

24. The population of India is about $6 \cdot 9 \times 10^8$ while that of France is about $5 \cdot 47 \times 10^7$.
    The area of India is about $3 \cdot 3 \times 10^6$ km² while that of France is about $5 \cdot 5 \times 10^5$ km².
    Find **(a)** the population density (i.e. the number of people per square kilometre) of India
          (b) the population density of France.

25.

Distance from Earth	
Sun	$1 \cdot 5 \times 10^6$ km
Nearest Star	$4 \cdot 0 \times 10^{13}$ km
Brightest Star	$8 \cdot 1 \times 10^{13}$ km
Centre of Milky Way	$2 \cdot 5 \times 10^{17}$ km
Nearest galaxies	$1 \cdot 6 \times 10^{18}$ km
Andromeda Galaxy	$1 \cdot 4 \times 10^{19}$ km
Galaxy in Virgo	$7 \cdot 1 \times 10^{20}$ km
Galaxy in Gt. Bear	$4 \cdot 5 \times 10^{22}$ km

(a) Is the Andromeda Galaxy closer to Earth than is the Centre of the Milky Way?
(b) How many times further from Earth is the Centre of the Milky Way than is the Brightest Star?
(c) What is about 50 times closer to the Earth than is the Galaxy in Virgo?
(d) The velocity of light is about $3 \cdot 0 \times 10^5$ km/sec. About how many kilometres will light travel in a year? (Give the answer to 2 s.f.)
(e) One light-year is the distance light will travel in one year. Using your answer for **(d)**, find the distance (in light-years) of the Nearest Star from Earth.

26. The surface area of a cube can be calculated from the
    formula: Surface Area = $6x^2$ where x is the length of
    an edge.
    Use this formula to find the surface area of the sketched
    cube.

    $1\frac{1}{3}$ m
    $1\frac{1}{3}$ m
    $1\frac{1}{3}$ m

27. Of a group of friends, $\frac{2}{5}$ are aged 16 or over. $\frac{1}{4}$ of those under 16 are also
    under 15.

    What fraction of this group of friends is 15?

28. Use the EXP key on the calculator to calculate:
    (a) $6\cdot1 \times 10^3 + 2\cdot7 \times 10^4$

    (b) $2\cdot71 \times 10^{-3} - 4\cdot6 \times 10^{-4}$

    (c) $5\,230\,000\,000 \times 68\,000\,000$

    (d) $\dfrac{0\cdot000\,000\,000\,452}{0\cdot000\,000\,028}$

29. The earth's crust was formed about $4\cdot5 \times 10^9$ years ago.
    The first land plants occurred about $4\cdot5 \times 10^8$ years ago.
    The first flowering plants occurred about $1\cdot35 \times 10^8$ years ago.

    (a) How many years after the earth's crust was formed did the first land plants
         occur?
    (b) How long before the first flowering plants occurred did the first land plants
         occur?

30. The fraction $\frac{13}{42}$ is formed by using two of the digits 1, 2, 3, 4 in the numerator and
    the other two in the denominator. What is the largest proper fraction that can be
    formed in this way from the digits 1, 2, 3, 4?

ALGEBRA

Algebra from Previous Levels

REVISION

Divisibility

A number is **divisible by 2** if it is an even number

divisible by 3 if the sum of its digits is divisible by 3

divisible by 4 if the number formed from the last two digits is divisible by 4

divisible by 5 if the last digit is 0 or 5

divisible by 6 if it is divisible by both 2 and 3

divisible by 8 if the number formed from the last three digits is divisible by 8

divisible by 9 if the sum of its digits is divisible by 9

divisible by 10 if the last digit is 0

Prime numbers, Factors, Multiples

A **prime number** is divisible by just two numbers, itself and 1.

The **multiples** of a number are found by multiplying the number by each of 1, 2, 3, . . . For instance, the multiples of 10 are 10, 20, 30, . . .

A **factor** of a given number is a whole number that divides exactly into the given number. For instance, the factors of 10 are 1, 2, 5, 10.

A **prime factor** is a factor that is a prime number. For instance, the prime factors of 10 are 2 and 5.

Spatial Arrangements of Numbers

The **square numbers** are $1^2, 2^2, 3^2, 4^2, \ldots$ i.e. 1, 4, 9, 16, . . .

The **cube numbers** are $1^3, 2^3, 3^3, 4^3, \ldots$ i.e. 1, 8, 27, 64, . . .

Finding a square and finding a square root are inverse operations as are finding a cube and a cube root. One operation "undoes" the other.

$\sqrt{64}$ is read as "the square root of 64". $\sqrt{64} = 8$, since $8^2 = 64$.

$\sqrt[3]{64}$ is read as "the cube root of 64". $\sqrt[3]{64} = 4$, since $4^3 = 64$.

The square numbers (1, 4, 9, 16, . . .), rectangular numbers (2, 6, 12, 20, . . .), triangular numbers (1, 3, 6, 10, . . .), pentagonal numbers (1, 5, 12, 22, . . .), hexagonal numbers (1, 6, 15, 28, . . .), can all be represented by a pattern of dots in the given geometric shape.

continued . . .

. . . *from previous page*

Sequences

A **sequence** is a list of numbers such as 3, 7, 11, 15, ...
t_1 means the first term, t_2 means the second term and so on. For instance, for the sequence 3, 7, 11, 15, ... $t_1 = 3$, $t_2 = 7$, $t_3 = 11$ etc.
t_n means the nth term. For instance, for the sequence 3, 7, 11, 15, ... $t_n = 4n - 1$.
Sometimes a letter other than t is used. For instance T_1 , a_1 , u_1 , all mean the first term.

Sequences are sometimes based on the following special numbers – odd numbers, even numbers, squares, cubes, multiples.
The terms of a sequence are sometimes found by adding the same number to each previous term or by multiplying each previous term by the same number.
Sometimes we can continue a sequence by using the **difference method**. For instance, the next term in the sequence 12, 14, 22, 36, 56, . . . can be found as follows.

$$
\begin{array}{ccccccccccc}
12 & & 14 & & 22 & & 36 & & 56 & & 82 \\
& 2 & & 8 & & 14 & & 20 & & 26 & \\
& & 6 & & 6 & & 6 & & 6 & &
\end{array}
$$

Simplifying

ab means $a \times b$.
2a means $2 \times a$.
a^2 means $a \times a$.

a + a can be simplified to 2a.
5a + 2a can be simplified to 7a.
5a + 3b – a + 2b can be simplified to 4a + 5b.
5 (2a – 3) can be expanded to 10a – 15.

3xa is usually written as 3ax. That is, the number is written first, then the letters are written in alphabetical order.

Powers. Indices.

3^4 is called a **power** of 3; 4 is called the **index**, 3 is called the **base**.

Indices is the plural of index. For instance, if we were speaking of the numbers 4 and 7 in 3^4 and 2^7 we would call 4 and 7 the indices.

The x^y key, on the calculator, may be used to find powers.

For instance, 2^7 is found by keying $\boxed{2}$ $\boxed{\text{INV}}$ $\boxed{x^y}$ $\boxed{7}$ $\boxed{=}$

continued . . .

. . . *from previous page*

Some of the laws of indices are: $a^m \times a^n = a^{m+n}$

$$\frac{a^m}{a^n} = a^{m-n}$$

$$(a^m)^n = a^{mn}.$$

For instance,
$$3^4 \times 3^5 = 3^{4+5} \qquad \frac{2^9}{2^4} = 2^{9-4} \qquad (5^2)^3 = 5^{2 \times 3}$$
$$= 3^9 \qquad\qquad\quad = 2^5 \qquad\qquad = 5^6$$

Formulae and Equations

$x + 3$ is an **expression**.

$p = x + 3$ is a **formula**. The value of p depends on the value of x.

$2p - 4 = 1$ is an **equation**. Here p can have only one value; $p = 2 \cdot 5$.

Three methods of **solving equations** are : trial and improvement, flowchart method, balance method. The **trial and improvement** method is particularly useful for solving polynomial equations ; that is, equations which involve a square such as x^2 or a cube such as x^3.

The **flowchart method** for solving $2a - 4 = 1$ is shown below.

$$\text{Begin with} \quad a \rightarrow \boxed{\times 2} \rightarrow 2a \rightarrow \boxed{-4} \rightarrow 2a - 4$$

$$2 \cdot 5 \leftarrow \boxed{\div 2} \leftarrow 5 \leftarrow \boxed{+4} \leftarrow \text{Begin with 1}$$

Hence $a = 2 \cdot 5$.

The **balance method** for solving $2a - 4 = 1$ is shown below.

$$2a - 4 = 1$$
$$2a = 5 \quad \text{(adding 4 to both sides)}$$
$$a = 2 \cdot 5 \quad \text{(dividing both sides by 2)}$$

The **"trial and improvement"** method for finding the solution (to 1 d.p.) for the equation $2x^3 - 1 = 9$ is shown below.

Try $x = 1$. If $x = 1$, $2x^3 - 1 = 1$ which is less than 9.

Try $x = 2$. If $x = 2$, $2x^3 - 1 = 15$ which is greater than 9.

Since 9 lies between 1 and 15, then the solution must be between 1 and 2.

Try $x = 1 \cdot 5$. If $x = 1 \cdot 5$, $2x^3 - 1 = 5 \cdot 75$ which is less than 9.

Try $x = 1 \cdot 8$. If $x = 1 \cdot 8$, $2x^3 - 1 = 10 \cdot 664$ which is greater than 9.

Try $x = 1 \cdot 7$. If $x = 1 \cdot 7$, $2x^3 - 1 = 8 \cdot 826$ which is less than 9.

The solution lies between $1 \cdot 7$ and $1 \cdot 8$. Since $8 \cdot 826$ is closer to 9 than is $10 \cdot 664$, the solution to 1 d.p. is $x = 1 \cdot 7$.

When solving an equation always **check your solution** by substituting your solution back into the equation. For instance, to check that $a = 2 \cdot 5$ is a solution for $2a - 4 = 1$ proceed as follows: If $a = 2 \cdot 5$, $2a - 4 = 2 \times 2 \cdot 5 - 4$
$$= 1 \quad \text{Correct.}$$

continued . . .

. . . *from previous page*

Reciprocals

The **reciprocal** of $\frac{a}{b}$ is $\frac{b}{a}$.

For instance, the reciprocal of $\frac{2}{7}$ is $\frac{7}{2}$; the reciprocal of 5 is $\frac{1}{5}$.

The $\frac{1}{x}$ key on the calculator is used to find the reciprocal of a number.

For instance, the reciprocal of 4 is found by keying $\boxed{4}$ $\boxed{\text{INV}}$ $\boxed{\frac{1}{x}}$.

The operation "take the reciprocal" is needed to solve some equations by the flowchart method. This operation is necessary if x is on the bottom line of the equation.
Remember that the inverse operation for "taking the reciprocal" is also "taking the reciprocal".

For instance, $\frac{3}{x} = 5$ is solved, using the flowchart method, as follows:

$$\text{Begin with x} \rightarrow \boxed{\text{Take the reciprocal}} \rightarrow \frac{1}{x} \rightarrow \boxed{\times 3} \rightarrow \frac{3}{x}$$

$$\frac{3}{5} \leftarrow \boxed{\text{Take the reciprocal}} \leftarrow \frac{5}{3} \leftarrow \boxed{\div 3} \leftarrow \text{Begin with 5}$$

The solution is $x = \frac{3}{5}$ or 0·6.

Graphs

The **x-axis** is the horizontal axis.
The **y-axis** is the vertical axis.

The **coordinates** of a point are a pair of numbers such as (3, –2).
The first number is the x-coordinate; the second number is the y-coordinate.

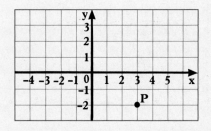

For the point P(3, –2), the x-coordinate is 3 and the y-coordinate is –2.

(3, –2), is also called an **ordered pair**. The ordered pair (3, –2) is different from the ordered pair (–2, 3).

The graph of a straight line may be drawn, from the equation of the line, as follows.
  Step 1   Find the coordinates of three points on the line.
  Step 2   Plot these points.
  Step 3   Draw the line that passes through these points.
Note: The line could be drawn by plotting just two points but for greater accuracy it is wise to plot three points.

continued . . .

. . . from previous page

For instance, to draw the line $y = 2x + 1$ proceed as follows.

Choose three values for x, say $-1, 0, 1$. Substitute these values for x into $y = 2x + 1$ to find the corresponding values of y – see the table below. Now plot the points $(-1, -1)$, $(0, 1)$, $(1, 3)$ and draw the line that goes through these points – see the graph below.

x	-1	0	1
y	-1	1	3

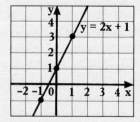

The **graph of a curve** may be drawn in a similar way to a straight line. Many points should be plotted and joined with a smooth curve.

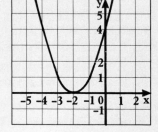

The curve shown on this graph is called a **parabola**.

On a **distance/time graph**, distance is on the vertical axis, time is on the horizontal axis.

The slope of the graph gives the **speed.**

The steeper the slope of the graph, the greater the speed.

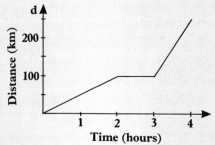

Inequalities such as $n \leq -2$, $n > 1$, $2 \leq n < 5$ may be graphed on a number line. To display an inequality on the number line proceed as follows.

Step 1 Draw a line over all the values included.

Step 2 If the end point of the line is one of values included, place the symbol ● on this end point; if the end point is not one of the values included, place the symbol O on this end point.

For instance,

is the graph of $n \leq -2$

is the graph of $n > 1$

is the graph of $2 \leq n < 5$

continued . . .

. . . *from previous page*

Simultaneous Equations

Equations such as $\begin{cases} 3x - 4y = 23 \\ 4x + 3y = 14 \end{cases}$, which need to be solved together to find the

value of x and y, are called **simultaneous equations.**
Some methods of solving these are: **trial and improvement, balance method**
(also called the **elimination** method), **substitution method, graphical method**.
In the graphical method, we draw the graphs of each equation on the same set of
axes. The x and y-coordinates of the point where the graphs meet give the solution of
the simultaneous equations.

The balance method depends on eliminating one of the unknowns.

$\begin{array}{l} 3x - 4y = 23 \\ 4x + 3y = 14 \end{array} \Big\}$ becomes $\begin{cases} 9x - 12y = 69 \quad \text{(multiplying both sides by 3)} \\ 16x + 12y = 56 \quad \text{(multiplying both sides by 4)} \end{cases}$

$$25x \quad\quad = 125 \quad \text{(adding the equations)}$$
$$x = 5 \quad \text{(dividing both sides by 25)}$$

When $x = 5$, $4x + 3y = 14$ becomes $20 + 3y = 14$

$$3y = -6 \quad \text{(subtracting 20 from both sides)}$$
$$y = -2 \quad \text{(dividing both sides by 3)}$$

Always check the solution by substituting the value of the unknowns into the original
equations.

Problem Solving

Three methods of problem solving are : **finding a pattern, solving a simpler
problem first, using equations.** We take the following steps to solve a problem
using equations.

Step 1 Choose a variable such as n or x for the unknown quantity.
Step 2 Rewrite the statements in mathematical symbols.
Step 3 Combine these statements into an equation.
Step 4 Solve the equation.
Step 5 Check the answer with the information in the problem.

REVISION EXERCISE

1.　　　1　　2　　3　　4　　6　　8　　11　　14　　16　　19　　20　　25　　30

   (a)　Which of these numbers are prime numbers?
   (b)　Which number is the cube of another number in the list?
   (c)　Which number is the square root of another number?
   (d)　Which numbers in the list are multiples of 4?
   (e)　Which numbers in the list are factors of 20?

2. Which inequality best describes the given statements.

    (a) The top speed of Jane's car is 140 km/h.
       A. $s > 140$ **B.** $s \geq 140$ **C.** $s < 140$ **D.** $s \leq 140$

    (b) Class sizes in a school range from 15 to 31.
       A. $15 < s < 31$ **B.** $31 \leq s \leq 15$ **C.** $15 \leq s \leq 31$ **D.** $31 < s < 15$

3. A patio is 2 metres longer than it is wide.

    (i) Write an expression, involving x, for
       (a) the length of the patio
       (b) the perimeter of the patio
       (c) the area of the patio.
    (ii) How wide is the patio if the perimeter is 22 metres?

    x metres

4. Solve these equations.

    (a) $3x - 5 = 16$ (b) $2(3a + 2) = 7$ (c) $3n + 4 = n - 1$

    (d) $\dfrac{2x}{5} = -4$ (e) $\dfrac{2}{x} = 0\cdot5$

5.

    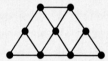 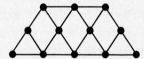 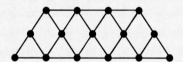

    "Garden Designs" are making screens by bolting short rods together. These diagrams represent their three smallest screens. In the smallest screen 14 rods and 9 bolts are used.

    (a) How many rods and how many bolts are used in the other two screens shown?
    (b) Selena wrote the relationship between r, the number of rods and b, the number of bolts as $r = b + 5$. She then realised this was not correct.
       What is the correct relationship between r and b?

6. Solve these simultaneous equations.

         (a) $2a + b = 8$ (b) $5m + 4n = 12$
             $3a - b = 17$ $5m - 2n = 9$

7. (i) Give the reciprocal of these as a fraction.   (a) 8   (b) 3a   (c) $\dfrac{x}{3}$

    (ii) Use the $\dfrac{1}{x}$ key on the calculator to find the reciprocal of each of the following. If rounding is necessary, round to two significant figures.

         (a) 25   (b) $1\cdot9$ (c) $0\cdot34$ (d) 90

8. Find the next three terms in the following sequences.

    (a) 1, 4, 9, 16, ...   (b) 1, 2, 3, 5, 8, ...

    (c) 3, 4, 6, 9, ...   (d) 1, 8, 27, 64, ...

    (e) 32, 16, 8, 4, ...

9. Write down the inequalities displayed on the number lines. Use n for the variable.

    (i)

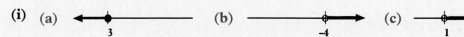

    (ii) (a) Display the inequality $-3 < x < 2$ on a number line.
         (b) Write down all the whole number solutions for x if $-3 < x < 2$.

10. Detectives from the "Snoopy" private detective agency charge an initial fee of £200 plus £75 for each day they are hired.
Detectives from the "Private Eye" agency charge no initial fee but their daily charge is £100 a day.

    (a) Write down an equation that would enable you to find the number of days for which the charge from both agencies would be the same. (Use d as the variable.)

    (b) Solve this equation.

11. Simplify   (a) $3n - 4a - 5n + a$ (b) $2x + 3(4 - x)$

12. Two school parties went to the theatre.

    (a) In the first party there were 2 adults and 26 students. They paid a total of £103.
        $2a + 26s = 103$ is an equation which describes this.
        What does a stand for? What does s stand for?

    (b) The second party paid £184 for 5 adults and 44 students.
        Write an equation, using a and s, which describes this.

    (c) Solve the two simultaneous equations from **(a)** and **(b)** to find the price paid by each adult and each student.

    (d) What total saving did these 77 people make by going to this theatre in a school party?
        What assumption did you have to make to be able to find this total saving?

13. Write as a single power of 4.   (a) $\frac{4^7}{4^2}$ (b) $(4^7)^2$ (c) $\frac{4^7}{16^2}$

14.

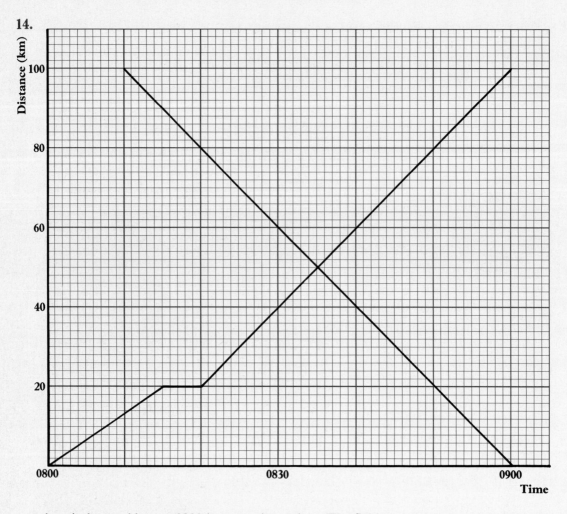

A train leaves Alton at 0800 hours and travels to Wayfield.
Another train leaves Wayfield arriving at Alton at 0900.

(a) At what time did the train from Wayfield leave?
(b) How far is it from Alton to Wayfield?
(c) At what time do these trains pass?
(d) How far from Wayfield do they pass?
(e) How many times did the train from Alton stop?
(f) What was the average speed of the train from Wayfield?
(g) What was the average speed of the train from Alton?

15. I think of a number.
    I divide by 3, then add 3.
    This gives the same result as subtracting 1, then dividing by 2.
    What is the number?

16. Use the x^y key on your calculator to find these powers of 7.
Continue finding answers for powers of 7.
What pattern do you notice if you look at the last digits?
Use this pattern to find the last digit of 7^{107}.

$7^2 =$

$7^3 =$

$7^4 =$

$7^5 =$

$7^6 =$

$7^7 =$

17. (a) Helen was using "trial and improvement" to solve the equation $2x^3 = 40$.
She wrote down this table of values.
Explain why there is a solution to the
equation $2x^3 = 40$ between $x = 2$
and $x = 3$.

x	1	2	3	4	5
$2x^3$	2	16	54	128	250

(b)

x	2·0	2·1	2·2	2·3	2·4	2·5	2·6	2·7	2·8	2·9
$2x^3$	16	18·522	21·296	24·334	27·648	31·25	35·152	39·366	43·904	48·778

Use this table to give the solution to $2x^3 = 40$ accurate to one decimal place.

(c) Find the solution to $2x^3 = 40$ accurate to 2 decimal places.

18. Use the rules of indices to simplify each of the following.

(a) $x^a \times x^b$ (b) $x^a \div x^b$ (c) $\dfrac{x^a}{x^b \times x^c}$ (d) $\dfrac{x^8 \times x^3}{x^5}$ (e) $(4x^3y)^2$

19.

t_1	t_2	t_3	t_4	. . .
2	5	8	11	. . .

t_1	t_2	t_3	t_4	. . .
6	18	54	162	. . .

The first 4 terms of two sequences are given in these tables.
(a) A formula for the nth term of one of these sequences is $t_n = 2 \times 3^n$. Which sequence is this? What is the 7th term of this sequence?
(b) Write down a formula for the nth term of the other sequence.

20. A group of students designed a game based on divisibility.
The digits 0 to 9 were written on cards. Part of the play consisted of the following:

Four cards are dealt, face up, to a player.
The player arranges these in as many different ways as possible to make 4-digit numbers which are divisible by a number the player nominates.
The larger the number nominated, the more points the player scores.

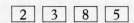

During the play of this game, Kwan was dealt the cards shown. She decided to make numbers divisible by 8.

(a) One arrangement she made was 　3　 　5　 　2　 　8　 . What other arrangements could she make?

(b) How many arrangements could Kwan have made if she had decided to make numbers divisible by 6?

21.

| 1 | 8 | 21 | 40 |

(a) Draw the next pattern in this sequence of octagonal numbers. How many dots are in this pattern?

(b) The following difference table can be formed from the numbers 1, 8, 21, 40.

$$1 \qquad 8 \qquad 21 \qquad 40$$
$$7 \qquad 13 \qquad 19$$
$$6 \qquad 6$$

Copy this difference table. Extend it to find the number of dots in the 8th pattern of octagonal numbers.

22. **(i)** **(a)** Draw a set of axes, with the x-axis from 0 to 6 and the y-axis from 0 to 10.

      (b) Copy and complete this table for $4x + 3y = 24$.
On your set of axes, draw the line $4x + 3y = 24$.

x	0	3	6
y			

      On the same set of axes, draw the line $2x + y = 10$.

  (ii) **(a)** A maths. test was in two sections. In the first section, each question was worth the same number of marks. More marks were given to the questions in the second section.
Let the questions in the first section each be worth f marks and those in the second section each be worth s marks.
On this test, Aidi correctly answered 4 questions in the first section and 3 questions in the second section for a total of 24 marks.
Write down an equation, involving f and s, which describes this.

      (b) $2f + s = 10$ is an equation which describes the number of questions Helen answered correctly and the marks she gained.
Use this equation and the equation from **(a)** to find how many marks were given to each question in the two sections.

 (iii) Is there a connection between **(i)** and **(ii)** of this question? Explain your answer.

23. A squash club charges £2·50 per game for non-members. Members pay a subscription of £20 per year and 50p per game.

  (a) $C = 20 + 0·5n$ is a formula which gives the total cost for a member who plays n games in a year. Draw the graph of $C = 20 + 0·5n$ using axes numbered as shown.

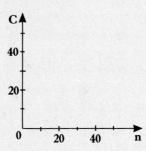

  (b) Write a formula for the total cost for a non-member who plays n games.

  (c) By drawing another graph on the same axes, find how many games could be played in a year before it becomes cheaper to be a member.

24. **(a)** Copy and complete this table for $y = x^2 - 3$.
  (b) Draw the graph of $y = x^2 - 3$ for values of x from –3 to 3.

x	-3	-2	-1	0	1	2	3
y	6			-3			

25.   1, 5, 9, 13, 17, 21, 25, 29, 33, 37, 41, 45, 49, 53, . . .
The 1st and 3rd terms of this sequence are square numbers. That is, t_1 and t_3 are square numbers.

  (a) For the numbers that are written down, there are two other values of n for which t_n is a square number. What are these values of n?

  (b) Use a difference table, or otherwise, to predict the next value of n for which t_n is a square number.

26. This diagram represents a rectangular garden. The shading represents the area in which an orchard is to be planted. The total area of the garden is 500 m².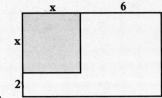

    (a) Show that $x^2 + 8x + 12 = 500$ is an equation which describes this situation.
    (b) Find the length of the orchard, to the nearest tenth of a metre. (*Hint*: use trial and improvement.)

27. Kirsten and Amanda live 2·4 km apart.
    They both leave their homes at the same time to jog to meet each other. Kirsten jogs at an average speed of 4 m/sec while Amanda jogs at an average speed of 5 m/sec.

    (a) How many metres does Kirsten jog in 1 minute?
    (b) How far does Amanda jog in 1 minute?
    (c) Draw a distance/time graph to find how far Kirsten has jogged before she meets Amanda. (Answer to the nearest 100 metres). On your graph have minutes, from 0 to 10, on the horizontal axis and metres, from 0 to 2400 on the vertical axis.

28.

    While on holiday, Edward wrote to 4 friends; Janine, Sarah, Emma and Debbie. His sister then put the letters in the envelopes in such a way that not one of the letters was in the correct envelope.
    Janine's letter was put into Sarah's envelope. Debbie's letter was not in Emma's envelope.
    Whose letter was in Emma's envelope?

29. (i) Consider the sequence of odd numbers 1, 3, 5, 7, 9, 11, . . .

    (a) Copy and complete
    $$1 + 3 = 4$$
    $$1 + 3 + 5 = 9$$
    $$1 + 3 + 5 + 7 =$$
    $$1 + 3 + 5 + 7 + 9 =$$

    (b) Write down a rule, in the form $S_n = . . .$, which gives the sum of the first n terms of 1, 3, 5, 7, 9, 11, . . .
    (c) Find the sum of the first 25 odd numbers.
    (d) The sum of the first n odd numbers is 361. What is n?

(ii) Darren and Julia were investigating odd numbers.

(a) One of the statements Darren made was "If you add together two or more consecutive odd numbers, you always get a square number". He wrote down three examples which supported this statement. What might these have been?

(b) Julia then wrote down an example which showed that Darren's statement wasn't correct. What might this example have been?

(c) Rewrite Darren's statement so it is correct.

Leonhard Euler

Leonhard Euler was born at Basel in Switzerland in 1707 and died at St. Petersburg (Leningrad) in Russia in 1783.

Leonhard's father was a clergyman who had studied mathematics. He passed his knowledge onto Leonhard and encouraged Leonhard in his studies of mathematics even although he had hoped his son would also become a clergyman.

Leonhard Euler became the most important mathematician of his time.

He studied theology, medicine, astronomy, physics, music and oriental languages as well as mathematics. At the age of 20, Euler went to the St. Petersburg Academy to teach medicine. This academy had been recently established by Catherine the Great. At the age of 26, Euler became the Academy's chief mathematician.

In 1741, he was invited by Frederick the Great to join the Berlin Academy. Euler spent 25 years there. His time in Germany was not altogether a happy time. Frederick was impressed with his mathematics but not with Euler as a person. Euler was not very sophisticated and Frederick called him "a mathematical cyclops". In 1766, Euler returned to the St. Petersburg Academy.

During his lifetime, Euler published more than 500 books on mathematics and many articles. His research averaged 800 pages a year. No mathematician has ever been such a prolific writer. He wrote on many aspects of mathematics, from elementary to advanced algebra, arithmetic and trigonometry. He wrote textbooks for use in Russian schools. He also wrote on mechanics, astronomy and music. Usually he wrote in Latin but sometimes in French, although his native tongue was German.

Euler was well known internationally. He frequently entered the competitions run by the Parisian Académie des Sciences and won 12 times. The essays he entered were on a variety of topics including the nature of fire, the masting of ships and tides.

Some of the notations we use today were developed by Euler. f(x) to mean "a function of x" is one such notation. He was not the first to use the symbol π for the ratio of a circle's circumference to its diameter but this symbol was not widely accepted until it appeared in one of Euler's books.

During Euler's time, attempts were made to find an expression that would give just prime numbers. An expression suggested by another mathematician was $2^{2^n} + 1$. Euler showed that although this expression gives prime numbers if $n = 1, 2, 3$ or 4 (we get the numbers 5, 17, 257 and 65537) it does not give a prime number if $n = 5$ (we then get 4 294 967 297).

Euler settled the question of the Königsberg bridge problem (see Level 5 and Level 6 books) by his work on Network theory.

It was said Euler could calculate without any apparent effort and was able to find the answers to complicated problems in his head.

Although Euler was blind for the last few years of his life he continued his work on mathematics until his death.

TRANSFORMING FORMULAE

Sometimes we need to rearrange a formula.

The formula $v = \frac{s}{t}$ can be rearranged as $s = vt$ or as $t = \frac{s}{v}$.

Written as $v = \frac{s}{t}$, v is said to be **the subject of the formula.**
Written as $s = vt$, s is the subject of the formula.
Written as $t = \frac{s}{v}$, t is the subject of the formula.

If a variable, such as s, is to be the subject of a formula then s must be written, on its own, on the left-hand side.

When we rearrange a formula, such as $v = \frac{s}{t}$, so that a variable other than v is the subject of the formula, we are said to have **transformed the formula.**

We can use a **flowchart** to transform formulae. On the flowchart, we make use of inverse operations. **Inverse operations** are operations which "undo" each other.

For instance, $4 \times 3 \div 3 = 4$ shows that multiplying and dividing are inverse operations.
For instance, $5 + 8 - 8 = 5$ shows that adding and subtracting are inverse operations.

Taking the reciprocal of **2** we get $\frac{1}{2}$. Now taking the reciprocal of $\frac{1}{2}$ we get

$\frac{1}{\frac{1}{2}} = 1 \times \frac{2}{1} = 2$. This shows that the inverse of "taking the reciprocal" is "taking the reciprocal".

Worked Example   Make b the subject of the formula A = bh.

Answer   Begin with b → $\boxed{\times h}$ → bh

$$\frac{A}{h} \leftarrow \boxed{\div h} \leftarrow \text{Begin with A}$$

Then $b = \frac{A}{h}$

Notes for using the flowchart method:
1. Always begin the first flowchart with the variable you want as the subject of the formula.
2. The first flowchart is completed once you have the expression that is on the right-hand side of the formula.
3. Always begin the second flowchart with the variable that is on the left-hand side of the formula.

Worked Example Make l the subject of the formula $S = \dfrac{n(a + l)}{2}$.

Answer Begin with $l \to \boxed{+ a} \to a + l \to \boxed{\times n} \to n(a + l) \to \boxed{\div 2} \to \dfrac{n(a + l)}{2}$

$$\dfrac{2S}{n} - a \leftarrow \boxed{- a} \leftarrow \dfrac{2S}{n} \leftarrow \boxed{\div n} \longleftarrow 2S \longleftarrow \boxed{\times 2} \leftarrow \text{Begin with S}$$

$$\text{Then } l = \dfrac{2S}{n} - a$$

Worked Example $x = \dfrac{a}{y}$. Express y in terms of x and a.

Answer Begin with $y \to \boxed{\begin{array}{c}\text{Take the} \\ \text{reciprocal}\end{array}} \to \dfrac{1}{y} \to \boxed{\times a} \to \dfrac{a}{y}$

$$\dfrac{a}{x} \leftarrow \boxed{\begin{array}{c}\text{Take the} \\ \text{reciprocal}\end{array}} \leftarrow \dfrac{x}{a} \leftarrow \boxed{\div a} \leftarrow \text{Begin with x}$$

$$\text{Then } y = \dfrac{a}{x}$$

DISCUSSION EXERCISE 6:1

"Changing the subject of a formula is similar to solving an equation". **Discuss** this statement.

Discuss ways, other than using a flowchart, of making x the subject of the following formulae: $y = mx + c, \quad a = c - x, \quad y = \dfrac{a}{4x}$.

EXERCISE 6:2

1. Make h the subject of these formulae.

    (a) $A = \frac{1}{2}bh$ **(b)** $A = \frac{1}{2}(a + b)h$ **(c)** $V = lbh$ **(d)** $V = \frac{1}{3}Ah$

2. Make r the subject of   (a) d = 2r   (b) C = 2πr.

3. Make *l* the subject of   (a) A = πr*l*   (b) P = 2(*l* + w).

4. Make m the subject of   (a) y = mx + c   (b) d = $\frac{m}{v}$ (c) a = $\frac{F}{m}$.

5. (a)   R = $\frac{V}{I}$. Express I in terms of R and V.

 (b)   Make x the subject of y = m(x + 3) + 2.

 (c)   The interest I, earned by a sum of money P, invested for T years at an interest rate of R% is given by I = $\frac{PRT}{100}$. Express P in terms of I, R and T.

 (d)   Make r the subject of the formula D = πr + 5s.

 (e) $v^2 = u^2 + 2as$. Express s in terms of v, u and a.

 (f)   The area of a trapezium is given by the formula A = $\frac{1}{2}$(a + b)h   where a and b are the lengths of the parallel sides and h is the distance between these sides. Make b the subject of this formula.

 (g)   Make R the subject of A = P($\frac{100 + R}{100}$).

 (h)   The area of metal needed to make a cylindrical tin of radius r and height h is given by A = 2πr (r + h). Express h in terms of A and r.

Review   (a)   m = $\frac{y}{x}$.   Make y the subject of this formula.

 (b)   m = $\frac{y}{x}$.   Express x in terms of m and y.

 (c)   v = u + at.   Express t in terms of v, u and a.

 (d)   F = $\frac{9}{5}$ C + 32 is a formula to convert temperatures given in degrees Celsius to degrees Fahrenheit. Make C the subject of this formula.

POWERS and ROOTS

$$4^2 = 4 \times 4 \qquad\qquad (-4)^2 = (-4) \times (-4)$$
$$= 16 \qquad\qquad\qquad\quad = 16$$

That is, both 4^2 and $(-4)^2$ have answer of 16.

Squaring and taking the square root are inverse operations. Since both 4^2 = 16 and $(-4)^2$ = 16, then both 4 and –4 are square roots of 16.

Since the symbol $\sqrt{\ }$ means the positive square root, then $\sqrt{16}$ = 4.
If we wish to use this symbol to refer to both the square roots of 16, we must use ± (read as "plus or minus") before $\sqrt{\ }$. For instance $\pm\sqrt{16}$ = 4 or –4.

DISCUSSION EXERCISE 6:3

- Do all numbers have two square roots? **Discuss.**

  $2^3 = 2 \times 2 \times 2$ That is, $2^3 = 8$. What is $(-2)^3$? What is $\sqrt[3]{8}$? Does 8 have more than one cube root? Do all numbers have a cube root? Does any number have more than one cube root? What is the inverse operation to cubing? **Discuss.**

- Suppose x is to be made the subject of the formula $a = x^2 + b$. Is $x = \sqrt{a - b}$ or $x = \pm\sqrt{a - b}$? **Discuss.**

  Suppose x is to be made the subject of the formula $a = x^3 + b$. Is $x = \sqrt[3]{a - b}$ or $x = \pm\sqrt[3]{a - b}$? **Discuss.**

- Suppose x is to be made the subject of the formula $a = \sqrt{x}$ + b. **Discuss** how this could be done.

TRANSFORMING FORMULAE involving POWERS and ROOTS

Worked Example $a = 5\sqrt{\frac{c}{b}}$.   Express b in terms of a and c.

Answer   Using a flowchart:

Begin with b → | Take the reciprocal | → $\frac{1}{b}$ → | × c | → $\frac{c}{b}$ → | Take the positive square root | → $\sqrt{\frac{c}{b}}$ → | × 5 | → $5\sqrt{\frac{c}{b}}$

$\frac{25c}{a^2}$ ← | Take the reciprocal | ← $\frac{a^2}{25c}$ ← | ÷ c | ← $\frac{a^2}{25}$ ← | Square | ← $\frac{a}{5}$ ← | ÷ 5 | ← Begin with a

Hence b = $\frac{25c}{a^2}$.

Worked Example   Make c the subject of $a = b + c^2$.

Answer   Using a flowchart:

Begin with c → | Square | ⟶ c^2 ⟶ | Add b | → $b + c^2$

$\pm\sqrt{a - b}$ ← | Take the square root | ← $a - b$ ← | Subtract b | ← Begin with a

Hence c = $\pm\sqrt{a - b}$.

102

Sometimes we know that the value of a variable cannot be negative. For instance, if we make r (the radius) the subject of the formula $A = \pi r^2$ (the formula for the area of a circle), we know that r must always be positive. In cases, such as this, when we take the square root we take just the positive square root.

Worked Example $V = \pi r^2 h$ is the formula for the volume of a cylinder of radius r and height h. Make r the subject of the formula.

Answer   Using a flowchart:

Begin with r → ☐ Square → r^2 → ☐ Multiply by πh → $\pi r^2 h$

$\pm \sqrt{\dfrac{V}{\pi h}}$ ← ☐ Take the square root ← $\dfrac{V}{\pi h}$ ← ☐ Divide by πh ← Begin with V

Since r must be positive, $r = \sqrt{\dfrac{V}{\pi h}}$.

EXERCISE 6:4

1. Make r the subject of   (a) $A = \pi r^2$ (b) $V = \frac{1}{3}\pi r^2 h$ if in each case r must be positive.

2. Make x the subject of the following. (x may take negative or positive values.)
   (a) $a = x^2$ (b) $b = 5x^2$ (c) $c = \dfrac{2}{x^2}$ (d) $d = \dfrac{ax^2}{b}$

3. $I = \frac{1}{3}ml^2$. Express l in terms of I and m. (l can take positive values only.)

4. $E = \frac{1}{2}mv^2$. Express v in terms of E and m. (v may take positive or negative values.)

5. If a stone is dropped from the top of a cliff the distance, s, it falls in time, t, is given by $s = \frac{1}{2}gt^2$. Make t the subject of this formula.

6. $x = \dfrac{y^2}{4a}$. Express y in terms of x and a. (y may take positive or negative values.)

7. Make r the subject of   (a) $V = r^3$ (b) $V = \frac{4}{3}\pi r^3$.

8. Make l the subject of   (a) $n = \sqrt{l}$ (b) $n = \sqrt{l-2}$ (c) $n = \dfrac{a}{\sqrt{l}}$ (d) $n = \sqrt{\dfrac{a}{l}}$

9. $T = 2\pi \sqrt{\dfrac{l}{g}}$. Express l in terms of T and g.

Review   (a) $I = \frac{c}{d^2}$. Express d in terms of I and c. (d may take positive values only).

(b)   The surface area of a sphere of radius r is given by the formula $A = 4\pi r^2$. Make r the subject of this formula.

(c) $y = \frac{x^2}{a^2}$. Express x in terms of y and a. (y may take positive or negative values.)

(d)   Make n the subject of $a = b\sqrt{n+1}$.

USING FORMULAE

Worked Example $V = \frac{4}{3}\pi r^3$.   (a)   Find V if r = 2·4.   (b)   Find r if V = 20·6.

Take $\pi = 3\cdot142$. Give the answers to 3 significant figures.

Answer   (a)   If r = 2·4, $V = \frac{4}{3} \times 3\cdot142 \times 2\cdot4^3$

$$= 57\cdot9 \text{ to 3 s.f.}$$

Keying $\boxed{4}$ $\boxed{\div}$ $\boxed{3}$ $\boxed{\times}$ $\boxed{3\cdot142}$ $\boxed{\times}$ $\boxed{2\cdot4}$ $\boxed{\text{INV}}$ $\boxed{x^y}$ $\boxed{3}$ $\boxed{=}$

(b)   If V = 20·6, $20\cdot6 = \frac{4}{3} \times 3\cdot142 \times r^3$. To find r, we need to rearrange this as r = ····. This can be done using a flowchart as shown below.

Begin with r → $\boxed{\text{Cube}}$ → r^3 → $\boxed{\begin{array}{c}\text{Multiply}\\\text{by}\\4 \times 3\cdot142\end{array}}$ → $4 \times 3\cdot142 \times r^3$ → $\boxed{\begin{array}{c}\text{Divide}\\\text{by 3}\end{array}}$ → $\frac{4}{3} \times 3\cdot142 \times r^3$

$\sqrt[3]{\frac{3 \times 20\cdot6}{4 \times 3\cdot142}}$ ← $\boxed{\begin{array}{c}\text{Take}\\\text{the}\\\text{cube}\\\text{root}\end{array}}$ ← $\frac{3 \times 20\cdot6}{4 \times 3\cdot142}$ ← $\boxed{\begin{array}{c}\text{Divide by}\\4 \times 3\cdot142\end{array}}$ ← $3 \times 20\cdot6$ ← $\boxed{\begin{array}{c}\text{Multiply}\\\text{by 3}\end{array}}$ ← Begin with 20·6

i.e. $r = \sqrt[3]{\frac{3 \times 20\cdot6}{4 \times 3\cdot142}}$

$$= 1\cdot70 \text{ to 3 s.f.}$$

Keying $\boxed{3}$ $\boxed{\times}$ $\boxed{20\cdot6}$ $\boxed{\div}$ $\boxed{[}$ $\boxed{4}$ $\boxed{\times}$ $\boxed{3\cdot142}$ $\boxed{]}$ $\boxed{=}$ $\boxed{\sqrt[3]{\ }}$

Note   Instead of pressing the $\sqrt[3]{\ }$ key we could have used the fact that $\sqrt[3]{x} = x^{\frac{1}{3}}$. The keying would then be:

$\boxed{3}$ $\boxed{\times}$ $\boxed{20\cdot6}$ $\boxed{\div}$ $\boxed{[}$ $\boxed{4}$ $\boxed{\times}$ $\boxed{3\cdot142}$ $\boxed{]}$ $\boxed{=}$ $\boxed{\text{INV}}$ $\boxed{x^{\frac{1}{y}}}$ $\boxed{3}$ $\boxed{=}$

Worked Example $v^2 = u^2 + 2as$. Find the two values for v if u = 25, a = 8·2, s = −20.

Answer $v^2 = u^2 + 2as$. $v = \pm\sqrt{u^2 + 2as}$

$$= \pm\sqrt{25^2 + 2 \times 8·2 \times (−20)}$$

$$= 17·2 \text{ or } −17·2 \text{ to 3 s.f.}$$

Keying ⟨25⟩ ⟨INV⟩ ⟨x²⟩ ⟨+⟩ ⟨2⟩ ⟨×⟩ ⟨8·2⟩ ⟨×⟩ ⟨20⟩ ⟨+/−⟩ ⟨=⟩ ⟨√⟩ gives the positive value 17·2.

DISCUSSION EXERCISE 6:5

Suppose we have to use the formula $V = \frac{4}{3}\pi r^3$ to find r for many different values of V. Instead of using a flowchart for each value of V we could rearrange $V = \frac{4}{3}\pi r^3$ to make r the subject. **Check** that we get $r = \sqrt[3]{\frac{3V}{4\pi}}$. We could then use this rearranged formula to find each value for r. Are there any disadvantages in doing this? **Discuss.**

What if just one value of r is to be found?

EXERCISE 6:6

Throughout this exercise take π = 3·142 or use the π key on the calculator. Give answers to 3 significant figures if rounding is necessary.

1. s = vt   Find the value of   **(a)**   s when v = 45 and t = 0·2
                                                   (b)   v when s = 120 and t = 3
                                                   (c)   t when s = 75 and v = 20
                                                   (d)   s when v = −15 and t = $\frac{1}{3}$.

2. The sum of the interior angles of a polygon is given by
S = 180 (n − 2)° where n is the number of sides.
  (a)   Find the sum of the interior angles of the sketched polygon.
  (b)   The sum of the interior angles of a polygon is 2700°. How many sides has this polygon?

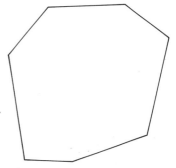

3. Use the formula $A = \pi r^2$ to find the radius of the circle which has an area of 7·6cm².

4. The formula for the surface area, A, of a cone is $A = \pi r l$.
   Find **(a)** the surface area if $r = 7\cdot57$ and $l = 2\cdot46$
   (b) the slant height, l, if $A = 22$ and $r = 3\cdot18$
   (c) the radius if $A = 984$ and $l = 26$.

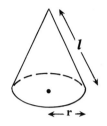

5. The sum of the first n odd numbers is given by $S = n^2$.
   (a) Find the sum of the first 20 odd numbers.
   (b) Find n if $S = 289$.

6. **(a)** Make x the subject of the formula $V = x^3$.
   (b) The volume of a cube is 80mm³. Find the length of an edge of this cube.

7. The surface area, A, of a sphere is given by the formula
   $A = 4\pi r^2$.
   (a) Find A if $r = 2\cdot36$.
   (b) Find r if $A = 18\cdot2$.

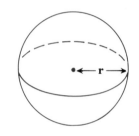

8. $s = \dfrac{v^2 - u^2}{2a}$ Find **(a)** s if $v = 6$, $u = 4\cdot2$, $a = 2$
   (b) the two values for v if $u = 24\cdot8$, $a = -2$, $s = 14$
   (c) a if $v = 40$, $u = 25$, $s = 120$.

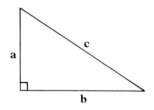

9. $c^2 = a^2 + b^2$ Find   **(a)** c if $a = 6\cdot1$, $b = 8\cdot5$
   (b) b if $c = 13$, $a = 5$
   (c) a if $b = 2\cdot71$, $c = 3\cdot84$.

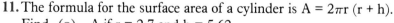

10. $T = 2\pi \sqrt{\dfrac{l}{g}}$ **(a)** Find T if $l = 10$ and $g = 9\cdot8$.
    (b) Find l if $T = 5\cdot2$ and $g = 9\cdot8$.

11. The formula for the surface area of a cylinder is $A = 2\pi r\,(r + h)$.
    Find **(a)** A if $r = 2\cdot7$ and $h = 5\cdot62$
    (b) h if $A = 226\cdot4$ and $r = 4\cdot25$.

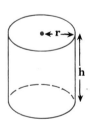

12. The formula $\dfrac{1}{R} = \dfrac{1}{R_1} + \dfrac{1}{R_2}$ is used in a Physics experiment.
    (a) Find the value of R if $R_1 = 6\cdot3$ and $R_2 = 7\cdot8$.
    (b) Find the value of R_1 if $R = 3\cdot6$ and $R_2 = 4$.

Review 1 $v = u + at$ Find the value of **(a)**   v when $u = 6 \cdot 8$, $a = 15$, $t = 25$
(b)   u when $v = 70$, $a = -10$, $t = 2$
(c)   a when $v = 8 \cdot 8$, $u = 6$, $t = 0 \cdot 4$
(d)   t when $v = 85$, $u = 100$, $a = -5$.

Review 2 $y = \dfrac{4a}{x^2}$ is the equation of a curve.

(a)   Find the value of y when $x = 2$ and $a = 1 \cdot 6$.
(b)   Find the values of x when $y = 0 \cdot 4$ and $a = 3 \cdot 6$.

Review 3 The area of a triangle can be found by using
the formula $A = \sqrt{s\,(s - a)\,(s - b)\,(s - c)}$ where
s is half the perimeter and a, b, c are the lengths of the sides.
Use this formula to find the area of this triangle.

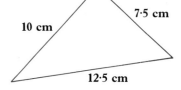
10 cm   7·5 cm   12·5 cm

EXPRESSING ONE FORMULA in terms of ANOTHER

Worked Example $x = at^2$, $y = 2at$. Express x in terms of y and a. Give the answer in its
simplest form.

Answer   Since x is to be expressed in terms of y and a but not in terms of t, we must
eliminate t. We do this as follows.

Rearrange $y = 2at$ to get $t = \dfrac{y}{2a}$.

Substitute $t = \dfrac{y}{2a}$ into $x = at^2$ to get $x = a\left(\dfrac{y}{2a}\right)^2$

$$= a \times \dfrac{y^2}{4a^2}$$

$$= \dfrac{ay^2}{4a^2}$$

$$x = \dfrac{y^2}{4a}$$

EXERCISE 6:7

1. For this square, the area $A = x^2$ and the perimeter $P = 4x$.
   Express A in terms of P.

2. $x = t^2$, $y = \dfrac{1}{t}$.
   Express x in terms of y.

3. $v = at$, $s = \dfrac{1}{2}at^2$.
   Express s in terms of v and a. Give the answer in its simplest form.

4. $x = t + 1$, $y = 3t - 2$.
   Express y in terms of x. Give the answer in its simplest form.

Review   For a circle $A = \pi r^2$, $C = 2\pi r$.
Express A in terms of C and π. Give the answer in its simplest form.

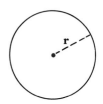

USING FUNCTION NOTATION

f(x) means "a function of x". That is, an expression in which the variable is x.
f(4) means "the value of the function when x is replaced by 4."

Worked Example $f(x) = \dfrac{x+3}{x-2}$. Find the value of f(5).

Answer $f(x) = \dfrac{x+3}{x-2}$

$\qquad f(5) = \dfrac{5+3}{5-2}$

$\qquad\qquad = \dfrac{8}{3}$

$\qquad\qquad = 2\tfrac{2}{3}$

Worked Example h(a) = 2a − 3. For what value of **a** is h(a) = 5?

Answer   h(a) = 2a − 3
$\qquad$ h(a) = 5
$\qquad$ Hence 2a − 3 = 5
$\qquad\qquad\qquad$ 2a = 8 (adding 3 to both sides)
$\qquad\qquad\qquad\quad$ a = 4 (dividing both sides by 2)

Worked Example $f(x) = (x + 3)^2$. Find the values of **x** for which $f(x) = 25$.

Answer $f(x) = (x + 3)^2$
$f(x) = 25$
Hence $(x + 3)^2 = 25$
$x + 3 = \pm 5$ (taking the square root of both sides)

If $x + 3 = 5$ If $x + 3 = -5$
$x = 2$ (subtracting 3 from both sides) $x = -8$ (subtracting 3 from both sides)

Hence $x = 2$ or -8.

DISCUSSION EXERCISE 6:8

● Suppose $g(x) = \dfrac{x + 4}{x - 1}$.

To evaluate $g(1)$ we begin as follows: $g(1) = \dfrac{1 + 4}{1 - 1}$

Continue this evaluation. What is the answer to $g(1)$? **Discuss.**

● Suppose $f(a) = \dfrac{2a - 7}{1 + a}$.

To find the value of **a** for which $f(a) = 4$ we begin as follows:

$f(a) = \dfrac{2a - 7}{1 + a}$

$f(a) = 4$

Hence $\dfrac{2a - 7}{1 + a} = 4$

$2a - 7 = 4(1 + a)$ [multiplying both sides by $(1 + a)$]

Discuss how to continue to find the value of a.

EXERCISE 6:9

1. $f(x) = 2x + 1$. Find $f(1)$, $f(2)$, $f(-2)$, $f(-5)$, $f(\frac{1}{2})$, $f(-\frac{3}{4})$.

2. $f(x) = \dfrac{x + 3}{2}$. Find $f(5)$, $f(1)$, $f(-3)$, $f(-7)$, $f(0)$, $f(\frac{2}{3})$, $f(1\frac{1}{2})$.

3. $f(a) = 3a^2 - 5$. Find $f(3)$, $f(2)$, $f(-1)$, $f(-2)$, $f(\frac{1}{3})$, $f(-\frac{1}{2})$.

4. $g(a) = \dfrac{2a + 3}{a}$. Find $g(4)$, $g(1)$, $g(0)$, $g(-2)$, $g(-\frac{1}{2})$.

5. $h(z) = \dfrac{z - 1}{z + 3}$. Find $h(1)$, $h(5)$, $h(0)$, $h(-1)$, $h(-3)$.

6. $g(x) = \dfrac{2x - 5}{x + 2}$. For what value of **x** does $g(x)$ have no answer?

7. **(a)** $h(x) = 3x - 4$. For what value of **x** is $h(x) = 11$?

   (b) $f(a) = 7 - 4a$. For what value of **a** is $f(a) = 3$?

   (c) $g(z) = 2(1 - 3z)$. For what value of **z** is $g(z) = -5$?

   (d) $f(x) = \dfrac{3x}{2} + 1$. For what value of **x** is $f(x) = \frac{1}{2}$?

   (e) $g(a) = 3(2a + 5)$. Find the value of **a** for which $g(a) = 12$.

   (f) $h(y) = 4 - \dfrac{y}{3}$. Find the value of **y** for which $h(y) = -1$.

   (g) $f(x) = 3 + 2(x - 1)$. Find the value of **x** for which $f(x) = \frac{3}{4}$.

8. **(a)** $f(x) = (x + 4)^2$. For what values of **x** is $f(x) = 36$?

   (b) $g(a) = (a - 1)^2$. For what values of **a** is $g(a) = 4$?

   (c) $h(b) = (b + 2)^2$. Find the values of **b** for which $h(b) = 9$.

   (d) $f(a) = (a + 5)^2$. For what values of **a** is $f(a) = 4$?

   (e) $g(x) = (x - 3)^2$. Find the values of **x** for which $g(x) = 1$.

9. **(a)** $g(a) = \dfrac{2 + a}{3 + a}$. For what value of **a** is $g(a) = 11$?

   (b) $h(z) = \dfrac{2z}{z + 1}$. For what value of **z** is $h(z) = -3$?

   (c) $f(a) = \dfrac{4a - 3}{1 - 2a}$. For what value of **a** is $f(a) = \frac{1}{2}$?

   (d) $g(x) = \dfrac{5(x - 2)}{x}$. For what value of **x** is $g(x) = 2$?

Review 1 $g(a) = 7 - 4a^2$. Find $g(2)$, $g(-2)$, $g(\frac{1}{2})$.

Review 2 $f(y) = (y - 3)^2$. Find the values of **y** for which $f(y) = 4$.

Review 3 $f(x) = \dfrac{2 - x}{3x}$. For what value of **x** is $f(x) = 5$?

Review 4 $h(z) = \dfrac{5z + 2}{z + 5}$. For what value of **z** has $h(z)$ no answer?

EXPANDING

Remember: To **expand** an expression such as 2(3a – 4) we remove the brackets. We do this by multiplying everything inside the brackets by the number outside. That is, 2(3a – 4) is expanded as 6a – 8.

The "rectangle method" of expanding is developed in the next discussion exercise.

DISCUSSION EXERCISE 6:10

-
$$5(2 + 7) = 5 \times 9$$
$$= 45$$

The expansion of 5(2 + 7) may be represented by this diagram.
Area of large rectangle = 5(2 + 7).
Sum of areas of small rectangles = 45.

	2	7
5	10	35

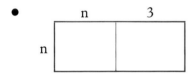

3(n + 2) = 3n + 6.
Discuss this statement, referring to the diagram.

-

How can this diagram be used to show that
$n(n + 3) = n^2 + 3n$? **Discuss.**

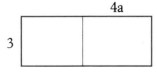

How can this diagram be used to show that
a(n + x) = an + ax? **Discuss.**

How can this diagram be used to show that
3(n + 4a) = 3n + 12a? **Discuss.**

How can this diagram be used to show that
$3x(2x + 4a) = 6x^2 + 12ax$? **Discuss.**

- $$8(7 - 2) = 8 \times 5$$
$$= 40$$

Is the expansion of $8(7 - 2)$ represented by this diagram?
Can we still talk about areas? **Discuss.**

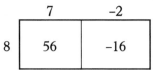

$2n(n - 4) = 2n^2 - 8n.$
Discuss this statement, referring to this diagram.

- **Discuss** diagrams which would show the following:

$$a(b - c) = ab - ac \qquad 2a(x - a) = 2ax - 2a^2$$

Worked Example Multiply out
  (a) $3(x + 2a)$
  (b) $n(4 - 3n)$
  (c) $\pi r \, (2h + r)$
  (d) $-2(x + 5)$
  (e) $-3x(1 - 2x)$

Answer Using the "rectangle method" the answers are:

(a)

$3(x + 2a) = 3x + 6a$

(b)

$n(4 - 3n) = 4n - 3n^2$

(c)

$\pi r \, (2h + r) = 2\pi rh + \pi r^2$

(d)

$-2(x + 5) = -2x - 10$

(e)

$-3x(1 - 2x) = 6x^2 - 3x$

Worked Example Expand and simplify
  (a) $4(n - 2) + 3n(4 + 5n)$
  (b) $9x - 5 - 2(3x - 2)$

Answer (a) $4(n - 2) + 3n(4 + 5n) = 4n - 8 + 12n + 15n^2$
$$= 16n - 8 + 15n^2$$

  (b) $9x - 5 - 2(3x - 2) = 9x - 5 - 6x + 4$
$$= 3x - 1$$

112

EXERCISE 6:11

1. Multiply out   (a) $5(x + 3)$ (b) $3(n - 4)$ (c) $2(5 + 3n)$ (d) $4(3 - 2a)$

              (e) $4(2x - 7)$ (f) $5(3p + 1)$ (g) $6(3 - 4n)$ (h) $2(1 - 3n)$

              (i) $n(5 + 3n)$ (j) $x(2x + 3)$ (k) $x(3 - 2x)$ (l) $a(a - 5)$

              (m) $2a(3 - a)$ (n) $4n(2n + 3)$.

2. Expand   (a) $-3(n + 2)$ (b) $-2(3 + 4a)$ (c) $-4(2n - 1)$ (d) $-5(3 - 4x)$

          (e) $-6(3x + 5)$ (f) $-5(4 - 5x)$ (g) $-2p(p + 2)$ (h) $-3a(2a + 5)$

          (i) $-3x(4 - x)$ (j) $-2n(3 - n)$ (k) $-3q(2q - 5)$.

3. Multiply out   (a) $4(x + b)$ (b) $3(x - a)$ (c) $x(n - 2a)$ (d) $n(4a + n)$

              (e) $3a(4 - 5x)$ (f) $2n(3 - 4a)$ (g) $5n(3a - 2n)$ (h) $-2x(3a + x)$

              (i) $-4x(x - a)$ (j) $-2a(3n - 4x)$ (k) $pq(p + q)$ (l) $\pi r(r + 2h)$

              (m) $ab(h - a)$ (n) $rs(s - r)$.

4. Expand and simplify   (a) $4 + 3(2n + 3)$ (b) $n - 5 + 2(3 - 2n)$

                        (c) $3n^2 + n(3 + 2n)$ (d) $2n(3 - n) + 5n$

                        (e) $x(2x + 5) - x$ (f) $2a(4 - a) + 5 + 6a$

                        (g) $3(2n + 5) - 6 - n$ (h) $3(x + 4) + 2(3 + 2x)$

                        (i) $5(2a - 1) - 3(1 - 2a)$ (j) $5n(n - 2) + 2n(1 - 2n)$

                        (k) $x(3 + 4x) + 2x(x - 2)$ (l) $x(2 + x) - 2(2 - x)$

                        (m) $5(2 - n) + 2n(n + 3)$ (n) $2x(2x - 3) - 3(4 - x)$.

5. The answer is $6n - 3$. What expressions could be expanded and simpified to give this answer?

Review 1 Multiply out   (a) $2(l + w)$ (b) $-3(1 - 2a)$ (c) $x(x + 4)$

                        (d) $2n(a - 5n)$ (e) $-3n(4 + 3n)$ (f) $ab(b - a)$.

Review 2 Expand and simplify.

        (a) $3 + 2(3n - 4)$ (b) $2 - 3a - a(2 + 3a)$ (c) $4n^2 - 3n(1 - 2n)$

        (d) $2(3x + 5) + 3(2 - 5x)$

FACTORISING — COMMON FACTOR

To **factorise** an expression, we write the expression with brackets. That is, factorising is the reverse of expanding.

For instance, $2x + 6$ is the expanded form of $2(x + 3)$ while $2(x + 3)$ is the factorised form of $2x + 6$.

Notice that in $2x + 6$ both 2x and 6 have a factor of 2. That is, 2 is a common factor of 2x and 6.

When we factorise $2x + 6$ as $2(x + 3)$ the common factor is placed outside the bracket.

We can use the "rectangle method" to factorise as shown in the following example.

Example To use the "rectangle method" to factorise $12x - 8$ take the following steps.

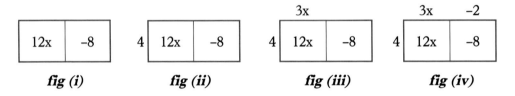

Step 1 Write the expression in a rectangle — *fig (i)*.
Step 2 Write the common factor on the left-hand side — *fig (ii)*.
Step 3 Divide the common factor into each part of the expression in the rectangle — *fig (iii)* and *fig (iv)*.
Step 4 Use *fig (iv)* to write down the factorised expression.
This is $4(3x - 2)$.
$12x - 8$ is factorised as $4(3x - 2)$.

DISCUSSION EXERCISE 6:12

- Karim's method of factorising is shown here. $12x - 8$ **Step 1** $4(\quad)$
  Step 2 $4(3x\quad)$
  Step 3 $4(3x - 2)$

  Discuss Karim's method.

- Gillian factorised $4x^2 + 6ax$ as $2(2x^2 + 3ax)$.
  Hamish factorised $4x^2 + 6ax$ as $x(4x + 6a)$.
  Although Gillian's and Hamish's factorising is not incorrect, neither has factorised $4x^2 + 6ax$ completely. How could $4x^2 + 6ax$ be factorised completely? **Discuss.**

  Discuss how to completely factorise $6a^2 - 2a$ and $a^2b + ab^2$.

Always factorise completely. If the expression in the brackets has a common factor, then the factorising is not complete.

For instance, $24x + 30$ may be factorised as $2(12x + 15)$. Since $12x$ and 15 have a common factor of 3 the factorising is not complete. $24x + 30$ is completely factorised as $6(4x + 5)$.

For instance $2\pi r^2 - \pi rh$ may be factorised as $\pi(2r^2 - rh)$. Since $2r^2$ and rh have a common factor of r, the factorising is not complete. $2\pi r^2 - \pi rh$ is completely factorised as $\pi r(2r - h)$.

It is a good idea to check your factorising by expanding. Suppose you have factorised $2n - 4$ as $2(n - 4)$. By expanding $2(n - 4)$ to $2n - 8$ you would see that you had incorrectly factorised.

EXERCISE 6:13

1. Copy and complete

   (a) $3x + 6 = 3(\cdots + \cdots)$ (b) $5a - 10 = 5(\cdots - \cdots)$ (c) $14x + 4 = 2(\cdots + \cdots)$

   (d) $16n - 12 = 4(\cdots - \cdots)$ (e) $4x + 4 = 4(\cdots + \cdots)$ (f) $12n - 4 = \cdots(3n - 1)$

   (g) $15d - 25 = \cdots(3d - 5)$ (h) $18 + 3n = \cdots(6 + n)$ (i) $6 - 3a = \cdots(\cdots - a)$

   (j) $6 + 9x = \cdots(2 + \cdots)$ (k) $15x - 10 = \cdots(\cdots - 2)$.

2. Factorise   (a) $2n + 2$ (b) $3 - 3a$ (c) $4x + 12$ (d) $6 + 12a$

             (e) $14y - 7$ (f) $9x + 3$ (g) $8 - 12y$ (h) $10x + 25$

             (i) $8n + 4$ (j) $11 - 22n$ (k) $10 + 15n$ (l) $9 - 21x$

             (m) $12n + 8$ (n) $40 - 15n$ (o) $2x - 20$ (p) $20n + 16$

             (q) $18 - 6a$ (r) $12 + 16n$ (s) $6x - 20$ (t) $21 - 6n$

             (u) $32x - 24$ (v) $18n + 24$ (w) $16y - 24$ (x) $24 - 36n$

             (y) $40 + 24a$ (z) $18a - 45$.

3. Copy and complete

   (a) $2n^2 + n = n(\cdots + \cdots)$ (b) $ax - a = a(\cdots - \cdots)$ (c) $4x + 3x^2 = x(\cdots + \cdots)$

   (d) $6x - x^2 = \cdots(6 - \cdots)$ (e) $10n^2 + 4 = 2(\cdots + \cdots)$ (f) $30n + 12n^2 = \cdots(\cdots + 2n)$

   (g) $6p^2q + 3p = \cdots(\cdots + 1)$ (h) $\pi r - \pi h = \cdots(r - \cdots)$.

4. Factorise   **(a)** $x^2 + 5x$ **(b)** $a^2 + 9a$ **(c)** $p^2 - 3p$ **(d)** $5y - y^2$

               (e) $x + x^2$ **(f)** $2y^2 - 5y$ **(g)** $a + 2a^2$ **(h)** $4n^2 - n$

               (i) $2p - 5p^2$ **(j)** $5a + 6a^2$ **(k)** $2a + a^2$ **(l)** $5a - a^2$

               (m) $5x^2 + 2x$ **(n)** $9n^2 + 4n$ **(o)** $2a^2 + 2$ **(p)** $5 + 5n^2$

               (q) $8x^2 + 4$ **(r)** $12 - 3y^2$.

5. Factorise completely   **(a)** $4x^2 + 2x$ **(b)** $9a^2 - 3a$ **(c)** $6b + 3b^2$

                         (d) $12n - 4n^2$ **(e)** $16a - 8a^2$ **(f)** $24n^2 + 32n$

                         (g) $30x - 12x^2$ **(h)** $8a^2 - 4an^2$ **(i)** $p^2q + pq^2$

                         (j) $ab^2 - a^2b$ **(k)** $6p^2q + 12q^2$ **(l)** $8p^2q - 4pq^2$

                         (m) $3a^2b - 6ab^2$ **(n)** $n^3 + n^2$ **(o)** $6a^2 - 8a^3$.

Review   Factorise   **(a)** $5a - 15$ **(b)** $12n - 32$ **(c)** $3a^2 + 5a$

                         (d) $15n - 20n^2$ **(e)** $\pi r^2 + \pi rh$ **(f)** $12ab^2 - 8a^2b$.

FURTHER EXPANDING

DISCUSSION EXERCISE 6:14

● $(2 + 6)(5 + 4) = 8 \times 9$
                                   $= 72$

This expansion can be represented on a diagram as shown below.

	5	4
2	10	8
6	30	24

Area of large rectangle $= (2 + 6)(5 + 4)$.
Sum of areas of small rectangles $= 72$.

$$(2 + 6)(5 - 4) = 8 \times 1$$
$$= 8$$

	5	-4
2	10	-8
6	30	-24

Is the expansion $(2 + 6)(5 - 4)$ represented by this diagram? Can we still talk about areas? **Discuss.**
What if 6 was replaced by -6?
What if 5 was replaced by -5?

●

	x	4
a		
3		

The first step in expanding $(a + 3)(x + 4)$, using the "rectangle method", is to draw this diagram.

How might you continue? **Discuss.**

What if you were asked to expand $(a + b)(p + q)$?

●

	2n	5
3n	$6n^2$	$15n$
–4	$–8n$	$–20$

Could we use this diagram to expand $(3n – 4)(2n + 5)$? **Discuss.** As part of your discussion, you may like to replace n with a number.

What if 5 was replaced by –5?

What if 2n was replaced by –2n?

● Jennifer's method for expanding $(3n – 4)(2n + 5)$ was:

$(3n – 4)(2n + 5) = 3n(2n + 5) – 4(2n + 5)$
$$= 6n^2 + 15n – 8n – 20$$

Jennifer simplified her expansion to $6n^2 + 7n – 20$. **Discuss** Jennifer's method.

Worked Example Expand and simplify **(a)** $(3x – 2)(x – 5)$
(b) $(a + 2b)(3a – b)$

Answer Using the "rectangle method", the expansions can be found from the following diagrams.

(a)

	x	–5
3x	$3x^2$	$–15x$
–2	$–2x$	10

(b)

	3a	–b
a	$3a^2$	$–ab$
2b	$6ab$	$–2b^2$

$(3x – 2)(x – 5) = 3x^2 – 15x – 2x + 10$
$$= 3x^2 – 17x + 10$$

$(a + 2b)(3a – b) = 3a^2 – ab + 6ab – 2b^2$
$$= 3a^2 + 5ab – 2b^2$$

EXERCISE 6:15

1. Expand and simplify.

   (a) $(2n + 3)(3n + 2)$ (b) $(2x + 1)(3x + 5)$ (c) $(4a + 3)(3a + 1)$

   (d) $(4n - 5)(3n + 1)$ (e) $(2a - 3)(a + 7)$ (f) $(2x + 3)(x - 4)$

   (g) $(5x - 1)(2x - 3)$ (h) $(n - 7)(n + 4)$ (i) $(x + 3)(2x - 5)$

   (j) $(5n - 1)(n - 4)$ (k) $(3x - 1)(x + 5)$ (l) $(3a + 2)(3a - 1)$

   (m) $(2x + 3)(3x + 2)$ (n) $(n - 3)(2n - 3)$ (o) $(5y - 2)(y + 2)$

   (p) $(3x - 2)(2 + x)$ (q) $(5a + 2)(5 + 2a)$ (r) $(2 - 3d)(d + 3)$

   (s) $(3 + 2x)(2 - 3x)$ (t) $(3 - n)(2n + 1)$ (u) $(3x + 2)(3x - 2)$

   (v) $(2 + n)(2 - n)$ (w) $(5x - 4)(5x + 4)$

2. Multiply out. Simplify if possible.

   (a) $(a + 2n)(a + 3n)$ (b) $(x + a)(3x + a)$ (c) $(2a + n)(3a + 5n)$

   (d) $(c - 3x)(2c + x)$ (e) $(2x - a)(5x + a)$ (f) $(3x - y)(2x - y)$

   (g) $(3a + 2n)(2a + 5n)$ (h) $(3x - 2n)(2x + n)$ (i) $(5a + 2n)(3a - 4n)$

   (j) $(2n - 3y)(5n - y)$ (k) $(3a + 2n)(5a - 3n)$ (l) $(4n - x)(3n - 2x)$

   (m) $(2x + n)(2x - n)$ (n) $(3n - 2a)(3n + 2a)$ (o) $(5x + 2y)(5x - 2y)$

   (p) $(ax + d)(x + c)$ (q) $(n + a)(bn + c)$ (r) $(an - x)(bn + y)$

   (s) $(ax + c)(bx - d)$ (t) $(q + px)(s - x)$ (u) $(p + q)(a + b)$

   (v) $(2p - a)(s + 3t)$ (w) $(5x + 2n)(a - 3b)$

3. Rectangular paving tiles come in different sizes.
   If the length of a tile is $3x - 1$ the width is $2x + 1$.
   (a) Write an expression for the area of a tile.
   (b) Multiply out and simplify your expression.

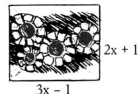

Review 1   Multiply out and simplify.

   (a) $(x + 5)(x + 2)$ (b) $(2n - 3)(3n - 1)$ (c) $(1 - 3a)(5 + 2a)$

   (d) $(2y - 3)(2 + 3y)$ (e) $(5x - 2)(5x + 2)$

Review 2   Expand. Simplify if possible.

   (a) $(a + 3b)(2a + b)$ (b) $(4x - n)(3x + 2n)$ (c) $(rx + s)(tx - u)$

   (d) $(3n + a)(p - 2q)$

USING EXPANDING AND FACTORISING

- The following steps may be taken to make x the subject of the formula $a = \dfrac{b - x}{c - x}$.
  Discuss each step.

$$a = \frac{b - x}{c - x}$$

Step 1 $a(c - x) = b - x$

Step 2 $ac - ax = b - x$

Step 3 $ac - b = ax - x$

Step 4 $ac - b = x(a - 1)$

Step 5 $\dfrac{ac - b}{a - 1} = x \; ; \; x = \dfrac{ac - b}{a - 1}$

- **Discuss** the steps that could be taken to make u the subject of $f = \dfrac{uv}{u + v}$.

119

William Oughtred

William Oughtred was born at Eton in 1574 and died at Albury in Surrey in 1660. He made popular the use of the × sign for multiplication . In fact he experimented with many new notations, including ∷ for ratio. Apart from the × sign, none of his notations became popular. His best known publication was his "Clavis mathematicae" (Key to mathematics) which he wrote for the purpose of teaching the Earl of Arundel. In this book he included Hindu-Arabic notation, decimals and algebra. His writings had a great influence on English mathematics at that time.

William was a student at Cambridge University and became a teacher there. In 1603 he left Cambridge and the following year he was appointed vicar of Shalford in Surrey. Later, he became rector of Albury. His time as a minister included the years of the Commonwealth when more than 8000 ministers were removed from their parishes. Oughtred was not removed from his. He continued to devote much of his time to mathematics and gave free lessons. One of his pupils was Christopher Wren, who designed and built St. Paul's Cathedral.

It is said that Oughtred was a much better mathematician than a preacher. Someone described his preaching as pitiful. He knew more mathematics than most professors.

William Oughtred is best known as the inventor of the slide rule which was widely used until quite recently. Most of the calculations we use the calculator for were able to be performed on the slide rule. Because hand-held calculators are now reasonably priced, students buy calculators rather than slide rules.

In a biography of William Oughtred the following is written.

He was a little man, had black haire, and blacke eies (with a great deal of spirit). His head was always working. He would drawe lines and diagrams on the dust ... did use to lye a bed till eleaven or twelve a clock ... Studyed late at night; went not to bed till 11 a clock; had his tinder box by him; and on the top of his bed-staffe, he had his inke-horne fix't. He slept but little. Sometimes he went not to bed in two or three nights.

7 Straight-Line Graphs: y = mx + c 7

INTRODUCTION

LINE GRAPHS

Throughout this investigation either **1.** *use a graphics calculator*

or **2.** *use a computer graphics package*

or **3.** *if neither a graphics calculator nor a computer*
with suitable software is available then draw the lines on graph paper. Do this by finding
the coordinates of 3 points and drawing the line that goes through these 3 points.

- Graph the lines $y = x + 2$ $y = -x + 2$
  $y = 2x + 2$ $y = -2x + 2$
  $y = 3x + 2$ $y = -3x + 2$.

  What do you notice about these 6 line equations? What do you notice about the 6 graphs? **Discuss.** As part of your discussion, make and test a statement about the position of the line $y = 4x + 2$.

  What if the lines were $y = 3x - 3, y = 2x - 3, y = x - 3, y = -x - 3, y = -2x - 3$?
  What if the lines were $y = 3x - 1, y = 2x - 1, y = x - 1, y = -x - 1, y = -2x - 1$?
  What if the lines were $y = 3x, y = 2x, y = x, y = -x, y = -2x, y = -3x$?
  What if ...

- Graph the lines $y = 2x + 2$ $y = 2x + 1$ $y = 2x$
  $y = 2x - 1$ $y = 2x - 2$

  What do you notice about these 5 line equations? What do you notice about the 5 graphs? **Discuss.** As part of your discussion, make and test a statement about the position of the lines $y = 2x + 3$ and $y = 2x - 3$.

  What if the lines were $y = 3x + 2, y = 3x + 1, y = 3x, y = 3x - 1, y = 3x - 2$?
  What if the lines were $y = x + 2, y = x + 1, y = x, y = x - 1, y = x - 2$?
  What if the lines were $y = -2x + 2, y = -2x + 1, y = -2x, y = -2x - 1, y = -2x - 2$?
  What if ...

GRADIENT

The **gradient** of a line is a measure of the slope, or the steepness of a line. The steeper the line the greater the gradient.

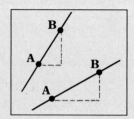

Gradient = $\dfrac{\text{vertical distance between two points on the line}}{\text{horizontal distance between these two points}}$

To find the gradient of a line take the following steps.

Step 1 Mark two points on the line as A and B. It is sensible to mark these points where grid lines meet.

Step 2 Find the vertical distance between A and B. Find the horizontal distance between A and B.

Step 3 Calculate the gradient by dividing the vertical distance by the horizontal distance.

DISCUSSION EXERCISE 7:2

The line in *fig (i)* has a **positive gradient.**
The line in *fig (ii)* has a **negative gradient.**

fig (i)   *fig (ii)*

One way of telling whether a line has a positive or negative gradient is as follows.
We "read" the line from left to right, the way we read a line of words. If we move up the line, the gradient is positive. If we move down the line the gradient is negative. **Discuss** this method.

Think of other ways of remembering which lines have a positive gradient and which have a negative gradient. **Discuss.**

Worked Example Find the gradient of these lines.

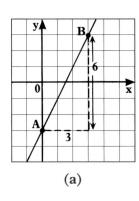 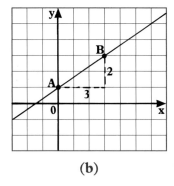 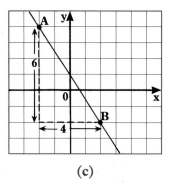

(a)   (b)   (c)

Answer (a) Vertical distance between A and B is 6; horizontal distance is 3.

Hence gradient = $\frac{6}{3}$. That is, gradient = 2.

(b) Vertical distance between A and B is 2; horizontal distance is 3.

Hence gradient = $\frac{2}{3}$.

(c) This line has a negative gradient. Vertical distance between A and B is 6; horizontal distance is 4. Hence gradient = $-\frac{6}{4}$. That is, gradient = $-\frac{3}{2}$.

Note In mathematics, a gradient is usually given as a whole number or a fraction.

EXERCISE 7:3

1.

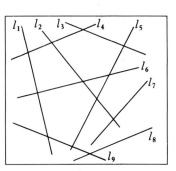

(a) Name the lines which have a positive gradient.
(b) Name the lines which have a negative gradient.
(c) There are two pairs of lines which have the same gradient. Name these pairs of lines.

2.

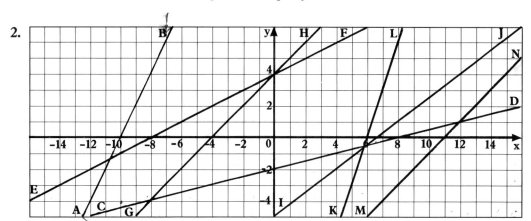

Find the gradient of these lines.

3.

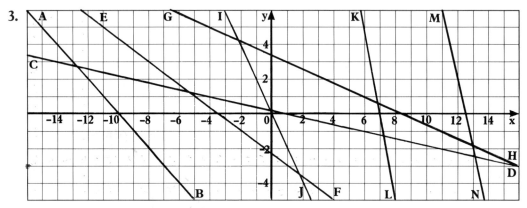

Find the gradient of these lines.

4.

Find the gradient of these lines.

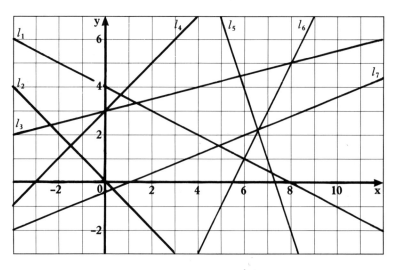

5. The three vertices of a triangle are P(2, 1), Q(4, –3), R(7, 0). Find the gradient of each side of this triangle.

6.

The gradient of a road is shown.
(a) What is the gradient as a fraction?
(b) Complete this statement "For every 100 metres horizontally, the road rises ... metres".

7.

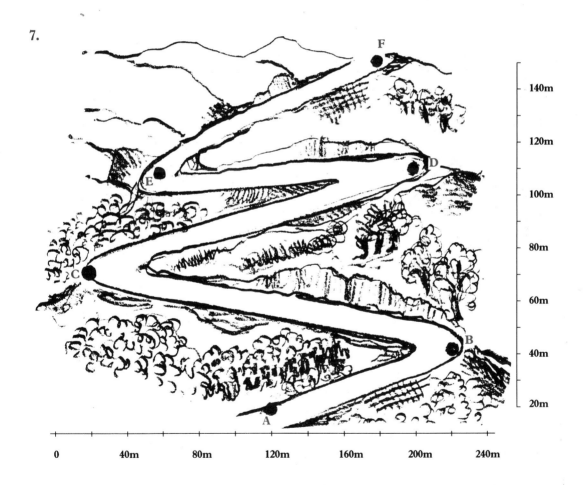

This diagram represents a road winding up a hill.
The scale, on the right, gives the distance above sea level.

Write the gradient, of each section of this road, as a percentage. Round your answers to the nearest 5%.

125

8.

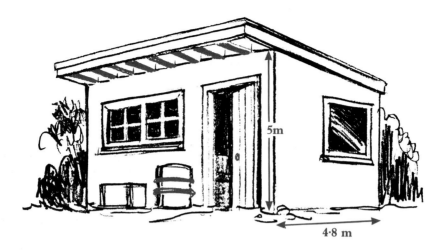

5m

4·8 m

The gradient of the roof on this shed is 1 : 12.

(a) Write this gradient as a fraction.

(b) At its highest point the shed is 5m high, as shown. How high is the shed at its lowest point?

Review 1

Find the gradient of each line on this graph.

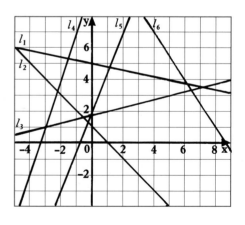

Review 2   The gradient of a ski-tow is 2 : 5.
Complete this statement "For every 10m horizontally, the ski-tow rises ... m".

Review 3   The vertices of a quadrilateral are (−3, 2), (1, 5), (7, 4), (3, −1).
Find the gradient of the diagonals of this quadrilateral.

126

The LINE EQUATION y = mx + c

INVESTIGATION 7:4

LINE EQUATIONS

● The coordinates of four points on the graph are (0, −1), (1, 1), (2, 3), (3, 5).

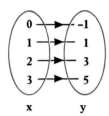

The coordinates of the four points are shown in this mapping diagram. What is the relation between x and y in this mapping diagram? What is the equation of the line?

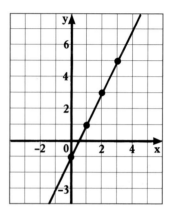

What is a possible connection between the numbers in the equation of the line and the graph of the line?

Investigate. Make a statement which includes the word gradient.

●

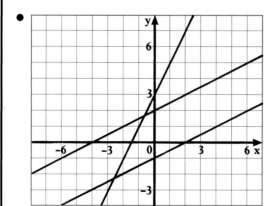 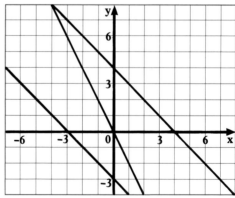

For each line shown on these graphs, find the equation by drawing a mapping diagram and finding the relation between x and y. What is the connection between the numbers in each line equation and the graph of the line? **Investigate.**
You may wish to draw some more lines as part of your investigation.

● Suppose you were to write a report on how to draw line graphs. What would you include in your report? Would you include examples? If so, which examples would you choose?

In the line equation $y = mx + c$, c gives the point where the line crosses the y-axis and m is the gradient.
We can use this to draw a line, instead of plotting points.

Worked Example   Draw the line $y = 3x - 4$.

Answer   The gradient of this line is 3, which may be written as $\frac{3}{1}$.

The line crosses the y-axis at –4.
The diagrams below show the steps to be taken to draw this line.

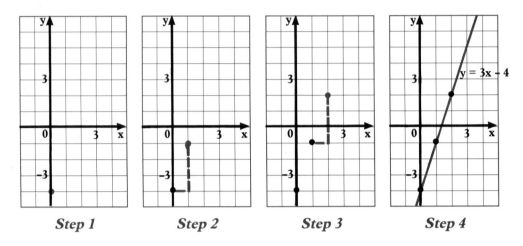

Step 1   Step 2   Step 3   Step 4

Step 1   Mark a point at –4 on the y-axis.
Step 2   Go along 1 and up 3 to mark the next point.
Step 3   Repeat Step 2 to mark the third point.
Step 4   Draw the line that goes through the marked points. Label the line.

Worked Example   Draw the line $y = 2 - x$.

Answer $y = 2 - x$ may be rewritten as $y = -1x + 2$.

The gradient is –1 which may be rewritten as $\frac{-1}{1}$.

The line crosses the y-axis at 2.

To draw the line: Begin at 2 on the y-axis; go along 1 and down 1 (up –1 is the same as down 1) to get another point; from this point go along 1 and down 1 to get another point. Draw the line through all 3 points. Label the line.

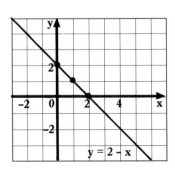

128

Worked Example Draw the line $y = 1\frac{1}{2}x$.

Answer $y = 1\frac{1}{2}x$ may be rewritten as $y = \frac{3}{2}x + 0$.

The gradient is $\frac{3}{2}$. The line crosses the y-axis at 0.

To draw the line: Begin at 0 on the y-axis; go along 2 and up 3 to get another point; from this point go along 2 and up 3 to get another point. Draw the line through all three points. Label the line.

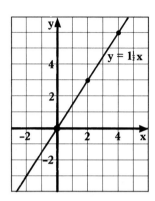

EXERCISE 7:5

1. Write down the gradient of each of these lines.

   (a) $y = 2x + 5$ (b) $y = \frac{1}{3}x$ (c) $y = x - 2$ (d) $y = -3x + 2$

   (e) $y = -\frac{1}{2}x + 6$ (f) $y = 2 + 3x$ (g) $y = 4 - x$ (h) $y = 3 + 5x$

   (i) $y = 3 - 5x$ (j) $y = \frac{2}{3}x - 7$ (k) $y = -\frac{3}{5}x$

2. Where do the lines, given in **question 1**, cross the y-axis?

3. Draw a pair of axes with values for both x and y from –5 to 8.
   On these axes, draw and clearly label the following lines.

   $y = 2x + 3$ $y = 3x - 4$ $y = x - 1$ $y = \frac{1}{2}x$

4. Draw a set of axes. Number both the x and y-axes from –4 to 10.
   On this set of axes, draw and label the following lines.

   $y = -3x + 5$ $y = -\frac{3}{2}x + 8$ $y = -x - 2$ $y = -2x$

5. Draw a pair of axes with values for both x and y from –6 to 6.
   On these axes, draw and label the following lines.

   $y = -x - 2$ $y = \frac{2}{3}x$ $y = 4 - \frac{1}{2}x$ $y = 2x - 5$ $y = 3 + \frac{1}{2}x$

6. Draw the following pairs of lines. (In each case, decide how large the axes should be.)
   Write down the coordinates of the point where the lines meet.

   (a) $y = 2x - 1$; $y = -x + 5$
   (b) $y = 3 - x$; $y = x - 3$
   (c) $y = \frac{1}{2}x + 2$; $y = x + 3$
   (d) $y = 3x$; $y = -2x - 5$
   (e) $y = x - 2$; $y = 5x - 2$
   (f) $y = 3 - 2x$; $y = 4x$
   (g) $y = \frac{5}{4}x + 3$; $y = 1 + \frac{1}{4}x$

7.

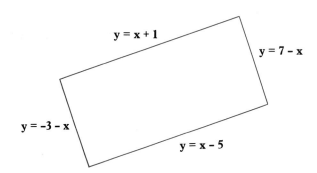

The equations of the four sides of a rectangle are shown.
Find the coordinates of the vertices of this rectangle.

Review 1   Write down the gradient of each of these lines.
   (a) $y = -2x + 7$ (b) $y = \frac{2}{3}x$ (c) $y = -8 + 3x$ (d) $y = 4 - x$

Review 2   Where do the lines, given in **question 1**, cross the y-axis?

Review 3   Draw the following pairs of lines. Write down the coordinates of the point
   where the lines meet. (On each graph, number both the x and y axes from –6
   to 6.)

   (a) $y = x - 4$; $y = -x$
   (b) $y = 2x + 5$; $y = -\frac{2}{3}x - 3$
   (c) $y = \frac{1}{2}x + 1$; $y = 6 - 2x$

REARRANGING LINE EQUATIONS into the form y = mx + c

$2y = 5x - 4$, $x + y = 3$, $2x - 3y = 12$, $y = \frac{1}{2}x + 3$ are all equations of straight lines. The last equation, $y = \frac{1}{2}x + 3$, is in the form $y = mx + c$. The other three equations may all be rearranged into the form $y = mx + c$ by using the technique of "changing the subject of a formula".

Worked Example Rearrange each of the following into the form $y = mx + c$.

(a) $2y = 5x - 4$ (b) $x + y = 3$ (c) $2x - 3y = 12$.

Answer We need to make y the subject of each. One method of doing this is to use a flowchart as follows.

(a) Begin with y → | Multiply by 2 | ⟶ 2y

$\dfrac{5x - 4}{2}$ ← | Divide by 2 | ⟵ Begin with 5x – 4

$$\text{Hence} \quad y = \frac{5x - 4}{2}$$
$$y = \frac{5x}{2} - \frac{4}{2}$$
$$y = \frac{5}{2}x - 2$$

(b) Begin with y → | Add x | ⟶ x + y

$3 - x$ ← | Subtract x | ⟵ Begin with 3

$$\text{Hence} \quad y = 3 - x$$
$$y = -x + 3$$

(c) Begin with y → |Multiply by –3| ⟶ –3y → | Add 2x | ⟶ 2x – 3y

$\dfrac{12 - 2x}{-3}$ ← | Divide by –3 | ← 12 – 2x ← | Subtract 2x | ← Begin with 12

$$\text{Hence} \quad y = \frac{12 - 2x}{-3}$$
$$y = \frac{12}{-3} - \frac{2x}{-3}$$
$$y = -4 + \frac{2}{3}x$$
$$y = \frac{2}{3}x - 4$$

DISCUSSION EXERCISE 7:6

$$2y = 5x - 4$$

$$y = \frac{5x - 4}{2} \qquad \text{(dividing both sides by 2)}$$

$$y = \frac{5x}{2} - \frac{4}{2}$$

$$y = \tfrac{5}{2}x - 2$$

Compare this "balance" method of rewriting $2y = 5x - 4$ in the form $y = mx + c$ with the "flowchart" method.

Discuss the advantages and disadvantages of each method. As part of your discussion, use the "balance" method to rewrite both $x + y = 3$ and $2x - 3y = 12$ in the form $y = mx + c$.

EXERCISE 7:7

1. Write each of the following line equations in the form $y = mx + c$.

   (a) $x + y = 3$ (b) $x + y = 6$ (c) $x + y = -7$
   (d) $3y = 2x + 6$ (e) $2y = x - 4$ (f) $4y = 6x + 8$
   (g) $x + 2y = 2$ (h) $x + 3y = -3$ (i) $2x + 2y = 1$
   (j) $3x + 2y = -4$ (k) $x + 2y - 1 = 0$ (l) $2x + y + 1 = 0$

2. Rearrange these line equations into the form $y = mx + c$.

   (a) $x - y = 4$ (b) $x - y = -1$ (c) $3x - y = 6$
   (d) $2x - y = -2$ (e) $2x - 3y = 12$ (f) $3x - 2y = -6$
   (g) $x - 4y = 4$ (h) $2x - 5y = 10$ (i) $x - y - 6 = 0$
   (j) $4x - 2y + 1 = 0$ (k) $3x - 4y - 12 = 0$

3. Draw a pair of axes with both x and y values from -6 to 6. On these axes draw and clearly label the following lines.

   $2x + y = 5$ $3y = 2x$ $y = 3x - 2$ $x + 2y = 8$

4. Draw a set of axes. Number both the x and y axes from -5 to 8. On this set of axes, draw and label the following lines.

   $2x - y = 0$ $x - y = 4$ $2x - 5y = 10$ $3x - 4y + 8 = 0$

5. Find the coordinates of the points of intersection of the following pairs of lines.

    (a) $y = x + 5$; $x + y = -1$
    (b) $x + y = 1$; $x - y = 5$
    (c) $x + 2y = 3$; $x - y = 0$
    (d) $2x + y = 1$; $x + y + 2 = 0$
    (e) $2x + y + 3 = 0$; $x + 2y = 0$

6.

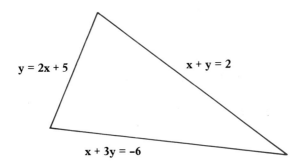

The equations of the three sides of a triangle are shown.
Find the coordinates of the vertices of this triangle.

Review 1   Write these line equations in the form $y = mx + c$.

    (a) $x + y = -2$ (b) $3y = x - 6$ (c) $x + 2y = 8$
    (d) $6x + 3y = 2$ (e) $x - y = 7$ (f) $2x - 3y = -18$
    (g) $x + y - 4 = 0$

Review 2   (a) Draw a set of axes. Number both the x and y axes from –6 to 8. On these axes, draw and label the following lines.
                $2x + y = 4$ $x - 2y = 6$ $2x + 5y = 10$ $2x - y = 0$
        (b) What are the coordinates of the point where the lines $x - 2y = 6$ and $2x - y = 0$ meet?

DISCUSSION EXERCISE 7:8

Compare the plotting points method of drawing a line with the $y = mx + c$ method.
Discuss.
As part of your discussion, compare these methods for line equations written in different ways.

HORIZONTAL and VERTICAL LINES

The coordinates of some points on the line l_1 are $(-4, 2)$, $(-1, 2)$, $(0, 2)$, $(3, 2)$. Regardless of the value of x, the value of y is always 2. The equation of this line is $y = 2$.

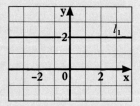

The coordinates of some points on the line l_2 are $(2, -1)$, $(2, 0)$, $(2, 2)$, $(2, 4)$. Regardless of the value of y, the value of x is always 2. The equation of this line is $x = 2$.

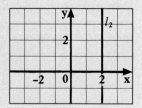

DISCUSSION EXERCISE 7:9

- Do all horizontal lines have equation $y = a$, where **a** is some number? Do all vertical lines have equation $x = a$, where **a** is some number? **Discuss.** As part of your discussion, draw many horizontal and vertical lines.

- Can you find the equation of a horizontal line, such as $y = 2$ shown above, by using $y = mx + c$? **Discuss.**
  Can you find the equation of a vertical line, such as $x = 2$ shown above, by using $y = mx + c$? **Discuss.**

FINDING EQUATIONS of GIVEN LINES

Take the following steps to write down the equation of a line drawn on a graph.
  Step 1 From the graph, find the values of c and m.
  Step 2 In the equation $y = mx + c$, replace c and m with these values.
  Step 3 Tidy up the equation. Use the guidelines that follow.

Guidelines for tidying up an equation.
  1. Do not leave fractions in the equation.
  2. Do not leave a negative at the beginning of either side of the equation.
  3. If both the x and y terms are on the left-hand side of the equation, begin with the x term.

Worked Example Find the equations of the lines l_1 , l_2 , l_3 , l_4 and l_5 .

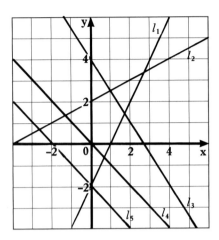

Answer **For l_1** $c = -2$, $m = \frac{2}{1}$ or 2.

The equation is $y = 2x - 2$.

For l_2 $c = 2$, $m = \frac{1}{2}$.

The equation is $y = \frac{1}{2}x + 2$

$2y = x + 4$ (multiplying both sides by 2)

For l_3 $c = 4$, $m = -\frac{3}{2}$.

The equation is $y = -\frac{3}{2}x + 4$

$2y = -3x + 8$ (multiplying both sides by 2)

$3x + 2y = 8$ (adding 3x to both sides)

Note An alternative way of tidying up the equation $2y = -3x + 8$ is
to write it as $2y = 8 - 3x$.

For l_4 $c = 0$, $m = -1$.

The equation is $y = -x + 0$

$x + y = 0$ (adding x to both sides)

For l_5 $c = -2$, $m = -1$.

The equation is $y = -x - 2$

$x + y = -2$ (adding x to both sides)

$x + y + 2 = 0$ (adding 2 to both sides)

Note We do not leave the equation as $x + y = -2$ since the right-
hand side begins with a negative.

EXERCISE 7:10

1. Tidy up these line equations.

   (a) $y = -x$ (b) $2y = -x + 3$ (c) $y = -3x + 1$ (d) $y = -4$

   (e) $x = -3$ (f) $2y = -x - 3$ (g) $y = -2x - 3$ (h) $y = \frac{1}{2}x + 1$

   (i) $y = -\frac{2}{3}x + 4$ (j) $y = \frac{2}{5}x$ (k) $y = 3x - \frac{1}{2}$ (l) $y = -x + \frac{2}{5}$

   (m) $y = 3 - \frac{1}{2}x$

2. Write down the equations of these lines.

   (a)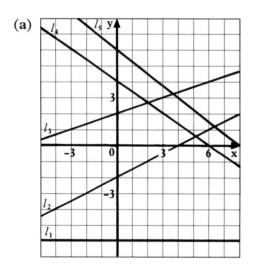
   (b)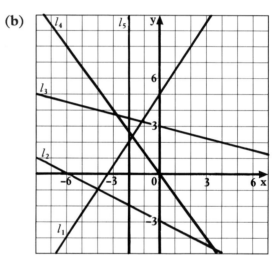

3. A(-2, 5), B(4, 2), C(6, 3) are the vertices of a triangle. Draw this triangle on a set of axes. (Number both the x and y axes from -10 to 10). Hence write down the equations of the sides of the triangle.

4.

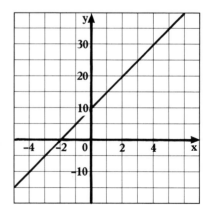

   The scale on the x-axis is different from the scale on the y-axis.
   The gradient of the line is *not* 1.

   (a) The gradient of the line is
        A. 2   **B.** 10   **C.** 5   **D.** 0·2
   (b) Find the equation of the line.

5.

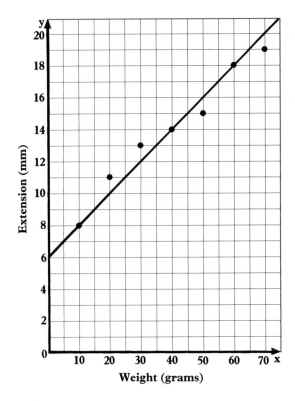

Helen gathered data on the extension of a spring for different weights hung from it.
She plotted the scatter diagram, then drew on this line of best fit.

Find the equation of this line of best fit.

Review 1   Tidy up these line equations.

    (a) $3y = -2x$ **(b)** $y = \frac{3}{4}x - 2$ **(c)** $2y = -x - 1$ **(d)** $x = -4$

Review 2   Write down the equation of these lines.

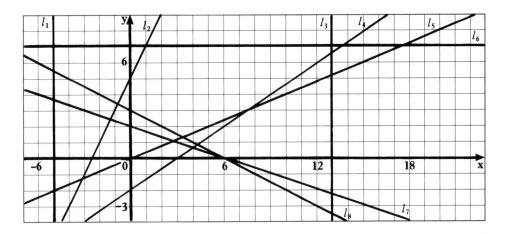

Sir Isaac Newton

Sir Isaac Newton was born at Woolsthorpe, Lincoln on Christmas Day in 1642 and died in 1727.

His father died shortly before Isaac was born. His mother remarried when he was two. Isaac then went to live with his grandmother. He went to a local school where it was reported that he paid little attention to his studies and was ranked among the lowest in the school. It is said that his main interests were carpentry, mechanics, writing poetry and drawing.

When Isaac was 14 his stepfather died. His mother then took Isaac from school to help on the farm. He showed no interest in farming. At the suggestion of an uncle, he returned to school when he was 18. The following year, 1661, he entered Trinity College at Cambridge.

In his first years at Trinity College he was not an outstanding student. It was not until about his fourth year that his genius became apparent. At first, chemistry was what interested Isaac most. Throughout his life he maintained this interest although he did his most famous work in mathematics and physics. During his early years at Trinity College he read books by Oughtred and Viète and other mathematicians.

In 1669 he became a Professor of Mathematics at Cambridge, a position he held until 1696. During the Black Plague of London he returned to Woolsthorpe where he had months of uninterrupted study. This time was the most creative of his career. By the time he was 25 he had invented calculus (a most important branch of mathematics), discovered the law of universal gravitation and proved that white light is a mixture of colours.

His research on light was published in 1672. His revolutionary ideas were criticized by many and Newton vowed to publish nothing further. Many of his other discoveries were not published for many years.

Newton's chief contribution to mathematics was the development of calculus. His laws of motion formed the basis for scientific development for centuries.

One of the most famous quarrels between mathematicians was between Newton and Gottfried Leibniz, a German mathematician. The argument was about who had invented calculus. Supporters of Newton accused Leibniz of stealing Newton's ideas. The quarrel developed into one of great bitterness. As a result of this, British mathematicians for generations afterwards were virtually ignored by those on the continent and the development of mathematics in Britain suffered as a consequence.

Newton was a famous man in his own lifetime. While at Cambridge he was a Member of Parliament. After he left Cambridge he was Warden of the Mint and later Master of the Mint, positions which involved him living in the Tower of London. He was a foreign associate of the Académie des Sciences and President of the Royal Society for many years. In 1705 he was knighted by Queen Anne.

Newton was a modest man. He once wrote *"If I have seen further than most men, it is because I have stood on the shoulders of giants"*.

He was also reported to be absent-minded. A story is told that while entertaining guests at dinner he left the room to get some wine. While out of the room he became distracted and didn't return to his guests. Another story is told that he dismounted his horse to lead it up a hill; when he attempted to remount the horse he found he had only the bridle in his hand and the horse was nowhere to be seen.

Newton was buried in Westminster Abbey, a great honour for one who began life as a farm boy. Voltaire, the French philosopher attended the funeral and said later *"I have seen a professor of mathematics, only because he was great in his vocation, buried like a king who had done good to his subjects"*.

SOLVING LINEAR INEQUALITIES

Remember: $n > -5$ is read as   "n is greater than – 5"
                $n \geq -5$ is read as   "n is greater than or equal to –5"
                $n < 3$ is read as   "n is less than 3"
                $n \leq 3$ is read as   "n is less than or equal to 3"
      $-4 < n < 7$ is read as   "n is between –4 and 7"
               or as   "n is greater than –4 but less than 7"

DISCUSSION EXERCISE 8:1

- The values of n for which the inequality $n - 3 > 1$ is true could be found by trial and improvement. We could begin with the following.

n	–2	–1	0	1	2	3	4	5	6	7
n – 3	–5	–4	–3	–2	–1	0	1	2	3	4

How could you use the above to solve the inequality $n - 3 > 1$? **Discuss.**

-

Which of these is the number line graph for $n - 3 > 1$? What are the others the graphs of? **Discuss.**

The solution of the equation $n - 3 = 1$ is $n = 4$.
The point 4 divides the number line into two regions; a region to the right of 4 and a region to the left of 4.
At the point 4, the equation $n - 3 = 1$ is true.
On one side of this point, the inequality $n - 3 < 1$ is true and on the other side the inequality $n - 3 > 1$ is true.

Solutions for inequalities such as $n - 3 > 1, 2n - 1 \leq 15$ etc. may be found by first solving the equations $n - 3 = 1, 2n - 1 = 15$ etc., then finding the region of the number line for which the inequality is true. The following worked example uses this method.

Inequalities

Example To find the solution of the inequality $2n - 1 \leq 15$ we can proceed as follows.

We first solve the equation $2n - 1 = 15$. The balance method is used below. Another method, such as trial and improvement or a flowchart, could be used.

$2n - 1 = 15$

$\qquad 2n = 16$ (adding 1 to both sides)

$\qquad\; n = 8$ (dividing both sides by 2)

The graph of the solution to $2n - 1 = 15$ is:

At the point 8, the equation $2n - 1 = 15$ is true. On one side of the point 8, the inequality $2n - 1 < 15$ is true.

In the inequality $2n - 1 < 15$, replace n with a value other than 8; check whether the inequality is true for this value.

We will choose to replace n with 10.

If $n = 10$, then $2n - 1 < 15$ becomes $2 \times 10 - 1 < 15$

$\qquad\qquad\qquad\qquad\qquad\qquad\qquad 19 < 15$ which is *not* true.

Since $n = 10$ is *not* one of the solutions of $2n - 1 < 15$ then the graph of $2n - 1 < 15$ is *not* to the right of 8. Hence the graph of $2n - 1 < 15$ is to the left of 8. The graph of $2n - 1 \leq 15$ is to the left of 8 and includes the point 8.

From this graph we can write down the solution of the inequality $2n - 1 \leq 15$. The solution is $n \leq 8$.

The previous worked example shows the steps that can be taken to solve a linear inequality.

Step 1 Replace the inequality sign with an = sign.
Solve the equation formed to find the point which divides the number line into two regions.

Step 2 Place the symbol ● or ○ on this point.
● is used if the sign of the inequality is $\geq$ or $\leq$, since this point is one of the solutions.
○ is used if the sign of the inequality is $>$ or $<$, since this point is not one of the solutions.

Step 3 Test a point in one of the regions to find the region for which the inequality is true.
Draw the number line graph.

Step 4 Use the number line graph to write down the solution.

Worked Example What can you say about x if $\frac{2-x}{4} < 1$?

Answer If $\frac{2-x}{4} = 1$ then $2 - x = 4$ (multiplying both sides by 4)

$\quad\quad\quad\quad\quad\quad\quad\quad\quad\quad - x = 2$ (subtracting 2 from both sides)

$\quad\quad\quad\quad\quad\quad\quad\quad\quad\quad\quad x = -2$ (dividing both sides by –1)

The point – 2 divides the number line into
two regions. The symbol O is placed on –2
since the inequality sign is $<$.

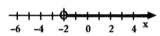

If x = 3, then $\frac{2-x}{4} < 1$ becomes $\frac{2-3}{4} < 1$

$\quad\quad\quad\quad\quad\quad\quad\quad\quad\quad -\frac{1}{4} < 1$ which is true.

The graph of $\frac{2-x}{4} < 1$ is then

We can say that x must be greater than –2.

Note A point other than x = 3 could have been tested.

The following discussion exercise develops another method of solving linear inequalities.

DISCUSSION EXERCISE 8:2

- "5 > 4" Is this true?
  "5 + 2 > 4 + 2 i.e. 7 > 6" Is this true?
  "5 + (–6) > 4 + (–6) i.e. –1 > –2" Is this true?
  "5 – 7 > 4 – 7 i.e. –2 > –3" Is this true?
  "5 – (–5) > 4 – (–5) i.e. 10 > 9" Is this true?

  If the same number is added to (or subtracted from) both sides of an inequality is the new inequality formed still true? **Discuss.**

- "2 < 6" Is this true?
  "3 × 2 < 3 × 6 i.e. 6 < 18" Is this true?
  "(–3) × 2 < (–3) × 6 i.e. –6 < –18" Is this true?
  "$\frac{2}{2} < \frac{6}{2}$ i.e. 1 < 3" Is this true?
  "$\frac{2}{-2} < \frac{6}{-2}$ i.e. –1 < –3" Is this true?

  Make and test statements about multiplying (or dividing) both sides of an inequality by the same number. **Discuss.**

- $2n - 3 = 15$ This equation may be solved using the "balance method" as follows.

$$2n - 3 = 15$$
$$2n = 18 \quad \text{(adding 3 to both sides)}$$
$$n = 9 \quad \text{(dividing both sides by 2)}$$

$2n - 3 < 15$ Can each line of the solution below be justified from your previous discussion? **Discuss.**

$$2n - 3 < 15$$
$$2n < 18$$
$$n < 9$$

- $5 - 3n = 29$ This equation may be solved by the "balance method" as follows.

$$5 - 3n = 29$$
$$-3n = 24 \quad \text{(subtracting 5 from both sides)}$$
$$n = -8 \quad \text{(dividing both sides by } -3)$$

$5 - 3n > 29$ Can each line of the solution below be justified from your previous discussion? **Discuss.**

$$5 - 3n > 29$$
$$-3n > 24$$
$$n < -8$$

Adding or **subtracting** a number from both sides of an inequality leaves the inequality sign unchanged. That is, $<$ remains $<$, $\leq$ remains $\leq$, $>$ remains $>$, $\geq$ remains $\geq$.

Multiplying or **dividing** both sides of an inequality **by a positive number** leaves the sign of the inequality unchanged.

If both sides of an inequality are **multiplied** (or **divided**) **by a negative number**, the sign of the inequality must be changed. That is, $<$ becomes $>$, $\leq$ becomes $\geq$, $>$ becomes $<$, $\geq$ becomes $\leq$.

Worked Example   Solve   (a) $\dfrac{x}{2} + 1 \geq 7$ (b) $2(3 - 2x) < -3$

Answer   (a) $\dfrac{x}{2} + 1 \geq 7$

$$\dfrac{x}{2} \geq 6 \quad \text{(subtracting 1 from both sides)}$$

$$x \geq 12 \quad \text{(multiplying both sides by 2)}$$

(b) $2(3 - 2x) < -3$

$$6 - 4x < -3 \quad \text{(expanding)}$$
$$-4x < -9 \quad \text{(subtracting 6 from both sides)}$$
$$x > \dfrac{-9}{-4} \quad \text{(dividing both sides by } -4)$$
$$x > 2 \cdot 25$$

Worked Example   **(a)**   Find the solution of $-2 \leq a + 3 < 5$.

                   (b)   List all the whole number solutions.

Answer   **(a)** $-2 \leq a + 3 < 5$

                   $-5 \leq$ a < 2 (subtracting 3 from each part of the inequality)

         (b)   The whole number solutions are $-5, -4, -3, -2, -1, 0, 1$.

DISCUSSION EXERCISE 8:3

Compare the two methods of solving linear inequalities — the "geometric" method shown at the beginning of this chapter and the "algebraic" method developed in Discussion Exercise 8:2. **Discuss** advantages and disadvantages of each method.

As part of your discussion, **discuss** how to solve the previous worked examples using the "geometric" method. (*Hint*: to solve $-2 \leq a + 3 < 5$ in this way rewrite as $a + 3 \geq -2$ and $a + 3 < 5$.)

EXERCISE 8:4

1. Solve these inequalities.

   (a) $x + 7 > 12$ **(b)** $n - 3 \leq -1$ **(c)** $a + 8 \geq 2$ **(d)** $4n < 12$

   (e) $2n > 3$ **(f)** $\dfrac{n}{2} \leq 3$ **(g)** $n - 2 < 3$ **(h)** $2a - 1 < 5$

   (i) $4x + 5 \geq -3$ **(j)** $\dfrac{a}{7} - 2 < 1$ **(k)** $\dfrac{n + 3}{2} < -2$ **(l)** $\dfrac{1 + 2n}{3} \geq 4$

2. Find the solution for these inequalities.

   (a) $2n > 5$ **(b)** $2n \geq -5$ **(c)** $-2n > 5$ **(d)** $-2n \geq -5$

   (e) $3 - 2x \leq 4$ **(f)** $2 - 5x > -8$ **(g)** $\dfrac{-5a}{3} < 4$ **(h)** $\dfrac{-2a}{5} \geq -1$

   (i) $2 - \dfrac{5n}{4} > 1$ **(j)** $\dfrac{3 - 2a}{2} \leq -4$ **(k)** $\dfrac{2 - n}{4} > 1$

3. Find the smallest whole number for which these inequalities are true.

   (a) $2(3 + 2n) > 10$ **(b)** $2(2n + 1) \leq -5$ **(c)** $2(2 - 3n) \geq 7$

   (d) $4(1 - n) \leq 15$ **(e)** $6n - n \geq -20$ **(f)** $2n + 5 > 5n - 2$

   (g) $2n + 1 < 3$ **(h)** $n - 6n < 4$

4. Solve these inequalities.

   (a) $-1 < x + 3 < 4$ (b) $2 \le a - 3 \le 7$ (c) $-6 < 2n \le 5$

   (d) $-5 \le 5n < 25$ (e) $-5 < \dfrac{n}{4} < 2$ (f) $-3 < \dfrac{x}{3} \le -1$

5. What can you say about n if: (a) $3n + 4 \le -11$ (b) $-3 < n - 2 < 8$

6. Write down the values of n, where n is a whole number, such that

   (a) $3(2 + n) > 10$ (b) $2 - 3n \le -5$ (c) $3n - 9 < 7 - 4n$

Review 1   Solve these inequalities.

   (a) $2a + 5 \ge 9$ (b) $3 + 5a < -7$ (c) $2(3 + 2x) > -1$ (d) $\dfrac{n + 5}{2} \le 6$

   (e) $2 + n < 5n - 4$ (f) $\dfrac{-2x}{3} \ge 5$

Review 2   Write down the values of n, where n is a whole number, such that

   (a) $-8 < 2n \le 6$ (b) $5 - 2n < 12$

INVESTIGATION 8:5

USING COUNTER-EXAMPLES

Consider the statement "2n is larger than n – 2".
We could test this statement by replacing n by 1, then 2, then
3, . . . If we continued in this way, it would seem that 2n is
always greater than n – 2.
However, if we replace n with –5, then $2n = -10$ and
$n - 2 = -7$. For this value of n, 2n is smaller than n – 2 . We
have found an example which disproves the statement "2n is
larger than n – 2". That is, we have found a counter-example.

n	2n	n – 2
1	2	–1
2	4	0
3	6	1
4	8	2
5	10	3

- **Investigate** the following statements. $3n > n - 3$
  $$n + 4 < 4n$$
  $$2n + 7 > n + 1$$

- Make other statements concerning inequalities. Test these statements.
  Try to find counter-examples which disprove your statements.

SOLVING QUADRATIC INEQUALITIES

The linear equation $2x = 6$ has just one solution; $x = 3$.
The point 3 divides the number line into two regions; a
region to the right of 3 and a region to the left of 3. In one of
these regions, the inequality $2x > 6$ is true; in the other
region, $2x < 6$ is true.

The quadratic equation $x^2 = 16$ has two solutions; $x = -4$ and $x = 4$.
The points -4 and 4 divide the number line into three
regions; a region to the left of -4, a region between -4 and 4
and a region to the right of 4. The inequality $x^2 > 16$ is true
in two of these regions while the inequality $x^2 < 16$ is true for the other region.
We may test a point in each of the three regions to find whether $x^2 > 16$ or $x^2 < 16$.

Worked Example   Solve the inequality $x^2 > 16$.

Answer   Find the end points of the regions by solving $x^2 = 16$.
If $x^2 = 16$, then $x = 4$ and $x = -4$.

Since the inequality sign is $>$, the symbol o
is placed on these end points.

Now test a point in each of the three regions.

Choose a point to the left of -4, say -5. In $x^2 > 16$, replace x with -5.
Is $(-5)^2 > 16$? That is, is $25 > 16$? Since the answer to this question is Yes,
solutions for the inequality are in the region to the left of -4.
So far we have

Choose a point between -4 and 4, say 3. In $x^2 > 16$, replace x with 3.
Is $(3)^2 > 16$? That is, is $9 > 16$? Since the answer to this question is No,
solutions for the inequality are not in the region between -4 and 4.

Choose a point to the right of 4, say $x = 6$. In $x^2 > 16$, replace x with 6.
Is $6^2 > 16$? That is, is $36 > 16$? Since the answer to this question is Yes,
solutions for the inequality are in the region to the right of 4. We now have

From this number line graph we see that the solutions for $x^2 > 16$ are
$x < -4$ and $x > 4$.

The previous worked example illustrates the steps to take when **using a number line graph to solve a quadratic inequality.**

Step 1 Replace the inequality sign with an = sign.
Solve the equation formed to find the end points of the regions into which the number line is divided.

Step 2 Place the symbol o or the symbol ● on these end points.
o is used if the sign of the inequality is > or <.
● is used if the sign of the inequality is ≥ or ≤.

Step 3 Test a point in each region to find the region (or regions) for which the inequality is true.
Build up the number line graph as you test the points.

Step 4 Use the number line graph to write down the solution.

Worked Example Solve the inequality $2x^2 - 5 \leq 13$.

Answer   If $2x^2 - 5 = 13$
then $2x^2 = 18$ (adding 5 to both sides)
$x^2 = 9$ (dividing both sides by 2)
$x = 3$ or $x = -3$

Since the inequality sign is ≤ , place the symbol ● on the –3 and 3.

Replace x with –4. $2(-4)^2 - 5 \leq 13$, i.e. $27 \leq 13$. Not true.

Replace x with 2. $2(2)^2 - 5 \leq 13$, i.e. $3 \leq 13$. True.

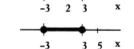

Replace x with 5. $2(5)^2 - 5 \leq 13$, i.e. $45 \leq 13$. Not true.

The completed number line graph is

The solution for $2x^2 - 5 \leq 13$ is $-3 \leq x \leq 3$.

EXERCISE 8:6

1. Solve these inequalities.

(a) $x^2 \geq 9$ (b) $x^2 > 4$ (c) $n^2 > 36$ (d) $n^2 \geq 100$

(e) $a^2 < 25$ (f) $a^2 < 100$ (g) $x^2 \leq 49$ (h) $x^2 > 64$

(i) $x^2 > 81$ (j) $n^2 \leq 4$

2. Solve these inequalities.

(a) $2x^2 \geq 8$ (b) $3x^2 \geq 48$ (c) $3x^2 < 12$ (d) $x^2 - 2 < 47$

(e) $x^2 + 5 > 30$ (f) $x^2 - 4 \leq 60$ (g) $2x^2 - 5 < 13$ (h) $\frac{x^2}{4} \leq 9$

(i) $3x^2 + 2 < 77$ (j) $7 + 2x^2 > 9$

3. Write down all the whole number values of n for which

(a) $n^2 \leq 25$ (b) $5n^2 < 45$ (c) $\frac{n^2}{2} < 8$ (d) $2n^2 + 11 \leq 13$

(e) $n^2 \geq 4$ (f) $3n^2 + 4 > 7$.

4. What can you say about p if   (a) $p^2 + 3 > 19$ (b) $2p^2 - 25 < 73$?

Review   Solve   (a) $n^2 > 25$ (b) $\frac{a^2}{4} \geq 16$ (c) $3x^2 - 1 \leq 11$.

GRAPHING LINEAR INEQUALITIES in 2 VARIABLES

$2x + 3 \geq 1$ is a linear inequality in one variable, x. A linear inequality in one variable can be graphed on a number line.

$2x + y \geq 1$ is a linear inequality in two variables, x and y. A linear inequality in two variables can be graphed on a plane.

DISCUSSION EXERCISE 8:7

- x = 2, y = –1. Is the inequality $2x + y > 1$ true for these values of x and y? Where, in relation to the line $2x + y = 1$, is the point $(2, -1)$? **Discuss.**

  What if x = 2, y = 3?   **What if** x = 1, y = 2?
  What if x = 0, y = –2?   **What if** x = –2, y = 3?
  What if x = $\frac{1}{2}$, y = –1?   **What if** x = 1, y = –1?
  What if x = 0, y = 1?   **What if** . . .

  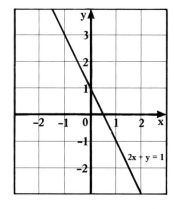

  Where, on the graph, are all the points for which the inequality $2x + y > 1$ is true? Where are all the points for which $2x + y < 1$ is true? Where are all the points for which $2x + y = 1$ is true? **Discuss.**

- Draw the line x – y = 2.
  Choose points; write down the x and y-coordinates of these points. Test these values of x and y in the inequality x – y < 2.
  Make and test a statement about regions of the plane for which the following are true:
  x – y < 2, x – y = 2, x – y > 2, x – y ≤ 2, x – y ≥ 2. **Discuss.**
  You may like to repeat this for other lines such as x + 2y = 4, x + 2y = –4, 2x – y = 2.

A line divides a plane into two regions; a region on one side of the line and a region on the other side of the line.
For instance, the line 3x – 2y = 6 divides the plane into a region above the line and a region below the line. In one of these regions 3x – 2y < 6 and in the other 3x – 2y > 6.

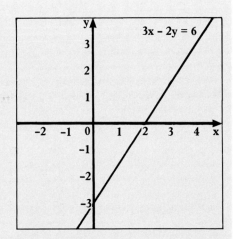

We take the following steps to shade the region given by an inequality.

Step 1   Draw the boundary line. The equation of this line is found by replacing the inequality sign with an = sign.
  If the inequality sign is ≥ or ≤ the boundary line is solid since the inequality is true for points on this line.
  If the inequality sign is > or < the boundary line is dotted since the inequality is not true for points on this line.

Step 2   Choose a point on the plane. (Don't choose a point on the boundary line.) Test the coordinates of this point in the inequality.
  If the inequality is true for these values of x and y shade this side of the boundary line.
  If the inequality is not true for these values of x and y shade the other side of the boundary line.

Note   We can draw the boundary line by plotting points or we can draw it by finding the gradient and where it crosses the y-axis.
  In the following worked examples the first method is used.

Worked Example   Shade the region for which x + 2y ≥ 4.

Answer   The boundary line has equation x + 2y = 4.

x	−2	0	2
y	3	2	1

The line goes through the points (−2, 3), (0, 2), (2, 1). Since the inequality
sign is ≥ this boundary line is a solid line.

Testing the coordinates of P(3, 2) in the inequality x + 2y ≥ 4 we get:
   3 + 2 × 2 ≥ 4
      7 ≥ 4   True
Since the inequality is true for these values of x and y, the point P is in the
region where the inequality is true. Hence we shade the region which includes P.

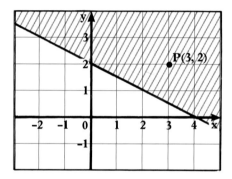

Worked Example   Shade the region for which 2x − y < −1.

Answer   The boundary line is the line 2x − y = −1.

x	−1	0	1
y	−1	1	3

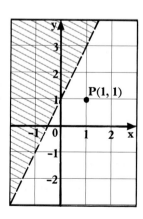

The line goes through the points (−1, −1), (0, 1), (1, 3).
Since the inequality sign is < this line is dotted.

Testing the coordinates of P(1, 1) in the inequality
2x − y < −1 we get 2 × 1 − 1 < −1 i.e. 1 < −1. False.
Hence P is not a point in the required region. We
shade the region which does not include P.

149

EXERCISE 8:8

1. Shade the region in which the following inequalities are true. Draw a separate graph for each. Number both the x and y-axes from –5 to 5.

   (a) $y \geq 2x + 1$ (b) $y \leq x - 4$ (c) $y > -x + 3$ (d) $x + y < 1$
   (e) $2x + y \geq -1$ (f) $x + 2y \leq 4$ (g) $x - y > 1$ (h) $x + 2y \geq 2$
   (i) $3x - 2y < 4$ (j) $4x - 2y \geq -1$ (k) $2x - 3y > 0$

2. The shaded area is given by

   (a)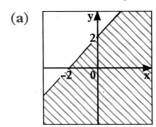

   A. $y \leq x + 2$
   B. $y < x + 2$
   C. $y \geq x + 2$
   D. $y > x + 2$

   (b)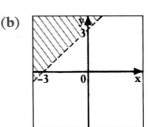

   A. $x - y \geq -3$
   B. $x - y > -3$
   C. $x - y \leq -3$
   D. $x - y < -3$

   (c)

   A. $2x + y > 2$
   B. $2x + y \geq 2$
   C. $2x + y < 2$
   D. $2x + y \leq 2$

Review   Draw graphs to show the region for which these inequalities are true.
   (a) $y < 2x - 4$ (b) $x + 2y \geq 4$ (c) $x - y \leq 3$ (d) $3x - 2y > 6$

FINDING REGIONS where a NUMBER of INEQUALITIES are TRUE

DISCUSSION EXERCISE 8:9

● The line $y = -1$ is shown on this graph.
   In which region of this graph are the following
   inequalities true: $y > -1, y \geq -1, y < -1, y \leq -1$?
   Discuss. Test points as part of your discussion.

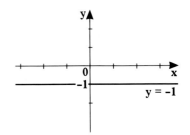

150

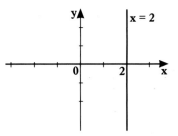

The line x = 2 is shown on this graph.
In which region of this graph are the following
inequalities true: x > 2, x ≥ 2, x < 2, x ≤ 2? **Discuss.**

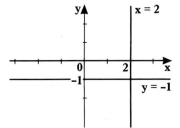

In which region of this graph are both x ≥ 2 *and*
y ≤ –1 true? **Discuss.**

● To shade the region in which both y ≥ 2x + 1 and x + 2y ≤ 4 we could begin by
drawing the lines y = 2x + 1 and x + 2y = 4 on the same set of axes.
How might we continue? **Discuss.**

Worked Example Draw a diagram to show where both of the inequalities
x < 3 and x + 2y ≥ –4 are true.

Answer The two diagrams below show the steps to be taken.

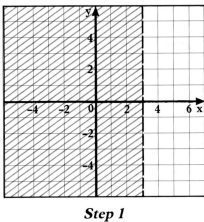

Step 1   **Step 2**

Step 1 shows the region where x < 3 shaded as

Step 2 shows the region where x + 2y ≥ –4 shaded as   on the same
graph as the region for x < 3.

The region that is shaded with both types of shading i.e. as   is the region
where both the inequalities x < 3 and x + 2y ≥ –4 are true.

Inequalities

Worked Example The region R is defined by the three inequalities $x < 3$, $y \le 2x$,
$x - y < 2$. Shade the region R.

Answer

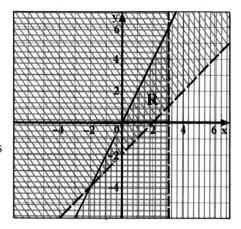

Begin by shading $x < 3$ as ⊟

Then shade $y \le 2x$ as ▥

Finally shade $x - y < 2$ as ⧄

R is the region shaded as ▦ Label this
region as R.

Note To make the required region more distinct it is a good idea to go over the shading,
and the boundaries, with a coloured pencil.

EXERCISE 8:10

In this exercise, number both the x and y-axes from –4 to 6.

1. Shade the region in which both of the inequalities are true.

   (a) $x < -1$ and $y \le 3$ (b) $x \ge 1$ and $y \ge 3$
   (c) $x > 3$ and $y < x$ (d) $y < 3$ and $y \ge x + 1$
   (e) $y \ge 2x - 1$ and $x \ge 1$ (f) $y > 3$ and $x - y > -3$
   (g) $x + y \le 0$ and $x \ge -3$

2. Draw a diagram to show where both inequalities are true.

   (a) $y \ge x - 2$ and $y < x + 4$ (b) $y < 2x$ and $y \ge x + 1$
   (c) $x + y > 2$ and $y > x - 3$ (d) $2x + y \ge 4$ and $2y \le x + 2$
   (e) $x - 2y < 4$ and $y \le x$ (f) $2x - 3y \le 6$ and $3x + 2y < 0$

3. The region A is defined by four inequalities. Shade this region A if the inequalities are

   (a) $y \le 4$, $y \ge -3$, $x \le 5$, $x \ge 0$ (b) $y \ge 0$, $x \ge -3$, $y \le 3$, $x \le 1$.

4. The region R is defined by three inequalities. Shade R in the following cases:

    (a) $x \geq 0, y \geq 0, y \geq x + 3$ (b) $y \leq x, x < 3, y \geq -3$
    (c) $y \geq -3, x \geq -1, y < 2x + 1$ (d) $x + y \leq 3, x \geq 0, y \geq 0$
    (e) $x > -3, y \geq -1, x + y < 2.$

Review 1 The region S is defined by two inequalities. Shade this region S if the inequalities are   (a) $x \leq 5, y \geq 1$
                                     (b) $y \geq x - 1, y < 3$
                                     (c) $2x - y > 1, x + y < 0.$

Review 2 Draw a diagram to show where all three inequalities are true.
          (a) $x \geq -2$ and $y \leq 4$ and $y > 2x - 3$
          (b) $x \geq 0$ and $4y \leq x - 4$ and $x - y \leq 4$

EXERCISE 8:11

1. Amanda bought a number of phone cards. Some cost £5 each and some cost £10 each. She spent less than £50. The inequality $5x + 10y < 50$ describes this.
    (a) What does x stand for? What does y stand for?
    (b) Can x or y have negative values?
    (c) Draw a graph to show the region that contains all possible values of x and y for which the inequalities are true.

2. Books in a sale are priced as shown.

    Kay went to this book sale prepared to spend up to £12. $2x + y \leq 12$ is an inequality which could be used to describe the amount of money Kay spent.
    (a) What does x stand for? What does y stand for?
    (b) Can either x or y have a negative value?
    (c) Draw a graph to show the region that contains all the possible numbers of books Kay bought.

3. Jon wants to get a total of more than 10 marks for his history and science projects. $h + s > 10$ is an inequality which describes this.
The history project is marked out of 12 and the science project out of 15.
That is, $h \leq 12$ and $s \leq 15$.
    (a) Can either h or s have a negative value?
    (b) Draw a diagram to show the region that contains all the possible marks which satisfy all the inequalities. (Have h on the vertical axis and s on the horizontal axis.)

4. Jon has two projects to do, one for history and the other for science. The inequality $h + s \leq 4$ defines the total time (in hours) he plans to spend on these projects.

   (a) Could either h or s be negative? Write down two more inequalities.

   (b) Jon plans to spend not more than 3 hours on either project. Use this information to write down another two inequalities.

   (c) Draw a diagram to show the region that contains all possible values of h and s that satisfy all the inequalities. (Have h on the vertical axis and s on the horizontal axis.)

Review   A committee is to have a maximum of 10 members.
At least 3 members are to be men. No more than 6 members may be women. If w stands for the number of women on the committee and m stands for the number of men, $m + w \leq 10$ is one of the inequalities which define the members of this committee.

   (a) Can m or w be negative?

   (b) Write down 3 more inequalities which define the members of this committee.

   (c) Draw a graph to show the region which gives all the possible numbers of men and women on the committee. (Have m on the vertical axis and w on the horizontal axis.)

WRITING INEQUALITIES for GIVEN REGIONS

Worked Example

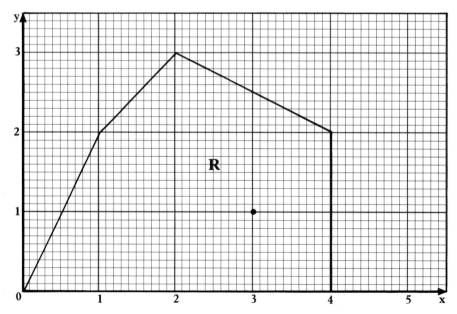

Five straight lines define the region R. Find the inequalities that define R.

Answer   Write down the equation of each of the five boundary lines.

These are $y = 0$, $y = 2x$, $y = x + 1$, $y = -\frac{1}{2}x + 4$ (which can be rearranged as $x + 2y = 8$), $x = 4$.

Choose a point within the region R, say $P(3, 1)$. Now test the coordinates of this point in an inequality formed from the equation of each boundary line. This is shown below.

Suppose $y \geq 0$. Testing $P(3, 1)$ in $y \geq 0$ we get $1 \geq 0$ which is true. Hence $y \geq 0$ is one of the inequalities.
Suppose $y \geq 2x$. Testing $P(3, 1)$ in $y \geq 2x$ we get $1 \geq 2 \times 3$ or $1 \geq 6$ which is not true. Hence $y \geq 2x$ is not one of the inequalities. The correct inequality must be $y \leq 2x$.
Suppose $y \geq x + 1$. Testing $P(3, 1)$ in $y \geq x + 1$ we get $1 \geq 3 + 1$ or $1 \geq 4$ which is not true. The correct inequality must be $y \leq x + 1$.
Suppose $x + 2y \geq 8$. Testing $P(3, 1)$ in $x + 2y \geq 8$ we get $3 + 2 \times 1 \geq 8$ or $5 \geq 8$ which is not true. The correct inequality must be $x + 2y \leq 8$.
Suppose $x \geq 4$. Testing $P(3, 1)$ in $x \geq 4$ we get $3 \geq 4$ which is not true. The correct inequality must be $x \leq 4$.

Hence R is defined by the inequalities $y \geq 0$, $y \leq 2x$, $y \leq x + 1$, $x + 2y \leq 8$, $x \leq 4$.

EXERCISE 8:12

1.

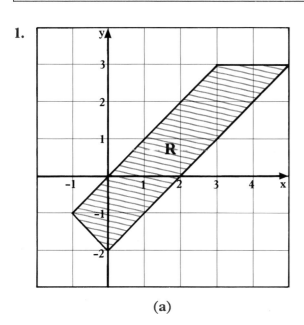

(a)

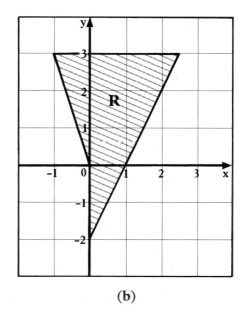

(b)

Four lines bound the region R. Find the four inequalities that define the region R.

2. The region R is defined by 3 inequalities.
Find these inequalities.

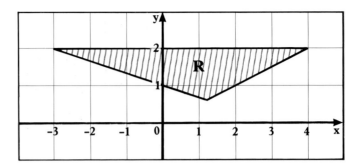

3.

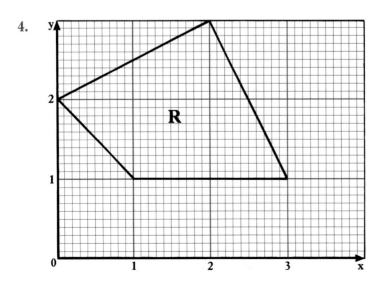

Write down the 6 inequalities that define the region R.

4.

The region R is defined by four inequalities, one of which is $2x + y \le 7$.

Find the other three inequalities.

5.

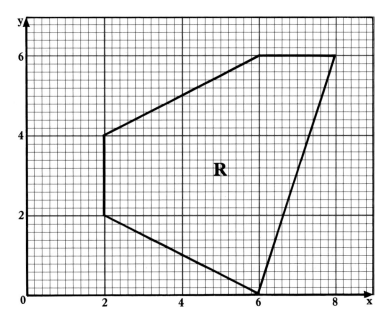

The region R is defined by five inequalities, two of which are
$3x - y \leq 18$,
$x - 2y \geq -6$.

Find the other three inequalities.

Review

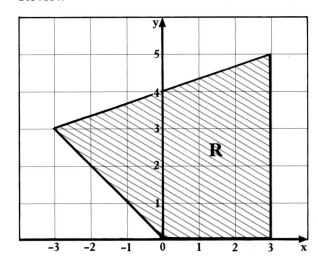

The region R is defined by four inequalities.

Find these inequalities.

Blaise Pascal

Blaise Pascal was born at Clermont in France in 1623 and died in 1662.

As a baby, he became ill with tuberculosis. At that time, many illnesses were blamed on witches. Some claim that an old lady said she had put a spell on Blaise when he was born and this spell could be lifted if an animal was killed. A cat was chosen to be sacrificed but it took fright and jumped out of a window — it hit the road below and died; Blaise recovered.

Blaise's father was interested in mathematics but he was reluctant to allow his son to begin studying mathematics when he was young. Some say this was because he wanted his son to develop other interests; others say it was because it was thought at that time that the study of mathematics overstretched the brain of children. Blaise showed such considerable mathematical talent by the age of 12 that his father relented and began to teach him.

At 14, Blaise joined his father in weekly meetings with other mathematicians at what was to become the Académie des Sciences.

At 16, Pascal published his first work. This was what is known as Pascal's Theorem which dealt with properties of a hexagon inscribed in a conic. (Both the hyperbola and parabola are conics.)

At 18, Pascal began work on a calculating machine and within a few years had built and sold 50 of these. He presented one to the king and one to the royal chancellor. At the time Pascal invented this calculating machine, his father was a collector of taxes. Some claim that Pascal invented the machine because his father needed a quick way of adding and subtracting.

At 23, Pascal and his brother-in-law performed a famous scientific experiment. They took a barometer to the top of a high hill and observed that the level of the mercury in the barometer decreased as they climbed higher and higher.

At 31, while trying to solve a famous gambling problem, Pascal connected the study of probability to the "Arithmetic Triangle", later to become known as Pascal's Triangle (see Level 6 and Level 7 books). This triangle had been known for about 600 years. It had been written about by an Arab mathematician in 1425 and by a Chinese scholar in 1261.

Pascal was a religious man. In 1646, with the encouragement of one of his sisters, he joined a very strict religious sect. A few years later he left the sect. He rejoined in 1654 after an accident. Some say he took the fact that he survived the accident as a sign that he should turn his back on the world. After this, he did little further mathematical work. Four years later he died, at the age of 39.

Mechanical Calculator made by Pascal in 1642

9 Graphs of some Special Functions and Real-Life Situations 9

INTRODUCTION

INVESTIGATION and DISCUSSION EXERCISE 9:1

$y = x^3,$ $y = x^2 - 9,$ $y = 2^x,$ $y = x^3 - 4x,$ $y = x + 2,$ $y = x^2,$

$y = 3^x,$ $y = 4 - x^3,$ $y = 2x,$ $y = 8 - 12x + 6x^2 - x^3,$ $y = -3x^2,$ $y = \frac{1}{x},$

$y = -x,$ $y = x^2 - 4x + 3,$ $y = \frac{-2}{x},$ $y = x^3 + x^2 - 6x + 3,$ $y = 3x - 4,$ $y = (\frac{1}{2})^x,$

$y = 2x^3,$ $y = 3 + 2x - x^2,$ $y = x^2 + 3x,$ $y = x^3 - x^2 - 2x,$ $y = \frac{3}{x},$ $y = -x^3,$

$y = -x^2,$ $y = (\frac{1}{3})^x,$ $y = \frac{-4}{x},$ $y = -x^3 - 2x^2 + 5x + 6$

The above functions can be grouped into 5 categories. The functions $y = x^3$, $y = x^3 - 4x$, $y = 4 - x^3$, $y = 8 - 12x + 6x^2 - x^3$, $y = x^3 + x^2 - 6x + 3$, $y = 2x^3$, $y = x^3 - x^2 - 2x$, $y = -x^3$, $y = -x^3 - 2x^2 + 5x + 6$ are all in one of these categories.

Which functions might be in each of the other 4 categories? **Discuss.**

As part of your discussion, draw the graph of each function. Use a graphics calculator or a computer graphics package to do this.

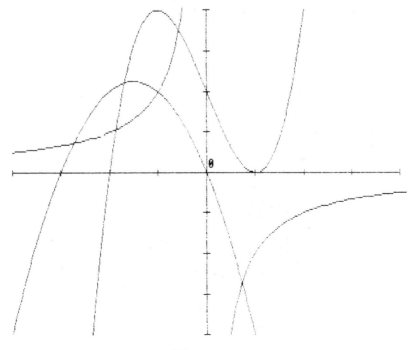

159

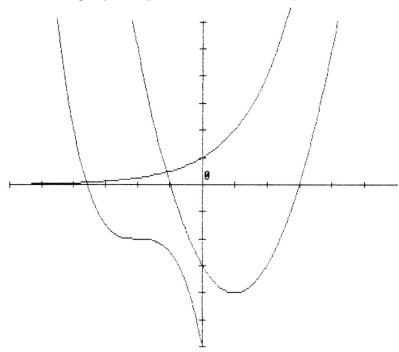

If you do not have a graphics calculator or a computer graphics package available, draw the graphs by plotting points.

For instance; for $y = x^2 - 9$, taking whole number values of x from –4 to 4 and using the calculator to find the y-values we get:

x	–4	–3	–2	–1	0	1	2	3	4
y	7	0	–5	–8	–9	–8	–5	0	7

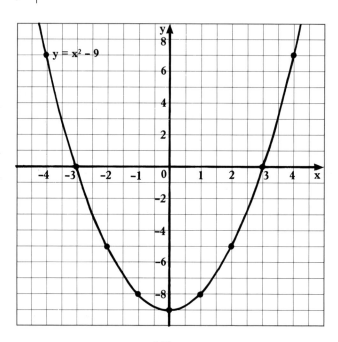

Look closely at the graphs in each of the 4 categories. **Discuss** what the graphs have in common. For instance, you should notice that the graph of $y = x^2 - 9$ and the other graphs in this category all have one turning point and an axis of symmetry.

Now draw the graphs of the functions $y = x^3$, $y = x^3 - 4x$, $y = 4 - x^3$, $y = 8 - 12x + 6x^2 - x^3$, $y = x^3 + x^2 - 6x + 3$, $y = 2x^3$, $y = x^3 - x^2 - 2x$, $y = -x^3$, $y = -x^3 - 2x^2 + 5x + 6$. Look closely at these. Do they all have something in common? **Discuss**

Once again, you could draw the graphs by plotting points if you do not have a graphics calculator or computer graphics package available.
For instance; for $y = -x^3 - 2x^2 + 5x + 6$, taking whole number values of x from –4 to 4 and using the calculator to find the y-values we get:

x	–4	–3	–2	–1	0	1	2	3	4
y	18	0	–4	0	6	8	0	–24	–70

Since the y-value corresponding to $x = 4$ is very large we will not include the point (4, –70) on our graph.

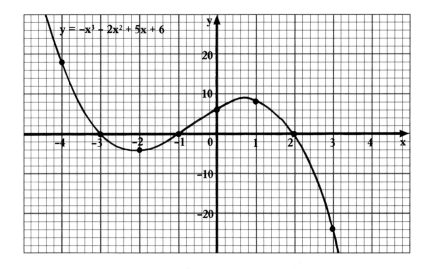

Write a short report on what you have discovered in the investigation.

RECOGNISING the GRAPHS

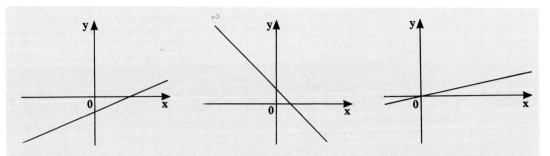

x, 2x, 3x + 4, –2x, 4 – $\frac{1}{2}$x are all **linear functions** of x. The graphs y = x, y = 2x, y = 3x + 4, y = –2x, y = 4 – $\frac{1}{2}$x are all **straight-line graphs.**

In a linear function of x, the highest power of x is x^1.

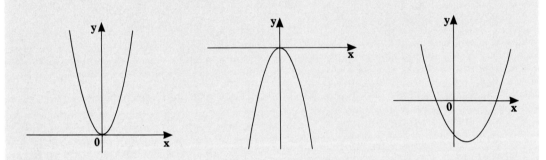

x^2, $2x^2 – 3$, $–5x^2$, $x^2 + 6x$, $2x^2 + 5x – 1$ are all **quadratic functions** of x. The graphs y = x^2, y = $2x^2 – 3$, y = $–5x^2$, y = $x^2 + 6x$, y = $2x^2 + 5x – 1$ are all **parabolas.** These graphs all have an axis of symmetry and one turning point.

In a quadratic function, the highest power of x is x^2.

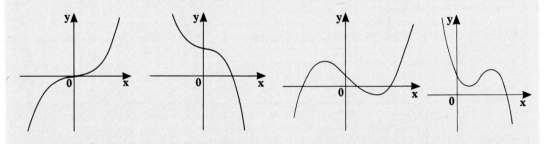

x^3, $–4x^3$, $2x^3 – 4x^2$, $2 – x^3$, $x^3 + 2x^2 – x + 1$ are all **cubic functions** of x. The graphs of y = x^3, y = $–4x^3$, y = $2x^3 – 4x^2$, y = $2 – x^3$, y = $x^3 + 2x^2 – x + 1$ are called **cubic graphs.** Some cubic graphs have two turning points, others have none.

In a cubic function, the highest power of x is x^3.

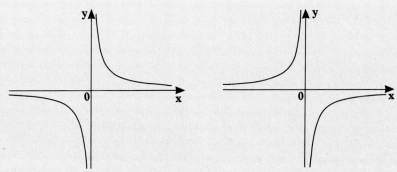

$\frac{1}{x}$, $\frac{3}{2x}$, $\frac{-4}{x}$ are all **reciprocal functions** of x. The graphs of $y = \frac{1}{x}$, $y = \frac{3}{2x}$, $y = \frac{-4}{x}$ are called **hyperbolas**. These graphs have two axes of symmetry. These graphs always consist of two separate congruent curves.

In a reciprocal function, the x is on the denominator.

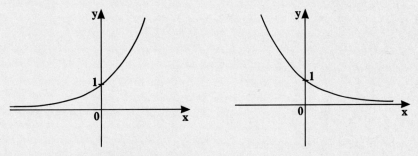

2^x, 3^x, $(\frac{1}{2})^x$ are all **exponential functions** of x. The graphs of $y = 2^x$, $y = 3^x$, $y = (\frac{1}{2})^x$ are called **exponential graphs**. These graphs always cross the y-axis at 1.

In an exponential function, the x is an index.

EXERCISE 9:2

1. (a) Which of the following could be the graph of $y = x^2 - 7x - 10$? Explain your choice.

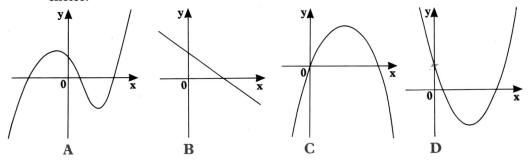

(b) Which of the following could be the graph of $y = -2x^3$? Give reasons for your choice.

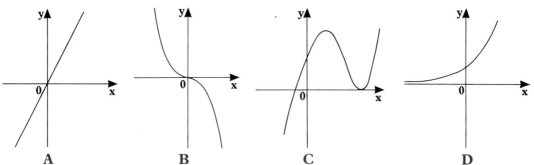

(c) Which of the following could be the graph of $y = 4x - x^2$? Explain your choice.

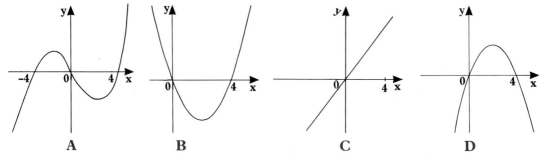

(d) Which of the following could be the graph of $y = \frac{3}{x}$? Explain your choice.

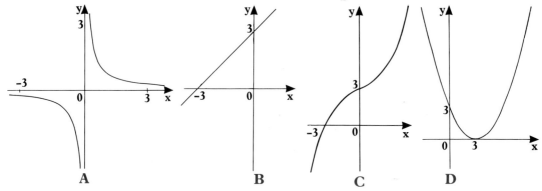

(e) Which of the following could be the graph of $y = 4^x$? Give reasons for your choice.

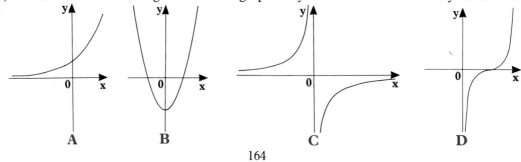

2. Choose sensible scales on the axes when you plot the graphs in this question. You should use different scales on the x and y-axes.

   (i) **(a)** Copy and complete the table for $y = \frac{x^3}{2}$.

x	−3	−2	−1	0	1	2	3
y	−13·5	−4					

   (b) Plot the graph of $y = \frac{x^3}{2}$.

   (ii) **(a)**

x	−4	−3	−2	−1	0	1	2	3	4
y				−4					11

   Copy and complete the table for $y = x^2 - 5$.

   (b) Draw the graph of $y = x^2 - 5$.

   (iii) **(a)**

x	−3	−2	−1	0	1	2	3
y		4			−5		

   Copy and complete the table for $y = x^3 - 6x$.

   (b) Plot the graph of $y = x^3 - 6x$. You may like to plot a few more points around the turning points.

   (iv) **(a)**

x	−5	−4	−3	−2	−1	$-\frac{1}{2}$	0	$\frac{1}{2}$	1	2	3	4	5
y			$3\frac{1}{3}$	5			no value						

   Copy and complete the table for $y = \frac{-10}{x}$.

   (b) Plot the graph of $y = \frac{-10}{x}$.

3. Match the graphs with the equations.

(a)

1. $y = 2x$

2. $y = 2x^2$

3. $y = 2x^3$

4. $y = \frac{2}{x}$

A   B   C   D

(b)

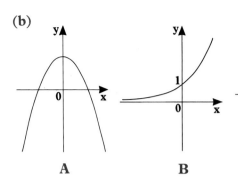

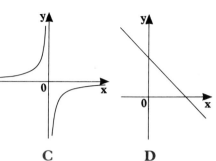

1. $y = 2 - x$

2. $y = 2^x$

3. $y = \dfrac{-2}{x}$

4. $y = 2 - x^2$

A   B   C   D

(c)

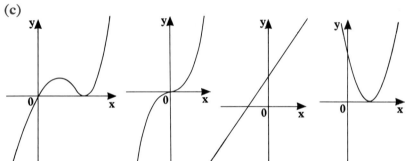

1. $y = x + 4$

2. $y = x^2 - 4x + 4$

3. $y = x^3 - 4x^2 + 4x$

4. $y = 4x^3$

A   B   C   D

4. For an exhibition of posters, the miniature posters were to have an area of 60 cm². If the width of one of these miniature posters is x cm and the height is y cm:

(a) Show that $y = \dfrac{60}{x}$.

(b) Copy and complete the table for $y = \dfrac{60}{x}$.

x	5	10	15	20	25	30
y					2·4	

(c) Draw the graph of $y = \dfrac{60}{x}$ for values of x from 5 to 30.

(d) One of the miniature posters in the exhibition had a width of 7·5 cm. Use your graph to find the height of this poster.

5. **(i)** Berryfields Orchard pack their cherries into wooden
   boxes which have square ends, as shown. These boxes are
   twice as long as they are wide.
   (a) If the width of one of these boxes is x centimetres,
   show that the volume is given by $V = 2x^3$ cubic
   centimetres.
   (b) Copy and complete the table for
   $V = 2x^3$.

x	5	10	15	20	25
V	250				31250

   (c) Draw the graph of $V = 2x^3$ for values of x from 5 to 25.
   (d) One of these cherry boxes has a volume of 20,000 cubic centimetres. Use
   your graph to find the approximate width of this box.

(ii) The cherry boxes do not have lids.
   (a) Show that the area of wood used in one of these boxes is $8x^2$ square
   centimetres.
   (b) Copy and complete the table for $A = 8x^2$.

x	5	10	15	20	25
A			1800		

   (c) Draw the graph of $A = 8x^2$ for values of x from 5 to 25.
   (d) 2500 cm² of wood is needed to make one of these boxes. Use your graph
   to find the approximate width of this box.

Review 1 Which of the following could be the graph of $y = x^3 - 2x^2 - x + 2$?
Explain your choice.

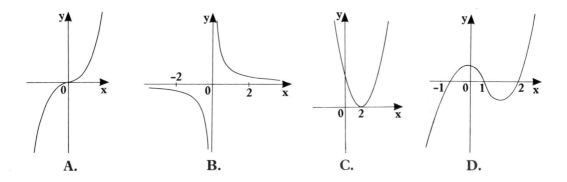

A.   B.   C.   D.

Review 2 Which of the graphs drawn in the previous question could have the
equation **(a)** $y = \frac{2}{x}$ **(b)** $y = x^2 - 4x + 4$ **(c)** $y = x^3$

Review 3 Plastic trays, on which rings are displayed in a jewellers', have square bases. The dimensions of these trays are shown in the diagram.

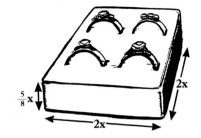

(a) Show that the area of plastic needed to make one of these trays is $A = 9x^2$.

(b) Copy and complete the table for $A = 9x^2$.

x	4	8	12	16	20
A	144			2304	

(c) Draw the graph of $A = 9x^2$ for values of x from 4 to 20. (Choose sensible scales for the x and A-axes.)

(d) Use the graph to find the approximate area of plastic needed to make a tray which is 15 cm long.

(e) 3000 square centimetres of plastic is needed to make a tray. Use your graph to find the approximate length of this tray.

Review 4 (a) Copy and complete the table for $y = 2^x$.
(b) Plot the graph of $y = 2^x$.

x	−3	−2	−1	0	1	2	3
y	$\frac{1}{8}$						8

DISCUSSION EXERCISE 9:3

Draw the graphs of $y = (\frac{1}{2})^x$ and $y = 2^{-x}$. **Discuss** the relationship between these graphs.

What if the graphs were $y = (\frac{1}{5})^x$ and $y = 5^{-x}$?

What if the graphs were $y = (\frac{1}{4})^x$ and $y = 4^{-x}$?

What if .....

In your discussion, you may like to discuss whether $(\frac{1}{2})^x$ is the same as $\frac{1}{2^x}$. You may also like to refer to the work on negative indices in **Chapter 4.**

INVESTIGATION and PRACTICAL EXERCISE 9:4

Make a parabolic reflector as follows:

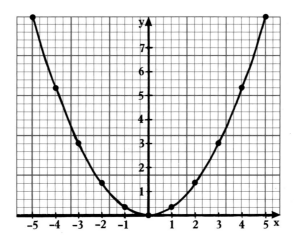

Step 1   Draw a grid of 1 cm squares on a sheet of A3 paper.

Plot the parabola $y = \frac{1}{3}x^2$, using the whole sheet (or nearly the whole sheet).

Step 2   Bend a piece of wire (or other strong but flexible material) to the shape of this parabola. Do this with 5 pieces of wire. (Each piece of wire will need to be about 60 cm long.)

Step 3   Use these 5 pieces of bent wire to make a skeleton shape as shown.
Have the wires placed symmetrically. To keep the shape rigid, tie the wire together at A.

Step 4   Line the inside of the shape with foil. Make this lining as smooth as possible.

What do you think will happen if you take your parabolic reflector outside and point the opening towards the sun? Talk about precautions you should take *before* you take the reflector outside.

What if   your reflector had been made using the parabola $y = x^2$?
What if   your reflector had been made using the parabola $y = 4x^2$?
What if   ...

MATCHING GRAPHS to REAL-LIFE SITUATIONS

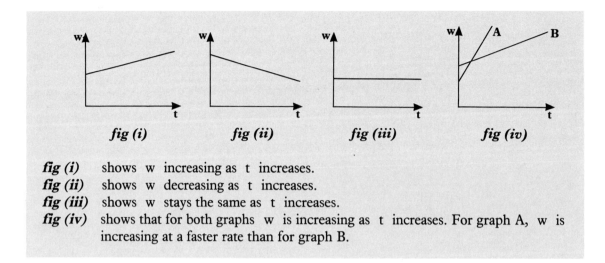

fig (i)   shows w increasing as t increases.
fig (ii)   shows w decreasing as t increases.
fig (iii)   shows w stays the same as t increases.
fig (iv)   shows that for both graphs w is increasing as t increases. For graph A, w is increasing at a faster rate than for graph B.

DISCUSSION EXERCISE 9:5

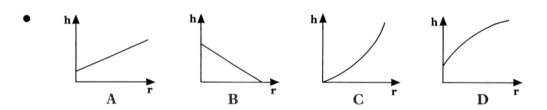

Graph D shows that as r increases, h at first increases quickly and then more slowly. What happens to h, as r increases, in the other graphs? **Discuss.**

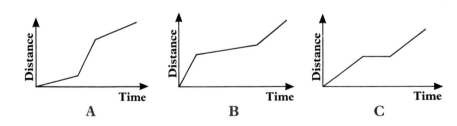

These are the graphs of three cycle journeys.
Graph A shows that at first the speed was quite slow, then the speed was quite fast, then the cyclist slowed down. The speed in the last section of the journey was not as slow as in the first part.
Describe the cycle journeys represented by graphs B and C. **Discuss.**

• At the beginning of an experiment, Josiah filled a measuring cylinder with water.
This graph shows that the measuring cylinder remained full for a time, then it was emptied.
The cylinder was emptied at a faster rate than it was filled.
How can we tell this from the graph? **Discuss.**

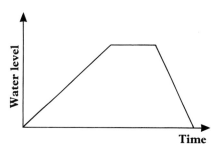

•
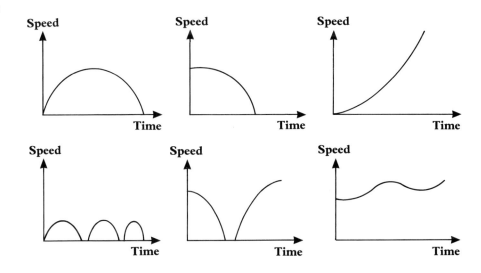

One of these graphs could represent a car in a traffic jam. Which one?
What might the other graphs represent? **Discuss.**

•
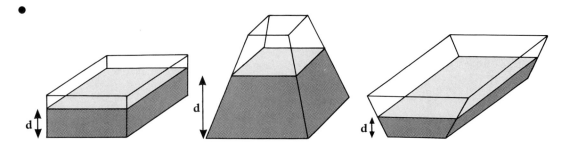

Suppose the above containers are being filled with a liquid at the rate of 200 m*l* per second. In each case the depth, d, of the liquid is increasing as time increases.
The graph, at the right, could represent how the depth changes with time for one of these containers. Which one? **Discuss.**
Discuss possible graphs for the other two containers.

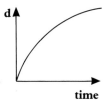

171

Worked Example   Match the graphs with the situations.

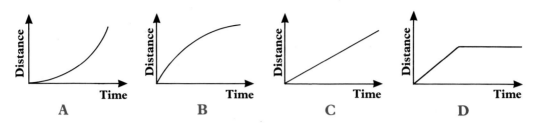

1. A car slowing down going up a hill.
2. A car cruising on the M4.
3. A car hitting a concrete wall.
4. A car rolling down a hill.

Answer   **Graph A** shows distance increasing slowly at first, then more quickly.
Situation **4.** could have this description.
Graph B shows distance increasing quickly at first, then more slowly.
Situation **1.** could have this description.
Graph C shows distance increasing at the same rate. Situation **2.** could have
this description.
Graph D shows distance increasing at the same rate at first, then the distance
is unchanged. Situation **3.** could have this description.
That is, A matches 4, B matches 1, C matches 2, D matches 4.

EXERCISE 9:6

1.

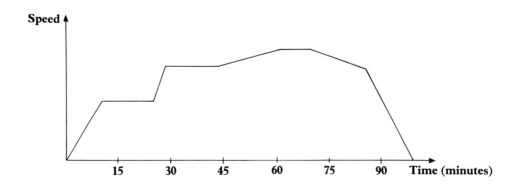

Beatrice took part in a charity run. This graph shows her speed during this run.
Describe Beatrice's run.

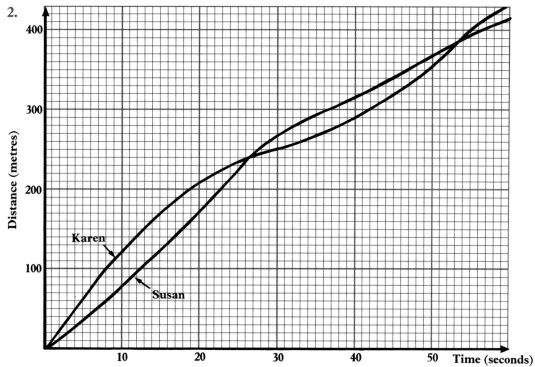

Karen and Susan were two of the runners in a 400m race.

(a) At what times were Karen and Susan level with each other?

(b) Did Karen finish before Susan or Susan before Karen?

(c) Who had the faster speed during the first 10 seconds?

(d) Who was leading after 50 seconds? About how far ahead was she?

(e) How might an announcer have spoken about Karen's and Susan's progress during this race? Write a short report on this.

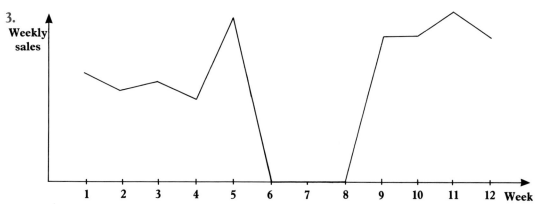

This graph shows the sales by "Best Bookshop" of a newly published book by a best-selling author.

What do you think happened in   (a)   the 6th week   (b)   the 9th week

                           (c)   the 5th week?

4.

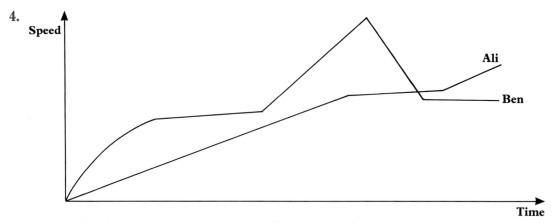

Ali and Ben both go for a morning jog. These graphs show Ali's and Ben's speeds on one morning.

Compare the times, distances and speeds. Write a short report.

5.

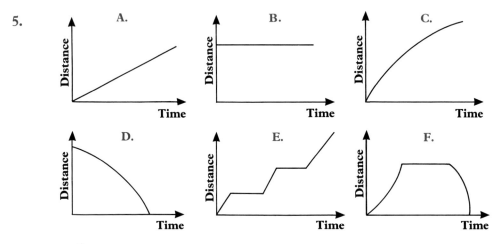

One of these graphs could represent a cricket ball thrown from one player to another. Which graph might this be?

What might the other graphs represent?

6.

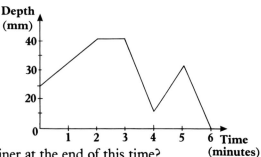

A beaker of liquid was used as part of an experiment. This graph shows the level of the liquid during this experiment.

(a) What was the depth of liquid at the beginning of this 6-minute experiment?

(b) How much liquid was in the container at the end of this time?

(c) Describe what was happening to the depth of liquid during the 6 minutes.

7.

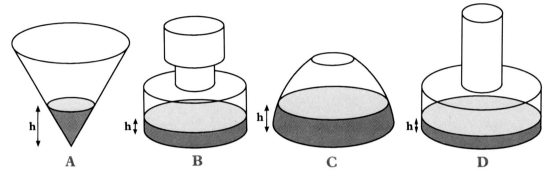

Water is poured into these containers at the rate of 150 m*l* per second. The graphs below show how the height of the water changes with time.
Match the containers with the graphs.

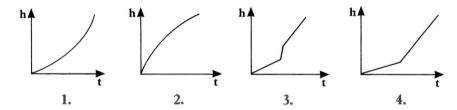

8.

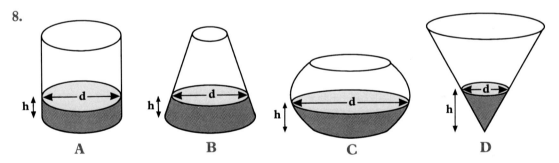

These containers are being filled with a liquid. The graphs below show how the diameter of the surface of the liquid changes as the height of the liquid increases. Which graph belongs to which container?

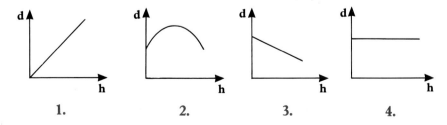

Review 1

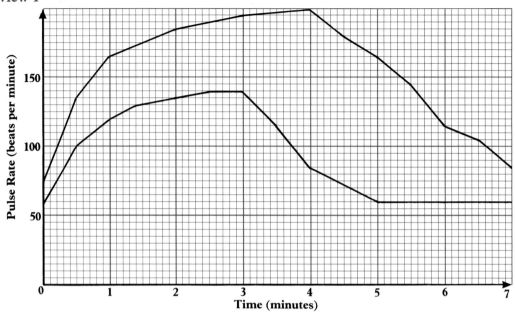

Before Felicity began an aerobics exercise programme, she did a 3-minute fitness test. The top graph shows her pulse rate during this test and for 4 minutes afterwards.

After six months on the aerobics programme, she did the same fitness test again. The bottom graph shows her pulse rate during and immediately after this test.

The gym. that Felicity was going to wrote a report based on these graphs.

What might have been written in this report?

Review 2

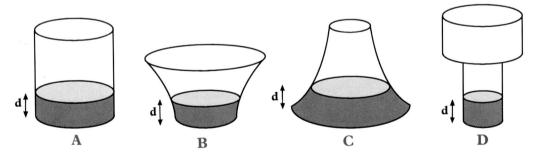

Water is poured at the rate of 100 m*l* per second into these containers. The graphs below show how the depth of water changes with time.

Match the containers with the graphs.

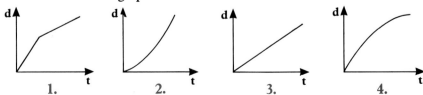

176

DISCUSSION EXERCISE 9:7

● Consider the following sequence of events: a cricket ball leaves the bowler's hand
the ball is hit by the batsman
the ball comes to rest against a fence
the ball is picked up
the ball is thrown to the bowler

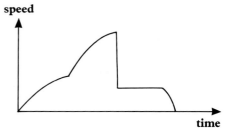

Does this graph show the change in speed of
the cricket ball in the above sequence of events?
Discuss.

● Can you think of sports which could produce graphs similar to those shown below?
Discuss.

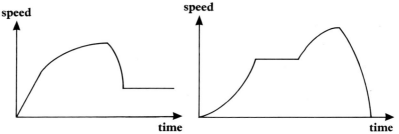

● Choose a sport. (Some suggestions follow.)
Draw a distance/time graph or a speed/time graph for a person or a ball or some other
equipment that is involved in this sport. **Discuss** your graph.
Suggestions: rowing, abseiling, football, netball, horse riding, car racing, gymnastics.

Emilie du Châtelet

Emilie du Châtelet was born in Paris in 1706 and died in Lunéville, France in 1749.

Emilie was a mathematician, physicist and philosopher. She did not do any original mathematical work of note. Her important contribution to mathematics was translating and analysing the work of others. Emilie published an explanation of the ideas of the German mathematician, Gottfried Leibniz and of the English mathematician, Sir Isaac Newton.

She is best known for her translation of Sir Isaac Newton's book "Principia Mathematica". Many of Newton's ideas on geometry were not accepted by the French. Some of the changes that Emilie made in her translation made these ideas more easily understood. Many mathematicians believed that Emilie's translation made better sense than Newton's original.

She published works on religion and philosophy as well as on science.

As a young girl, Emilie was clumsy, plump and not at all attractive. Her parents, who were wealthy, gave her an excellent education as they thought it unlikely that she would ever marry. In fact, she grew into a tall, beautiful woman. She was educated firstly by governesses and tutors and then at private girls' schools in Paris. She was a brilliant student, excelling at mathematics, literature and languages. Her education also included music and science.

At the age of nineteen, she married the Marquis du Châtelet. Five years after they were married, Emilie's husband took up a military career. After this, they seldom saw each other.

In 1730 Emilie formed a lasting friendship with Voltaire, the famous French philosopher. She had an influence on his literary works. From 1734 until her death in 1749, Voltaire and Emilie lived at her chateau in the country. At this chateau, which had a well equipped laboratory, they continued their writing and scientific work.

In 1738, the Académie des Sciences offered a prize for an essay on the nature of fire. Both Emilie and Voltaire entered this competition which was won by the Swiss mathematician Leonhard Euler. Emilie's essay was considered to be worthy of publication and was published at the expense of the Académie.

Emilie became well known and students came to study with her. This was unusual in the 18th century when women were not well regarded as educators.

Emilie died at the age of 43, a few days after giving birth to her third child.

based on an article from the book "Women Sum It Up" — Hazard Press

DIRECT PROPORTION

DISCUSSION EXERCISE 10:1

- This table shows the distance travelled by a car.

t (min)	1	2	3	4	5
s (km)	2	4	6	8	10

  For $t = 4$, the value of the ratio $\frac{s}{t}$ is $\frac{8}{4} = 2$.

  What is the value of the ratio $\frac{s}{t}$ for other values of t?

  Is the car travelling at constant speed?

  Can the relationship between s and t be written as $s = kt$ where k is some constant number? If so, what is k?

  What does the distance/time graph look like?

  Discuss.

- To make scones, $\frac{1}{2}$ cup of milk is needed for every 2 cups of flour. How much milk is needed with 5 cups of flour?

  Can the relationship between the amount of milk (m) and flour (f) be written as $m = kf$ where k is some constant number? If so, what is k?

  What does the graph of m plotted against f look like?

  Discuss.

-

l	2	4	5	8	10	15	20	30
P	8							

What values for P, the perimeter of a square, correspond to the other values of l, the length of the square?

Is the value of $\frac{P}{l}$ always the same? If the relationship between P and l is written as

$P = kl$, where k is some constant number, what is the value of k?

What does the graph of P plotted against l look like? **Discuss.**

If two quantities increase at the same rate, so that if one is doubled so is the other, the quantities are said to be **directly proportional.**

The symbol $\propto$ is read as "is proportional to".
For instance, the statement "perimeter is proportional to length" could be written as "$P \propto l$" where P stands for perimeter and l stands for length.

$a \propto b$ means $a = kb$ where k is some positive number. If we know one pair of values for a and b we can find the value of k.

Worked Example

x	2	5	10	20	50
y			15		

Given that y is proportional to x, find the missing values of y.

Answer   Since $y \propto x$, then $y = kx$.
From the table, when $x = 10$, $y = 15$. Hence $15 = k \times 10$.

$$\frac{15}{10} = k$$

$$1{\cdot}5 = k$$

The relationship between x and y is then $y = 1{\cdot}5x$.
We now use $y = 1{\cdot}5x$ to find the values of y for $x = 2, 5, 20$ and 50.

x	2	5	10	20	50
y	3	7·5	15	30	75

Worked Example   The current, I, in a particular type of wire is proportional to the voltage, V.
If $I = 8$ amps when $V = 5$ volts, find
    (a)   the current when the voltage is 8 volts
    (b)   the voltage if the current is 10 amps.

Answer   Since $I \propto V$, then $I = kV$.
When $I = 8$, $V = 5$. Hence $8 = k \times 5$ which gives $k = 1{\cdot}6$.
The relationship between I and V is $I = 1{\cdot}6V$.
   (a) Using $I = 1{\cdot}6V$, $I = 1{\cdot}6 \times 8$
$$= 12{\cdot}8 \text{ amps.}$$

   (b) Using $I = 1{\cdot}6V$, $10 = 1{\cdot}6V$

$$\frac{10}{1{\cdot}6} = V$$

$$6{\cdot}25 = V \quad \text{That is, } V = 6{\cdot}25 \text{ volts.}$$

EXERCISE 10:2

1. This table shows the cost of tickets to a concert.

Number, N	3	6	8
Cost, C, in £	13·5	27	36

   (a)   Copy and complete: If $C \propto N$, then ... = kN.
   (b)   Use one set of values for C and N to find the value of k.
   (c)   Replace k in C = kN to find the relationship between C and N.
   (d)   Use this relationship to find the cost of 19 tickets.
   (e)   A school party went to this concert. The total cost of the tickets was £153. How many were in this school party?

2. In each of the following y is proportional to x; that is y = kx.
   For each, find the value of k then copy and complete the tables.

x	3	5		20
y	18		54	

(a)

x	2		16	35
y		35	56	

(b)

x	1	3	5	
y			2	2·8

(c)

3. Map distances, m, are proportional to distances on the ground, g.
   (a)   Write this statement using the symbol $\propto$.
   (b)   2 mm on the map corresponds to 5 km on the ground. Find the relationship between m and g.
   (c)   Two villages are 12 km apart. How far apart are they on the map?
   (d)   The length of a lake on the map is 7 mm. What is the actual length of this lake?

4. The distance a cyclist travels is directly proportional to the number of revolutions of the front wheel of the bicycle.
   (a)   Write down the relationship between the distance s, the number of revolutions r and a constant k.
   (b)   The cyclist travels 24 m for 10 revolutions of the front wheel. Find the relationship between s and r.
   (c)   How far does the cyclist travel for 120 revolutions?
   (d)   How many revolutions are needed to travel 120 m?

5. The extension, e, of a spring is proportional to the mass, m, hung from the spring. A mass of 2 kg gives an extension of 5 cm.
   (a)   Find the relationship between e and m.
   (b)   Use this relationship to find the mass needed to give an extension of 40 mm.

6. The acceleration of a moving object is proportional to the force acting on the object. If a force of 150 Newtons produces an acceleration of 18 metres per sec² find
   (a) the relationship between the acceleration, a, and the force, F
   (b) the force needed to give an acceleration of 4·5 m/sec²
   (c) the acceleration produced by a force of 200 Newtons.

7.

x	1	2	3
y	3	5	7

(a)

x	3	5	7
y	1	−0·5	−2

(b)

x	1	2	3
y	0·4	0·1	−0·8

(c)

x	2	3	4
y	4	7	9

(d)

x	1	2	3
y	−2	−4	−6

(e)

In which of the above relationships is y proportional to x? Explain your answer.
Plot the graphs of each relationship to help answer this question.

8. The formula v = u + at gives the velocity (v) after time (t) of an object which has initial velocity (u) and constant acceleration (a).
   Are there any values of u for which v is proportional to t? Explain your answer.

Review 1 At constant speed, the distance (s) travelled by a car is directly proportional to the time (t).
   (a) Write this statement using the symbol ∝.
   (b) Rewrite this statement using the symbol = .
   (c) At constant speed, a car travels 160 km in 2 hours.
       Find the relationship between s and t .
   (d) Use the relationship to find the distance travelled in $2\frac{1}{4}$ hours.
   (e) How long does it take to travel 280 km?

Review 2 The cost, C, of furnishing fabric is proportional to the width, W, of the fabric.
   (a) Write down the relationship between C, W and a constant k.
   (b) The cost of one yard of 45″ wide furnishing fabric is £13·50. What is the cost of one yard of 54″ wide fabric?

a ∝ b is read as "a is proportional to b". It may also be read as "a varies as b".

a ∝ b² is read as "a is proportional to the square of b" or as "a varies as the square of b".

a ∝ √b is read as "a is proportional to the square root of b" or as "a varies as the square root of b".

Just as a ∝ b means a = kb, where k is some positive number, a ∝ b² means a = kb²; a ∝ b³ means a = kb³, a ∝ b⁴ means a = kb⁴, a ∝ √b means a = k√b etc.

k is known as the **constant of variation.**

Worked Example   The energy of a moving object is proportional to the square of its speed. If the object has 45 units of energy when it is moving at a speed of 5 metres per second, how many units of energy does it have at a speed of 8 metres per second?

Answer   Using E for energy and v for speed, $E \propto v^2$ or $E = kv^2$.
Since $v = 5$ when $E = 45$ then $45 = k \times 5^2$

$$\frac{45}{25} = k$$

$$k = 1 \cdot 8$$

The relationship between E and v is $E = 1 \cdot 8v^2$.
When $v = 8$, $E = 1 \cdot 8 \times 8^2$
$$= 115 \cdot 2 \text{ units.}$$

Worked Example   The distance a person can see, when looking at the horizon, varies as the square root of the height of the person above sea level. A person who is 16 m above sea level can see for a distance of 14 km.

   (a)   Find the relationship between d, the distance of the horizon and h, the height of the person above sea level.

   (b)   Use this relationship to find the distance a person could see, when looking at the horizon, if the person was 46 m above sea level.

   (c)   What height above sea level would Andrew be if he could see for 20 km?

Answer   (a) $d \propto \sqrt{h}$ or $d = k\sqrt{h}$
   Since $d = 14$ when $h = 16$ then $14 = k\sqrt{16}$
$$14 = 4k$$
$$k = 3 \cdot 5$$
   The relationship between d and h is $d = 3 \cdot 5\sqrt{h}$.

   (b)   We have to find d when $h = 46$. $d = 3 \cdot 5\sqrt{h}$
$$= 3 \cdot 5\sqrt{46}$$
$$= 24 \text{ km (to the nearest km)}$$

   (c)   We have to find h when $d = 20$. $20 = 3 \cdot 5\sqrt{h}$
$$\frac{20}{3 \cdot 5} = \sqrt{h}$$
$$\left(\frac{20}{3 \cdot 5}\right)^2 = h \text{ (squaring both sides)}$$
$$h = 33 \text{ m (to the nearest metre)}$$

EXERCISE 10:3

1. Using k as the constant of variation, write down the relationship between the following.
   (a) The area (A) of a square varies as the square of the length of a side (*l*).
   (b) The volume (V) of a sphere is proportional to the cube of the radius (r).
   (c) Total price (P) of chocolate fish is proportional to the number bought (n).
   (d) The surface area (A) of a cube varies as the square of the length of an edge (*l*).
   (e) The time (T) it takes for a pendulum to swing back and forth once is proportional to the square root of the length (*l*) of the pendulum.
   (f) The air-resistance (r) to a bullet varies as the square of the speed (v) of the bullet.

2. It is known that a is proportional to the square of n.
   (a) Find k, the constant of variation.
   (b) Find the relationship between n and a.
   (c) Copy and complete the table.

n	2		5	8	20
a		8			200

3.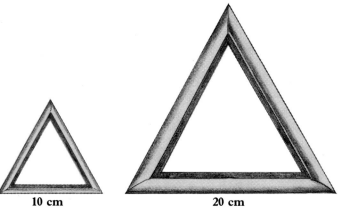

10 cm   20 cm

"Designer" photo frames are shaped like equilateral triangles. The mass of each frame is proportional to the square of the length of a side.
If the mass of the large photo frame is 500 g find the mass of the small one.

4. When a ball is thrown up in the air, the height it reaches varies as the square of the speed with which it is thrown.
   A ball, which was thrown with a speed of 29·4 m/sec reaches a height of 44·1 m.
   With what speed must a ball be thrown if it is to reach a maximum height of 10 m?

5. The mass, m, of a cube is proportional to the cube of the length, *l*, of an edge.
   (a) Write down the relationship between m, *l* and a constant k.
   (b) A cube of length 5 cm has a mass of 400 g. Use this information to find the value of k.
   (c) What is the mass of a cube which is 8 cm long?

6.

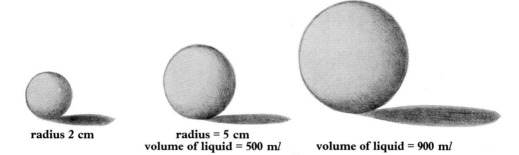

| radius 2 cm | radius = 5 cm
volume of liquid = 500 m*l* | volume of liquid = 900 m*l* |

These spheres are filled with liquid.
The volume of liquid in each varies as the cube of the radius.
Find **(a)** the volume of liquid in the small sphere
 (b) the radius of the large sphere.

7. It is known that $m \propto \sqrt{a}$.
 (a) Show that the value of k, the constant of
  variation, is 6·8.
 (b) Find the value of m if $a = 20$.
 (c) Find the value of a if $m = 15$.

a	4	9	16	25
m	13·6	20·4	27·2	34

8. If a stone is dropped from the top of a building, the time (t) it takes to reach the ground is proportional to the square root of the height (h) of the building.
A stone takes 4·5 seconds to reach the ground after being dropped from a building 100 feet high.
A stone is dropped from a building 50 feet high. How long does it take to reach the ground?

Review 1 The energy, E, stored in a spring is proportional to the square of the extension, e.
 (a) Write down the relationship between E, e, and a constant k.
 (b) If the extension is 4 cm, the energy stored is 320 joules. Use this information to find the value of k.
 (c) How much energy is stored in the spring if the extension is 2 cm?

Review 2 It is known that y is proportional to x^3.
 (a) Find the value of y if $x = 50$.
 (b) Find the value of x if $y = 6·75$.

x	10	20	30	40
y	2	16	54	128

Review 3 The current (I) in an electrical circuit varies as the square root of the power (P).
If the current is 3·5 amps when the power is 25 watts, find the current when the power is 36 watts.

DISCUSSION EXERCISE 10:4

● The formula for the circumference of a circle is $C = \pi d$.
Is C proportional to d?
What happens to C if d is doubled?
What happens to C if d is halved?
What effect does increasing the diameter have on the
circumference? What effect does decreasing the diameter have?
Discuss.

● $A = \pi r^2$ is the formula for the area of a circle.
Discuss the statement "A is proportional to r^2".
What happens to A if r is doubled?
What happens to A if r is trebled?
What happens to A if r is halved?
What effect does increasing the radius have on the area? What
effect does decreasing the area have on the radius?
Discuss.

●

Is the perimeter of a square proportional to the length of a side?
Is the area of a square proportional to the length of a side?
Is the area of a square proportional to the perimeter?
Discuss. Use formulae to justify the arguments you use in your
discussion.

What happens to the perimeter if the length of a side is doubled?
What happens to the area if the length of a side is doubled?
What happens to the area if the perimeter is doubled?
Discuss.

● **Discuss** what happens to the volume of a cube if the length
of an edge is doubled.
What if the length of an edge is trebled?
What if the length of an edge is halved?

Each edge on a cube is five times the length of an edge of
the cube shown. What can you say about the volumes of
these two cubes? **Discuss.**

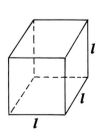

INVERSE PROPORTION

DISCUSSION EXERCISE 10:5

- The following table gives the time taken to complete a 200 km journey for various average speeds.

Average speed, v (km/hr)	20	40	50	80	100
Time, t (hours)	10	5	4	2·5	2

For t = 10, the product vt = 200.
What is the product vt for other values of t?

Can the relationship between t and v be written as $t = \frac{k}{v}$ where k is some constant number? If so, what is the value of k?
What does the graph of t plotted against v look like?
Discuss.

- Simone plans to spend £60 on theatre tickets next year. All the shows she plans to see cost from £5 for the cheapest seats to £20 for the best seats. The table shows the number of shows Simone can see if she always buys the same priced tickets.

Price, P (in £)	20	15	12	10	5
Number, n	3	4	5	6	12

Discuss the relationship between n and P. As part of your discussion, draw a graph.

-

Hourly rate, r (in £)	2	4	5	8	10
Hours, h	50	25	20	12·5	10

This table shows the time taken to earn £100 at different rates of pay.
Discuss the relationship between h and r.

- What was similar about the three examples given above? **Discuss.** As part of your discussion, consider the tables, the graphs and the relationships between the two variables.

If two quantities increase at opposite rates, so that if one is doubled the other is halved, the quantities are said to be **indirectly proportional.** Indirect proportion is usually called inverse proportion. Quantities that are indirectly proportional are usually said to be **inversely proportional.**

If a is inversely proportional to b, then $a \propto \frac{1}{b}$ or $a = \frac{k}{b}$ where k is some positive number.

Just as for direct proportion, where we could have a quantity directly proportional to the square of another so we can have a quantity inversely proportional to the square of another. For instance, a may be inversely proportional to the square of b. The relationship between a and b in this case is $a = \frac{k}{b^2}$, where k is some positive number. This is sometimes called the **inverse square law.**

DISCUSSION EXERCISE 10:6

● For each statement, **discuss** whether the quantities are likely to be directly proportional or inversely proportional or not proportional.

The weight of a sheet of paper and its area.
The weight of a sheet of paper and its length.
The number of chocolates in a box and the size of the box.
The cost of a box of chocolates and the weight of chocolates in the box.
The rate of pay and the earnings for a 40 hour week.
The age of a kitten and its weight.
The cost of a phone call and the time taken for this call.
The area of an isosceles triangle and the length of a side.
The size of an exterior angle and the number of sides of regular polygons.
The base length and height of right-angled triangles which have the same area.

● Think of quantities, others than those mentioned already in this chapter, which could be directly proportional or inversely proportional. Write statements, similar to those above but include the words "is proportional to" or "is inversely proportional to". **Discuss** your statements.

Worked Example   Boyle's law states that at a constant temperature, the volume of a gas is inversely proportional to its pressure.
  (a) Find the relationship between volume V, pressure P and a constant k.
  (b) When the pressure is 400 N/m², the volume is 2 m³. Use this information to find the value of k.
  (c) Find the volume when the pressure is 200 N/m².
  (d) Find the pressure when the volume of the gas is 2·5 m³.

Answer (a) Since $V \propto \frac{1}{P}$ then $V = \frac{k}{P}$.

(b) Since $V = 2$ when $P = 400$ then $2 = \frac{k}{400}$

$$800 = k$$

(c) The relationship between V and P is $V = \frac{800}{P}$.

When $P = 200$, $V = \frac{800}{200}$

$$= 4 \text{ m}^3$$

(d) When $V = 2\cdot5$, $2\cdot5 = \frac{800}{P}$

$$2\cdot5P = 800 \text{ (multiplying both sides by P)}$$

$$P = \frac{800}{2\cdot5}$$

$$= 320 \text{ N/m}^2$$

Worked Example The intensity of a light on an object is inversely proportional to the square of the distance of the object from the light.
If the intensity of the light is 8 units at a distance of 5 metres, find the intensity at a distance of 3 metres.

Answer Using I for intensity and d for distance, $I \propto \frac{1}{d^2}$ or $I = \frac{k}{d^2}$.

Since $I = 8$ when $d = 5$, $8 = \frac{k}{5^2}$

$$5^2 \times 8 = k$$
$$200 = k$$

Then $I = \frac{200}{d^2}$.

When $d = 3$, $I = \frac{200}{3^2}$

$$= 22 \text{ units (to the nearest unit)}$$

EXERCISE 10:7

1. Write down the relationship between the two variables using k as the constant of variation.
   (a) m is inversely proportional to n.
   (b) x varies inversely as the square of y.
   (c) b is inversely proportional to the square of d.
   (d) *l* varies inversely as p.
   (e) t varies inversely as the square root of u.
   (f) a is inversely proportional to the cube of h.

2. For parallelograms of the same area, height varies inversely as the length of the base. If the height is 5 cm when the base is 8 cm find
   (a) the relationship between height h, length of the base l and a constant k expressed as h = ...
   (b) the value of the constant k
   (c) the height when the length of the base is 2·5 cm.

3. The wavelength of sound waves is inversely proportional to the frequency. If the frequency of the note G is 387 cycles per second and the wavelength is 0·853 metres find the wavelength of the note C which has frequency of 256 cycles per second.

4. It is known that y is inversely proportional to x^2.

x	0·1	0·2	0·4	0·5	1
y	200	50	12·5	8	2

   (a) Write down the relationship between y, x and a constant k.
   (b) Find the value of k.
   (c) Find the value of y when x = 2.

5. The resistance R, in a fixed length of wire varies inversely as the square of the diameter d. If the diameter is 5 mm the resistance is 0·08 ohms.
   Find the resistance if the diameter is 4 mm.

6. The air pressure available from a bicycle pump is inversely proportional to the square of the diameter of the pump.
   If a pressure of 8 units is available from a pump of diameter 25 mm find
   (a) the pressure available from a pump of diameter 14 mm
   (b) the diameter of the pump which can deliver 15 units of pressure.

7. The frequency of radio waves varies inversely as the wavelength. Radio M broadcasts on a wavelength of 212 metres and frequency of $1·42 \times 10^6$ cycles per second.
   (a) Radio P broadcasts on 384 m. What frequency is this?
   (b) For Radio Q, the frequency is $6·2 \times 10^5$ cycles per second. What wavelength is this?

8. At a constant temperature, the volume V of a gas is inversely proportional to its pressure P. The gas in a cylindrical container of radius 2m is at a pressure of 500 N/m². The gas is transferred into another cylindrical container. This new container is the same height but twice the radius of the first one. What is the pressure of the gas in the new container?

Review 1 It is known that m is inversely proportional to n.
Copy and complete the table.

m		2	5		20
n	100		10	5	

Review 2 The force of attraction between two bodies varies inversely as the square of their distance apart.
If the force of attraction is 2 units when the bodies are 100 km apart, find the force of attraction when they are 50 km apart.

INVESTIGATION 10:8

PROPORTION and GRAPHS

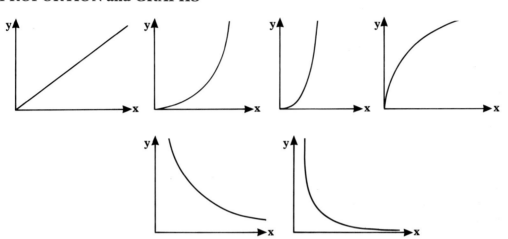

Investigate the graphs associated with proportion. You could include $y \propto x$, $y \propto x^2$, $y \propto x^3$, $y \propto x^4$, $y \propto \sqrt{x}$, $y \propto \sqrt[3]{x}$, $y \propto \frac{1}{x}$, $y \propto \frac{1}{x^2}$, $y \propto \frac{1}{x^3}$, $y \propto \frac{1}{\sqrt{x}}$.

You could include the following in your investigation.
Considering $y \propto x^2$; if $k = 3$ then $y = 3x^2$.

x	1	2	3	4	5
y	3	12	27	48	75

Now plot the graph on these axes.

x^2	1	4	9	16	25
y	3	12	27	48	75

Now plot the graph on these axes.

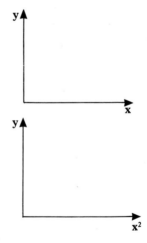

Continue by plotting similar graphs for other values of k such as $k = 1, k = 2, k = 4$ etc.

Write a report on your investigation. Use tables and graphs in your report.

PRACTICAL EXERCISE 10:9

Make a pendulum similar to that shown. You will need the following equipment.

Equipment   A piece of string about 50 cm long.
Some nuts or bolts of different weights.
A stopwatch or a watch from which you
can read seconds.

As well as the above equipment you will need some way of
suspending your pendulum a little way out from a wall.

Use your pendulum to investigate the relationship between the time (T) for a complete
swing and the length of the string.
You could also investigate the relationship between T and the weight attached to the end
of the string.
Note Start your pendulum swinging by pulling the weight to the side, keeping the string
taut. T is the time taken for the weight to move through one swing from this starting
position back to the same position.

Write a report on your investigation. Include graphs in your report. Mention proportion in
your report.

INVESTIGATION 10:10

PROPORTION and DIFFERENCE TABLES

x	1	2	3	4	5
y	4	16	36	64	100

Which of the following is true : $y \propto x$, $y \propto x^2$, $y \propto x^3$?

Consider the following "difference table" for the y-values.

4		16		36		64		100	
	12		20		28		36		⟵ —— 1st differences
		8		8		8			⟵ —— 2nd differences

x	1	2	3	4	5
y	2	16	54	128	250

Which of the following is true : $y \propto x$, $y \propto x^2$, $y \propto x^3$?
What do you think will happen if a difference table
is formed?

continued . . .

. . . from previous page

Investigate the relationship between proportion and difference tables. For your difference tables, you could use the following program.

```
10    MODE 3
20    INPUT "HOW MANY Y-VALUES WILL YOU ENTER? (MINIMUM 4)" N
30    DIM Y(N), D1(N - 1), D2(N - 2), D3(N - 3)
40    PRINT "ENTER THE Y-VALUES, PRESSING < RETURN > AFTER EACH ONE"
50    FOR J = 1 TO N
60    INPUT Y(J)
70    NEXT J
80    PRINT "Y-VALUES";
90    FOR J = 1 TO N
100   PRINT SPC(5); Y(J);
110   NEXT J
120   PRINT : PRINT "1ST DIFF"; SPC(5);
130   FOR J = 1 TO N-1
140   D1(J) = Y(J + 1) - Y(J)
150   PRINT SPC(5); D1(J);
160   NEXT J
170   PRINT : PRINT "2ND DIFF"; SPC(10);
180   FOR J = 1 TO N - 2
190   D2(J) = D1(J + 1) - D1(J)
200   PRINT SPC(5); D2(J);
210   NEXT J
220   PRINT : PRINT "3RD DIFF"; SPC(14);
230   FOR J = 1 TO N - 3
240   D3(J) = D2(J + 1) - D2(J)
250   PRINT SPC(5) ; D3(J);
260   NEXT J
270   PRINT
400   END
```

Note   If you want to include another row of differences you must change line 30 and insert extra lines after line 270.

If you wish, you could use a spreadsheed instead of the program.

	A	B	C	
1	= 2	= A2 – A1	= B2 – B1	
2	= 16	= A3 – A2	= B3 – B2	
3	= 54	= A4 – A3	= B4	
4	= 128	= A		
5	=			

1. Multiply out   **(a)** $3(a - b)$ **(b)** $a(2a - 5)$ **(c)** $mn(m - n)$

2. The gradient of a road is shown.
   - **(a)** Write this gradient as a fraction.
   - **(b)** How high does the road rise for every 200 metres horizontally?

3. Solve these inequalities.   **(a)** $5a - 4 < 9$ **(b)** $2 - x \geq 1$

4. **(a)** Make P the subject of the formula $k = PVT$.
   (b) $A = 2\pi rh + \pi r^2$. Make h the subject of this formula.
   (c) $S = \frac{1}{2}(a + b + c)$. Express b in terms of S, a and c.

5. At Christmas time, a shop wraps small gifts and places them in boxes. These boxes are made from cardboard and are shaped as shown.
   - **(a)** Show that the area of cardboard needed for one of these boxes is given by $A = 9x^2$.
   - **(b)** Draw the graph of $A = 9x^2$ for values of x between 1 and 10.
   - **(c)** One of these boxes is made from 780 cm² of cardboard. Use your graph to find the approximate length of this box.

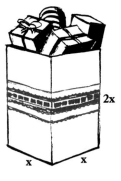

6. The time for a journey varies inversely as the speed. If a journey takes 4 hours at a speed of 75 km/h find
   - **(a)** the time for this journey if the speed is 100 km/h
   - **(b)** the speed if the time for this journey is 5 hours.

7. **(i)** Rearrange these line equations into the form $y = mx + c$.
        (a) $5x + y = 7$ **(b)** $x + 2y - 6 = 0$ **(c)** $3x - y = 1$
   (ii) Write down the gradient of each of the lines.
   (iii) Where does each line cross the y-axis?

8. The volume of a cone is given by $V = \frac{1}{3}\pi r^2 h$, where r is the radius of the base and h is the height.
   - **(a)** Find the volume of the sketched cone.
   - **(b)** Find the radius of the cone for which $V = 150$ cm³ and $h = 20$ cm.

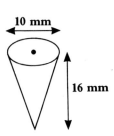

9. One way of estimating the adult height, in metres, to which a baby is expected to grow is by using one of the formulae:

$$g = \frac{m + f - 0.13}{2} \qquad\qquad b = \frac{m + f + 0.13}{2}$$

In these formulae, g is the adult height of a baby girl, b is the adult height of a baby boy, m is the mother's height and h is the father's height.

Rearrange the formula $g = \dfrac{m + f - 0.13}{2}$ to make f the subject.

10. The illumination from a source of light is inversely proportional to the square of the distance from the light.
   At a distance of 6m, the illumination from a particular source of light is 5 units.
   What is the illumination at a distance of 3m?

11. For what whole number values of n is the following true?
$$-6 \leq 4n < 12$$

12.

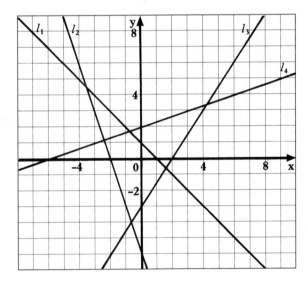

   (a) Find the gradient of each of these lines.
   (b) Use the line equation $y = mx + c$ to write down the equations of these lines.

13. Expand and simplify
   (a) $2(3 - 2x) + 5x$
   (b) $3a - 2 + a(2a - 5)$
   (c) $5n - (2n - 1)$
   (d) $3(2n - 3) - 2(n + 3)$.

14. What can you say about p if
   (a) $p^2 \leq 25$
   (b) $3p^2 + 5 > 17$?

15. Factorise
   (a) $6 - 8n$
   (b) $2a + 3a^2$
   (c) $16x - 10x^2$
   (d) $\pi r^2 h + 2\pi r$
   (e) $x^2 y - xy^2$

16.

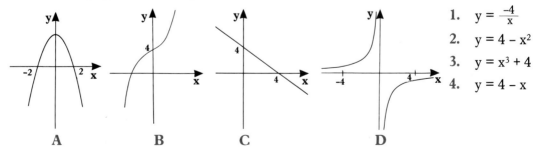

Which of the above could be the graph of $y = x^2 - 2$? Explain your choice.

17. Draw a set of axes. Number both the x and y-axes from –5 to 5.
On this set of axes draw the following lines.
  (a) $y = 2x$ (b) $y = 2$ (c) $x + 4 = 0$ (d) $x + 2y = 6$ (e) $3x - y = 4$

18. (a) $C = \frac{5}{9}(F - 32)$ is a formula to convert temperatures given in degrees Celsius to degrees Fahrenheit. Rearrange this formula to make F the subject.

   (b) The volume of a cylinder is given by $V = \pi r^2 h$.
   Express r in terms of V and h.

   (c) The time, T, for a pendulum to make one complete swing to and fro is given by

   $T = 2\pi\sqrt{\frac{l}{g}}$ where l is the length of the pendulum and g is the acceleration due to gravity. Make l the subject of this formula.

19. (i) Rashid used this diagram to help to expand $(3n + 2)(n + 5)$.
How should Rashid fill in the second row?

	n	5
3n	$3n^2$	15n
2		

   (ii) Use Rashid's method or some other method to expand and simplify the following.

   (a) $(3n + 2)(n + 5)$ (b) $(2n - 5)(3n - 2)$ (c) $(4x + y)(x - 2y)$
   (d) $(a + bx)(c + dx)$

20. Match the graphs with the equations.

A	B	C	D

1. $y = \frac{-4}{x}$
2. $y = 4 - x^2$
3. $y = x^3 + 4$
4. $y = 4 - x$

21. Draw graphs to show the region in which each of these inequalities is true. (Draw a separate graph for each.)

    (a) $y \geq 0$ (b) $x < 2$ (c) $y \geq 2x - 1$ (d) $x - 2y > 2$

22. In a kite-flying competition, all kites must have an area of 4m². If **a** and **b** are the lengths of the diagonals of the kites, the relationship between **a** and **b** is $a = \frac{8}{b}$.

    (a) Copy and complete this table.

b	1	2	3	4	5	6	7	8
a			2·7				1·1	

    (b) Draw the graph of **a** against **b**.
    (c) Use your graph to estimate the value of a when b = 4·5.

23.

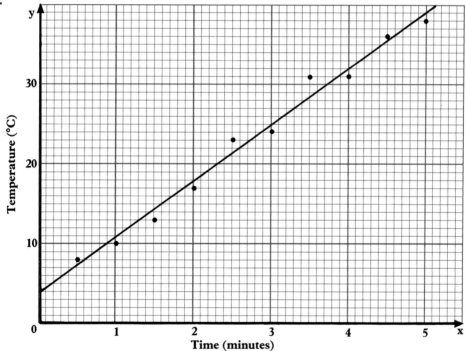

Yasmin heated a liquid for 5 minutes. Every 30 seconds she took the temperature.
Yasmin drew this scatter diagram to illustrate her results.
Find the equation of the line of best fit that Yasmin drew.

24. Draw a diagram to show where both of the following inequalities are true.

$$y < x \ , \ 2x + 3y \geq 6$$

25.

Shortest stopping distances — in metres and feet				
mph	Thinking distance	Braking distance	Overall stopping distance	On a dry road, a good car with good brakes and tyres and an alert driver will stop in the distances shown. Remember these are shortest stopping distances. Stopping distances increase greatly with wet and slippery roads, poor brakes and tyres, and tired drivers.
20	6 20	6 20	12 40	
30	9 30	14 45	23 75	
40	12 40	24 80	36 120	
50	15 50	38 125	53 175	
60	18 60	55 180	73 240	
70	21 70	75 245	96 315	

The table above is from the Highway Code.
(a) Which figures are in metres and which are in feet?
(b) Show that thinking distance, in metres, is proportional to speed.
(c) What thinking distance in metres, is needed if the speed is 100mph?
(d) Show that the braking distance, in feet, is proportional to the square of the speed.
(e) At what speed is the braking distance 100 feet?

26. Peter was prepared to spend up to £20 buying CDs and Tapes in this sale.
$2x + 5y \le 20$ is an inequality which could be used to describe the amount of money Peter spent.
(a) What does x stand for? What does y stand for?
(b) Can x have a negative value? Can y have a negative value?
(c) Draw a graph to show the region which contains all the possible numbers of CDs and Tapes that Peter could have bought.

27. The equations of the three sides of a triangle are shown. (The diagram is not drawn to scale.)
The line PQ, which has equation $y = 2x - 4$, is parallel to one of the sides of this triangle. Which one?

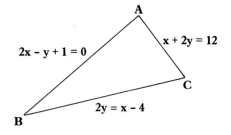

28. (i) $f(x) = 3 + 2x^2$. Find (a) $f(1)$ (b) $f(3)$ (c) $f(-3)$ (d) $f(\frac{1}{2})$.

(ii) $g(a) = \dfrac{2a + 3}{a + 1}$. (a) For what value of a is $g(a) = -3$?
(b) For what value of a does $g(a)$ have no answer?

29.

This graph shows the speed of a chainsaw blade during the felling of a tree.
Describe what is happening.

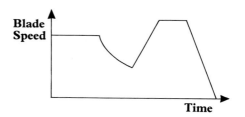

30. (a) The surface area of a sphere varies as the square of the diameter. A sphere of diameter 10 cm has surface area of 314 cm². Find the diameter of a sphere which has surface area of 212 cm².

(b) The volume of a sphere varies as the cube of the diameter. A sphere of diameter 10 cm has a volume of 523·6 cm³. Find the volume of a sphere with diameter of 5 cm.

31.

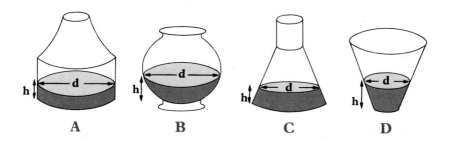

A   B   C   D

These containers are being filled with a liquid at the rate of 200 m*l* per second.

(a) These graphs show how the height of the liquid is increasing with time. Match the containers with the graphs.

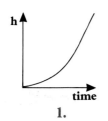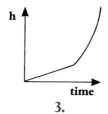

1.   2.   3.   4.

(b) These graphs show how the diameter of the surface of the liquid changes as the height increases. Match the containers with the graphs.

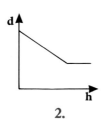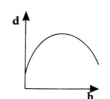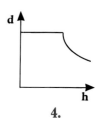

1.   2.   3.   4.

32.

The formula for the area of a circle is $A = \pi r^2$.
The relationship between the radius and the diameter is $d = 2r$.
Express A in terms of d and π. Give your answer in its simplest form.

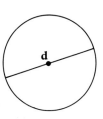

33. The formula $\dfrac{1}{u} + \dfrac{1}{v} = \dfrac{1}{f}$ is used in a Physics experiment on light.

    (a) Find the value of f if $u = 6{\cdot}2$ and $v = 10$.

    (b) Find the value of u if $f = 4{\cdot}6$ and $v = 8{\cdot}2$.

34.

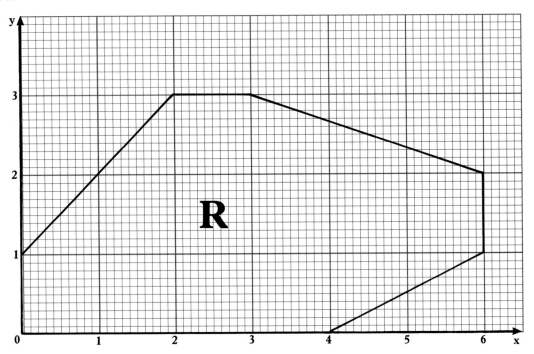

The region R is defined by seven inequalities, three of which are $y \geq 0$, $x - 2y \leq 4$, $x \leq 6$. Find the other four inequalities.

SHAPE and SPACE

Shape and Space from Previous Levels

REVISION

Congruence. Symmetry

Congruent shapes are shapes of the same size and the same shape. Corresponding lengths are equal ; corresponding angles are equal.

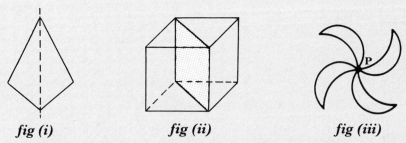

fig (i)   *fig (ii)*   *fig (iii)*

A **line of symmetry (axis of symmetry)** divides a 2–D shape into two congruent shapes – see *fig (i)*.

A **plane of symmetry** divides a 3–D shape into two congruent shapes – see *fig (ii)*. A shape has **reflective symmetry** if it has a line or a plane of symmetry – both *fig (i)* and *fig (ii)* have reflective symmetry.

A shape has **rotational symmetry** if it coincides with itself more than once when it is rotated a complete turn about some point. The point about which it is rotated is called the **centre of rotational symmetry**. The number of times the shape coincides with itself during one complete turn is called the **order of rotational symmetry**. For instance, *fig (iii)* has rotational symmetry of order 4. P is the centre of rotational symmetry for *fig (iii)*.

Naming Polygons

A 3-sided polygon is a **triangle**.   A 4-sided polygon is a **quadrilateral**.
A 5-sided polygon is a **pentagon**.   A 6-sided polygon is a **hexagon**.
A 7-sided polygon is a **heptagon**.   An 8-sided polygon is an **octagon**.
A 9-sided polygon is a **nonagon**.   A 10-sided polygon is a **decagon**.
A **regular polygon** has all its sides equal and all its angles equal.

Special Quadrilaterals

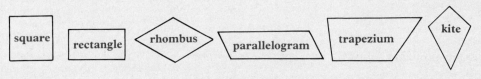

continued . . .

. . . *from previous page*

Some of the properties of these special quadrilaterals are shown in the following table.

	Square	Rhombus	Rectangle	Parallelogram	Kite	Trapezium
one pair of opposite sides parallel	√	√	√	√		√
two pairs of opposite sides parallel	√	√	√	√		
all sides equal	√	√				
opposite sides equal	√	√	√	√		
all angles equal	√		√			
opposite angles equal	√	√	√	√		
diagonals equal	√		√			
diagonals bisect each other	√	√	√	√		
diagonals perpendicular	√	√			√	
diagonals bisect the angles	√	√				

Angles made with Intersecting Lines

vertically opposite angles
$a = b$

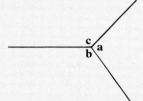

angles at a point
$a + b + c = 360°$

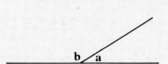

adjacent angles on a line
$a + b = 180°$

Angles made with Parallel Lines

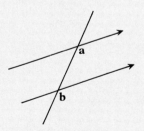

corresponding angles
$a = b$

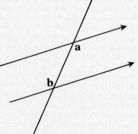

alternate angles
$a = b$

interior angles
$a + b = 180°$

continued . . .

. . . from previous page

Triangles

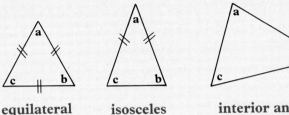
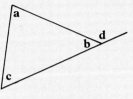

equilateral	isosceles	interior angles	exterior angle
$a = b = c$	$b = c$	$a + b + c = 180°$	$d = a + c$

In a right-angled triangle, the longest side (the side opposite the right-angle) is called the **hypotenuse.**

Pythagoras' Theorem: $r^2 = x^2 + y^2$ (In a right-angled triangle, the square on the hypotenuse equals the sum of the squares on the other two sides.)

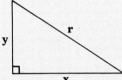

Angles of a Polygon

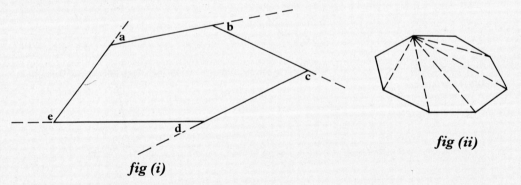

fig (i)

fig (ii)

The sum of the **exterior angles** of any polygon is equal to 360°. Hence in *fig (i)* $a + b + c + d + e = 360°$.

The sum of the **interior angles** of any polygon may be found as follows.

> *Step 1* From one vertex, draw all the diagonals to divide the polygon into triangles – see *fig (ii)*.
>
> *Step 2* Find the sum of the angles in all of these triangles.

For instance, *fig (ii)* can be divided into 6 triangles. Hence the sum of the interior angles of this 8-sided polygon is $6 × 180° = 1080°$.

continued . . .

. . . *from previous page*

2-D representation of 3-D shapes

Look down to find the plan.

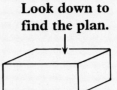

What we see when we look directly down onto a 3–D shape is called the **plan**.

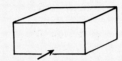

What we see when we look from the front at a 3–D shape is called the **front elevation**.

Look from the front to find the front elevation.

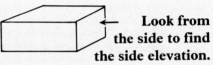

What we see when we look from the side at a 3–D shape is called the **side elevation**.

Look from the side to find the side elevation.

3-D Coordinates

In 2-D we have x and y axes. The x-axis is horizontal and the y-axis is vertical.
In 3-D we have x, y and z axes. These axes are at right-angles to each other. There are many ways of drawing these axes, four of which are shown below.

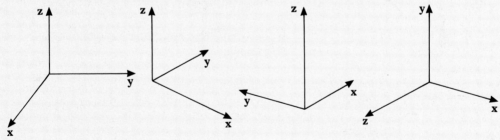

In 3-D, the position of a point is described by giving three coordinates; the x-coordinate, the y-coordinate and the z-coordinate.

For instance, the point P shown on this diagram is P(2, 5, 4).

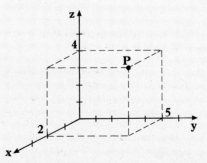

continued . . .

. . . from previous page

Area, Perimeter, Volume

The formulae for the **area** of some common shapes are given below.

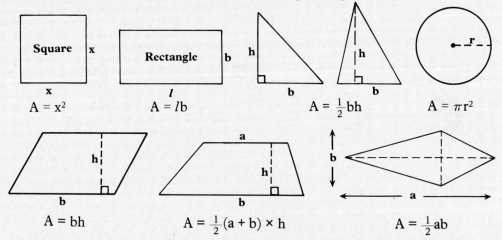

$$A = x^2 \qquad A = lb \qquad A = \tfrac{1}{2}bh \qquad A = \pi r^2$$

$$A = bh \qquad A = \tfrac{1}{2}(a + b) \times h \qquad A = \tfrac{1}{2}ab$$

Common metric units for land area are the **hectare** (ha) and **square kilometre** (km^2). The hectare is derived from the unit of land measure, the **are**.

Some small land areas, such as building plots, are measured in m^2.

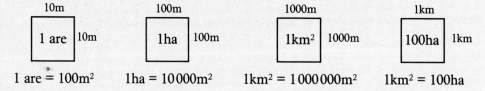

$$1 \text{ are} = 100m^2 \qquad 1ha = 10\,000m^2 \qquad 1km^2 = 1\,000\,000m^2 \qquad 1km^2 = 100ha$$

The acre is an imperial unit used for land areas. The approximate relationship between acres and hectares is **1ha = 2·5 acres.**

The **perimeter** is the distance right around the outside. The perimeter of a circle is called the **circumference**. The formula for the circumference of a circle is $C = 2\pi r$ or $C = \pi d$; r is the radius and d is the diameter of the circle, the value of π to 3 d.p. is 3·142.

The formulae for the **volume** of some common shapes are given below.

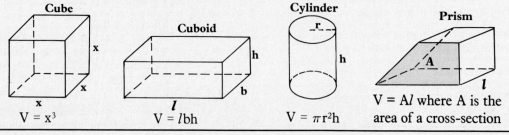

$$V = x^3 \qquad V = lbh \qquad V = \pi r^2 h$$

V = A*l* where A is the area of a cross-section

continued . . .

. . . *from previous page*

Movements — Reflection, Translation, Rotation. Tessellations

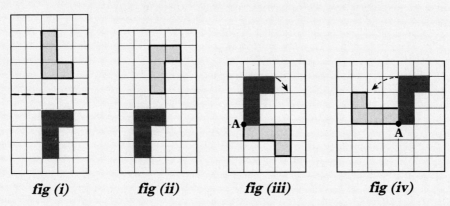

| *fig (i)* | *fig (ii)* | *fig (iii)* | *fig (iv)* |

fig (i) illustrates a **reflection** (or **flip movement**). The red shape has been reflected in the dotted line to the shaded shape. The dotted line is called the **mirror line**. A point and its image are the same distance from the mirror line.

fig (ii) illustrates a **translation** (or **straight movement**). The red shape has been translated 1 square to the right and 4 squares up to the shaded shape.

fig (iii) and *fig (iv)* illustrate **rotation** (or **turning movement**). In *fig (iii)* the red shape has been rotated clockwise about A, through $\frac{1}{4}$ turn or 1 right angle.

In *fig (iv)* the red shape has been rotated anticlockwise about A, through $\frac{1}{4}$ turn.

A shape is **tessellated** if, when it is translated and/or reflected and/or rotated, it completely fills a space leaving no gaps.

Enlargement

The **scale factor** of an **enlargement** can be found by taking the ratio of the length of a side on the image shape to the length of the corresponding side on the original shape.

For instance, in the diagram, ABC has been enlarged to A′B′C′. Scale factor = $\frac{\text{length of A′B′}}{\text{length of AB}}$

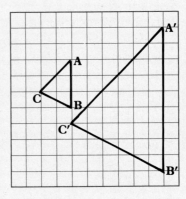

$$= \frac{9}{3}$$

$$= 3$$

continued . . .

207

. . . from previous page

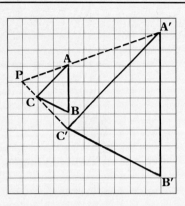

This diagram shows how the **centre of enlargement** can be found. The steps needed to find the centre of enlargement in this case are:

Step 1 Join A′ and A.

Step 2 Join C′ and C.

Step 3 Extend the lines A′A and C′C. The point P, where these lines meet, is the centre of enlargement.

This diagram shows how to draw an enlargement of the triangle PQR, scale factor 2, centre of enlargement C. Beginning with just the point C and the triangle PQR we proceed as follows:

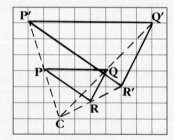

Step 1 Join C to P, C to Q and C to R.

Step 2 Extend the line CP to P′ so that the length of CP′ = twice the length of CP.

Step 3 Extend the line CQ to Q′ so that the length of CQ′ = twice the length of CQ.

Step 4 Extend the line CR to R′ so that the length of CR′ = twice the length of CR.

Step 5 Join P′, Q′ and R′ to form the image triangle P′Q′R′.

If the scale factor is greater than 1, the image is larger than the original.

If the scale factor is between 0 and 1, the image is smaller than the original — see ***fig (i)*** below where ABC has been enlarged, centre P, scale factor $\frac{1}{2}$.

If the scale factor is negative, the image and original are on opposite sides of the centre of enlargement — see ***fig (ii)*** below where ABC has been enlarged, centre P, scale factor $-\frac{1}{2}$.

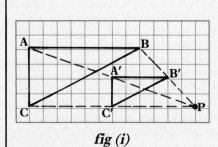

fig (i)

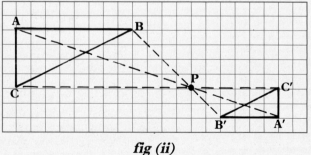

fig (ii)

continued . . .

. . . from previous page

Compass Points

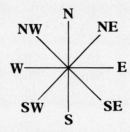

The angle between any two adjacent compass points is 45°.

Bearings from North

Bearings from North are always given as 3 digits.
To find the bearing of A from B proceed as follows.

Step 1 Join AB.
Step 2 Draw a North line from B.
Step 3 Measure the angle (in a *clockwise* direction) between this North line and the line AB.

In this diagram, the bearing of A from B is 342°.

Networks

The **nodes** (vertices) are marked with dots.
The **arcs** are the lines or curves that join the nodes.

Odd nodes have an odd number of arcs coming from them.
Even nodes have an even number of arcs coming from them.

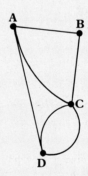

If a path can be found that goes over each arc once and only once, the network is said to be **traceable**. A network must have either 0 or 2 odd nodes to be traceable. If this path is to begin and finish at the same point, the network must have 0 odd nodes.

In the network shown there are four nodes. Nodes A and D are odd nodes ; nodes B and C are even nodes. Since this network has 2 odd nodes it is traceable. However, a path cannot be found which goes over every arc once and only once *and* begins and ends at the same point.

continued . . .

. . . *from previous page*

Compass Constructions

The following diagrams show **the construction of the bisector of the line BC.**

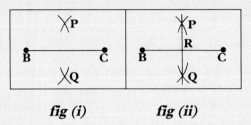

fig (i)   **fig (ii)**

Step 1   Open out the compass so the length on the compass is a little more than half the length of the line BC. Keep this length on the compass throughout.

Step 2   With compass point firstly on B and then on C, draw arcs to meet at P and Q – see **fig (i)**.

Step 3   Draw the line through P and Q – see **fig (ii)**. This line is the required bisector of the line BC.

Note   The point R, where PQ meets BC, is the **mid-point** of the line BC.

The following diagrams show **the construction of the line through A that is perpendicular to the line BC.**

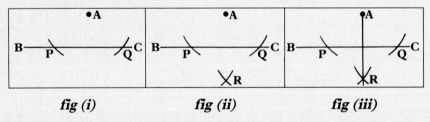

fig (i)   **fig (ii)**   **fig (iii)**

Step 1   Open out the compass to any reasonable length. This length should be such that when the compass point is placed at A two arcs can be drawn that will cross BC. Keep this length on the compass throughout.

Step 2   With compass point on A, draw two arcs to meet BC at P and Q – see **fig (i)**.

Step 3   With compass point firstly on P, then on Q, draw two arcs to meet at R – see **fig (ii)**.

Step 4   Join AR – see **fig (iii)**. AR is the required line.

continued . . .

. . . *from previous page*

The following diagrams show **the construction of the line through A that is parallel to the line BC.**

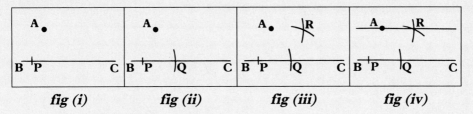

| fig (i) | fig (ii) | fig (iii) | fig (iv) |

Step 1   Mark any point P on BC – see **fig (i)**.

Step 2   Open out the compass to the length AP. Keep this length on the compass throughout.

Step 3   With compass point on P, draw an arc to meet BC at Q – see **fig (ii)**.

Step 4   With compass point firstly on Q and then on A, draw two arcs to meet at R – see **fig (iii)**.

Step 5   Draw the line through A and R – see **fig (iv)**. This is the required line.

The following diagrams show **the construction of the bisector of the angle P.**

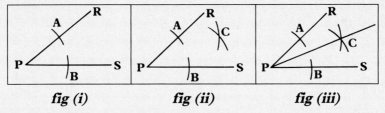

| fig (i) | fig (ii) | fig (iii) |

Step 1   Open out the compass to any reasonable length. This length should be less than the length of either arm (PR or PS) of the angle P. Keep this length on the compass throughout.

Step 2   With compass point on P, draw arcs to meet PR and PS at A and B – see **fig (i)**.

Step 3   With compass point firstly on A and then on B, draw two arcs to meet at C – see **fig (ii)**.

Step 4   Draw the line from P through C – see **fig (iii)**. This line is the required bisector of the angle P.

continued . . .

. . . from previous page

Locus

The **locus** of an object is the set of all possible positions that this object can occupy. The path of an object, moving according to some rule, is the locus of the object. Some well known loci are shown below.

1. The locus of a point which is a constant distance from a fixed point is a circle.

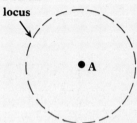

2. The locus of a point which is a constant distance from a fixed line is a pair of parallel lines.

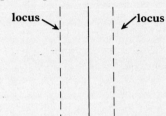

3. The locus of a point which is equidistant from two fixed points is the mediator (perpendicular bisector) of the line joining the fixed points.

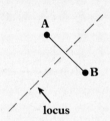

4. The locus of a point which is equidistant from two intersecting lines is the pair of lines which bisect the angles between the fixed lines.

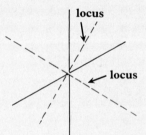

REVISION EXERCISE

In this exercise, use the calculator value for π or $\pi = 3\cdot14$.

1.

In this diagram, BCJ is an equilateral triangle. What name is given to the following shapes?

(a) ABDEFH   (b) ABJI   (c) DEF
(d) KLNM   (e) DONL   (f) HKMPG

2. (a) Name this 3-D shape.

(b) Name all the vertices on the vertical faces.

(c) Which edges are perpendicular to the edge BF?

(d) Name the parallel faces.

(e) How many lines of symmetry does the face BCGF have?

(f) Does this 3-D shape have any horizontal planes of symmetry?

(g) Name pairs of congruent faces.

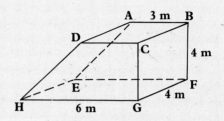

3. Copy this diagram.

(a) A is reflected in the x-axis to B. Draw B on your diagram. Write down the coordinates of the vertices of B.

(b) A is rotated about the point (–1, 0), through a $\frac{1}{4}$ turn clockwise, to C. Draw C on your diagram. Write down the coordinates of the vertices of C.

(c) B is reflected in the line x = –1 to D. Draw D on your diagram. Write down the coordinates of the vertices of D.

(d) Describe the rotation which would map A onto D.

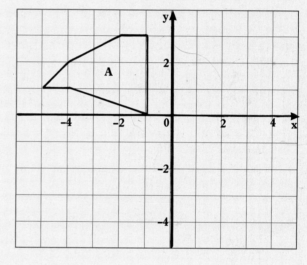

4.

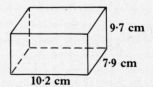

(a) Find the area of the base of this cylindrical soup tin.

(b) If this tin is filled to the top, how many m*l* of soup does it hold? (Answer to the nearest 10m*l*.)

(c) The soup is poured into a microwave container, shaped as shown. Estimate the depth of soup in this container.

(d) Calculate the depth of soup in the microwave container. (Answer to the nearest mm.) Use your estimate as a check.

213

5. (a) Find the value of x.

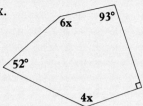

(b) Each exterior angle of a regular polygon is equal to 36°. How many sides does this polygon have?

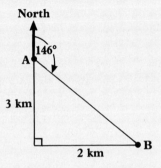

6. Annabel jogs from A to B, across the centre of a park. B is on a bearing of 146° from A.

From B, Annabel jogs due West for 2 km, then due North for 3 km. She is then back at A.

(a) Use Pythagoras' Theorem to find the distance AB.

(b) Find the size of angle B in the triangle.

(c) What is the bearing of A from B?

7. (i) This shape is drawn on "square dot" paper.

(a) What is the name of this shape?

(b) What is the size of angle A (the marked angle)?

(c) What other angles are equal to angle A?

(d) Is this a regular shape? Explain your answer.

(e) What is the order of rotational symmetry of this shape?

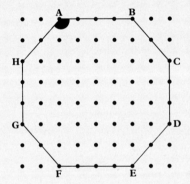

(ii)

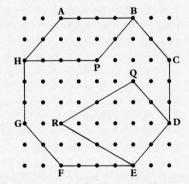

If the length of AB is 8 cm, find

(a) the lengths of the diagonals of the kite DERQ

(b) the area of the kite DERQ

(c) the area of the parallelogram ABPH.

(iii) Two triangles can be drawn by joining B, P, Q and C, D, Q. Are these triangles congruent? Explain your answer.

8.

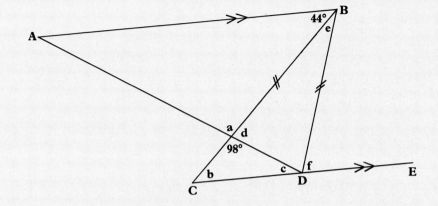

The lines AB and CE are parallel; BF = BD.
Find the size of the angles marked a, b, c, d, e and f.

9.

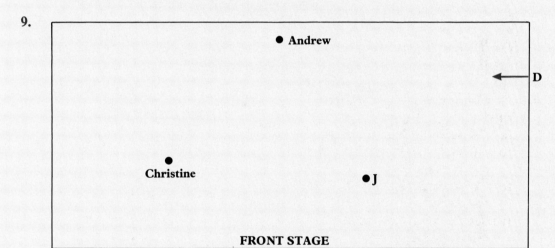

Scale 1 cm represents 2 m

This diagram represents an outdoor stage. Andrew and Christine are standing on the
stage when John comes onto the stage at D.
John walks in the direction shown by the arrow. He walks until he is the same distance
from Andrew and the chair at J. He then stops.

(a) Use your compass and ruler to construct the set of points which are the same
distance from Andrew and the chair at J. Hence mark the point where John
stops. Label this point as P.

(b) From P, John walks in a straight line to the chair at J. How far is it from P to J?

(c) Andrew now walks towards the front of the stage in such a way that he is always
the same distance from Christine and John. Use your compass and ruler to
construct the path Andrew takes.

(d) Andrew stops when he is 6 m from Christine.
Use your compass to construct the set of points that are 6 m from Christine.
Hence mark the point where Andrew stops. How far has Andrew walked?

10. Copy this diagram.

    (a) A′ is an enlargement of A.
    What is the scale factor of this enlargement?
    What are the coordinates of the centre of this enlargement?

    (b) A′ is enlarged, centre (–1, 3), scale factor $\frac{1}{2}$ to A″.

    Draw A″ on your diagram. Write down the coordinates of the vertices of A″.

    (c) B is an enlargement of A. The scale factor of this enlargement is:
    A. 0   B. 1   C. –1   D. (3, 2)

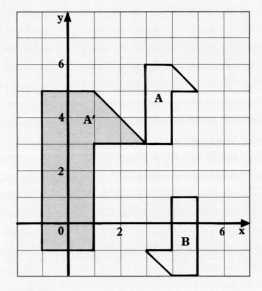

11.

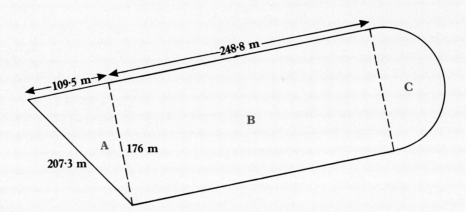

This sketch shows the shape and dimensions of Helford Common. C is a semicircle, A is a right-angled triangle and B is a rectangle.

(a) Susie estimates the area of A as follows: $\frac{1}{2} \times 100 \times 200 = 10000$ m². Estimate the area of B and the area of C.

(b) Calculate the area of Helford Common, to the nearest 10 m². Use your estimate as a check.

(c) Susie wrote the area of Helford Common in hectares, to 2 d.p. What answer should she have written?

(d) About how many acres is Helford Common? (Answer to the nearest acre.)

(e) Each day, Susie jogs around Helford Common twice. About how many kilometres does she jog each day?

12. Shirdia wanted to find the surface area of a circular ice-skating rink. She decided she could do this if she measured the circumference.
Explain how Shirdia could then calculate the area.

13.

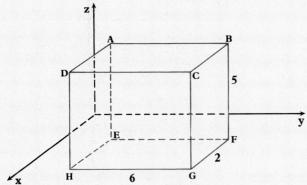

G is the point (3, 8, 0); A is the point (1, 2, 5).
Write down the coordinates of B, C, D, E, F and H.

14.

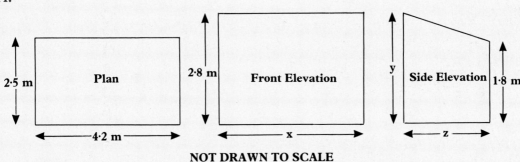

NOT DRAWN TO SCALE

The plan, front elevation and side elevation of a shed are shown above.
(a)   What are the measurements x, y and z?
(b)   Find the perimeter of the floor of this shed.
(c)   What is the area of the smallest wall of this shed?

15.

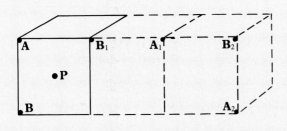

Jack moves a wool bale by rolling it along the ground, as shown by the dotted lines. The wool bale is a cube. A_1 , B_1 give the positions of A and B after it has been rolled once; A_2 , B_2 give the positions after it has been rolled twice.

Sketch the locus of
(a)   P, the midpoint of the front face
(b)   the point B.

16.

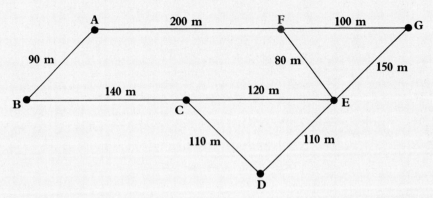

Hester works for a florist. The florist's shop is at F. The diagram is a network for the roads around this shop.

(a) How many odd nodes are there in the network shown?

(b) Is it possible for Hester to deliver flowers to each of the places A, B, C, D, E and G without retracing her steps? Is it possible for Hester to do this, ending at the florist's shop?

(c) Hester is to deliver to each place, ending at C. What is the distance of Hester's shortest route.

(d) Hester is to deliver to each place, ending at the florist's shop. What is the distance of her shortest route?

17. (a) Make a sketch of this isosceles triangle.
On your sketch, draw the axis of symmetry.

(b) Use your sketch to calculate the area of the triangle.
(**Hint:** You will need to use Pythagoras' Theorem.)

(c)

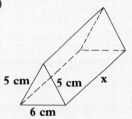

The volume of this chocolate packet is 120 cm³.
What is the length of the packet? (x in the diagram.)

(d) The net for the packet in **(c)** is cut from a piece of rectangular cardboard as shown in this sketch. Show that 104 cm² of this cardboard is wasted.

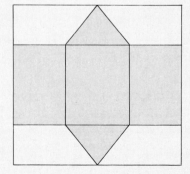

218

18.

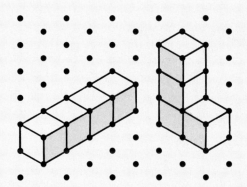

These shapes are built from 4 cubes. On isometric paper, draw another three shapes which could be built from 4 cubes. Each shape must *not* be a rotation or reflection of any of the other shapes.

19. Rebecca and Kylie are making patchwork quilts. They know they could make them by cutting material in the shape of regular hexagons. They draw the following sketch.

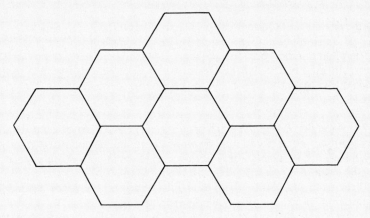

(a) They decide to experiment with different shapes. The first shape they experiment with is an octagon. They decide that octagons won't tessellate. Are they correct?

(b) They then decide to use octagons with another shape as a "filler". Could they use a square as a "filler"?

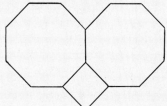

(c) Could they use a combination of octagons, and the rhombus shown?

(d) Could they use a square as a "filler" with the hexagons? If not, what shape could they use as a "filler"?

219

Emmy Noether

Emmy Noether was born in Germany in 1882 and died in the USA in 1935.

Emmy was the only girl in her family. Her father was a professor of Mathematics. When Emmy was young, he recognised her mathematical ability and encouraged her to study mathematics.

In 1907, Emmy gained a Ph.D. from the University of Erlangen. She wished to teach at a University but had difficulty getting a job. At the beginning of this century, it was not acceptable for a woman to teach mathematics at this level. From 1913 to 1915 she occasionally taught her father's students. From 1915 to 1919 she lectured, on a casual basis, at the University of Göttingen. Some of the other mathematicians, who recognised her mathematical and teaching ability, strongly supported her application to become a permanent member of the staff. The university authorities were concerned. It is said that one of them voiced this concern as *"What will our soldiers think when they return from the war and find they are expected to learn at the feet of a woman?"* In 1919 she overcame this opposition and was made a permanent lecturer. However her salary was low compared with that of the male mathematicians.

Emmy Noether was a Jew. Because of this, she was forced by the Nazis to leave the University of Göttingen in 1933. She went to the USA to become a professor of mathematics at Bryn Mawr College. She also conducted research at the Institute for Advanced Study at Princeton. Her talents as a mathematician and a teacher were fully appreciated in the USA. She had been in the USA for less than 2 years when she died after an operation for cancer.

Emmy Noether specialised in algebra and became known as one of the most creative mathematicians of her time. She developed mathematics which is used in modern physics; in particular, in the theory of relativity. Much of her work was on non-commutative algebra. In this algebra, the order in which numbers are added or multiplied affects the answer. She published 37 papers on mathematics.

Many of Emmy Noether's colleagues and students developed important mathematical theories from an idea of hers. She was an enthusiastic and lively teacher. It has been reported that her hair, which she wore up, often fell down when she became excited during her lecturing.

After her death, the *New York Times* published a tribute to her. In this, Einstein wrote *"In the judgement of the most competent living mathematicians, Fraulein Noether was the most significant mathematical genius thus far produced since the higher education of women began"*.

based on an article from the book "Women Sum It Up" — Hazard Press

DIMENSIONS for LENGTH, AREA, VOLUME

The perimeter of this rectangle is 16 m. The unit of measurement used is metres (m).
The area of this rectangle is 15 m². The unit of measurement used is square metres (m²).

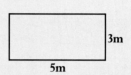

The volume of this cuboid is 60 m³. The unit of measurement used is cubic metres (m³).

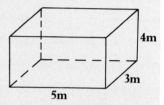

That is,   for perimeter the unit used is m
         for area the unit used is m²
         for volume the unit used is m³
These units are all related. They all refer to the unit of length, m.

We say,   **the dimension of perimeter is length (L)**
         the dimension of area is length × length (L²)
         the dimension of volume is length × length × length (L³)

DISCUSSION EXERCISE 12:1

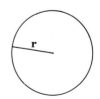

The formula for the area of a circle is $A = \pi r^2$.
If r is measured in metres, what unit of measurement is used for A?
What is the dimension of r? What is the dimension of A?

Consider πr^2. This is a number (π) × a length (r) × a length (r). What can you say about the dimension of π? **Discuss.**

Consider the formula for the circumference of a circle, $C = 2\pi r$.
What is the dimension of r? What is the dimension of C? What can you say about the dimension of the number 2? **Discuss.**

We can use dimensions to check whether a formula is reasonable.

Example   Garth cannot remember if the formula for the area of a circle is $A = 2\pi r$ or $A = \pi d$ or $A = \pi^2 r$ or $A = \pi r^2$. He checks the dimensions of these formulae as follows.

$2\pi r$ number × number × length   Dimension is L
πd number × length   Dimension is L
$\pi^2 r$ number × number × length   Dimension is L
πr^2 number × length × length   Dimension is L^2

Garth then decides that the area formula must be $A = \pi r^2$ since the dimension of area is L^2.

Worked Example   This diagram represents a piece of cheese. Which of the following expressions could be an expression for
(a)   the surface area   (b)   the volume?

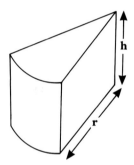

$\frac{1}{4}\pi rh + rh^2$ $\frac{1}{8}\pi r + 2h$

$\frac{1}{8}\pi r^2 h$ $\frac{1}{8}\pi r^2 h + \frac{1}{4}\pi rh$

$2rh + \frac{1}{4}\pi r$ $\frac{1}{4}\pi r^2 + 2rh + \frac{1}{4}\pi rh$

Answer   Dimension of $\frac{1}{4}\pi rh + rh^2$ is $L^2 + L^3$.

Dimension of $\frac{1}{8}\pi r + 2h$ is $L + L$; i.e. L.

Dimension of $\frac{1}{8}\pi r^2 h$ is L^3. This could be the expression for the volume.

Dimension of $\frac{1}{8}\pi r^2 h + \frac{1}{4}\pi rh$ is $L^3 + L^2$.

Dimension of $2rh + \frac{1}{4}\pi r$ is $L^2 + L$.

Dimension of $\frac{1}{4}\pi r^2 + 2rh + \frac{1}{4}\pi rh$ is $L^2 + L^2 + L^2$; i.e. L^2. This could be an expression for the surface area.

The answers are then   (a) $\frac{1}{4}\pi r^2 + 2rh + \frac{1}{4}\pi rh$ (b) $\frac{1}{8}\pi r^2 h$.

EXERCISE 12:2

1. Tariq worked out that the volume of this shape
   was given by $V = \frac{7}{3}\pi r^2 l^2$.
   Use dimensions to show that this formula
   cannot be correct.

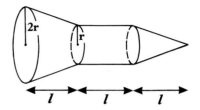

2. Angela wrote down the formula $A = \frac{4}{3}\pi r^3$ for the surface area of a sphere.
   Use dimensions to explain why this formula cannot be correct.

3. This diagram represents a running track.
   Which of the following could be an expression for
   (a) the perimeter   (b) the area?

   $2l + \pi dl$ $dl + \frac{1}{4}\pi d^2$ $2\pi d^2 l + 2l^2 d$

   $2l + \pi d$ $\frac{1}{4}\pi d^2 + d^2 l$

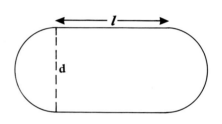

4. Which of the following could be a formula for the volume of this glass?

   $V = \frac{26}{27}\pi^2 rh$ $V = \frac{26}{27}\pi r^2 h$

   $V = \frac{1}{9}\pi r^2 h - \frac{1}{27}\pi rh$ $V = \frac{26}{27}\pi rh$

   $V = \frac{1}{3}\pi^2 rh + \frac{1}{27}\pi r^2 h$

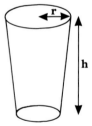

5.

   Which of the following could be a formula for the volume of this pencil?

   $V = \frac{1}{4}\pi dl + \frac{1}{12}\pi d^2 h$ $V = \pi^2 dl^2 + \frac{1}{12}\pi d^2 l^2$

   $V = \frac{1}{4}\pi d^2 l + \frac{1}{12}\pi dh$ $V = \frac{1}{4}\pi^2 d^2 l + \pi dh$

   $V = \frac{1}{4}\pi d^2 l + \frac{1}{12}\pi^2 dh$ $V = \frac{1}{4}\pi d^2 l + \frac{1}{12}\pi d^2 h$

6.

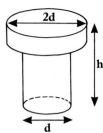

A piece of equipment in a workshop is shaped like this. Which of the following could be an expression for **(a)** the surface area **(b)** the volume?

$\frac{1}{4}\pi(8d + 5h)$ $\frac{1}{4}\pi d(8d + 5h)$ $\frac{1}{4}\pi dh(5\pi + 8d)$ $\frac{7}{16}\pi d^2h^2$

$\frac{7}{16}\pi d + 5\pi dh$ $\frac{7}{16}\pi d^2h$ $\frac{7}{16}\pi dh + \pi d$

7.

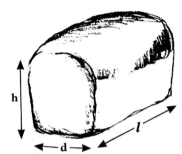

$V = \frac{1}{2}dl\,(2h - d) + \frac{1}{8}\pi d^2l$

$V = \frac{1}{2}d\,(l + h) + \frac{1}{8}\pi dl$

$V = \frac{1}{2}l\,(2h - d) + \frac{1}{8}\pi d^2l$

$V = \frac{1}{2}dl\,(2h - d) + \frac{1}{8}\pi d^2l^2$

A bakery bakes bread of this shape. Which of the formulae in the list could be a formula for the volume of this bread? Is there more than one possible formula in this list?

8. This drawing represents a rubbish bin.
Which of the following could be an expression for
    (a) the surface area   **(b)** the volume?

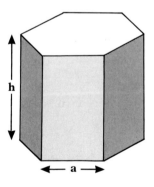

$6ah + \frac{3}{2}\sqrt{3}\,a$ $\frac{3}{2}\sqrt{3}\,a$ $\frac{3}{2}\sqrt{3}\,a^2h^2$

$\frac{3}{2}\sqrt{3}\,a^2h^2 + 6a$ $\frac{3}{2}\sqrt{3}\,a^2h$ $6ah + \frac{3}{2}\sqrt{3}\,a^2$

9. Which of the following expressions could be for   **(a)** perimeter
                                                  (b) area
                                                  (c) volume?

$\pi r + \frac{1}{2}r$ $4\pi r^2h$ $\pi r l$ $\frac{1}{4}\pi d^2$ $\frac{1}{3}\pi r^2h$

$\pi r(r + l)$ $r(\pi + 3)$ $\frac{4}{3}\pi r^3$ $\frac{1}{3}\pi r$ $\frac{4}{3}\pi r^2$

$\pi r + 4l$ $4\pi r l$ $4l^2h$ $3lh^2$ $\frac{1}{3}\pi r h$

Review 1

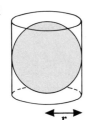

A ball is placed in a hollow cylinder, as shown in this diagram. Michael worked out a formula for the space not occupied by the ball. His formula was $V = \frac{2}{3}\pi r^2$.

Use dimensions to explain why Michael's formula cannot be correct.

Review 2

This diagram represents a test-tube.
Which of the following expressions could be for
   (a)   the volume   (b)   the surface area?

$\frac{2}{3}\pi^3 r + \pi r^2 h$ $2\pi r(h + r)$ $\frac{2}{3}\pi r^2 + \pi r^2 h$

$2\pi r(h + \pi)$ $\frac{2}{3}\pi r^3 + \pi r^2 h$ $2\pi^2(h + r)$

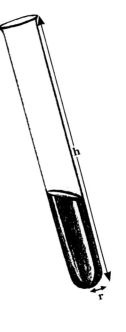

Carl Friedrich Gauss

Carl Gauss was born in 1777 at Brunswick and died in 1855 at Göttingen. He never left Germany, not even for a visit. He was the greatest mathematician of his time, perhaps of all time. Someone once described him as the last mathematician to know everything in his subject.

Carl's father was a labourer and contractor, as was his father before him. He did not approve of Carl becoming educated. He had hoped his son would join him in his work. Carl's mother who, as her husband, was uneducated, encouraged Carl in his studies and was always very proud of her son's achievements. She lived to see many of them, not dying until she was 97.

Carl was a child prodigy. When he was 3, he corrected the wages account his father was working on, much to his father's astonishment. He went to the local school and at 10, knew a great deal of maths. A teacher once asked Carl's class to add all the integers from 1 to 100 and was most surprised when Carl produced the correct answer immediately, with no written working.

When he was 14, one of Carl's teachers arranged a meeting with the Duke of Brunswick. The Duke was impressed with Carl and sponsored his education from then on. At 15, he went to a college in Brunswick; then at 18 he went to Göttingen University.

Just before his 19th birthday, Carl discovered how to construct, using compass and ruler only, a regular polygon of 17 sides. He then began to keep a diary, recording in this all his mathematical discoveries. Although this diary is only 19 pages long, it is one of the most valued mathematics documents of all time. Another entry in the diary, made when Carl was 19, was the discovery that every integer is the sum of three, or fewer, triangular numbers.

In 1798, Gauss received a doctorate from the University of Helmstädt. In his thesis for this doctorate he proved that every equation has a solution.

Gauss did a great deal of work on prime numbers and made many discoveries. He once said *"Mathematics is the queen of the sciences and number theory the queen of mathematics"*.

In the early 19th century, Gauss began to concentrate on subjects such as astronomy and physics. He later regretted having taken his attention away from number theory.

In 1807 he was made Director of the Göttingen Observatory and a Professor of Astronomy. He had been offered positions as Professor of Mathematics, both at Göttingen University and at St. Petersburg Academy. He did not accept these offers as he hated teaching. In a letter to a friend, he once wrote *"This winter, I am giving two courses of lectures to three students, of which one is only moderately prepared, the other less than moderately, and the third lacks both preparation and ability. Such are the onera of a mathematical profession."*

He remained at the Göttingen Observatory for the rest of his life. His health was good and his mind active, right up until the time he died.

Gauss is known as the founder of modern German mathematics. Some of his work, on mathematical applications, laid the groundwork for Einstein's theory of relativity and worldwide communications. He is said to have been frightened by the idea of international communications. His methods for calculating the orbits of heavenly bodies are still in use today.

RECOGNISING SIMILAR SHAPES

Shapes that are identical in every way are called congruent shapes.
These shapes are congruent.

Shapes that are the same shape but different sizes are called **similar shapes**.
These shapes are similar.

DISCUSSION EXERCISE 13:1

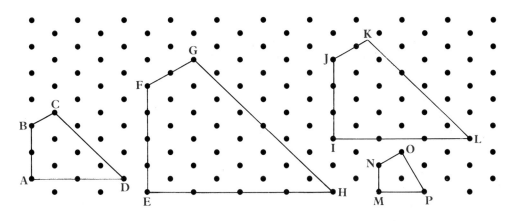

If a shape is enlarged, do we get similar shapes?
Which of the shapes above are similar shapes? **Discuss.**

What can you say about the angles B and J?
Which angles are equal to angle C? Which angles are equal to angle D?
What other equal angles can you find? **Discuss.**

Make a statement about the angles of two similar shapes. **Discuss** your statement.

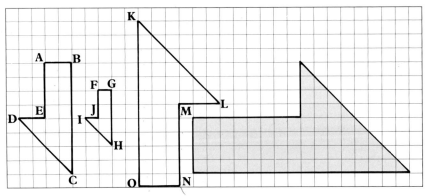

The shapes ABCDE and FGHIJ are similar. $\dfrac{\text{Length BC}}{\text{Length GH}} = \dfrac{8}{4} = 2.$

Make a statement about the ratio of the lengths of the sides in similar shapes. **Discuss** your statement.

Is the shape KLMNO similar to shape ABCDE? Find the ratio of the lengths of the shortest sides of these two shapes. Make and test a statement about the ratios of the lengths of other sides on these two shapes. **Discuss.**

Choose a shape that is similar to the pink shape.
Which sides are in the same ratio? **Discuss.**

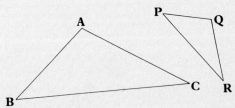

In similar shapes, the angles that are equal are called **corresponding angles.**
For instance, in these similar shapes, the corresponding angles are A and Q, C and R, B and P.

In similar shapes, the sides that are in corresponding positions are called **corresponding sides.** In similar triangles, the corresponding sides are opposite the corresponding angles. For instance, in the similar triangles above, sides BC and PR are corresponding sides since these are opposite the corresponding angles A and Q. Sides AB and PQ are also corresponding sides as are the sides AC and QR.

In the similar quadrilaterals shown here, AB and SP are corresponding sides as they both lie between the 100° and 105° angles. The other corresponding sides are BC and PQ, CD and QR, DA and RS.

228

EXERCISE 13:2

1. Name the similar shapes.

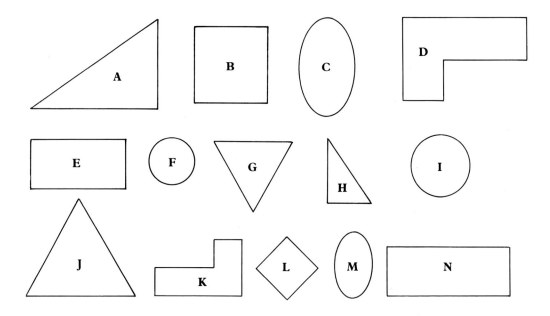

2. Which of the diagrams are similar?

(a)   (b)

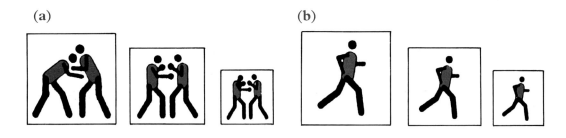

3. The following pairs of shapes are similar.
   Name the angle which corresponds to angle B.

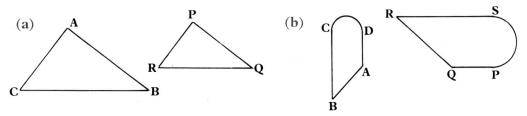

4. In the diagrams in **question 3**, name the side which corresponds to the side AB.

5.

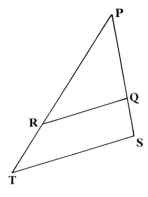

In this diagram there are two similar triangles.
One is △PTS.
    (a) Name the other similar triangle.
    (b) Which angle corresponds to ∠PRQ?
    (c) Which side corresponds to PS?

6.

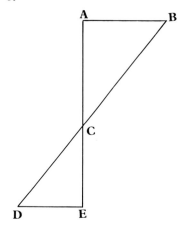

In this diagram there are two similar triangles.
    (a) Name these similar triangles.
    (b) Which angle corresponds to angle B?
    (c) Which angle corresponds to ∠DCE?
    (d) Which side corresponds to AB?
    (e) Which side corresponds to EC?

7. Are the following pairs of triangles similar? (The triangles are NOT drawn to scale.)

    (a)   **(b)**

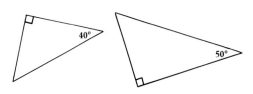   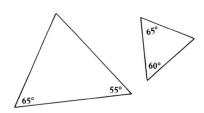

8. Which word, **always** or **sometimes**, is missing in these statements?
    (a) A guitar in a photo and the guitar in the negative of the photo are . . . similar
           shapes.
    (b) A building and its shadow are . . . similar shapes.
    (c) A slide and its image on a screen are . . . similar shapes.
    (d) The floor plan of a house and the floor itself are . . . similar shapes.

(e) A photo of the front view of a racing car and the front view of the racing car itself are . . . similar shapes.

(f) An oil painting of a daisy and the daisy itself are . . . similar shapes.

Review 1

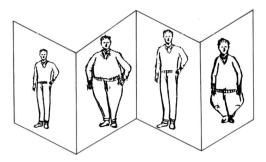

Wayne went into the "Hall of Mirrors" at a fairground. This is how he saw himself at the first set of mirrors.

Are any of these images similar? If so, which ones?

Review 2 These two quadrilaterals are similar.

(a) Which angle corresponds to angle B?

(b) Which angle corresponds to angle F?

(c) Which side corresponds to DC?

(d) Which side corresponds to HG?

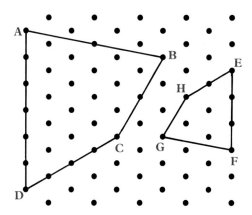

Review 3 Are the following pairs of triangles similar? (The triangles are NOT drawn to scale.)

(a)   (b)

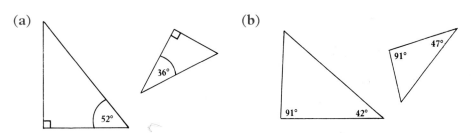

PRACTICAL EXERCISE 13:3

Enlarge a picture or a photograph from a book or brochure or magazine or newspaper using the following technique. (This is an enlargement technique used by artists.)

Step 1 Either draw a grid of 5 mm squares over your selected picture or firmly attach a transparent grid (drawn up in 5 mm squares) over your picture.

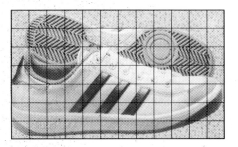

Step 2 In pencil, draw up a grid of 1 cm squares. On each square of this grid, draw that part of the picture that is in the corresponding square on the original picture.

Use pen for this drawing. Rub out the pencilled grid when you have finished.

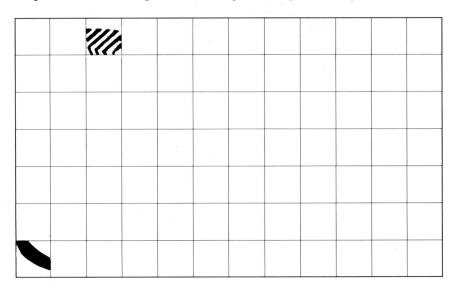

Notes
- You could make your drawing larger by using a grid of 2 cm squares or 5 cm squares or ... .
- If you want to make a very large picture, you could cut down sheets of A4 paper so they are square; then use one of these for each grid square. If you do this, you could work on this as a group with each student enlarging part of the picture.

FINDING UNKNOWN LENGTHS

If two shapes are similar then **1.** corresponding angles are equal

2. corresponding sides are in the same ratio.

We use the fact that corresponding sides are in the same ratio to find unknown lengths.

Worked Example When Jayne planted a tree 5 m from a window the tree just blocked from view a building 50 m away. If the building was 20 m tall, how tall was the tree?

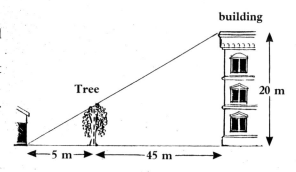

NOT DRAWN TO SCALE

Answer

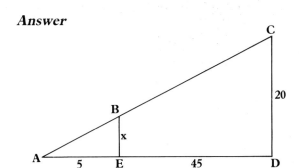

Label the diagram as shown.
Let x be the height of the tree.
Since $\triangle ABE$ is similar to $\triangle ACD$

then $\dfrac{BE}{CD} = \dfrac{AE}{AD}$

$\dfrac{x}{20} = \dfrac{5}{50}$

$x = 20 \times \dfrac{5}{50}$

$x = 2$

That is, the tree was 2 m tall.

Worked Example A light, 3·4 metres above the floor, produces a circular patch of light on the floor. The radius of this patch of light is 1·8 metres.
A table, which is 1·2 m high, is placed directly under the light. What is the radius of the patch of light on the table?

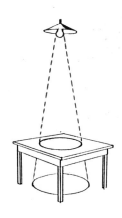

Answer   The problem can be represented by the following diagrams.

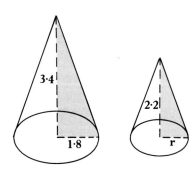

Since the shaded triangles are similar,

$$\frac{r}{1\cdot8} = \frac{2\cdot2}{3\cdot4}$$

$$r = 1\cdot8 \times \frac{2\cdot2}{3\cdot4}$$

$$= 1\cdot2 \text{ to 1 d.p.}$$

That is, the radius of the patch of light on the table is 1·2 m, to the nearest tenth of a metre.

Worked Example   The triangles ABE and CBD are similar.
Find the length of DB and AB.

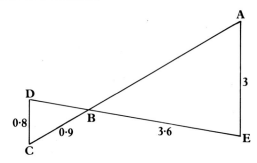

Answer   Corresponding angles are A and C, E and D, ∠ABE and ∠CBD.
Corresponding sides are BE and BD, AB and CB, AE and CD.

$$\frac{BD}{BE} = \frac{CD}{AE}$$

$$\frac{BD}{3\cdot6} = \frac{0\cdot8}{3}$$

$$BD = 3\cdot6 \times \frac{0\cdot8}{3}$$

$$= 0\cdot96$$

$$\frac{AB}{CB} = \frac{AE}{CD}$$

$$\frac{AB}{0\cdot9} = \frac{3}{0\cdot8}$$

$$AB = 0\cdot9 \times \frac{3}{0\cdot8}$$

$$= 3\cdot375$$

EXERCISE 13:4

1. Find the length marked as x.

(a) **(b)**

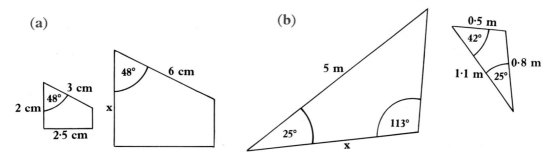

2. Beth, who is 1·53 m tall, gets her friend Jill to help her find the height of a building. Jill measures Beth's shadow as 2·42 m.
Beth measures the shadow of the building as 19·24 m. Beth then used similar triangles to find the height of the building. What answer should she get?

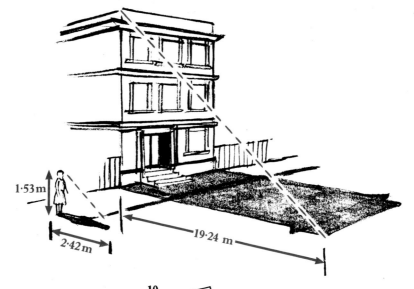

3. Find the value of *l*.

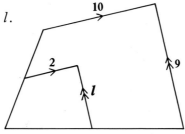

4.

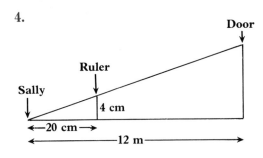

Sally is making a scale drawing of the front of a house. She is 12 m from the house.
When she holds a transparent ruler vertically in front of her, she measures the door as being 4 cm high.
Find the actual height of this door if Sally held the ruler 20 cm from her.

5. A tall man, who is sitting up straight in his seat, is completely blocking John's view at the cinema.
John is 10 m from the 4 m high screen. The man is 1 m in front of John.
How far would the man need to lower his head and shoulders if John is to be able to see all of the screen?

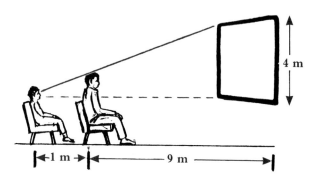

6.

A magazine gave a pattern for a shirt. The instructions stated that each pattern piece needed to be enlarged. The diagram shows one of the pattern pieces.
Measure the length of DC and AB on this pattern piece.

When Amanda enlarged this pattern piece she made DC 36 cm long.
Use similar shapes to find the length Amanda made AB on her pattern.

7.

Hamish was doing an experiment
on light. This is one of the
diagrams he drew.

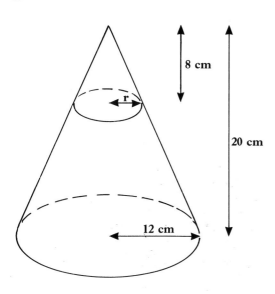

When u was 18 cm the image of the straw was 5 cm high. What was the distance v?

8.

A cone is cut parallel to its base to form a
smaller cone.
Find the radius of this smaller cone.

9.

A light is shone onto a screen, through a hole in
a piece of cardboard.
The hole is 4 cm wide. The spot of light on the
screen has a diameter of 10 cm.
If the cardboard is 5 cm from the light, show
that the screen is 12·5 cm from the light.

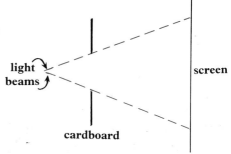

10.

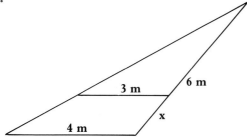

The two triangles in this diagram are similar.
Find the value of x.

11.

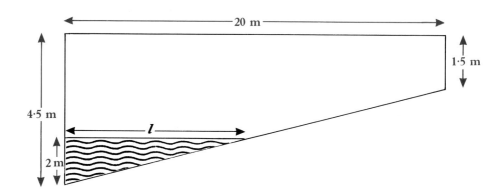

A swimming pool is being filled.
Find the length, *l*, of the surface of the water when the pool has been filled to a depth of 2 m.

Review 1   Sarah found the height of a tree by placing a 30 cm ruler upright in the shadow of the tree. She placed the ruler so that the end of its shadow was at the same place as the end of the shadow of the tree.
How high was this tree?

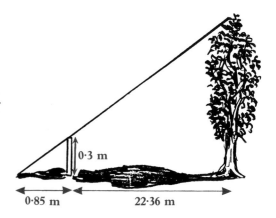

Review 2   Zeke calculated the width, w, of a river by taking the measurements shown, then using similar triangles.
What answer should Zeke get for the width?

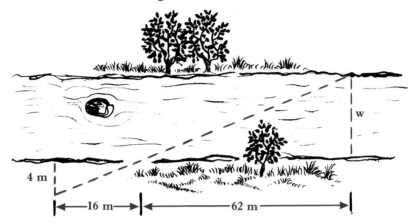

Review 3   A cylinder of radius 10 cm just fits inside a hollow cone of height 24 cm, as shown in the diagram. If the radius of the cone is 16 cm, how tall is the cylinder?

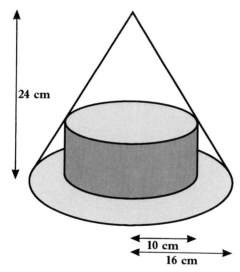

PRACTICAL EXERCISE 13:5

Use similar shapes to find the height of a tree (or a building) or the width of a road (or a stream).
You could use one of the methods shown in **questions 2, 4, Review 1** or **Review 2** of the previous exercise.

INVESTIGATION 13:6

SIMILAR TRIANGLES

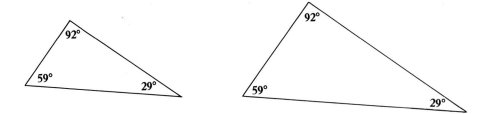

These triangles are similar since the angles of one triangle are the same as the angles of the other.

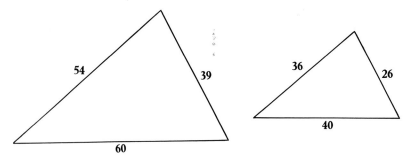

These triangles are similar since corresponding sides are in the same ratio.

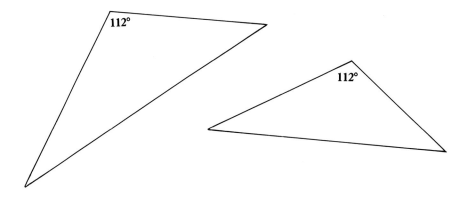

Suppose we are given just one pair of equal angles, as shown in these triangles. What is the least amount of information you need to be given about the sides to be sure the triangles are similar? **Investigate.**

PRACTICAL EXERCISE 13:7

Choose a business. Design a suitable logo for this business.
Adapt your logo for various uses such as: letterhead, newspaper advertisement, advertisement on the London Underground, sign outside the business premises, business cards.

Instead of designing a logo for a business you could design a logo for a sports team or an organization such as a charity.

You may like to draw the enlargements and reductions of your logo using the "ray" method of enlargement (see **page 208**) or you may like to use the method used in **Practical Exercise 13:3**.

Tycho Brahe

Tycho Brahe was born in 1546 at Knudstrup, in what was Denmark but is now Sweden. He died in 1601 at Prague.

Tycho was born into a noble family. When very young, he was abducted by a wealthy uncle who had no children of his own. After some time, his parents gave the uncle permission to continue to raise Tycho. Tycho spent his early childhood at his uncle's castle in Tostrup. At the age of 13, he was sent to the University of Copenhagen to study law. Tycho spent 3 years at this University then another 3 years at the University of Leipzig. He was more interested in astronomy than law. He spent the daytime attending law lectures, to satisfy his uncle, and the night-time watching the stars. At the University of Copenhagen, the professor of mathematics and other maths. lecturers helped Tycho with his astronomy.

It is said that Tycho became fascinated with astronomy in 1560. A total eclipse of the Sun was predicted for August 21st of that year. When the eclipse occurred on that day Tycho was most impressed by the accuracy of the prediction. When, in 1563, another solar event was less accurately predicted Tycho decided to devote his life to gathering accurate information on the position and movement of the planets and other heavenly bodies. He needed this information to rewrite the existing inaccurate tables of data.

Considering that Brahe lived so long ago, he made an outstanding contribution to astronomy. The accuracy of his measurements is apparent from the fact that his calculation for the length of a year was only a few seconds less than its actual value.

The illustration shows Brahe with one of the very large instruments he built and used. The one shown is called a quadrant and was used to measure the angle of elevation of a heavenly body. This instrument was much more accurate than any of those used by previous astronomers. It could be used to measure angles to an accuracy of about one-tenth of a degree.

The system of movements of the planets which Brahe worked out is known as the Tychonic System. It was later shown that this system was based on incorrect assumptions. However, Brahe's work laid the foundation for Kepler and later astronomers.

After leaving University in 1565, Brahe travelled widely throughout Europe. He studied at various places and also acquired many mathematical and astronomical instruments. About 1571, Brahe built his first observatory. By this time his father and uncle had died and Brahe inherited both estates. In 1576, he planned to leave Denmark and establish an observatory in Germany. The King of Denmark, Frederick II, gave Brahe an island and financial support to persuade him to stay. The new observatory built on this island became the centre of European astronomical research. However, in 1597 Brahe did leave Denmark after he had fallen out with the King, the church and the nobility. He settled in Prague in 1599 under the patronage of Emperor Rudolf II. Brahe died in 1601. Johannes Kepler, who was Brahe's pupil and assistant, continued with his work.

As did many of the astronomers of his time, Brahe believed in astrology. That is, he believed in the power of the stars to influence human behaviour. He also believed, quite unreasonably considering his measurements, that the Earth was the centre of the Universe, and that the Sun revolved round it. He claimed that to believe otherwise was irreligious.

At times, Brahe was a quarrelsome man. He once got into a bitter argument over a geometry problem. This led to a duel in which the end of his nose was cut off with a sword.

INTRODUCTION

> ### INVESTIGATION and DISCUSSION EXERCISE 14:1

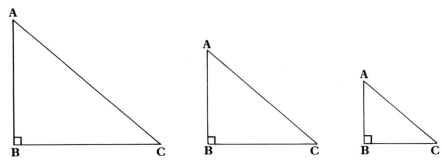

In each of these right-angled triangles, use a protractor to find the size of angle C.
In each triangle, measure the lengths of AB and BC; then calculate the ratio

$\dfrac{\text{length of AB}}{\text{length of BC}}$ to two decimal places. **Discuss** your answers.

What if you had found the ratio $\dfrac{\text{length of AB}}{\text{length of AC}}$ or $\dfrac{\text{length of BC}}{\text{length of AC}}$?

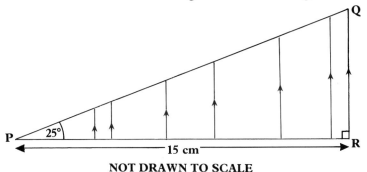

NOT DRAWN TO SCALE

Use a ruler and protractor to accurately draw the right-angled triangle PQR. Draw
lines parallel to QR to form a number of triangles.

Do you expect the ratio $\dfrac{\text{length of shortest side}}{\text{length of longest side}}$ to be the same for each triangle

formed? **Discuss.** As part of your discussion find this ratio for each triangle.
Draw other diagrams, similar to that shown.
On one diagram make angle P equal to 30°, on another 35°, on another 40° and so on.

Is there a relationship between the ratio $\dfrac{\text{length of shortest side}}{\text{length of longest side}}$ and the size of the
angle P? **Investigate.**

What if you considered the ratio of two other sides?

NAMING SIDES of a TRIANGLE

It is convenient to give "names" to the sides of a right-angled triangle.
From previous work on Pythagoras' theorem, we know that the side opposite the right angle is called the **hypotenuse.**

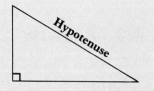

The "names" of the other two sides are **opposite side** and **adjacent side.** These "names" depend on the angle we consider.

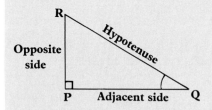

Consider the angle Q.
Since the side opposite angle Q is PR then, **for angle Q, PR is called the opposite side.**
There are two sides next to angle Q, the hypotenuse and PQ. **For angle Q, PQ is called the adjacent side.**

Consider the angle R.
Since the side opposite angle R is PQ then, **for angle R, PQ is called the opposite side.**
The side next to angle R, that is not the hypotenuse, is PR. **For angle R, PR is called the adjacent side.**

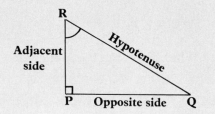

Example

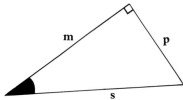

In this triangle, the hypotenuse is s. For the marked angle, the opposite side is p and the adjacent side is m.

Greek letters are often used to name angles. Greek letters commonly used for angles are α (alpha), β (beta), θ (theta).

Example

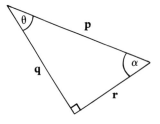

For θ, the opposite side is r and the adjacent side is q.

For α, the opposite side is q and the adjacent side is r.

EXERCISE 14:2

1. Name the hypotenuse in each of these triangles.

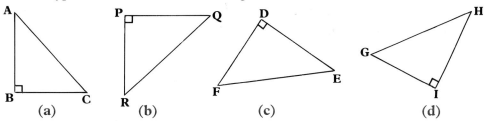

2. Refer to the triangles in **question 1.**
  (a) For angle A, name the opposite side.
  (b) For angle Q, name the adjacent side.
  (c) For angle F, name the opposite side.
  (d) For angle G, name the adjacent side.

3. Which side completes the statement for the marked angle?

(a)
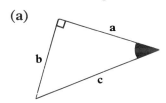

(b)
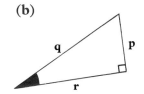

(c)
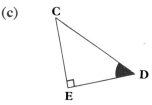

The opposite side is ...   The adjacent side is ...   The adjacent side is ...

4.
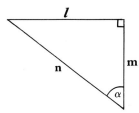

  (a) Name the hypotenuse in this triangle.
  (b) For α, name the adjacent side.
  (c) For α, name the opposite side.

Review

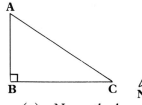
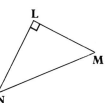
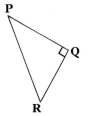
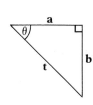

  (a) Name the hypotenuse in $\triangle$ PQR.
  (b) For angle N, name the opposite side.
  (c) For angle A, name the adjacent side.
  (d) For angle R, name the opposite side.
  (e) For θ, name the adjacent side.

The ratios SINE, COSINE, TANGENT

The hypotenuse, opposite side and adjacent side have been labelled on these triangles for the 40° angle.

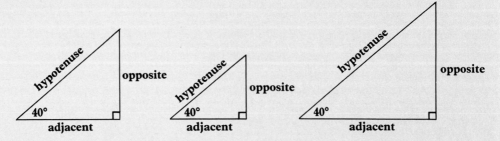

In Investigation 14:1, you found that the ratio $\dfrac{\text{shortest side}}{\text{longest side}}$ i.e. $\dfrac{\text{opposite}}{\text{hypotenuse}}$ is the same for each of these triangles.

This ratio $\dfrac{\text{opposite}}{\text{hypotenuse}}$ is given a special name. It is called the sine of 40° or **sine 40°**.

The ratio $\dfrac{\text{adjacent}}{\text{hypotenuse}}$ is called **cosine 40°**. The ratio $\dfrac{\text{opposite}}{\text{adjacent}}$ is called **tangent 40°**.

The abbreviations sin, cos, tan are used for sine, cosine, tangent.
The ratios sin A, cos A, tan A are called **trigonometrical ratios**, or **trig. ratios**.

DISCUSSION EXERCISE 14:3

- To find the value of sin 72° we could begin by accurately drawing a right-angled triangle in which one of the angles is 72°.
  Does it matter how large or small we make the triangle? How could we continue? **Discuss.**

  The calculator can be used to find the value of sin 72°. The calculator value of sin 72° is 0·9511 to 4 decimal places. Which keys do you press to find this? **Discuss.**

- **Discuss** how to use the calculator to find the cosine or tangent of an angle.
  Choose some angles. Draw right-angled triangles to work out the value of the cosine of some of your chosen angles, the tangent of some of the others and the sine of the rest.
  Compare your values with the calculator values.

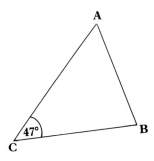
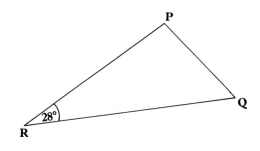

Could you use triangles, such as those shown, to work out the value of sin 47° or cos 28°? **Discuss.**

● $\sin \theta = \dfrac{\text{opposite}}{\text{hypotenuse}}$

$\cos \theta = \dfrac{\text{adjacent}}{\text{hypotenuse}}$

$\tan \theta = \dfrac{\text{opposite}}{\text{adjacent}}$

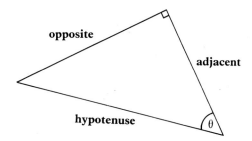

One way of remembering these trig. ratios is by using SOHCAHTOA. How can this be used to help you remember these ratios? **Discuss.**

Make up a mnemonic to help remember SOHCAHTOA. Your mnemonic could begin "**S**cience **O**r **H**istory ..." or "**S**ome **O**ld **H**orses **C**an ...". **Discuss** your mnemonic.

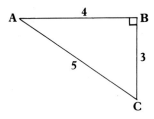

Worked Example Write, as a fraction

    (a)   sin A   (b)   cos A

    (c)   tan C   (d)   sin C.

Answer

For angle A, AC is the hypotenuse

              BC is the opposite side

              AB is the adjacent side

(a) $\sin A = \frac{3}{5}$ (using $\sin A = \dfrac{\text{opposite}}{\text{hypotenuse}}$)

(b) $\cos A = \frac{4}{5}$ (using $\cos A = \dfrac{\text{adjacent}}{\text{hypotenuse}}$)

For angle C, AC is the hypotenuse

              AB is the opposite side

              BC is the adjacent side

(c) $\tan C = \frac{4}{3}$ (using $\tan C = \dfrac{\text{opposite}}{\text{adjacent}}$)

(d) $\sin C = \frac{4}{5}$ (using $\sin C = \dfrac{\text{opposite}}{\text{hypotenuse}}$)

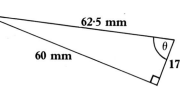

Worked Example

62·5 mm

60 mm

θ

17·5 mm

Find the values of sin θ, cos θ, tan θ giving the answers to 2 d.p.

Answer $\sin\theta = \dfrac{60}{62\cdot5}$ $\cos\theta = \dfrac{17\cdot5}{62\cdot5}$ $\tan\theta = \dfrac{60}{17\cdot5}$

$= 0\cdot96$ $= 0\cdot28$ $= 3\cdot43$ (2 d.p.)

EXERCISE 14:4

1. What is the missing side in each of the following?

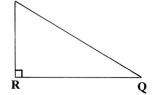

(a) $\sin Q = \dfrac{PR}{\cdots}$ (b) $\cos Q = \dfrac{\cdots}{PQ}$ (c) $\tan Q = \dfrac{\cdots}{QR}$

(d) $\tan P = \dfrac{QR}{\cdots}$ (e) $\cos P = \dfrac{\cdots}{PQ}$ (f) $\sin P = \dfrac{\cdots}{PQ}$

2. Write sin θ, as a fraction.

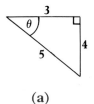 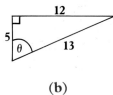 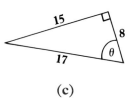 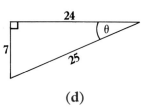

(a)   (b)   (c)   (d)

3. For the triangles in **question 2**, write tan θ as a fraction.

4. For the triangles in **question 2**, write cos θ as a fraction.

5. Complete each trig. ratio giving the answers as decimals. Round to 2 d.p. if rounding is necessary.

(a) 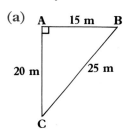   (b) 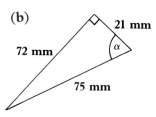   (c)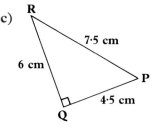

sin B = · · ·   cos α = · · ·   tan R = · · ·
cos C = · · ·   tan α = · · ·   sin P = · · ·
tan B = · · ·   sin α = · · ·   cos R = · · ·
sin C = · · ·   tan P = · · ·

Review   Copy and complete.

(a) $\cos M = \dfrac{\cdots}{MP}$

(b) $\tan P = \dfrac{30}{\cdots}$

(c) $\sin M = \cdots$ (to 2 d.p.)

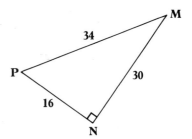

Calculator keying sequences to find the values of sin 14°, cos 14°, tan 14° are as follows.

For sin 14°:   **Key** $\boxed{14}\ \boxed{\sin}$ to get answer of 0·2419 to 4 d.p.

For cos 14°:   **Key** $\boxed{14}\ \boxed{\cos}$ to get answer of 0·9703 to 4 d.p.

For tan 14°:   **Key** $\boxed{14}\ \boxed{\tan}$ to get answer of 0·2493 to 4 d.p.

Note   Make sure your calculator is operating in Degree Mode.
This is MODE 4. You do not need to remember Mode 4 is Degree mode as 4 is
written above DEG on the calculator.

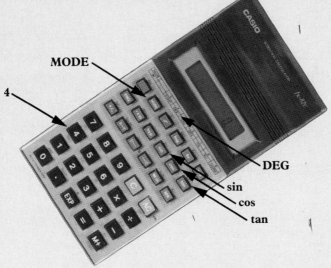

EXERCISE 14:5

Use the calculator to find the value of the following trig. ratios, giving each answer to 3 d.p.

1. cos 70°	2. sin 13°	3. tan 54°	4. tan 18°	5. sin 84°
6. sin 60·7°	7. cos 24·1°	8. cos 82·7°	9. tan 58·7°	10. tan 45°
11. sin 15°	12. sin 35°	13. sin 55°	14. sin 75°	15. sin 90°
16. cos 10°	17. cos 60°	18. cos 90°	19. tan 2°	20. tan 89·9°

Review 1 tan 34°   Review 2 sin 72°   Review 3 cos 40·3°

DISCUSSION EXERCISE 14:6

Referring to the angle θ, which of x, y or r is the hypotenuse, which is the opposite side, which is the adjacent side?

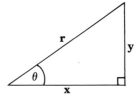

Discuss how the ratios $\sin \theta$, $\cos \theta$, $\tan \theta$ may be written in terms of x, y and r.

To find the length x, we may use the formula $x = r \cos \theta$.
What formula could be used to find y? Is there more than one possible formula? **Discuss.**

Make a summary of your discussion.

FINDING the length of a SIDE

In a right-angled triangle, if we are given the length of one side and the size of an angle (other than the right angle) we can use one of the trig. ratios to find the length of one of the other sides.

Worked Example

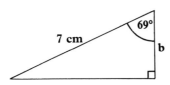

Find the length of the side marked as b.

Answer $\cos 69° = \dfrac{b}{7}$ or $\dfrac{b}{7} = \cos 69°$

$b = 7 \times \cos 69°$ (multiplying both sides by 7)
$b = 2\cdot5$ cm (1 d.p.)

Keying $\boxed{7}$ $\boxed{\times}$ $\boxed{69}$ $\boxed{\cos}$ $\boxed{=}$

Note   Just as x × y is usually written as xy so is 7 × cos 69° usually written as 7 cos 69°.

Worked Example   (a)

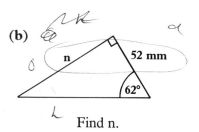

Find m.

(b)

Find n.

Answer   (a) $\sin 51° = \dfrac{m}{2·7}$ or $\dfrac{m}{2·7} = \sin 51°$

$m = 2·7 \sin 51°$ (multiplying both sides by 2·7)
$m = 2·1$ cm (1 d.p.)

Keying   [2·7] [×] [51] [sin] [=]

(b) $\tan 62° = \dfrac{n}{52}$ or $\dfrac{n}{52} = \tan 62°$

$n = 52 \tan 62°$ (multiplying both sides by 52)
$n = 98$ mm (to the nearest mm)

Keying   [52] [×] [62] [tan] [=]

Worked Example   Find the length of the
side marked as t.

Answer $\sin 35° = \dfrac{6·8}{t}$

$t \sin 35° = 6·8$ (multiplying both sides by t)

$t = \dfrac{6·8}{\sin 35°}$ (dividing both sides by $\sin 35°$)

$t = 11·9$ cm (1 d.p.)

Keying   [6·8] [÷] [35] [sin] [=]

The previous worked examples show the steps to be taken to find an unknown side. These steps are:
Step 1   Write down a trig. ratio for the given angle. This ratio must involve the unknown side and a known side.
If these sides are the hypotenuse and the opposite side the trig. ratio used is sine.
If these sides are the hypotenuse and the adjacent side the trig. ratio used is cosine.
If these sides are the opposite and the adjacent sides the trig. ratio used is tangent.
Step 2   Solve the equation formed to find the unknown side.

EXERCISE 14:7

1. Which trig. ratio (sin, cos or tan) would you use to find d?

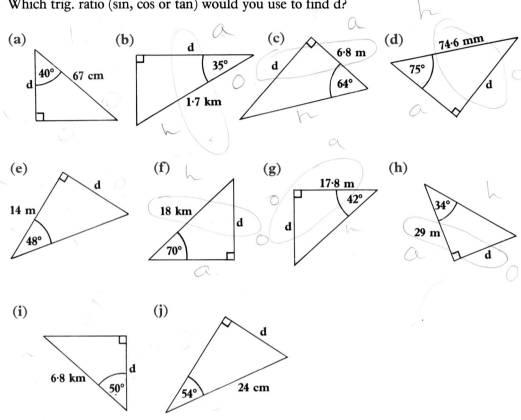

(a)

40° 67 cm
d

(b)

d
35°
1·7 km

(c)

6·8 m
d
64°

(d)

74·6 mm
75°
d

(e)

d
14 m
48°

(f)

18 km
d
70°

(g)

17·8 m
42°
d

(h)

34°
29 m
d

(i)

6·8 km
d
50°

(j)

d
54°
24 cm

2. For each of the triangles in **question 1**, find d. Round your answers sensibly.

3. A 5·2 metre ladder leans against a wall as shown.
   How far is the bottom of this ladder from the wall?

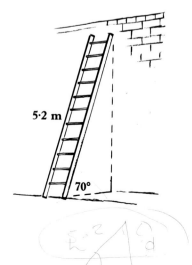

5·2 m

70°

4.

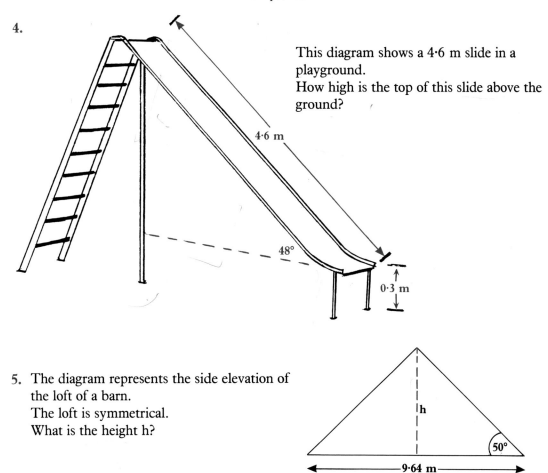

This diagram shows a 4·6 m slide in a playground.
How high is the top of this slide above the ground?

4·6 m

48°

0·3 m

5. The diagram represents the side elevation of the loft of a barn.
The loft is symmetrical.
What is the height h?

h

9·64 m

50°

4·082

6. Find the length of **a**.

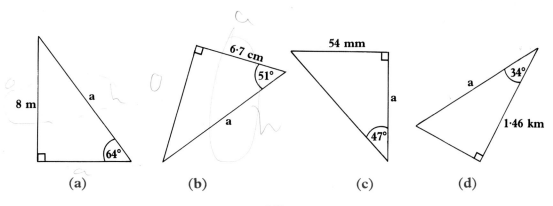

8 m

a

64°

(a)

6·7 cm

51°

a

(b)

54 mm

a

47°

(c)

34°

a

1·46 km

(d)

7. When an aeroplane is at a height of 1000 metres, it is picked up on radar.
The diagram represents this situation. How far is the aeroplane from the radar?

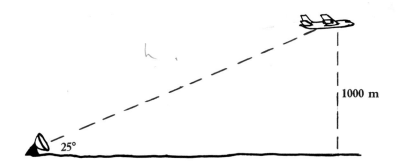

8.

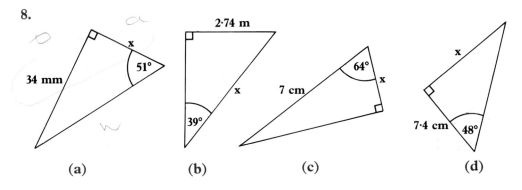

(a)   (b)   (c)   (d)

Find the length of x.

Review 1   Bob is pulling a trolley along the ground, as shown in this diagram.
Find the height of Bob's hand above the ground.

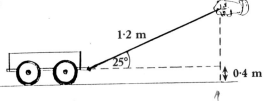

Review 2   Find d in each of these triangles.

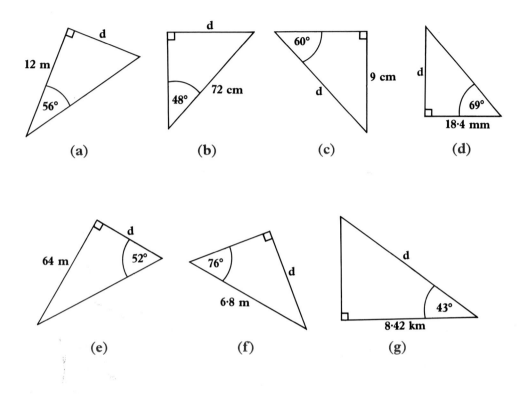

(a)   (b)   (c)   (d)

(e)   (f)   (g)

FINDING the size of an ANGLE

DISCUSSION EXERCISE 14:8

- If $\sin \theta = 0.89$, then $\theta = 62.9°$ to one decimal place.
  What keying sequence on the calculator gives this answer for θ ? **Discuss.**

- The angle α could be found as follows.

    $\tan \alpha = \dfrac{4.6}{5.9}$

    $\alpha = 37.9°$ (1 d.p.), using the

Keying sequence [4·6] [÷] [5·9] [=] [INV] [tan⁻¹]

Discuss each part of this keying sequence.

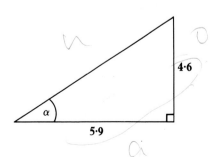

If we are given the lengths of two of the sides of a right-angled triangle we can use a trig. ratio (sin, cos or tan) to find the size of an unknown angle.

We use tan if we are given the lengths of the opposite and adjacent sides.

We use cos if we are given the lengths of the adjacent side and the hypotenuse.

We use sin if we are given the lengths of the opposite side and the hypotenuse.

Worked Example Find the size of θ if (a) $\tan \theta = 1.5$ (b) $\cos \theta = 0.6$
(c) $\sin \theta = 0.2834$

Answer (a) $\tan \theta = 1.5$
$\theta = 56.3°$ (1 d.p.) **Keying** $\boxed{1.5}$ $\boxed{\text{INV}}$ $\boxed{\tan^{-1}}$

(b) $\cos \theta = 0.6$
$\theta = 53.1°$ (1 d.p.) **Keying** $\boxed{0.6}$ $\boxed{\text{INV}}$ $\boxed{\cos^{-1}}$

(c) $\sin \theta = 0.2834$
$\theta = 16.5°$ (1 d.p.) **Keying** $\boxed{0.2834}$ $\boxed{\text{INV}}$ $\boxed{\sin^{-1}}$

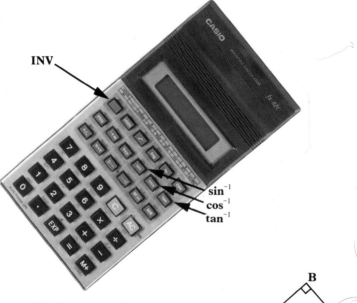

Worked Example Find the size of angle A.

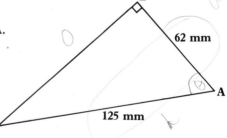

Answer The given lengths are AB and AC. For angle A, AC is the hypotenuse and AB is the adjacent side. Hence we use cos A to find angle A.

$$\cos A = \frac{62}{125}$$

$A = 60.3°$ (1 d.p.) **Keying** $\boxed{62}$ $\boxed{\div}$ $\boxed{125}$ $\boxed{=}$ $\boxed{\text{INV}}$ $\boxed{\cos^{-1}}$

EXERCISE 14:9

1. Find, to one decimal place, the size of angle P if:

   (a) sin P = 0·83   (b) cos P = 0·462   (c) tan P = 0·945   (d) tan P = 14·6

   (e) sin P = 0·345   (f) cos P = 0·8236 (g) tan P = 56   (h) cos P = 0·125

   (i) tan P = 0·82   (j) sin P = $\frac{1}{4}$ (k) tan P = $\frac{2}{5}$ (l) cos P = $\frac{2}{3}$

   (m) tan P = $\frac{14}{9}$ (n) sin P = $\frac{8}{11}$

2. Which of sin, cos, tan would you use to find θ ?

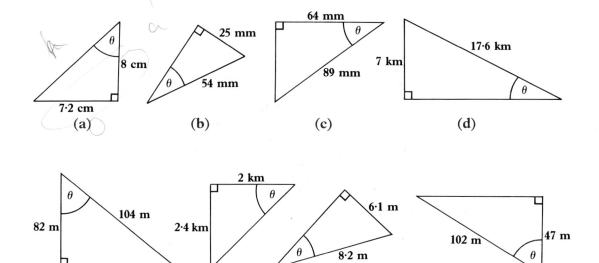

(a)   (b)   (c)   (d)

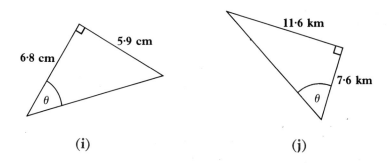

(e)   (f)   (g)   (h)

(i)   (j)

3. For the triangles drawn in **question 2**, find the size of θ. Give your answers to the nearest degree.

4.

Judy was abseiling down a building.
When she was a vertical distance of
10 m from where she began, her hips
were 1 m from the side of the building.
What angle did Judy's rope make with
the building?

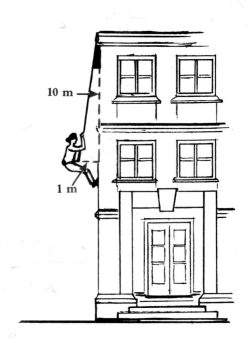

10 m

1 m

5.

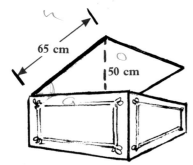

65 cm

50 cm

The play "Pandora's Box" was being produced by
Highfield School Drama Club.
The lid of the box they were using was 65 cm wide.
It was decided to prop this lid open so there was a
50 cm wide gap.
At what angle was the lid propped open?

6. Drainage pipes were being laid along
the diagonal of a rectangular field, as
shown in this diagram.
At what angle, to the shorter sides of
this field, were the pipes laid?

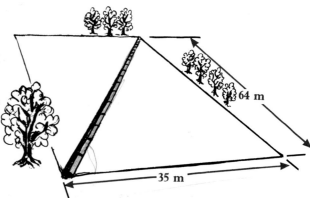

64 m

35 m

Review 1 Find, to the nearest degree, the size of α if

(a) $\cos\alpha = 0{\cdot}687$ (b) $\tan\alpha = 2{\cdot}7$ (c) $\sin\alpha = 0{\cdot}8$ (d) $\sin\alpha = \frac{2}{7}$

(e) $\tan\alpha = \frac{14}{5}$ (f) $\cos\alpha = \frac{3}{8}$.

Review 2

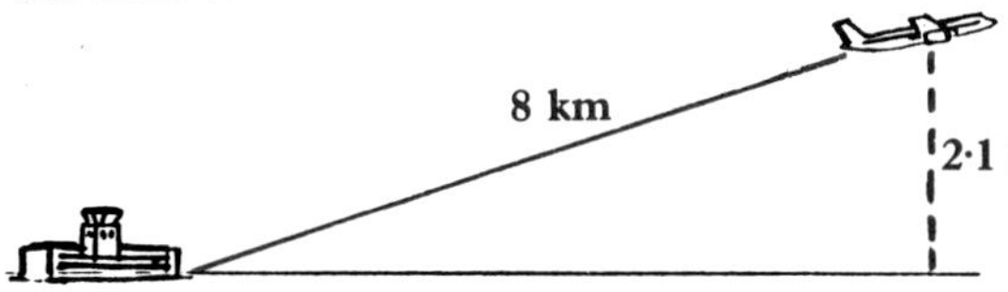

A plane, which took off from Manchester Airport, had gained an altitude of 2·1 km after it had travelled 8 km.
At what angle was this plane climbing?

APPLICATIONS to NAVIGATION

Navigation problems involve bearings.
Pythagoras' theorem as well as trigonometry is often needed to solve these.

Worked Example A ship travels due East from A to B, a distance of 74 km. It then travels due South to C. C is 47 km from B.

(a) What is the bearing of C from A?
(b) Use Pythagoras' theorem to find the distance from A to C.

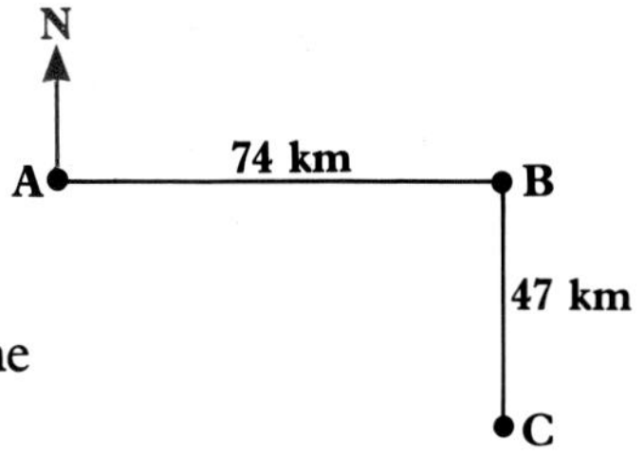

Answer (a) The required bearing is given by the angle θ. $\theta = 90° + \text{angle BAC}$.

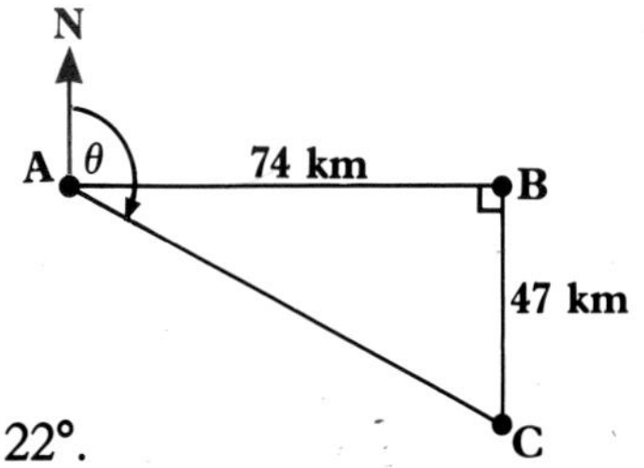

$\tan \text{BAC} = \frac{47}{74}$

angle BAC = 32° (to the nearest degree).

Keying [47] [÷] [74] [=] [$\tan^{-1}$]

Then $\theta = 122°$. The bearing of C from A is 122°.

(b) $AC^2 = BC^2 + AB^2$ (Pythagoras' theorem)

$= 47^2 + 74^2$

AC = 88 km (to the nearest kilometre)

Keying [47] [INV] [x^2] [+] [74] [INV] [x^2] [=] [$\sqrt{\ }$]

Worked Example   A yacht sails from Wicklow on a bearing of 055°. By the end of the first day the yacht has travelled 39 km.
How far East of Wicklow is the yacht at the end of this day?

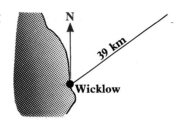

Answer   We need to find d in this diagram.

$\theta = 90° - 55°$

$\quad = 35°$

$\dfrac{d}{39} = \cos 35°$

$d = 39 \cos 35°$ (multiplying both sides by 39)

$d = 32$ km (to the nearest km)

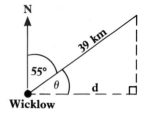

DISCUSSION EXERCISE 14:10

In both of the previous worked examples, we found a length in a right-angled triangle. We used Pythagoras' theorem to find the length in the first example and trigonometry to find the length in the second example.
Could we have used Pythagoras' theorem both times? Could we have used trigonometry both times? **Discuss.**

EXERCISE 14:11

1. B is 10 km East of A and 8 km North of C.

    (a)   Use trigonometry to find the size of angle BCA.

    (b)   What is the bearing of A from C?

    (c)   Use Pythagoras' theorem to find the distance from A to C.

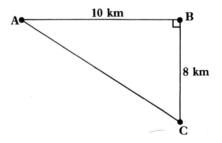

2.

A car begins its journey at R. It travels due West to Q, a distance of 17 km; then due South to P.
The bearing of R from P is 048°.

(a)   Which angle in this diagram is 48°?

(b)   What total distance did the car travel?

3. A plane flies from P to Q on a bearing of 146°.
   Q is 229 km from P.

   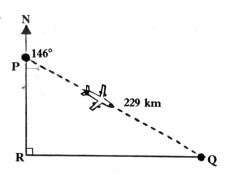

   (a) What is the size of angle RPQ?
   (b) Use trigonometry to find how far further
       East Q is than P.
   (c) Use Pythagoras' theorem to find how far
       further South Q is than P.

4.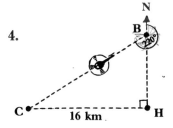

   A helicopter leaves its base (B) and flies on a bearing of
   220° to pick up an injured climber at C. It then flies the
   climber 16 km to the nearest hospital (H). The hospital is
   due South of B and due East of C, as shown in the
   diagram.

   (a) What is the size of angle CBH?
   (b) Use trigonometry to find how far the hospital is from B.
   (c) Use Pythagoras' theorem to find how far the injured climber was from the
       helicopter base.

5.

   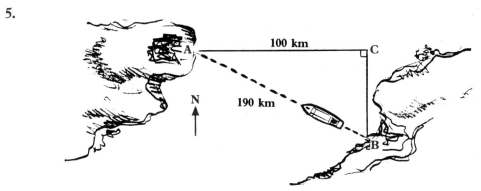

   A ship sails from B to A, a distance of 190 km. A is 100 km further West than B.
   (a) Use Pythagoras' theorem to find how far further North A is than B.
   (b) Find the size of angle ABC. Hence find the bearing on which the ship sailed.

Review   A North Sea oil pipeline runs from
             W to R.
             R is 84 km South and 48 km West of W.

   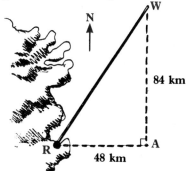

   (a) Use Pythagoras' theorem to find the
       length of this pipeline.
   (b) Use trigonometry to find the size of
       angle WRA.
   (c) What is the bearing of W from R?

APPLICATIONS to SURVEYING

In surveying, distances which are difficult to measure are calculated by measuring angles, then using trigonometry.

Worked Example   A surveyor, on top of a mountain, measures the angle below the horizontal to another mountain as 15°. It is known that the two mountains are 1800 m apart and that the lower mountain is 1050 m high.
How high is the higher mountain?

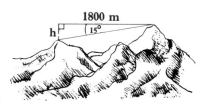

Answer   The height of the higher mountain = 1050 + h.

$$\frac{h}{1800} = \tan 15°$$

h = 1800 tan 15° (multiplying both sides by 1800)
h = 482 m (to the nearest metre)
Hence, the height of the higher mountain = 1050 + 482
= 1532 m.

When we look **up** at something, the angle between the horizontal and the direction in which we are looking is called the **angle of elevation**. In this diagram, θ is the angle of elevation.

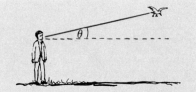

When we look **down** at something, the angle between the horizontal and the direction in which we are looking is called the **angle of depression**. In this diagram, θ is the angle of depression.

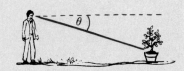

Worked Example

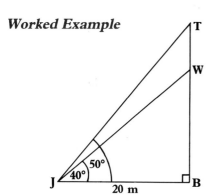

Jill found the distance of a windowsill from the top of a building as follows.

From a point 20 m from the base of the building, she measured the angle of elevation of the windowsill to be 40° and the angle of elevation of the top of the building to be 50°. She drew this sketch then used trigonometry to calculate TB and WB.

(a) What further calculation did Jill need to make?
(b) How far is the windowsill from the top of the building?

Answer (a) Once TB and WB are calculated, the only further calculation to be made is subtracting WB from TB.

(b)

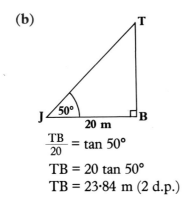

$$\frac{TB}{20} = \tan 50°$$

$$TB = 20 \tan 50°$$

$$TB = 23{\cdot}84 \text{ m (2 d.p.)}$$

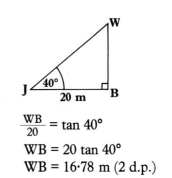

$$\frac{WB}{20} = \tan 40°$$

$$WB = 20 \tan 40°$$

$$WB = 16{\cdot}78 \text{ m (2 d.p.)}$$

$$TW = TB - WB$$
$$= 23{\cdot}84 - 16{\cdot}78$$
$$= 7{\cdot}06 \text{ m}$$

Hence, to the nearest metre, the windowsill is 7 m from the top of the building.

EXERCISE 14:12

1. Anita used the following method to find the width of a street.
   She walked along the street until she found two houses (P and Q) that were directly opposite each other. She walked a further 20 m to R, then measured the angle PRQ as 37°. From these measurements she calculated w, the width of the street. What answer should Anita get?

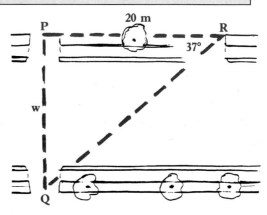

2.

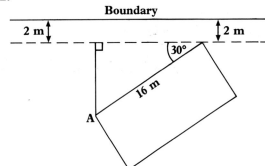

A surveyor has been asked to set out the four corners of a rectangular house at 30° to the front boundary. The surveyor starts by marking a line 2 metres from the boundary. One corner of the house is to be on this line, as shown in the diagram.
How far from the boundary is the corner of the house marked as A?

3. At a distance of 80 m from a church tower, Donald measured the angle of elevation of the top of the tower as 24°.

How high is this church tower?

24°

80 m

4.

28°

25 m

From the top of a 25 m high cliff, the angle of depression of a canoe is 28°.
How far is this canoe from the foot of the cliff?

5. At the edge of a beach, which is 8 m wide, there is a 6 m high wall. From the top of this wall, Simon measures the angle of depression of a swimmer as 16°.
How far out to sea is the swimmer?

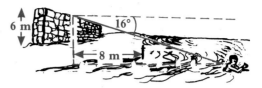

6.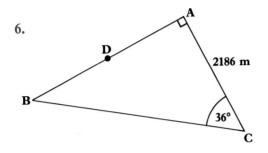

There is a trig. station at each of A, B and C. The distance AC = 2186 m.
A surveyor measures the angle ACB to be 36° and the angle CAB to be 90°.

   (a)   Use trigonometry to find how far B is from C.
   (b)   Use Pythagoras' theorem to find how far A is from B.
   (c)   D is a point halfway between A and B.
        The surveyor measures the angle between AC and CD. What answer should the surveyor get?

7.

A flagpole is on the top of a building.
From the point D, 40 m from the base of the building, Joanne measures the angles of elevation of the top, A, and the bottom, B, of the flagpole. Her measurements are shown on the diagram.

   (a)   Find the length AC.
   (b)   Find the length BC. Hence find the height of the flagpole.

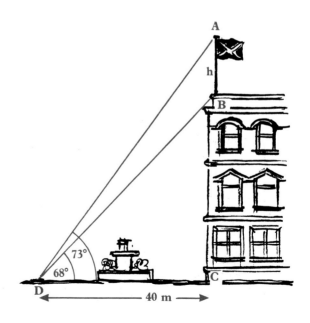

8.

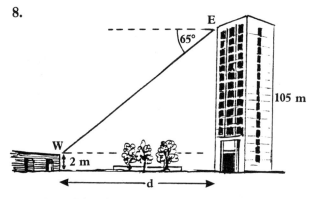

From the top of a 105 m high building Ellen measures the angle of depression of the top of a 2 m high wall as 65°.

Ellen then calculates the distance of the wall from the building.

(a) List the steps Ellen needs to take.
(b) What answer should Ellen get?

Review 1 A rock ledge overhangs a path. Dianne stood directly under the end of this ledge, then walked back towards the rock face for 2 m. At this point she measured the angle of elevation of the end of the ledge as 74°.

What is the height of the end of the ledge above the path?

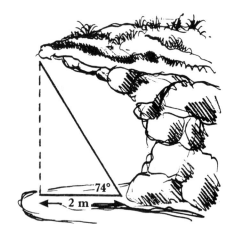

Review 2

Gareth stood 5 m from the foot of a tree. He measured the angle of elevation of the top of the tree as 59° and the angle of depression of the foot of the tree as 20°.

(a) What is the length of GH?
(b) Use trigonometry to find TH.
(c) What other calculations need to be made to find the height of the tree?
(d) What is the height of the tree?

Review 3 Minami finds the distance between two houseboats, P and R, on the other side of the river as follows.

She begins at A, opposite houseboat P. From A she walks to B, a distance of 54 m. She measures the angle ABP as 42° and angle CBR as 47°. From these measurements she is able to find the distance PR, between the two houseboats.

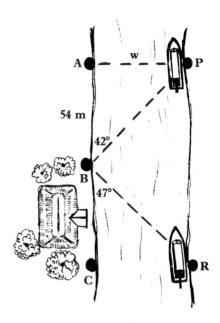

(a) Calculate w, the width of the river, using the triangle APB.

(b) Using triangle CBR, calculate the distance BC. Hence find the distance between the houseboats.

PRACTICAL EXERCISE 14:3

Use trigonometry to find the height of an object or the distance of an object from an observation point.

You could base your work on one of the examples given in the previous exercise.

Use a trundle wheel or long measuring tape to measure distances. Use a theodolite or clinometer to measure angles.

Évariste Galois

Évariste Galois was born in 1811 at a village near Paris and died in 1832 at Paris.

Although his maths. writing consisted of only 60 pages, he is considered one of the greatest mathematicians of all times. He was certainly the youngest mathematician (he was 20 when he died) to make important discoveries.

Évariste's parents were well educated but had no particular talent for mathematics. His father was the mayor of the village in which the family lived. His mother was a strong-willed, unconventional woman who taught Évariste at home until he was 12.

At school, Évariste was considered to be eccentric, both by his teachers and his fellow students. He was teased by the students who regarded him with fear and anger. Évariste was so inarticulate that he was unable to make his teachers understand him. His classwork was quite poor; so poor that in one year he was demoted. During this year he became fascinated with a book on Geometry and read and understood the contents in a very short time. This book was written for mathematicians, not for school pupils.

By 16, Évariste knew he was a mathematical genius; a view not supported by his teachers. He did most of his mathematics in his head and refused to write down what he thought were obvious, trivial details. He frequently lost his temper with his teachers when they insisted that he show all his working. To Évariste, stupidity was an "unpardonable sin" — he regarded both his teachers and fellow students as stupid. It is claimed that one of his teachers said *"The mathematical madness dominates this boy. I think his parents had better let him take only mathematics. He is wasting his time here, and all he does is to torment his teachers and get into trouble"*.

Before he was 17, Évariste attempted to enter the École Polytechnique, famous for its mathematics teaching. He failed the entrance examination; the examiners did not recognise his ability because he showed so little working. The examiners suggested he prepare himself better and apply again. He did apply again but again he failed. It is claimed that during this second examination he was asked to show his working on the blackboard; he lost his temper and threw the blackboard duster at the examiner, hitting him on the head.

Just before his second attempt to enter the École Polytechnique, Évariste wrote up his maths. discoveries which he asked a famous mathematician to present at a meeting of the Académie des Sciences. The mathematician forgot to do this. To make matters worse, he also lost the article Évariste had written. Évariste became very bitter and disillusioned.

At 18, Évariste entered the École Normale where he continued his research and prepared for a career of teaching.

In 1830, he entered the Académie des Sciences mathematics competition. The secretary took Évariste's paper home to read; the secretary died and the paper was lost! It seemed that Évariste was never going to get any of his work recognised or published.

Évariste became involved in politics and was a most outspoken supporter of the 1830 revolution. Because of this, he was expelled from the École Normale. Shortly after this he was jailed for proposing a toast, at a republican meeting, that was interpreted as a threat to King Louis-Philippe. Soon after his release from jail, he was shot in a duel and left to die. Some say the duel was the result of a quarrel over a woman, others say he was challenged by those who disagreed with his political views. Évariste expected to be killed and spent the night before writing down his mathematical discoveries. These were published in 1846.

Évariste Galois is famous for developing group theory, an important branch of algebra. This theory is also important in the study of the behaviour of electrons and molecules.

VECTOR and SCALAR QUANTITIES

Quantities which have both size and direction are called **vector quantities.**
Quantities which have just size are called **scalar quantities.**

DISCUSSION EXERCISE 15:1

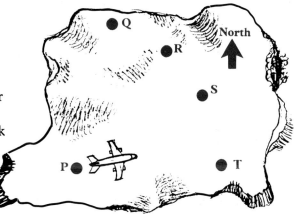

- An aeroplane leaves P and flies for
  400 km.
  Can you tell from this information
  whether the aeroplane flies to Q or R or
  S or T or to some other place? What
  further information do you need? Think
  of many different ways in which this
  further information could be given.
  Discuss.

Scale 1 cm represents 100 km

Gavin kicks a football in the direction of the goal.
Can you tell from this information whether or not the ball is
likely to go into the goal? **Discuss.**

- Which of the quantities mentioned in the following statements are vector quantities and
  which are scalar quantities? **Discuss.**
     The journey took 6 hours.
     We travelled for 250 km.
     The coach travelled West.
     The ship travelled for 70 km on a bearing of 157°.
     The plane flew North at an average speed of 250 km/h.
     There was a current of 5 km/h in the river.

Write some sentences in which the quantity mentioned is a vector quantity and some in
which the quantity is a scalar quantity. **Discuss** your sentences.

VECTOR NOTATION

Vector quantities may be represented by a line.
The length of the line represents the size of the vector. An arrow is placed on the line to show the direction of the vector.

For instance, the vector **a** represents a velocity of 5 km/h in a North-East direction.

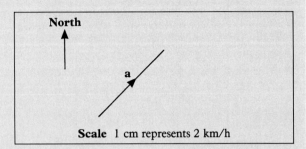

Vectors are sometimes labelled with a single lower-case letter such as a. In hand-written material we place a wavy line underneath the letter. That is, $\underset{\sim}{a}$, $\underset{\sim}{b}$, $\underset{\sim}{d}$, $\underset{\sim}{m}$ etc. are used to label vectors. In typed material, the lower-case letters are usually written in bold type-face and the wavy line is omitted. That is, **a**, **b**, **d**, **m** etc. are used to label vectors.

Vectors are sometimes labelled with two upper-case letters such as AB. A is the point where the vector begins; B is the point where the vector ends. We place an arrow over the AB to indicate the vector. That is,

$\overrightarrow{AB}$ represents the vector which begins at A and finishes at B.

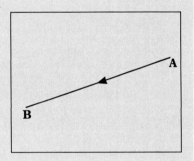

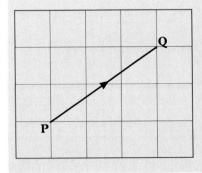

Vectors drawn on a grid can be described by giving the position of the end point in relation to the start point. Since Q is 3 squares in the x-direction and 2 squares in the y-direction from P, the vector $\overrightarrow{PQ}$ can be described by $\overrightarrow{PQ} = \begin{pmatrix} 3 \\ 2 \end{pmatrix}$. When a vector is written like this it is said to be written as a **column vector**.

Note We cannot write $\overrightarrow{PQ} = (3, 2)$ since (3, 2) refers to a point.

Worked Example Draw the vectors (a) $\overrightarrow{EF} = \begin{pmatrix} 4 \\ -1 \end{pmatrix}$ (b) $\mathbf{m} = \begin{pmatrix} -3 \\ 4 \end{pmatrix}$

Answer (a) These diagrams show the steps to take.

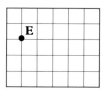

Step 1 Start at any point E.

Step 1   Step 2   Step 3

Step 2 From E, move 4 in the x-direction, then –1 in the y-direction to find the point F.

Step 3 Join E and F with a line. Place an arrow on this line in the direction from E to F.

(b) Start at any point, move –3 in the x-direction then 4 in the y-direction to find the end of the vector.

Join the start and end points with a line. Place an arrow on the line in the direction from the start point to the end point.

Label the vector as **m**.

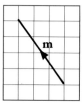

Worked Example Write these vectors in column form.

Answer $\overrightarrow{AB} = \begin{pmatrix} -4 \\ -1 \end{pmatrix}$ $\mathbf{p} = \begin{pmatrix} 2 \\ 4 \end{pmatrix}$ $\overrightarrow{ML} = \begin{pmatrix} 0 \\ 4 \end{pmatrix}$

$\mathbf{q} = \begin{pmatrix} 2 \\ -5 \end{pmatrix}$ $\mathbf{b} = \begin{pmatrix} -4 \\ 0 \end{pmatrix}$

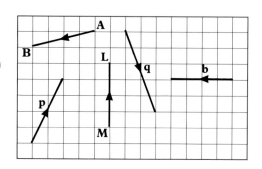

EXERCISE 15:2

1. Draw these vectors.

$\overrightarrow{AB} = \begin{pmatrix} 2 \\ 1 \end{pmatrix}$ $\overrightarrow{CD} = \begin{pmatrix} 3 \\ 2 \end{pmatrix}$ $\overrightarrow{EF} = \begin{pmatrix} 1 \\ 3 \end{pmatrix}$ $\overrightarrow{GH} = \begin{pmatrix} 1 \\ 2 \end{pmatrix}$ $\overrightarrow{KL} = \begin{pmatrix} -2 \\ 3 \end{pmatrix}$

$\overrightarrow{MN} = \begin{pmatrix} 3 \\ -2 \end{pmatrix}$ $\overrightarrow{PQ} = \begin{pmatrix} -2 \\ -3 \end{pmatrix}$ $\overrightarrow{RS} = \begin{pmatrix} -1 \\ -2 \end{pmatrix}$ $\mathbf{a} = \begin{pmatrix} 3 \\ 1 \end{pmatrix}$ $\mathbf{b} = \begin{pmatrix} -3 \\ -1 \end{pmatrix}$

$\mathbf{c} = \begin{pmatrix} 1 \\ -3 \end{pmatrix}$ $\mathbf{d} = \begin{pmatrix} 2 \\ -3 \end{pmatrix}$ $\mathbf{p} = \begin{pmatrix} -3 \\ 2 \end{pmatrix}$ $\mathbf{o} = \begin{pmatrix} -3 \\ -2 \end{pmatrix}$ $\mathbf{u} = \begin{pmatrix} 3 \\ 3 \end{pmatrix}$

$\mathbf{v} = \begin{pmatrix} -2 \\ -2 \end{pmatrix}$ $\mathbf{e} = \begin{pmatrix} 2 \\ 0 \end{pmatrix}$ $\mathbf{s} = \begin{pmatrix} 0 \\ 2 \end{pmatrix}$ $\mathbf{f} = \begin{pmatrix} -3 \\ 0 \end{pmatrix}$ $\mathbf{r} = \begin{pmatrix} 0 \\ -3 \end{pmatrix}$

2. Write these vectors as column vectors.

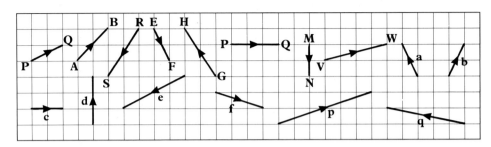

3.

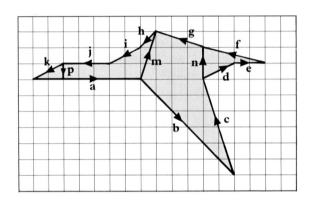

(a) Write each of the vectors, shown on this diagram, as a column vector.

(b) Draw the following vectors, one after the other. (Begin at the centre of an 8 × 8 grid.) What picture do you get?

$$\binom{-1}{0}, \binom{0}{-1}, \binom{-1}{-1}, \binom{3}{0}, \binom{1}{1}, \binom{0}{1}, \binom{-1}{-1}, \binom{0}{1}, \binom{-1}{2}, \binom{-1}{0}$$

$$\binom{-1}{1}, \binom{1}{0}, \binom{2}{1}, \binom{-2}{0}, \binom{-2}{-2}, \binom{0}{-1}, \binom{1}{0}, \binom{0}{-2}, \binom{-1}{-1}, \binom{1}{0}$$

4. P shows the starting position of a car on a racing track. The car moves around this track, from P to A to B to C ... to L, as described by the following vectors.

P to A: $\binom{2}{1}$ A to B: $\binom{3}{-1}$ B to C: $\binom{4}{-4}$ C to D: $\binom{3}{-2}$

D to E: $\binom{-2}{-1}$ E to F: $\binom{-1}{-1}$ F to G: $\binom{-7}{0}$ G to H: $\binom{-2}{-1}$

H to I: $\binom{-3}{2}$ I to J: $\binom{-1}{1}$ J to K: $\binom{1}{3}$ K to L: $\binom{3}{3}$

(a) How many times did the car go off the track?

(b) Describe, using vectors, a possible route around the track in which the car does not go off the track at any stage.

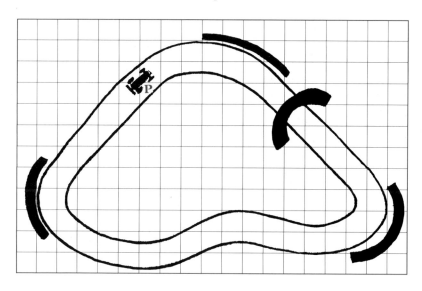

5. A journey from P to Q can be described by the vector $\begin{pmatrix} -4 \\ 2 \end{pmatrix}$.

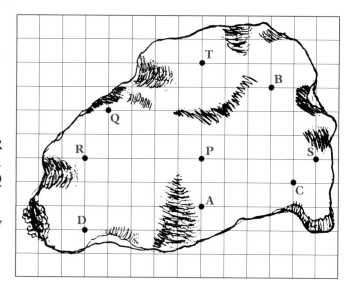

(i) What vector describes the following journeys?

(a) P to R   (b) P to S
(c) B to S   (d) D to R
(e) A to C   (f) T to A
(g) S to P   (h) A to Q
(i) Q to A

(ii) A journey is described by the vector $\begin{pmatrix} -3 \\ 1 \end{pmatrix}$. What journey is this?

6. Draw a pair of axes. Number both the x and y-axes from –5 to 5. Plot points to answer this question.

The coordinates of two points, P and Q are given. Write the vector $\overrightarrow{PQ}$ as a column vector.

(a) P(3, 1) Q(4, 3)   (b) P(–2, 0) Q(4, 1)   (c) P(1, 4) Q(–2, 4)
(d) P(–3, 0) Q(–1, –3)   (e) P(2, 4) Q(0, 0)

Review

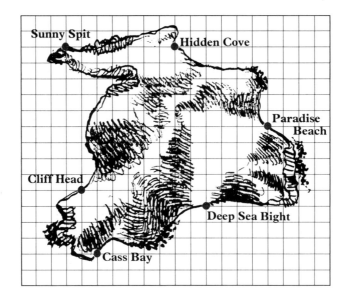

(i) Groups of people travelled by boat to this island. Each group was dropped off at a different place. These groups then made the journeys described below.
Which group, or groups, finished their journeys where they began?

Ann's group   Began at Hidden Cove.
From here their journey is described by these vectors:

$\begin{pmatrix} 0 \\ -4 \end{pmatrix}$ then $\begin{pmatrix} 6 \\ -1 \end{pmatrix}$ then $\begin{pmatrix} -4 \\ -5 \end{pmatrix}$ then $\begin{pmatrix} -5 \\ 0 \end{pmatrix}$ then $\begin{pmatrix} 2 \\ 6 \end{pmatrix}$
then $\begin{pmatrix} -5 \\ -5 \end{pmatrix}$.

Simon's group   Began at Cliff Head.
From here their journey is described by these vectors:

$\begin{pmatrix} 2 \\ -2 \end{pmatrix}$ then $\begin{pmatrix} 3 \\ 4 \end{pmatrix}$ then $\begin{pmatrix} -2 \\ 4 \end{pmatrix}$ then $\begin{pmatrix} 3 \\ 2 \end{pmatrix}$ then $\begin{pmatrix} 6 \\ -4 \end{pmatrix}$
then $\begin{pmatrix} -4 \\ -5 \end{pmatrix}$ then $\begin{pmatrix} -8 \\ 1 \end{pmatrix}$.

Bik's group   Began at Paradise Beach.
From here their journey is described by these vectors:

$\begin{pmatrix} -4 \\ -5 \end{pmatrix}$ then $\begin{pmatrix} -8 \\ 1 \end{pmatrix}$ then $\begin{pmatrix} 6 \\ 9 \end{pmatrix}$ then $\begin{pmatrix} -1 \\ -2 \end{pmatrix}$ then $\begin{pmatrix} 7 \\ -3 \end{pmatrix}$.

(ii) Write one column vector to describe each of these journeys.
     (a) From Cliff Head to Deep Sea Bight.
     (b) From Cass Bay to Hidden Cove.
     (c) From Paradise Beach to Deep Sea Bight.
     (d) From Hidden Cove to Paradise Beach.
     (e) From Paradise Beach to Hidden Cove.

RELATIONSHIPS BETWEEN VECTORS

DISCUSSION EXERCISE 15:3

- P is the point (2, 3). Q is the point (5, 1).

  The vector $\overrightarrow{PQ} = \begin{pmatrix} 3 \\ -2 \end{pmatrix}$.

  Write the vector $\overrightarrow{AB}$ as a column vector. What do you notice about the column vectors for $\overrightarrow{PQ}$ and $\overrightarrow{AB}$? What do you notice about the vectors $\overrightarrow{PQ}$ and $\overrightarrow{AB}$ on the diagram? **Discuss.**

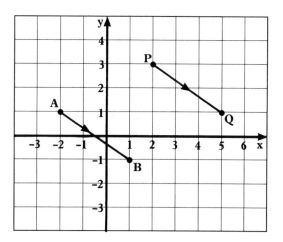

- In the above diagram the vector $\overrightarrow{PQ} = \begin{pmatrix} 3 \\ -2 \end{pmatrix}$.

  Write the vector $\overrightarrow{QP}$ as a column vector. What do you notice?

  What if the points P and Q were P(0, 1), Q(4, 3) or P(-1, 5), Q(-2, 2)? **Discuss.**

- $\mathbf{a} = \begin{pmatrix} 4 \\ 2 \end{pmatrix}$, $\mathbf{b} = \begin{pmatrix} 8 \\ 4 \end{pmatrix}$. What do you notice about **a** and **b** on the diagram?

  $\mathbf{a} = \begin{pmatrix} 4 \\ 2 \end{pmatrix}$, $\mathbf{c} = \begin{pmatrix} 2 \\ 1 \end{pmatrix}$. What do you notice about **a** and **c** on the diagram?

  Could we write **b** as 2**a**? Could we write **c** as $\frac{1}{2}$**a**? What would the vector 3**a** look like? What would the vector -2**a** look like? **Discuss.**

  As part of your discussion, make and test a statement which begins "If a vector **a** is multiplied by a number then ...".

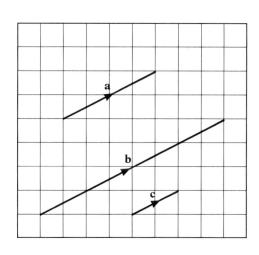

Vectors are equal if they have the same length and are in the same direction.
The vectors shown on this diagram are all equal.

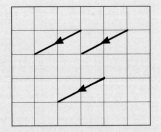

The vector **−a** has the same length as **a** but is in the opposite direction.
The vectors **a** and **−a** are shown on this diagram.

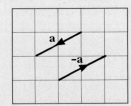

The vector **2a** is in the same direction as **a** but twice as long as **a**.
The vector **3a** is in the same direction as **a** but three times as long as **a**.
The vector $\frac{1}{2}$**a** is in the same direction as **a** but half the length of **a**.

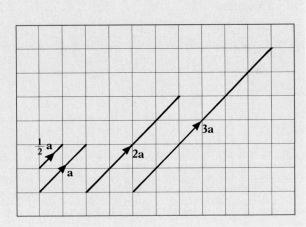

EXERCISE 15:4

1.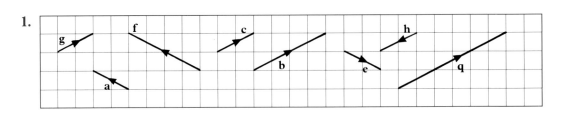

Name the vector equal to (a) **g**   (b) **−c**   (c) **2a**   (d) **2g**   (e) **3c**

(f) **−a**   (g) **−2h**   (h) $\frac{1}{2}$**f**   (i) $-\frac{1}{3}$**q**

2. Draw up a 20 × 10 grid, as
   shown here.
   Continue the diagram using
   each of the following vectors
   at least once:
   −a, −b, −c, −d, 2a, 3a,

   4c, $\frac{1}{2}$**d, a, b, c, d.**

   Make your diagram into an
   interesting pattern.

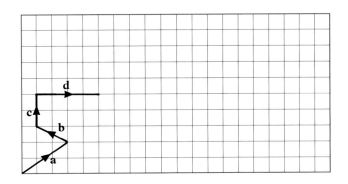

3. $\mathbf{p} = \begin{pmatrix} -3 \\ 3 \end{pmatrix}$, $\mathbf{q} = \begin{pmatrix} -4 \\ -1 \end{pmatrix}$, $\mathbf{r} = \begin{pmatrix} 6 \\ 2 \end{pmatrix}$

   Draw the vectors $2\mathbf{p}$, $-\mathbf{p}$, $3\mathbf{q}$, $\frac{1}{2}\mathbf{r}$, $-\frac{1}{3}\mathbf{p}$.

4. $\overrightarrow{PQ} = \begin{pmatrix} 5 \\ 2 \end{pmatrix}$ as shown on the diagram.

   (a) Write the vector $\overrightarrow{QP}$ as a column vecto

   (b) Copy and complete: $\overrightarrow{QP} = \dots \overrightarrow{PQ}$.

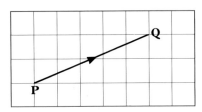

5.

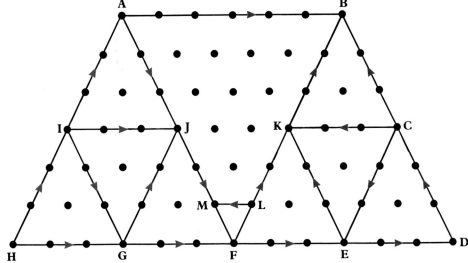

Copy and complete the following.

   (a) $\overrightarrow{CK} = \dots \overrightarrow{KC}$ (b) $\overrightarrow{AB} = \dots \overrightarrow{ED}$ (c) $\overrightarrow{AF} = \dots \overrightarrow{IG}$ (d) $\overrightarrow{AB} = \dots \overrightarrow{CK}$

   (e) $\overrightarrow{LM} = \dots \overrightarrow{CK}$ (f) $\overrightarrow{DC} = \dots \overrightarrow{AF}$ (g) $\overrightarrow{LM} = \dots \overrightarrow{ED}$

Review 1

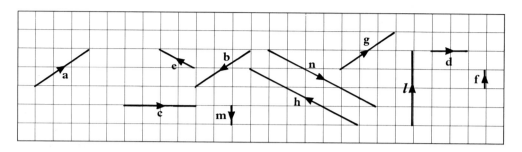

Name a vector equal to   (a) **a**   (b) **−a**   (c) **2d**   (d) $\frac{1}{2}$**c**   (e) **3e**

                               (f) $\frac{1}{4}$**l**   (g) **−m**   (h) **−3e**

Review 2 $\mathbf{a} = \begin{pmatrix} 1 \\ 2 \end{pmatrix}$ $\mathbf{m} = \begin{pmatrix} 3 \\ -2 \end{pmatrix}$ $\mathbf{p} = \begin{pmatrix} -8 \\ 4 \end{pmatrix}$

         Draw the vectors   **2m**,   **−m**, $\frac{1}{4}$**p**,   **3a**, $-\frac{1}{2}$**p**.

VECTORS and TRANSLATION

Translations can be described using vectors.

For instance, consider the translation of the red arrow
onto the grey arrow.
This translation could be described as "5 squares in the
x-direction and 1 square in the negative y-direction"

or as $\begin{pmatrix} 5 \\ -1 \end{pmatrix}$.

The translation described by the vector $\begin{pmatrix} 5 \\ -1 \end{pmatrix}$ moves,

or maps, the red arrow onto the grey arrow.

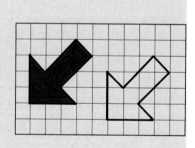

Worked Example   The point (2, 3) is translated to the point (−2, 2). What is the vector
that describes this translation?

Answer   Plot the points (2, 3) and (−2, 2) as shown.
To move from (2, 3) to (−2, 2) we move −4 in the
x-direction and −1 in the y-direction. Hence the

vector of the translation is $\begin{pmatrix} -4 \\ -1 \end{pmatrix}$.

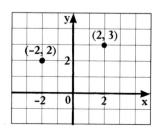

Worked Example (a) Draw the triangle ABC that has vertices A(2, 0), B(5, 3), C(7, 1).

(b) Draw the image triangle A'B'C' after a translation given by the vector $\left(\begin{smallmatrix} -3 \\ 2 \end{smallmatrix}\right)$.

(c) Write down the coordinates of A', B' and C'.

(d) What is the vector of the translation that would map triangle A'B'C' onto triangle ABC?

Answer (a) The triangle ABC is shown drawn here.

(b) Each of the vertices A, B and C is translated –3 in the x-direction and 2 in the y-direction to get the vertices A', B' and C' of the image triangle. The image triangle is then drawn.

(c) A'(–1, 2), B'(2, 5), C'(4, 3).

(d) To map A' onto A we move 3 in the x-direction and –2 in the y-direction. Hence the vector of this translation is $\left(\begin{smallmatrix} 3 \\ -2 \end{smallmatrix}\right)$.

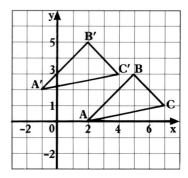

EXERCISE 15:5

1.

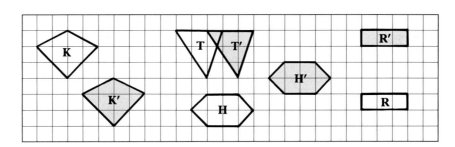

What is the vector for the following translations?

(a) K onto K' (b) T onto T' (c) H to H' (d) R to R'
(e) H' to H (f) R' onto R (g) T' onto T (h) K' to K

2.

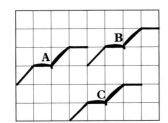

What vector maps (a) B onto C
(b) C onto A
(c) B onto A?

3. Find the vector which describes these translations.
   (a) (2, 3) maps onto (–1, 6)
   (b) (3, –1) maps onto (3, 6)
   (c) (1, 2) maps onto (0, –3)
   (d) (–1, 0) maps onto (4, 0)
   (e) (–1, –3) maps onto (–3, –1)

4. Each point A is translated by the vector **p**. Write down the coordinates of A′, the image of A.
   (a) A(–1, 5) $\mathbf{p} = \begin{pmatrix} 2 \\ -1 \end{pmatrix}$ (b) A(3, –1) $\mathbf{p} = \begin{pmatrix} -3 \\ 4 \end{pmatrix}$ (c) A(2, 0) $\mathbf{p} = \begin{pmatrix} -3 \\ -5 \end{pmatrix}$

5. This arrow, A, is translated to A′. The vector of the translation is $\begin{pmatrix} -5 \\ 3 \end{pmatrix}$.

   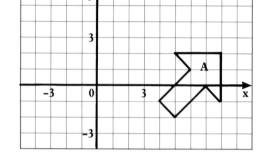

   (a) Copy this diagram.
       Draw A′ on your diagram.
   (b) The arrow A′ is now translated to A″. The vector of this translation is $\begin{pmatrix} 4 \\ -1 \end{pmatrix}$. Draw A″ on your diagram.
   (c) Write down the vector that would translate A directly onto A″.
   (d) A is translated so that the tip of the arrow is at the point (0, 0). What is the vector of this translation?

6. Draw up a set of axes with both the x and y-values from –4 to 6.
   (a) Draw the rectangle with vertices at A(3, 1), B(6, –2), C(4, –4), D(1, –1).
   (b) The rectangle is translated by the vector $\begin{pmatrix} -2 \\ 3 \end{pmatrix}$. Draw the image rectangle.
   (c) Write down the coordinates of A′, B′, C′ and D′.
   (d) What is the vector of the translation which would map A′B′C′D′ onto ABCD?

Review 1   A translation maps the point (–1, 2) onto the point (–2, 5).
   Which of the following is the vector of this translation?

   $\begin{pmatrix} 3 \\ 1 \end{pmatrix}$ $\begin{pmatrix} -3 \\ -1 \end{pmatrix}$ $\begin{pmatrix} 1 \\ -3 \end{pmatrix}$ $\begin{pmatrix} -1 \\ 3 \end{pmatrix}$ $\begin{pmatrix} -1 \\ -3 \end{pmatrix}$ $\begin{pmatrix} 1 \\ 3 \end{pmatrix}$

Review 2   (a) P is translated to Q. What is the vector of this translation?
   (b) Q is translated to R. What is the vector of this translation?
   (c) What vector translates P directly to R?

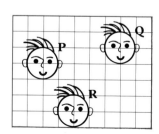

Review 3

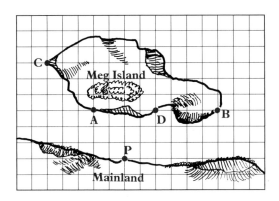

A picnic party is translated from the mainland to Meg Island.

(i) If the boat leaves from P, find the vector of translation if it lands at
   (a) A (b) C (c) D (d) B.

(ii) On the return journey the picnic party lands at P. Where did they leave from if the vector of the translation is $\begin{pmatrix} 2 \\ -3 \end{pmatrix}$?

Review 4 A(0, –2) , B(3, 0) , C(1, 4)

   (a) Draw the triangle ABC.

   (b) The triangle ABC is translated to triangle A′B′C′. If the vector describing this translation is $\begin{pmatrix} -4 \\ 3 \end{pmatrix}$ write down the coordinates of A′, B′ and C′.

   (c) What vector will translate triangle A′B′C′ to triangle ABC?

PUZZLE 15:6

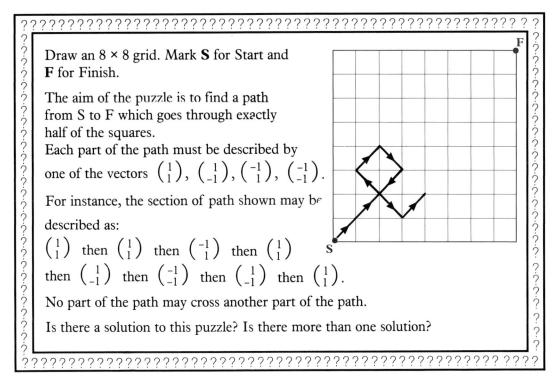

Draw an 8 × 8 grid. Mark **S** for Start and **F** for Finish.

The aim of the puzzle is to find a path from S to F which goes through exactly half of the squares.

Each part of the path must be described by one of the vectors $\begin{pmatrix} 1 \\ 1 \end{pmatrix}$, $\begin{pmatrix} 1 \\ -1 \end{pmatrix}$, $\begin{pmatrix} -1 \\ 1 \end{pmatrix}$, $\begin{pmatrix} -1 \\ -1 \end{pmatrix}$.

For instance, the section of path shown may be described as:

$\begin{pmatrix} 1 \\ 1 \end{pmatrix}$ then $\begin{pmatrix} 1 \\ 1 \end{pmatrix}$ then $\begin{pmatrix} -1 \\ 1 \end{pmatrix}$ then $\begin{pmatrix} 1 \\ 1 \end{pmatrix}$ then $\begin{pmatrix} 1 \\ -1 \end{pmatrix}$ then $\begin{pmatrix} -1 \\ -1 \end{pmatrix}$ then $\begin{pmatrix} 1 \\ -1 \end{pmatrix}$ then $\begin{pmatrix} 1 \\ 1 \end{pmatrix}$.

No part of the path may cross another part of the path.

Is there a solution to this puzzle? Is there more than one solution?

GAME 15:7

VECTOR CAPTURE: a game for 2 players

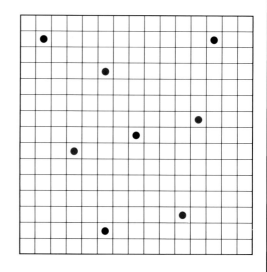

Equipment A 15 × 15 grid of 1cm squares.
Two dice; one white, the other red.
Eight counters; 4 of one colour for one player, 4 of another colour for the other player.

The Play Both players place all their counters on the grid.
The players take it in turn to throw the dice together.
The number on the red die gives a translation in the x-direction (either positive or negative); the number on the white die gives a translation in the y-direction (either positive or negative).
For instance, at the throw of the dice shown, one of the translations $\begin{pmatrix} 3 \\ 4 \end{pmatrix}$, $\begin{pmatrix} 3 \\ -4 \end{pmatrix}$, $\begin{pmatrix} -3 \\ 4 \end{pmatrix}$ $\begin{pmatrix} -3 \\ -4 \end{pmatrix}$ may be chosen. The player then moves one of his or her counters according to one of these vectors. If the counter is moved onto a square occupied by an opponent's counter then the opponent's counter is removed.

Aim of the Game The aim of the game is to capture all the opponent's counters.

Variations A larger grid may be used.
Each player may begin with more counters.

PRACTICAL EXERCISE 15:8

Make up a board game which involves vectors.

You could base your game on **Game 15:7** or on **question 4** in **Exercise 15:2** or on **Puzzle 15:6** or you could design quite a different sort of game.

You may like to base the design of your board on the board shown below.

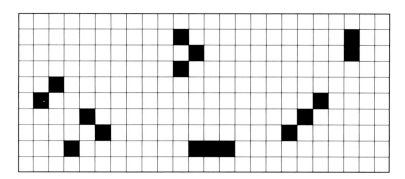

1.

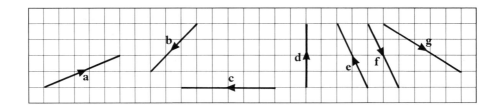

    (a)   Write these vectors as column vectors.
    (b)   What is the relationship between vectors **e** and **f**?

2. (i) Find, to two decimal places, the values
       of (a) $\sin R$
           (b) $\tan Q$
           (c) $\cos Q$

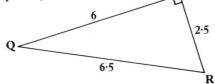

  (ii) Use the calculator to find the size of the angle θ (to the nearest tenth of a degree) if
      (a) $\cos \theta = 0\cdot26$
      (b) $\tan \theta = 5$
      (c) $\sin \theta = \frac{2}{5}$

3.

Are any of these diagrams similar?
If so, which ones?

4.

Copy and complete: (a) $\overrightarrow{CB} = \overrightarrow{D...}$

                    (b) $\overrightarrow{CF} = ... \overrightarrow{DE}$

                    (c) $\overrightarrow{EF} = ... \overrightarrow{DA}$

                    (d) $\overrightarrow{AF} = ... \overrightarrow{CD}$

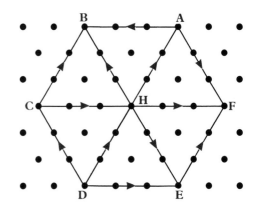

5. (a)

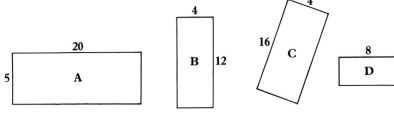

Not Drawn to Scale

One of the rectangles is not similar to the other three. Which one is not similar?

(b)

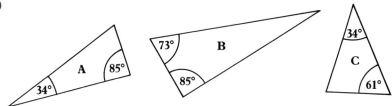

Not Drawn to Scale

Two of these triangles are similar. Which ones are these?

6. A ladder makes an angle of 70° with the ground. The foot of the ladder is 1·2 m from the wall. How long is this ladder?

7. Marie used the formula $A = \frac{1}{3}\pi r^2 h$ for the surface area of a cone of radius r and height h.
Use dimensions to explain why this formula cannot be correct.

285

8.

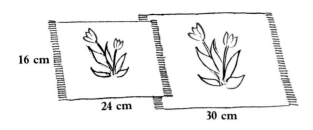

Hilary is making rectangular tablemats in two sizes. The small size measures 24 cm by 16 cm. The large size is 30 cm long.
If Hilary's tablemats are similar shapes, find the width of a large mat.

9. What is the vector of the translation which
maps   (a)   Q onto P
       (b)   P onto R
       (c)   Q onto R?

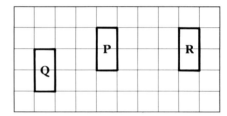

10.

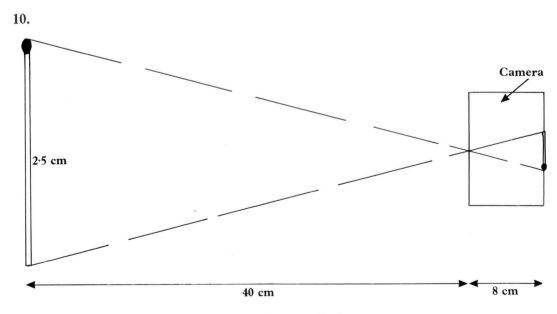

Not Drawn to Scale

This diagram represents a match and its image on the screen of a pinhole camera. The match, which is 2·5 cm tall, is placed 40 cm from the pinhole. If the pinhole is 8 cm from the screen, how high is the image of the match?

11.

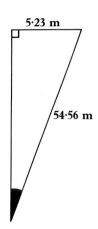

5·23 m

54·56 m

It is believed that the Leaning Tower of Pisa will collapse once its top is more than 5·23 metres from the vertical. The Tower is 54·56 metres tall.

Find the greatest angle the Tower can make with the vertical.

12.

61	62	63	64	65	66	67	68	69	70
60	59	58	57	56	55	54	53	52	51
41	42	43	44	45	46	47	48	49	50
40	39	38	37	36	35	34	33	32	31
21	22	23	24	25	26	27	28	29	30
20	19	18	17	16	15	14	13	12	11
1	2	3	4	5	6	7	8	9	10

This diagram represents a game of "snakes and ladders". If a player goes up the ladder from square 16 the movement could be described by the vector $\begin{pmatrix} -2 \\ 3 \end{pmatrix}$.

What vectors describe the following movements?   **(a)**   Up the ladder from square 14.

                                                    (b)   Up the ladder from square 45.

                                                    (c)   Down the snake from square 58.

13. Ahmed stands at A, directly under the end of a crane. From A, he walks 10 m to B. At B, he measures the angle of elevation of the end of the crane as 73°.

How high is the end of the crane?

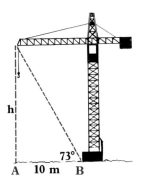

h

73°

A   10 m   B

14. The point A(2, 5) is translated to the point A′(4, 1).

Which of the following vectors describes this translation?

     A. $\begin{pmatrix} 2 \\ 4 \end{pmatrix}$ **B.** $\begin{pmatrix} 4 \\ 2 \end{pmatrix}$ **C.** $\begin{pmatrix} -4 \\ 2 \end{pmatrix}$ **D.** $\begin{pmatrix} 2 \\ -4 \end{pmatrix}$ **E.** $\begin{pmatrix} -2 \\ -4 \end{pmatrix}$

15. Anne was making a scale drawing of a school building.
    The first thing Anne did was to find the actual height of this building. At a distance of
    20 metres from the building, Anne's friend held a 1 metre ruler upright. When Anne
    lay on the ground 3·42 metres from this ruler she could just see the top of the
    building.
    Anne then drew the following sketch and used similar shapes to calculate the height of
    the building.
    What answer should she get?

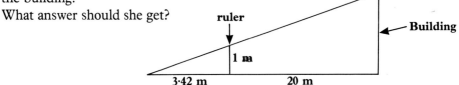

16.

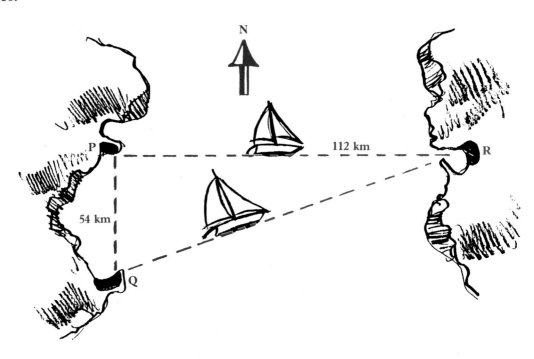

Two yachts sail into the harbour at R.
One yacht sails from P, which is 112 km due West of R. The other sails from Q,
which is 54 km due South of P.

   (a) Use Pythagoras' theorem to find the distance from Q to R.
   (b) Which angle in the diagram gives the bearing of R from Q?
        Use trigonometry to find the size of this angle and hence the bearing of R
        from Q.

17. Draw up a pair of axes. Number both the x and y axes from –6 to 6.

    (a) Draw the triangle with vertices at P(–2, –3), Q(0, 1), R(2, –2).

    (b) The triangle PQR is translated to triangle P′Q′R′. This translation is described by the vector $\begin{pmatrix} 4 \\ -1 \end{pmatrix}$. Draw the triangle P′Q′R′.

    (c) Write down the coordinates of P′, Q′ and R′.

    (d) What is the vector of the translation which would map triangle P′Q′R′ onto triangle PQR?

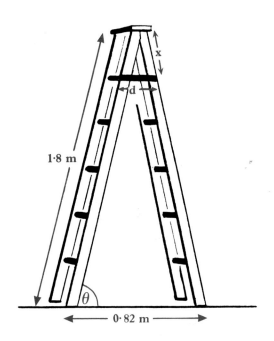

18. A symmetrical stepladder has five equally spaced steps as shown in the diagram. When the stepladder is being used it is kept stable with a bar connecting the top steps.

    (a) Find the distance between each step (x in the diagram).

    (b) Use similar shapes to find the length of the connecting bar (d in the diagram).

    (c) Use trigonometry to find the angle each side of the stepladder makes with the ground (θ in the diagram).

19.

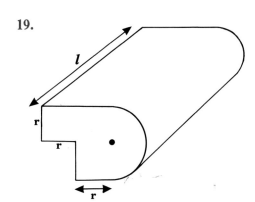

This diagram represents a brick of an unusual shape.

Which of the following expressions could be for

    (a) the volume

    (b) the surface area of the front face

    (c) the perimeter of the front face?

$3rl + \frac{1}{2}\pi r^2 l$ $6\pi r^2 + \pi r$ $6r + \pi r$ $6r^2 + \pi r$ $3r^2 l + \frac{1}{2}\pi l$

$3r^2 l + \frac{1}{2}\pi r^2 l$ $3r^2 + \frac{1}{2}\pi r$ $3r^2 + \frac{1}{2}\pi r^2$ $3r + \frac{1}{2}\pi r^2$ $3r^2 l^2 + \frac{1}{2}\pi rl$

20. A helicopter is flying at a height of 120 metres. From this helicopter, the angle of depression of a liferaft is measured as 42°. At the same time, the angle of depression of another liferaft is measured as 31°.

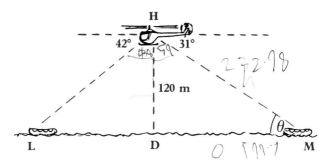

(a) What is the size of the angle θ?
(b) Use trigonometry to find the distance DM.
(c) How far apart are the two liferafts?

21.

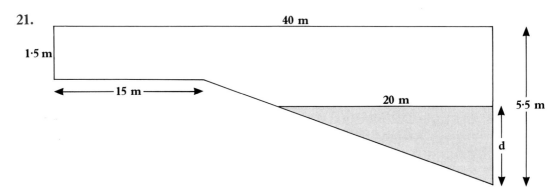

This sketch represents a swimming pool which is being emptied.
How deep is the water in this pool when the length of the surface of the water is 20 m?

DATA HANDLING

Data Handling from Previous Levels

REVISION

Types of Data

Discrete data can take only particular values, usually whole numbers.
Continuous data can take any value within a given range.
For instance, size of shoes is discrete data; length of shoes is continuous data.

Tables, Charts, Graphs

This **bar chart** or **bar graph** shows the number of hours of sunshine on each of the days of one week.

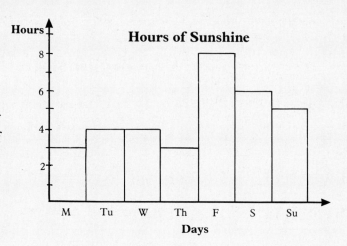

27   29   28   28   30   29   27   27   29   28   29   27   30   29   28   27   28   29   29   27
This data, which gives the number of biscuits in each of 20 packets, is summarized on the **tally chart** below and graphed on a **bar-line graph**. Since the tally chart includes a column for frequency, it is a combined tally chart and **frequency table**.

Biscuits Tally Chart

Number	Tally	Frequency
27	⫽⫽⫽⫽ I	6
28	⫽⫽⫽⫽	5
29	⫽⫽⫽⫽ II	7
30	II	2

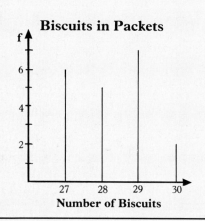

continued . . .

. . . from previous page

The following figures give the number of times the letter e appears in each sentence on the last page of "The Clan of the Cave Bear".

1 2 2 1 6 10 2 8 3 3 5 5 3 1 6 7 3 9 3 4 5 2 4 9 11 15 0 8

This discrete data has been grouped into 6 categories on the combined tally chart and frequency table, shown below.

Notice that each category is the same **width**. The first column on the table (Number of e's) could also be labelled **"class interval"**. When we group data, we should have between 6 and 15 class intervals.

The information on the tally chart is graphed as a **frequency diagram.** This type of graph is often called a **histogram.**

e's Frequency Table

Number of e's	Tally	Frequency
0–2	𝍢𝍢 III	8
3–5	𝍢𝍢 𝍢𝍢	10
6–8	𝍢𝍢	5
9–11	IIII	4
12–14		0
15–17	I	1

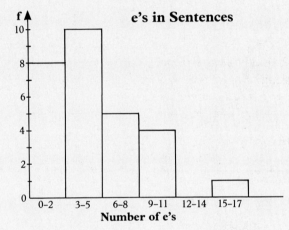

Pie Charts are circle graphs.
The circle is divided into sections.
The number of degrees in the angle at the centre of each section represents the frequency.

Hockey Matches

Won	3
Lost	15
Drawn	6

The continuous data from this table is shown graphed, on the next page, as a histogram and as a **frequency polygon.**

Handspan of Students	
Class interval (mm)	Frequency
$170 \leq l < 180$	2
$180 \leq l < 190$	3
$190 \leq l < 200$	5
$200 \leq l < 210$	4
$210 \leq l < 220$	4

continued . . .

. . . from previous page

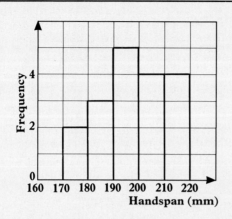

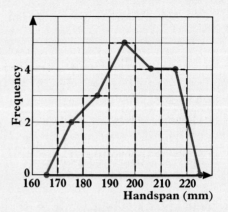

During Jane's first 12 hours in hospital her temperature was taken at 4-hourly intervals.

At 8 a.m. it was 37°C, at Noon it was 38°C, at 4 p.m. it was 37·5°C and at 8 p.m. it was 37·8°C.

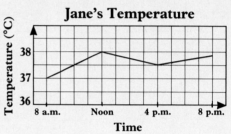

This **line graph** shows these temperatures. It was drawn by plotting the temperatures at 8 a.m., Noon, 4 p.m., 8 p.m. and joining the points with straight lines.

A **conversion graph** is a line graph which shows the relationship between two different units of measurement. Conversion graphs may be drawn to convert kilometres to miles, ounces to grams, °F to °C, litres to gallons, $U.S. to £ sterling etc.

A **scatter graph** displays two aspects of data. For instance, both the length and weight of dogs could be displayed on a scatter graph. A scatter graph is sometimes called a **scatter diagram** or a **scattergram.**

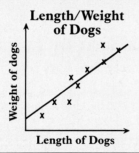

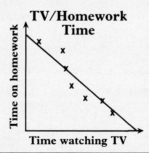

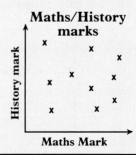

continued . . .

. . . *from previous page*

The word **correlation** is used to describe the relationship between the variables on a scatter graph. If the data shows some correlation, we can draw a line of best fit. The **line of best fit** has about the same number of points above and below it. Also, the sum of the vertical distances (to this line) from the points above is about the same as the sum of the vertical distances (to the line) from the points below.

For **positive correlation** the points must be clustered around a line that slopes upwards. The scatter graph for Length/Weight of dogs shows positive correlation. For **negative correlation** the points must be clustered around a line that slopes downwards. The scatter graph for TV/Homework time shows negative correlation. If there is neither positive nor negative correlation, as in the scatter graph for Maths/History marks, we say there is **no correlation**.

Two-way tables are tables which display two aspects of data. On a two-way table, the total of all the columns is equal to the total of all the rows. The following table is a two-way table.

Year \ Sport	Cricket	Athletics	Tennis	Swimming	Totals
Year 7	14	35	52	18	119
Year 8	26	26	48	21	121
Year 9	34	22	25	32	113
Year 10	19	18	19	24	80
Year 11	21	15	34	17	87
Totals	114	116	178	112	520

Mean, median, mode, range

The **range** of a set of data is the difference between the largest and smallest data values. For instance, the range of 3, 2, 6, 2, 2, 3, 7 is $7 - 2 = 5$.

$$\text{Mean} = \frac{\textbf{Sum of all data values}}{\textbf{No. of items of data}}$$ For instance the mean of 3, 2, 6, 2, 2, 3, 7 is

$$\frac{3 + 2 + 6 + 2 + 2 + 3 + 7}{7} = 3 \cdot 6 \text{ to 1 d.p.}$$

If the data is given as a **frequency distribution**, $\text{mean} = \dfrac{\Sigma \, fx}{\Sigma \, f}$

For instance,

x	3	4	5	6
f	2	3	0	5

; $\text{mean} = \dfrac{2 \times 3 + 3 \times 4 + 0 \times 5 + 5 \times 6}{2 + 3 + 0 + 5} = 4 \cdot 8.$

continued . . .

. . . from previous page

If the data is **grouped,** we can find an approximate value for the mean by assuming that all the items of data in a given class interval have the value of the mid-point of that interval.

For instance,

Test mark	1–20	21–40	41–60	61–80	81–100
Mid-point	10·5	30·5	50·5	70·5	90·5
Frequency	2	5	7	10	1

$$\text{mean} = \frac{2 \times 10{\cdot}5 + 5 \times 30{\cdot}5 + 7 \times 50{\cdot}5 + 10 \times 70{\cdot}5 + 1 \times 90{\cdot}5}{2 + 5 + 7 + 10 + 1} = 52{\cdot}9$$

The **mode** is the value that occurs most often. For instance, the mode of 3, 2, 6, 2, 2, 3, 7 is 2. A set of data may have more than one mode or no mode. If the data is grouped we may talk about the **modal class** which is the class interval that contains more data values than any other. For instance, the modal class for the Test Marks shown above is the interval 61–80.

The **median** is the middle value of a set of data which is arranged in order. For instance, arranged in order 3, 2, 6, 2, 2, 3, 7 is 2, 2, 2, 3, 3, 6, 7. The median is the 4th value which is 3. If there is an even number of values, the median is the mean of the middle two values. If the data is grouped we can talk about the class interval which contains the median. For instance, for the previous Test Marks, the class interval which contains the median is 41–60 since the middle value (the 13th value) lies in this interval.

Flow Diagrams

The following shapes are used for the "boxes" in flow diagrams.

Start, stop	Decisions	Other instructions Calculations

Probability

The probability of an event that is certain to happen is 1.
The probability of an event that will never happen is 0.
The probability of any other event is between 0 and 1.

Choosing at **random** means every item has the same chance of being chosen.
Equally likely outcomes are outcomes which have the same probability of occurring. For instance, when a coin is tossed the outcomes "a head", "a tail" are equally likely; each of these outcomes has probability of $\frac{1}{2}$.

The probability of an event may be calculated if all the possible outcomes are equally likely.

For equally likely outcomes, $P(\text{an event occurring}) = \dfrac{\text{Number of favourable outcomes}}{\text{Number of possible outcomes}}$

continued . . .

. . . *from previous page*

For instance, the probability of getting a prime number when a die is tossed is calculated as follows.

Possible equally likely outcomes are 1, 2, 3, 4, 5, 6. Number of possible outcomes = 6.
Favourable outcomes are 2, 3, 5. Number of favourable outcomes = 3.

P(prime number) = $\frac{3}{6}$ or $\frac{1}{2}$.

Outcomes may be given as a **list**, in a **table** or in a **diagram**. For instance, the possible equally likely outcomes when two coins are tossed could be shown in any of the ways below.

Table:

1st coin \ 2nd coin	H	T
H	HH	HT
T	TH	TT

List: HH HT TH TT

Diagram:

1st coin	2nd coin	Possible outcome
H	H	HH
	T	HT
T	H	TH
	T	TT

The **probability of an event not happening** is equal to 1 – P(A), where P(A) is the probability of the event happening. For instance, when a card is chosen at random from a pack, the probability of getting the Jack of spades = $\frac{1}{52}$; the probability of not getting the Jack of spades = $\frac{51}{52}$.

Exhaustive events account for all possible outcomes. If events are exhaustive, it is certain that one of them will happen. For instance, when a die is thrown the events "an odd number", "an even number" are exhaustive events.

Events which cannot happen at the same time are called **mutually exclusive events.** For instance, if a die is tossed the events "a four", "a prime number" are mutually exclusive since both of these events cannot happen together.

The **addition principle for probability** is: If events A and B are mutually exclusive, then P(A **or** B) = P(A) + P(B). For instance, when a die is tossed

P(four **or** prime no.) = P(four) + P(prime no.)

$$= \frac{1}{6} + \frac{3}{6}$$

$$= \frac{4}{6} \text{ or } \frac{2}{3}$$

continued . . .

. . . *from previous page*

Probability may be estimated from experiments. The **frequency** of an event is the number of times that event occurs in a number of trials. The **relative frequency** of an event compares the frequency with the number of trials. It is the proportion of times the event occurs in a number of trials.

$$\text{Relative frequency of an event} = \frac{\text{Number of times the event occurs}}{\text{Number of trials}}$$

If an experiment is repeated a great number of times, the relative frequency of an event occurring can be used as an estimate of the probability of that event occurring. The more often the experiment is repeated, the better the estimate will be. For instance, if in 1000 tosses of an unfair die, a "six" came up 620 times, we can estimate the probability of getting a "six" the next time we toss this die as $\frac{620}{1000}$ or 0·62.

The **expected number** of times an event will occur is equal to the product of the number of trials and the probability of the event occurring in any one trial. For instance, if we toss the unfair die, above, 200 times we expect to get a "six" 0·62 × 200 or 124 times.

Subjective estimates of probability are a way of saying how strongly we believe an event will occur. Subjective estimates are made if we cannot either calculate the probability of the event occurring or estimate the probability by carrying out an experiment. An example where a subjective estimate is necessary is: "The probability of humans landing on Mars next century".

Surveys

The steps taken to **conduct a survey** are:
Step 1 **Decide** on the purpose of the survey.
Step 2 **Design** an observation sheet or a questionnaire.
Step 3 **Collect** the data. If necessary, collate the data.
Step 4 **Organize** the data onto tables and graphs or into a computer database.
Step 5 **Analyse** the data i.e. make some conclusions.

Some **guidelines for designing a questionnaire** are:
- Decide how the collected data is to be collated and analysed.
- Allow for *all* possible answers.
- Give clear instructions on how the questions are to be answered.
- Do not ask for information that is not needed.
- Avoid questions which people may not be willing to answer.
- Make the questions clear and concise.
- If your questions are asking for opinions, word them so that *your* opinion is not evident.
- Keep the questionnaire as short as possible.

continued . . .

> An **hypothesis** is a statement of one person's opinion about an issue. For instance, the statement "most students do not eat breakfast" is an hypothesis. A survey could be conducted to test this hypothesis; that is, to find whether the hypothesis is true or false.

REVISION EXERCISE

1. An unfair die is tossed many times. The results are shown on the table.

Number on die	1	2	3	4	5	6
Frequency	72	69	82	221	203	353

   (a) What is the relative frequency of tossing a 6?
   (b) Estimate the probability of getting an even number the next time this die is tossed.

2. (a) As part of Dean and Joanne's survey on traffic, Dean decided to display this data on a bar-line graph.
   Draw this bar-line graph.
   (b) Joanne decided to display the data on a pie chart. What angle should Joanne have for each of the 5 categories?
   Draw the pie chart.

Vehicle	Frequency
Lorry	5
Bus	3
Car	28
Motorbike	7
Bicycle	17

3.

Black \ Red	1	2	3	4	5	6
1						
2						
3						
4						
5						
6				10	11	12

The two dice are tossed together.
   (a) Copy and complete the table for the possible totals.
   (b) What is the probability of getting a total of more than 8?
   (c) What is the most likely total to get?

4.

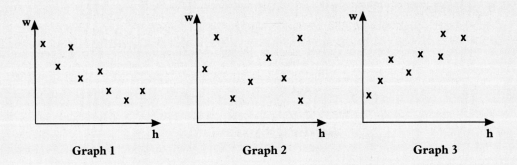

Graph 1   Graph 2   Graph 3

(a)   Which of these graphs shows positive correlation between the variables h and w?
(b)   Which shows negative correlation?
(c)   Which shows no correlation?

5. These line graphs show
the midday temperatures
at Carlisle and Calais for
one week in June.
Compare these
temperatures. In your
comparison, refer to the
ranges and the means.

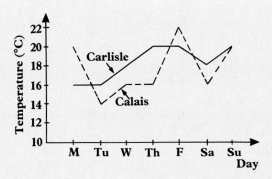

6.   During the opening night at a new disco, some people completed a questionnaire on
the lights, the music, the decoration and the service. Each of these was to given one of
the ratings: excellent, good, acceptable or poor. The results are shown in the table.

	Excellent	Good	Acceptable	Poor	Totals
Lights	52	34	9	5	
Music	38	31	24	7	
Decoration	24	18	43	15	
Service	15	41	14	30	
Totals					

(a)   Copy the table. Complete the totals.
(b)   How many people completed the questionnaire?
(c)   How many people rated the music as excellent or good?
(d)   Can you tell from this table how many people gave both the music and the lights
an excellent rating?
(e)   What type of graphs could be used to display the results of the questionnaire?

7. **(a)** Work through this flow diagram with the data 3, 4, 6, 9, 10, 11.
    State what the output is.
    In words, state what the flow diagram does.

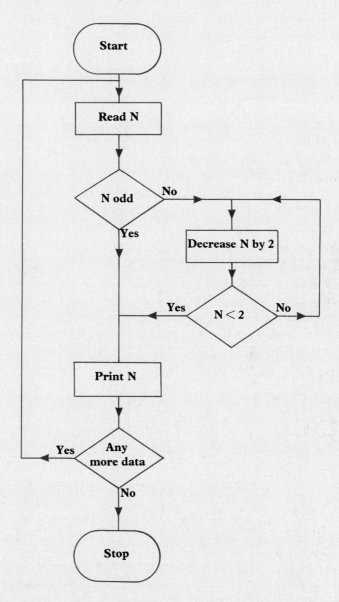

(b) The flow diagram, shown above, is not very efficient. The loop on the right-hand
side can be replaced with a simpler loop.
Rewrite the flow diagram so it is more efficient.

8. Three coins are tossed together.
    (a) Copy and complete this list of possible outcomes: HHH, HHT, HTH, ...
    (b) What is the probability of getting at least two heads?

301

9.

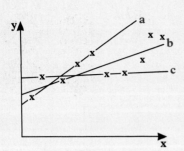

Which of the lines **a**, **b** or **c** is a line of best fit for the data shown?

10. Adrian made this spinner as part of a game he designed. When this spinner is spun find the probability of it stopping in the following sections:

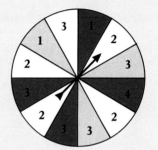

   (a) Red   (b) 3
   (c) Red 3   (d) prime number
   (e) number less than 5   (f) number greater than 4
   (g) either Red or Grey

11. As part of the comparison of the marks of her class on two tests, Ms Hassell drew the frequency polygons on the same set of axes.

The histogram and frequency polygon for Test A are shown.

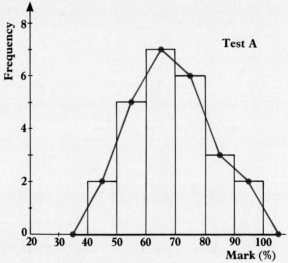

  (a) Copy the frequency polygon for Test A.
  (b) The marks in Test B are given in the table.

Mark Range	40–49	50–59	60–69	70–79	80–89	90–99
Frequency	3	4	3	6	8	1

      On the same set of axes used in **(a)**, draw the frequency polygon for Test B.
  (c) Comment on any similarities or differences between the two frequency polygons.

12. These four discs are placed in a bag. The discs are all the same shape and size. Melanie chooses two of these discs at random. She replaces the first disc before choosing the second. What is the probability that the two discs she chooses, total less than 30p?

13. Would you expect there to be positive correlation, negative correlation or no correlation between the following:
    (a) the weight of suitcases filled with clothes and the volume of the suitcases
    (b) the distance cars travel on 10 litres of petrol and the weight of the cars
    (c) the time students take to run 100 m and the time they take to run 200 m
    (d) the time students take to run 100 m and the time they take to swim 100 m
    (e) the height of the oldest child in a family and the height of the youngest child?

14. Part of the analysis of a dentist's patients is shown on this table.
    (a) Find the probability that a patient is either an adult or a school pupil.
    (b) The probability that a patient is either a school pupil or female is *not* 0·3 + 0·45. Why not?
    (c) What is the probability that a patient is not an adult?
    (d) Find the probability of a patient having dental work other than a tooth filled.
    (e) Of the next 150 patients, how many do you expect will be adults?

	Probability
Male	0·55
Female	0·45
Under school age	0·1
School pupil	0·3
Adult	0·6
Tooth filled	0·38
Reconstruction work	0·09
Tooth extract	
Teeth	

15. The data in the table gives the height of some 16-year old boys and their height as 3-year olds.

	Jon	Ian	Tim	Evan	Adam	Luke	Brett	Ryan	Mark	Rob
Height at 16 (m)	1·85	1·72	1·74	1·88	1·77	1·79	1·63	1·80	1·61	1·73
Height at 3 (m)	1·03	0·93	0·94	1·04	0·96	0·99	0·85	0·95	0·84	0·93

(a) Plot this data on a scatter diagram. (Have height at 16 on the horizontal axis and height at 3 on the vertical axis.)
(b) Draw the line of best fit.
(c) At 16, Matthew is 1·68 m tall. Estimate how tall Matthew was at 3.
(d) When Ian's younger brother was 3, he was 1·01 m tall. Estimate his height at 16.

16.   1.   *The probability that Gloria will be absent from school next Wednesday is 0·09.*
2.   *That probability that the captain of Gloria's cricket team wins the toss at the beginning of the next game is 0·5.*
3.   *The probability of a family living on the moon in Gloria's lifetime is 0·00001.*

(a)   Which of the above probabilities is a subjective estimate?

(b)   Which can be calculated by considering equally likely outcomes?

(c)   Which can be estimated by carrying out an experiment or a survey?

17. Write a flow diagram to find the median of a list of data.
Use the following instructions. Place each instruction in the correct type of operation or decision box.

Start	Write down this value	Odd number of data values?
Stop	Find the middle value	Find the mean of these values
Data in order?	Put the data in order	Find the middle two values
Read the data		

18. Part of William's survey on traffic involved counting the number of people in cars. William collected the data shown.

People in Cars

4	1	1	2	2	3	2	1	2	
1	5	2	1	1	2	3	2	3	
2	1	4	2	1	2	1	3	1	
4	2	5	2	2	1	1	1	3	
1	2	1	1	1	2	2	4	2	
3	1	4	1	1	3	1	5	1	

(a)   William could have collected this data using a better designed observation sheet. Suggest a way he could have done this.

(b)   William collected his data between 2.00 p.m. and 2.15 p.m. How useful would this data be? Explain your answer.

19. Julian's family own an apple orchard. Julian conducted a survey for his family.

(i)   Julian counted the number of trees in each row. His results are shown on this frequency table.

Number of trees	15	16	17	18	19	20	21	22	23
Frequency	1	0	1	3	1	3	0	1	1

(a)   How many rows of trees are there on this orchard?

(b)   How many trees are there?

(c)   What is the mean number of trees per row? (Answer to 1 d.p.)

(d)   What is the mode?

(e)   Find the median number of trees per row.

(f)   Find the range.

(ii)   Julian collected data on the number of apples produced last season by each of the trees. He organized this data onto the following frequency table.

Apples produced	600–799	800–999	1000–1199	1200–1399	1400–1599	1600–1799
Frequency	8	14	10	34	68	76

Julian then displayed this data on a histogram. Draw the histogram.

(iii)   Julian estimated the height of each tree. He entered the height of each tree on this observation sheet.
Julian then wrote up the frequency table shown below.

Height (m)	Tally
1 –	卌 I
2 –	卌 卌 卌 卌 IIII
3 –	卌 卌 卌 卌 卌 卌 卌 卌 卌 卌 卌 卌 卌 卌 卌 卌 卌 IIII
4 –	卌 卌 卌 卌 卌 卌 卌 卌 卌 卌 卌 卌 卌 卌 卌 卌 卌 II
5 – 6	卌 IIII

Class interval	1m –	2m –	3m –	4m –	5m – 6m
Mid-point	1·5m				
Frequency	6	24			

(a)   Copy and complete this frequency table.
(b)   Calculate an approximate value for the mean height.
(c)   Which class interval contains the median?
(d)   What is the modal class?

20. In a bag there are caramel and peppermint chocolates. One of these chocolates is chosen at random.
Sue claims that the events "choosing a caramel chocolate", "choosing a peppermint chocolate" are mutually exclusive.
Nigel claims that these events are exhaustive.
Who is correct: Sue or Nigel? Explain your answer.

21. Rule some parallel lines on a sheet of plain paper.
Make the distance between these lines about $1\frac{1}{2}$ times the length of a toothpick or some other small object.
If the toothpick is held above the paper, then dropped, it may land on one of the lines.
Design and conduct an experiment to find the relative frequency of the toothpick landing on a line.
Use your results to estimate the probability that the next time the toothpick is dropped, it will land on a line.

Robert Recorde

Robert Recorde was born in 1510 at Tenby, in Wales. He died in 1558 at London.

At the age of 15, Robert entered Oxford University. He studied and taught mathematics there, then went to Cambridge University where he gained a medical degree in 1545. He then went to London and served as physician to King Edward VI and Queen Mary.

In 1549, Recorde became Comptroller of His Majesty's Mint in Bristol. In 1551, he became Surveyor of the King's Mines and Monies in Ireland.

Robert Recorde was the most important mathematician in England in the 16th century. He introduced algebra into England. He wrote books on mathematics, astronomy and medicine. His mathematics text books were used in England for more than a century.

His first book was "The Grounde of Artes", published in 1542. This book is often referred to as the first arithmetic book to be written in the English language. This is not true. Recorde himself said of this book *"I doubt not but some will like this my booke aboue any other English Arithmetike hitherto written, & namely such as shal lacke instructers, for whose sake I haue plain-ly set forth the exāples, as no book (that I haue seene) hath hitherto."*

"The Grounde of Artes", which was dedicated to King Edward VI, was a most popular arithmetic book. 28 editions were published, from 1542 to 1699. In this book, Recorde used the abacus to teach addition and subtraction. He also used the + and – signs. The book was well written with the theory carefully developed and hence easily understood. It contained many interesting practical applications. The following is an extract: *"Then what say you to this question? If I sold unto you an horse having 4 shoes, and in every shoe 6 nayles, with this condition, that you shall pay for the first nayle one ob : for the second nayle two ob : for the third nayle foure ob : and so forth, doubling untill the end of all the nayles, now I ask you, how much would the price of the horse come unto?"*

Recorde's most famous book was "The Whetstone of Witte", published in 1557. In this book he proposed and used the symbol = . He said the following: *"I will sette as I doe often in woorke use, a paire of paralleles, or Gemowe (twin) lines of one lengthe, thus: ══════ , bicause noe 2. thynges, can be moare equalle."*

The symbol = was not the only notation in use at that time for "equals". In fact, it was more than a century after Recorde used it in "The Whetstone of Witte" before it became the accepted notation. Both Sir Isaac Newton and Gottfried Leibniz helped to make it popular.

In his work on astronomy, Recorde agreed with the theory that the Earth revolves around the Sun.

A year after the "Whetstone of Witte" was published, Robert Recorde died in prison. The reason for his imprisonment is not known. It is thought to have been for some dishonest transaction carried out in connection with his position as surveyor of the King's Mines and Monies in Ireland.

Testing Hypotheses: Surveys and Experiments

RESPONSES to QUESTIONS on a QUESTIONNAIRE

DISCUSSION EXERCISE 17:1

- Schofied School is surveying parents about the school's reports. Think of questions, or statements, that might be included in the questionnaire for which the following responses would be suitable. **Discuss.**

  Yes ☐   No ☐

  Yes ☐   No ☐   Undecided ☐

  Always ☐   Usually ☐   Sometimes ☐   Seldom ☐   Never ☐

  Strongly agree ☐   Agree ☐   Disagree ☐   Strongly disagree ☐

  Agree ☐   Neither agree nor disagree ☐   Disagree ☐

- One of the questions on the Schofield School questionnaire was:
  Which of these do you consider the most important and the least important to have on a report? We would like you to rank them in order of importance to you, with 1 the most important and 8 the least important.

  ☐ *General Comment*
  ☐ *Comment with each subject*
  ☐ *Activities outside the classroom*
  ☐ *% marks (or grades) for each subject*
  ☐ *Level achieved in each subject*
  ☐ *Some reference to attitude*
  ☐ *Some reference to effort*
  ☐ *Some reference to behaviour*

  Discuss other questions that could be ranked in this way.

- Think of responses, other than those already mentioned, that could be used for a question on a questionnaire. **Discuss.** As part of your discussion, discuss questions for which these responses would be suitable.

Responses to a question should "fit" the question. In other words, the responses must be consistent with the wording of a question.

Example   *Question: Do you prefer typed or handwritten reports?*

Responses: Yes ☐   No ☐

These responses do not "fit" the question. The responses could be rewritten as   Typed ☐   Handwritten ☐   or the question could be reworded as "Do you prefer typed to handwritten reports?".

Responses should allow for all possible answers to a question.

Example   *Question: Do you discuss reports with your child?*

Responses: *Always* ☐   *Sometimes* ☐   *Never* ☐

Parents who had discussed every report, except one, with their child would find it difficult to respond to this question. These parents need the response *Usually* ☐.

Responses should be "balanced". That is, there should be the same number of positive and negative responses.

Example   The responses   Strongly agree ☐   Agree ☐   Disagree ☐ are "unbalanced" since there are two positive responses and only one negative response. The following responses are balanced:

Agree ☐   Neither agree nor disagree ☐   Disagree ☐

If the same responses are used for more than one question, or statement, these responses should be written in the same order.

Example   *I would like the reports posted.*   ☐ Yes ☐ No
           I would like a report twice a term.   ☐ Yes ☐ No
           I would like separate reports for each subject.   ☐ Yes ☐ No
           I would like just comments and no marks (or grades).   ☐ No   ☐ Yes

The responses for the last statement should be   ☐ Yes ☐ No
It is possible that people will assume that the first response for all the statements will be   ☐ Yes.

The responses should be placed so they clearly relate to the question or statement. This is very important if a list of statements is being ranked.

Example In each of the following, the same statements are to be ranked from the most important to the least important. The position of the response "boxes" is better on A than on B.

A.

> **Rank**   from 1 to 8; with 1 for the most important and 8 for the least important.
> ☐   General Comment
> ☐   Comment with each subject
> ☐   Activities outside the classroom
> ☐   % marks (or grades) for each subject
> ☐   Level achieved in each subject
> ☐   Some reference to attitude
> ☐   Some reference to effort
> ☐   Some reference to behaviour

B.

> | | **Rank (1 to 8)** |
> |---|---|
> | General Comment | ☐ |
> | Comment with each subject | ☐ |
> | Activities outside the classroom | ☐ |
> | % marks (or grades) for each subject | ☐ |
> | Level achieved in each subject | ☐ |
> | Some reference to attitude | ☐ |
> | Some reference to effort | ☐ |
> | Some reference to behaviour | ☐ |

COLLATING and ANALYSING SURVEY RESULTS

An example of **collating and analysing the results of a question with multiple responses** is shown below.

Example A questionnaire on school reports for Year 10 students is given to all the parents of these students.
One of the questions is:

Do you discuss reports with your child?

Always ☐   *Usually* ☐   *Sometimes* ☐   *Seldom* ☐   *Never* ☐

The responses to this question could be collated using a tally chart, as shown below on the left.

To analyse these responses, percentages could be worked out as shown below on the right. Some conclusions could then be made from these percentages.

Response	Tally	Frequency	Response	%
Always	ℍℍ ℍℍ ℍℍ ℍℍ ℍℍ ℍℍ ℍℍ ℍℍ ℍℍ ℍℍ ℍℍ	55	Always	48%
Usually	ℍℍ ℍℍ ℍℍ ℍℍ ℍℍ ℍℍ IIII	34	Usually	30%
Sometimes	ℍℍ ℍℍ III	13	Sometimes	11%
Seldom	ℍℍ II	7	Seldom	6%
Never	ℍℍ I	6	Never	5%

An example of **collating and analysing the results of ranking a list** is shown below.

Example   Rasha works part-time in a cafe. This cafe is about to introduce a new menu to attract more teenagers. Rasha has been asked to survey two different age groups about their preferences. Rasha chose to survey all the 13-year olds and 16-year olds in her school.

Rasha's questionnaire, her collation and analysis is shown below.

Rasha's Questionnaire

Place a √ in the box for your age.   13 ☐   16 ☐   other ☐

Rank the following meals in order of preference.

Place   1 beside your 1st preference,   2 beside your 2nd preference,
3 beside your 3rd preference,   4 beside your 4th preference,
5 beside your 5th preference.

Fish & Chips   ☐
Hamburger   ☐
Nachos   ☐
Curry   ☐
Pizza   ☐

Rasha's Collation

Rasha divided the completed questionnaires into 3 groups; those from 13-year olds, those from 16-year olds and those who had given their age as other than 13 or 16.

She then drew up two tally charts; one for 13-year olds, the other for 16-year olds. Rasha transferred the results from the questionnaires onto these tally charts.

The tally marks she used for a 13-year old whose questionnaire rankings are shown, at the right, are in red on the tally chart below.

Fish & Chips   2
Hamburger   1
Nachos   5
Curry   3
Pizza   4

	Tally: 13 year-olds				
Meal / Rank	**Fish & Chips**	**Hamburger**	**Nachos**	**Curry**	**Pizza**
1.	THL THL THL THL THL THL THL III	THL THL THL THL THL THL THL THL THL THL II	III	THL THL THL	THL III
2.	THL THL THL THL THL THL THL THL IIII	THL THL THL THL THL III	II	THL III	THL THL THL THL THL THL IIII
3.	THL THL THL THL III	THL THL THL	THL THL THL THL THL THL	THL THL	THL THL THL THL THL THL THL III
4.	THL II	THL THL THL II	THL THL THL THL THL II	THL THL THL THL THL THL THL THL THL III	THL THL THL II
5.	IIII	IIII	THL THL THL THL THL THL THL THL THL THL THL IIII	THL THL THL THL THL THL	THL THL THL IIII

Rasha now displayed the results on a two-way table. The 13-year old results are shown in red, the 16-year old results are in black.

Meal / Rank	**Fish & Chips**	**Hamburger**	**Nachos**	**Curry**	**Pizza**	**Totals**
1.	38 / 9	52 / 39	3 / 1	15 / 7	8 / 28	116 / 84
2.	44 / 30	28 / 14	2 / 3	8 / 6	34 / 31	116 / 84
3.	23 / 11	15 / 18	30 / 21	10 / 28	38 / 6	116 / 84
4.	7 / 22	17 / 2	27 / 19	48 / 31	17 / 10	116 / 84
5.	4 / 12	4 / 11	54 / 40	35 / 12	19 / 9	116 / 84
Totals	116 / 84	116 / 84	116 / 84	116 / 84	116 / 84	

Key
Red figures:
13 year old
Black figures:
16 year old

Rasha's Analysis

From the two-way table, Rasha made some comparisons. She could see that just under half of both age groups chose Hamburgers as their 1st preference. It was also obvious that a much higher proportion of 13-year olds gave Fish & Chips as their 1st preference ($\frac{38}{116}$) than 16-year olds ($\frac{9}{84}$).

Since not all of the results were obvious from the two-way table, Rasha decided to convert the figures to percentages and then continue with her analysis. The first row of her percentage table is shown below.

Meal / Rank	Fish & Chips	Hamburger	Nachos	Curry	Pizza
1.	33%	45%	3%	13%	7%
	11%	46%	1%	8%	33%
2.					

DISCUSSION EXERCISE 17:2

- Neither the 13-year old nor the 16-year old percentages, shown above, add to 100%. Why not? Should adjustments be made to these percentages so they do add to 100%? If so, how could the adjustments be made? **Discuss.**

- Rasha drew some graphs of her results. What types of graphs would be suitable? **Discuss.**

- Apart from analysing the percentages of students who chose particular rankings of the meals how else might Rasha have analysed the results of her survey? **Discuss.**

- Brian suggested that Rasha could have found the overall popularity of each meal. He suggested that this could have been done as follows.

  13 year-olds   Fish & Chips: $38 \times 1 + 44 \times 2 + 23 \times 3 + 7 \times 4 + 4 \times 5 = 243$

               Hamburger: $52 \times 1 + 28 \times 2 + 15 \times 3 + 17 \times 4 + 4 \times 5 = 241$

               Nachos: $3 \times 1 + 2 \times 2 + 30 \times 3 + 27 \times 4 + 54 \times 5 = 475$

               Curry: $15 \times 1 + 8 \times 2 + 10 \times 3 + 48 \times 4 + 35 \times 5 = 428$

               Pizza: $8 \times 1 + 34 \times 2 + 38 \times 3 + 17 \times 4 + 19 \times 5 = 353$

  From these figures, Brian concluded that Hamburgers were the most popular, then Fish & Chips, Pizza, Curry and Nachos in that order.
  Discuss Brian's analysis.

- Barbara suggested that Rasha could have analysed her results by adding the number of times each meal was given as the 1st, 2nd or 3rd preference.
  13-year olds Fish & Chips 105, Hamburger 95, Nachos 35, Curry 33, Pizza 80.
          Discuss Barbara's analysis.
          What if the 1st or 2nd preference only are added?

- Could the computer be used to collate and/or analyse the results of Rasha's survey? **Discuss.** As part of your discussion consider a spreadsheet, a database and any commercial statistical package that your school owns.

SURVEYS to TEST HYPOTHESES

Remember that an hypothesis is one person's opinion about an issue. There are usually 4 steps in making and testing an hypothesis.
    Step 1   State the hypothesis.
    Step 2   Collect data related to this hypothesis.
    Step 3   Collate and analyse the data.
    Step 4   Use the analysis to test the hypothesis.

Example   Before Rasha carried out her survey on menu preferences she could have made an hypothesis such as "Hamburgers are the most popular meal with 13-year olds".
        Step 1   Stating this hypothesis.
        Step 2   Designing the questionnaire.
                 Using the questionnaire to collect the data from the 13-year olds.
        Step 3   Collating the results.
                 Displaying the results on the two-way table.
                 Analysing the data.
        Step 4   Testing the hypothesis. Rasha's data supports the hypothesis "Hamburgers are the most popular meal with 13-year olds."

Example   The question "Do you discuss reports with your child?" and the responses
        "Always ☐   Usually ☐   Sometimes ☐   Seldom ☐   Never ☐ "
        could have been written to test the hypothesis "Most parents always discuss reports with students".
        The data collected and analysed on page 310, does not support this hypothesis.

PRACTICAL EXERCISE 17:3

Wherever possible in this exercise, use a computer to collate and/or analyse the data collected. You could use a spreadsheet or database or a commercial statistical package.

Use the guidelines given on page 298 for Designing a Questionnaire.

Make and test an hypothesis in at least one of your surveys.

1. Decide on an issue. Some suggestions follow.
   Write a questionnaire to find people's opinion on this issue. Have some questions with multiple responses.
   Collect the data.
   Collate and analyse the data. Use suitable tables and graphs.

   Suggestions: *What makes a good holiday?*
                       What makes a good magazine?
                       Recreational facilities in your area.
                       Pollution: problems and solutions.

2. Design and use a questionnaire to rank a list. This list could be a list of products or activities etc. to be ranked in order of preference or it could be a list of statements to be ranked in order of preference. Some suggestions follow.
   Collect the data.
   Collate and analyse the data. Use suitable tables and graphs.

   Suggestions: *Colour preferences of students from one year group.*
                       Ranking of hamburgers for taste or presentation or value for money.
                       Popularity of TV programmes.
                       Preferred type of video watched.

EXPERIMENTS to TEST HYPOTHESES

Experiments which involve several variables should be carefully planned.

With the exception of the variable being changed, all other conditions should remain the same throughout the experiment.
For instance, if we are looking at the effect of light, temperature and fertilizer on the growth of poppy seedlings, all seedlings should be the same height, strength and colour at the beginning of the experiment. One tray of these seedlings should be used as a "control", one tray should have just the light varied, one tray should have just the temperature varied and another should have just the fertilizer varied.

Planning should consist of: Deciding which conditions to vary.

Deciding what data to collect.

Deciding how and when the data will be collected.

Deciding how the data will be collated and displayed.

Deciding how the data will be analysed.

Experiments can be carried out to test an hypothesis.

For instance, an experiment could be carried out to test one or more of the following hypotheses about the growth of poppy seedlings.

"The better the light, the faster poppy seedlings grow".

"Fertilized poppy seedlings grow taller than unfertilized seedlings".

"Good light is more important than fertilizer for the fast growth of poppy seedlings".

PRACTICAL EXERCISE 17:4

1. Make an hypothesis that can be tested by carrying out an experiment. Some suggestions follow.

   Plan your experiment thoroughly before you begin. This planning should include all aspects, from the setting up of the experiment to the analysis of the data to test the hypothesis.

   Suggested hypotheses:

   "People with large feet can walk backwards faster than those with small feet".

   "Blind-folded short people can walk in a straight line for a greater distance than blind-folded tall people".

   "The reaction time of 15-year olds is better in the afternoon than the morning".

   "Drinking coffee has more effect on the pulse rate than jogging".

2. Conduct an experiment with several variables. Some suggestions follow.

   Begin your planning by making an hypothesis.

   Collate and analyse the data collected to test the hypothesis.

   Suggested experiments: *The growth of yeast.*

   The drying of paint.

   Germination rates of seeds.

   Effect of the weather on mood.

   Effect of astrology on plant growth.

Sofya Kovalevskaya

Sofya Kovalevskaya was born in Moscow in 1850 and died in Stockholm in 1891. She was the daughter of a Russian general who disciplined his troops but not his daughter!

Sofya was first exposed to mathematics by an uncle who talked to her about maths. when she was quite young; too young to understand. Her father encouraged her when she showed interest in the subject and provided maths. tutors for her.

Sofya married at 18 and she and her husband went to study in Germany. Women, at that time, were not allowed to study at Russian Universities. Some claim that Sofya married in order to be able to travel abroad to continue her studies. It was not acceptable for Russian women to travel if they were not married. The situation regarding women studying at Universities in Germany was similar to that in Russia. However, Sofya had private lessons in Berlin with a famous mathematician who recognised her remarkable ability.

At the age of 24, she gained a Doctorate in Mathematics from the University of Göttingen. Sofya hadn't studied there; she was granted her degree "in absentia." Her thesis was on differential equations, an important area of mathematics. Throughout her life she continued to work in this area and made valuable contributions to the theory of differential equations.

In 1884 she was appointed to the University of Stockholm as a lecturer. Shortly after this she became the editor of the important international journal "Acta Mathematica." In 1889, she became Professor of Mathematics at Stockholm University.

In 1888 she won a prestigious prize, the Prix Borodin awarded by the French Académie des Sciences. Her entry, on the rotation of a solid body about a fixed point, impressed the judges so much that they raised the prize money from 3000 francs to 5000 francs.

In 1889, she was elected to the Russian Imperial Academy of Sciences; a great honour. She was the first woman to be elected.

Sofya had talents other than mathematical talents. She was a well known writer. Her most famous novel was "Vera Vorontzoff", published in 1893. This novel, and others she wrote, were based on her early life in Russia. She also wrote plays and poetry.

Sofya was a political activist; often taking a radical point of view and always a champion of women's rights. She was particularly outspoken about the role of women in Russian society and their limited educational opportunities.

In the past, Sofya's achievements have often been ignored by historians. In recent times, the opposite has been true — many feminist writers have made exaggerated claims about her achievements. This is a shame since her achievements were quite remarkable and do not need any exaggeration. She was the first woman mathematician to achieve international fame; the first woman to gain a Doctorate in mathematics; the first woman Professor of Mathematics and the first woman to be the editor of a major mathematical journal.

At the age of 41, Sofya died from pneumonia, a complication arising after having had influenza.

based on an article from the book "Women Sum It Up" — Hazard Press

ANALYSING DATA: quartiles, interquartile range

We may use the statistical measures, **mean, median, mode** and **range** to analyse data. Other statistical measures we may use are the **quartiles** and the **interquartile range.**

For a set of data arranged in order, the median is the middle value, the **lower quartile** is the middle value of the lower half of the data and the **upper quartile** is the middle value of the upper half of the data.
The **interquartile range** is the difference between the upper and lower quartiles.

That is , | **interquartile range = upper quartile – lower quartile** |

Examples   **1.**

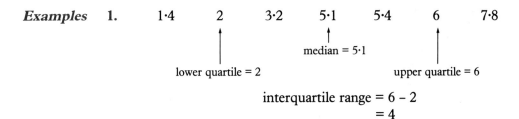

| 1·4 | 2 | 3·2 | 5·1 | 5·4 | 6 | 7·8 |

lower quartile = 2   median = 5·1   upper quartile = 6

interquartile range = 6 – 2
= 4

2.

| 8 | 8 | 9 | 10 | 12 | 13 | 14 | 16 | 17 | 17 |

lower quartile = 9   median = 12·5   upper quartile = 16

interquartile range = 16 – 9
= 7

3.

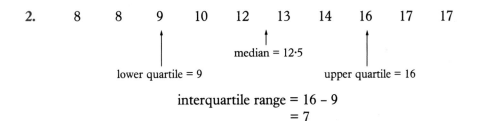

| 8 | 11 | 12 | 13 | 15 | 15 | 18 | 19 |

lower quartile = 11·5   median = 14   upper quartile = 16·5

interquartile range = 16·5 – 11·5
= 5

DISCUSSION EXERCISE 18:1

- 16   17   18   20   24   25   28   31   33   34   35   39   40
  This data gives the marks of 13 students for a history assignment. The median is 28, the lower quartile is 19, the upper quartile is 34·5, the interquartile range is 15·5, the range is 24.

  1   4   17   21   27   27   28   28   28   30   39   50   70
  This data gives the marks of the same 13 students for a science assignment. The median, the lower quartile, the upper quartile and the interquartile range are the same as for the history assignment; the range is 69.

  Do you think the interquartile range describes the spread of these sets of data well? **Discuss.**

- **Discuss** the advantages and disadvantages of using the interquartile range as one of the measures to describe a set of data. As part of your discussion write down several sets of data, some of which have the same interquartile range but different quartiles, some of which have the same range but different interquartile ranges, some of which have the same quartiles but different medians and so on.

-

Number of children	1	2	3	4	5	6	7	8
Frequency	16	21	18	9	5	4	0	1

  This frequency distribution shows the number of children in the families of the members of a youth club.
  How could you find the quartiles for this data? **Discuss.**

- **Discuss** how the following statements could be completed.

  "The median divides a set of data in ..."
  "The quartiles divide a set of data into ..."

  "One half of the data values lie below the ..."
  "One-quarter of the data values lie below the ..."
  "Three-quarters of the data values lie below the ..."
  "The interquartile range is the range of the central ... of the data".

Worked Example   Margaret gathered data on the ages of the people in her modern dance class. Her data was:
12 15 15 14 13 15 15 16 17 11 17 14 16 14 12 16
What is the interquartile range for this data?

Answer In order, the data is:

11 12 12 13 14 14 14 15 15 15 15 16 16 16 17 17

lower quartile = 13·5   median = 15   upper quartile = 16

Interquartile range = upper quartile – lower quartile
$$= 16 - 13·5$$
$$= 2·5$$

EXERCISE 18:2

1. Find the lower quartile and the upper quartile for the following sets of data.
   (a) 12 14 14 16 18 24 27
   (b) 3 5 6 6 7 8 9 11 12 13 15 19 24 24 25
   (c) 1 1 2 3 5 7 10 10 11 14
   (d) 28 34 25 27 14 18 25 27 13 14 26 29 20
   (e) 12 10 3 7 9 5 2 11 8 4 1 15 14 16
   (f) 3 9 4 5 1 2 9 6 8 3 2 4 9 4 3 2 5 8 7 2

2. Find the interquartile range for the sets of data given in **question 1.**

3. The following data gives the marks obtained, by the students in two classes, for a maths. test.
   Mr Benzoni's class: 14 7 12 17 18 8 9 11 13 10 15 9 18 6 19 18 7 13 20 15 16 9
   Ms Patel's class: 8 11 13 12 14 10 15 12 12 16 13 9 12 10 9 15 8 11 14
   Find the range, median, lower quartile, upper quartile and interquartile range for each class.
   Write a sentence or two comparing the marks.

4. Jane gathered data on the number of videos the students in her class watched during one week. This data is shown in the frequency table below.

No. of videos watched	0	1	2	3	4	5	6	7	8
Frequency	7	9	3	4	1	1	0	0	1

As part of Jane's analysis of this data she found the median, the lower quartile, the upper quartile, the interquartile range and the range.
What answers should Jane get for these?

Review 1. Find the lower and upper quartiles and the interquartile range.

(a) 5   5   7   8   9   10   10   11   13   14   14   15   16   17   18   20

(b) 5   4   1   3   2   4   3   5   6   5

Review 2. As part of a project on school attendance, Hari wrote up the following frequency tables.

Girls' absences during June

No. of days absent	0	1	2	3	4	5	6	7	8	9	10	11	12	13
Frequency	14	5	7	1	0	4	3	0	1	4	0	0	0	1

Boys' absences during June

No. of days absent	0	1	2	3	4	5	6	7	8	9	10	11
Frequency	8	12	3	5	0	4	0	1	4	3	3	2

Hari compared the data for girls with the data for boys. As part of his comparison, he found the lower quartiles, the upper quartiles, the interquartile ranges, the medians and the ranges. What values should he get for these?

Write a few sentences comparing the data.

CUMULATIVE FREQUENCY GRAPHS

This frequency distribution shows the time taken, by the 26 students in a class, to correctly answer a trigonometry problem.

It is difficult to find the median, the lower quartile or the upper quartile from this table. However, we can find these easily by drawing a **cumulative frequency graph**.

Time (sec)	Frequency
10–20	1
20–30	0
30–40	2
40–50	5
50–60	6
60–70	7
70–80	3
80–90	2

To draw a cumulative frequency graph we firstly write a cumulative frequency column on the frequency table. In this column we add up the frequencies as we go along; that is, the cumulative frequency column gives a "running total" of the frequencies as shown below.

Time (sec)	Frequency	Cumulative Frequency	
10–20	1	1	← This means 1 student took less than 20 sec.
20–30	0	$1 + 0 = 1$ 1	← This means 1 student took less than 30 sec.
30–40	2	$1 + 2 = 3$ 3	← This means 3 students took less than 40 sec.
40–50	5	$3 + 5 = 8$ 8	← This means 8 students took less than 50 sec.
50–60	6	$8 + 6 = 14$ 14	← This means 14 students took less than 60 sec.
60–70	7	$14 + 7 = 21$ 21	← This means 21 students took less than 70 sec.
70–80	3	$21 + 3 = 24$ 24	← This means 24 students took less than 80 sec.
80–90	2	$24 + 2 = 26$ 26	← This means 26 students took less than 90 sec.

To draw the cumulative frequency graph we plot the points $(20, 1)$, $(30, 1)$, $(40, 3)$, $(50, 8)$, $(60, 14)$, $(70, 21)$, $(80, 24)$, $(90, 26)$. That is, we **plot the cumulative frequency against the upper boundary of each class interval.**

Since 0 students took less than 10 sec., another point on the cumulative frequency graph is $(10, 0)$. We plot this point along with the others. **We always begin a cumulative frequency graph on the horizontal axis.**

The cumulative frequency graph is shown below.
The points on the graph are joined with a smooth curve or with straight lines, as shown. **Use straight lines, rather than a curve, only if the completed graph closely approximates a smooth curve.**

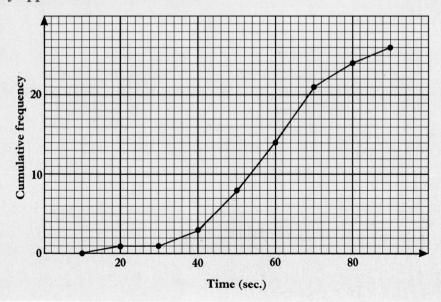

We can find the median, the lower quartile and upper quartile from the cumulative frequency graph, as shown below.

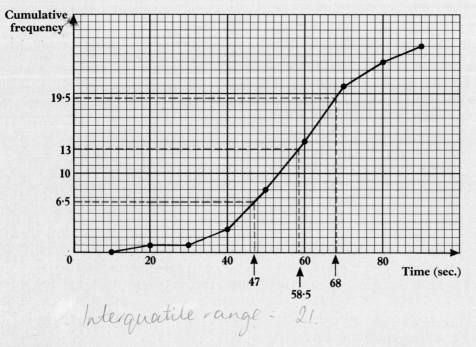

Interquartile range = 21.

To find the median: Since $\frac{1}{2}$ of 26 = 13, 13 students have times less than the median time.

Reading from the graph, 13 students have times less than 58·5 sec.

The median time is 58·5 sec.

To find the lower quartile: Since $\frac{1}{4}$ of 26 = 6·5, 6·5 students have times less than the lower quartile.

Reading from the graph, 6·5 students have times less than 47 sec.

The lower quartile is 47 sec.

To find the upper quartile: Since $\frac{3}{4}$ of 26 = 19·5, 19·5 students have times less than the upper quartile.

Reading from the graph, 19·5 students have times less than 68 sec.

The upper quartile is 68 sec.

EXERCISE 18:3

1.

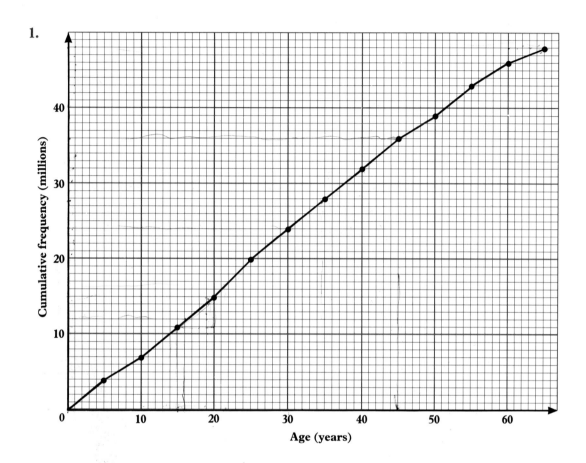

This graph is the cumulative frequency graph for the ages of people in the United Kingdom who are under the age of 65.
(a) What is the median age of these people?
(b) Find the lower and upper quartiles.
(c) What is the interquartile range?
(d) How many people are aged under 20?
(e) How many people are aged under 15?
(f) How many people are aged between 15 and 20?
(g) How many people are aged between 60 and 65?

2.

Temperature (°C)	Frequency	Cumulative Frequency
12 –	3	3
14 –	5	8
16 –	15	23
18 –	9	32
20 –	16	48
22 –	9	57
24 –	3	60
26 – 28	1	61

During June and July, Susan kept a record of the maximum daily temperature. She organized the data as shown in this table. Susan then drew the cumulative frequency graph.

(a) Three of the points Susan plotted for the cumulative frequency graph were (12, 0), (14, 3), (16, 8).
What other points should Susan plot?

(b) Draw the cumulative frequency graph.

(c) Use the cumulative frequency graph to find the median, the lower quartile, the upper quartile and the interquartile range.

3. Copy and complete the following cumulative frequency tables.

(a)

Height of Seedlings (cm)	Frequency	Cumulative Frequency
0 – 1	9	9
1 – 2	3	12
2 – 3	10	
3 – 4	15	
4 – 5	12	
5 – 6	7	
6 – 7	4	

(b)

Time Spent on Leisure	Frequency	Cumulative Frequency
$10 \leq t < 15$	1	
$15 \leq t < 20$	4	
$20 \leq t < 25$	7	
$25 \leq t < 30$	15	
$30 \leq t < 35$	13	
$35 \leq t < 40$	5	
$40 \leq t < 45$	3	
$45 \leq t < 50$	2	

(c)

Weight of fruit (kg)	0·5 –	1·0 –	1·5 –	2·0 –	2·5 –	3·0 –	3·5 –	4·0 –
Frequency	6	5	8	7	14	18	27	12
Cumulative Frequency								

(d)

Handspan (mm) at least	Handspan (mm) below	Frequency	Cumulative Frequency
160	170	2	
170	180	0	
180	190	4	
190	200	10	
200	210	7	
210	220	3	
220	230	1	
230	240	1	

4. Plot the cumulative frequency graphs for the data given in **question 3.**
   Find the median, lower quartile, upper quartile and interquartile range for each set of data.

5. In the spring, Mrs. Eade fertilized one of her two rhubarb plants. Two months later, she measured the length of each stick of rhubarb on these plants. The lengths are given in the following tables.

Length of Rhubarb on Unfertilized Plant (cm)	25 –	30 –	35 –	40 –	45 –	50 – 55
Frequency	2	5	8	7	5	3

Length of Rhubarb on Fertilized Plant (cm)	25 –	30 –	35 –	40 –	45 –	50 – 55
Frequency	4	2	6	6	9	1

(a) Copy the tables. Complete a cumulative frequency row on both tables.
(b) On the same set of axes, draw both cumulative frequency graphs.
(c) Find the median length, the lower and upper quartiles and the interquartile range for each.
(d) Write a sentence or two comparing the length of the sticks of rhubarb on these plants. Use the median, quartiles and interquartile range in your comparison.

6.

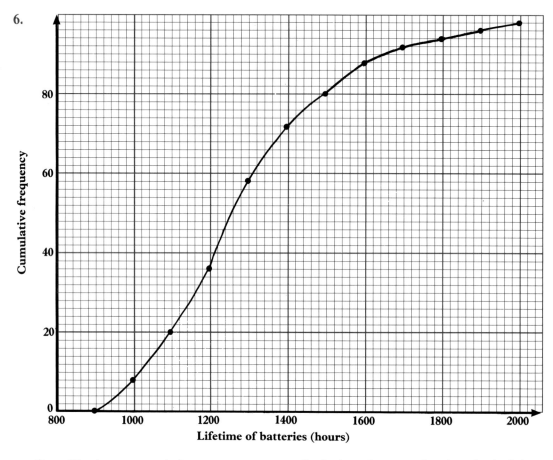

Lifetime of batteries (hours)

(i)   Testing was carried out on a new type of calculator battery. One hundred of these batteries were tested. The time these batteries worked for (the lifetime) is shown on this cumulative frequency graph.

   (a)   How can you tell from this graph that 2 of the batteries were still working after 2000 hours of use?

   (b)   What is the median lifetime of the 100 batteries tested?

   (c)   What is the interquartile range?

(ii)   One hundred calculator batteries of another type were also tested. The results are shown in the table below.

Lifetime (hours)	1000–1100	1100–1200	1200–1300	1300–1400	1400–1500	1500–1600	1600–1700	1700–1800
Frequency	3	5	9	21	33	16	7	6

   (a)   Draw the cumulative frequency graph for this data.

   (b)   Use the cumulative frequency graph to find the median, the quartiles and the interquartile range.

(iii) Write a sentence or two comparing the two different types of calculator batteries.

326

7.

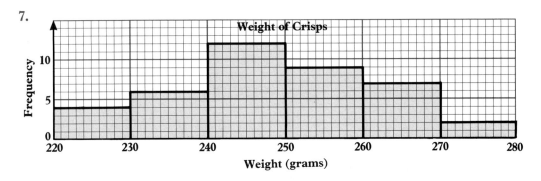

Pamela weighed a number of packets of crisps. She drew this histogram and then a cumulative frequency graph. From the cumulative frequency graph she found the median and quartiles.

(a) Two of the points Pamela plotted on the cumulative frequency graph were (220, 0) and (230, 4). What other points should Pamela plot?

(b) Draw the cumulative frequency graph.

(c) What is the median weight of these packets of crisps?

(d) What is the interquartile range?

Review 1   Kate weighed the ripe tomatoes from two different varieties of tomato plants. The weights are shown in the following frequency tables.

Variety: Top Tom

Weight (grams)	Frequency	Cumulative Frequency
50–	4	
70–	6	
90–	10	
110–	12	
130–	24	
150–	25	
170–190	2	

Variety: Goliath

Weight (grams)	Frequency	Cumulative Frequency
50–	4	
70–	8	
90–	13	
110–	9	
130–	24	
150–	15	
170–	11	
190–210	4	

(a) Copy the tables. Complete the cumulative frequency on both.

(b) Draw the cumulative frequency graphs.

(c) Find the median, lower quartile, upper quartile and interquartile range for both varieties of tomatoes.

(d) Write a sentence or two comparing the Top Tom tomatoes with the Goliath tomatoes.

Review 2

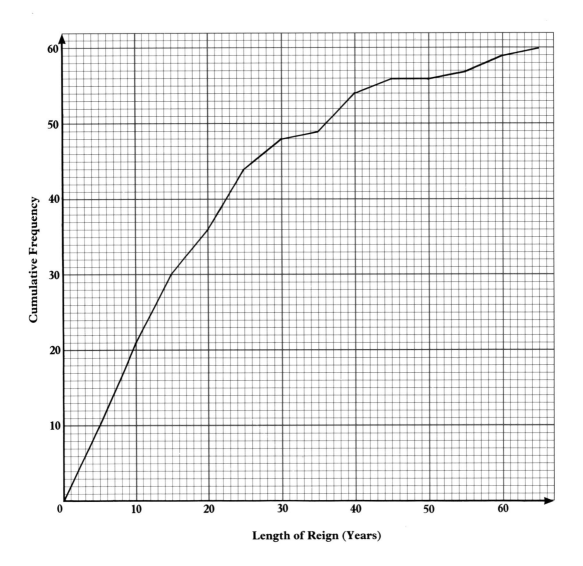

This cumulative frequency graph shows the length of the reign of English monarchs.
(a) How many monarchs reigned for less than 5 years?
(b) How many monarchs reigned for less than 10 years?
(c) How many monarchs reigned for between 5 and 10 years?
(d) How many monarchs has England had?
(e) What is the median length of reign?
(f) Find the lower and upper quartiles.
(g) What is the interquartile range?

DISCUSSION EXERCISE 18:4

Frequency

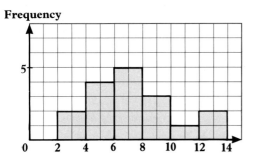

Frequency

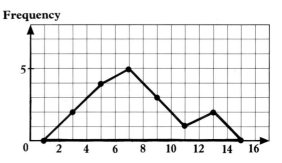

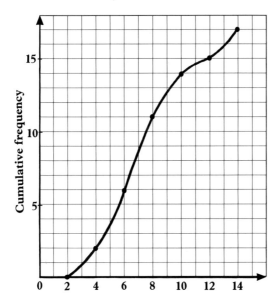

The histogram, frequency polygon and cumulative frequency graph, above, all display the same data.

"Which graphs are drawn depends on the way in which we are going to analyse the data". **Discuss** this statement.

"The frequency polygon has greater visual impact than either the histogram or the cumulative frequency graph". **Discuss** this statement.

Is it sensible to draw all three of the above graphs to display a set of data? Is one of these graphs more useful than the others? **Discuss.** As part of your discussion, you could refer to data given in the previous exercise.

The cumulative frequency graphs drawn so far in this chapter have all been for continuous data.
Cumulative frequency curves are also drawn for **grouped discrete data.**

For **continuous data**, the cumulative frequency values are the number of data values that are **less than** the upper boundaries of each class interval.
For **discrete data**, the cumulative frequency values are the number of data values that are **less than or equal to** the upper boundaries of each class interval.

Example   Melanie threw a dart 30 times. The following frequency table shows Melanie's scores.

Score	Frequency	Cumulative Frequency
1–5	2	2
6–10	7	9
11–15	8	17
16–20	11	28
21–25	2	30

← This means 2 scores were less than or equal to 5.
← This means 9 scores were less than or equal to 10.
← This means 17 scores were less than or equal to 15.
← This means 28 scores were less than or equal to 20.
← This means 30 scores were less than or equal to 25.

The culmulative frequency graph is shown below. The points plotted are (5, 2), (10, 9), (15, 17), (20, 28), (25, 30) and (0, 0).

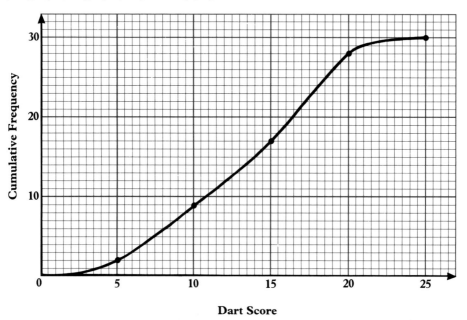

Dart Score

330

EXERCISE 18:5

1. The following table gives the prices of 35 different types of computers.

Price range (£)	1–200	201–400	401–600	601–800	801–1000	1001–1200	1201–1400	1401–1600
Frequency	1	2	6	8	7	4	5	2

(a) Copy and complete the following cumulative frequency table for these computers.

Price (£)	≤ 200	≤ 400	≤ 600	≤ 800	≤ 1000	≤ 1200	≤ 1400	≤ 1600
Cumulative Frequency	1	3	9					

(b) Draw the cumulative frequency graph.
(c) Use your graph to find the median price and the interquartile range.

2.

Claim (£)		Number of claims	Cumulative Frequency
at least	below		
0	100	15	
100	200	62	
200	300	89	
300	400	54	
400	500	28	

This table shows the number of insurance claims, under £500, during one week.

(a) Copy the table and fill in the cumulative frequency column.
(b) Draw the cumulative frequency graph.
(c) Find the median insurance claim.
(d) Find the interquartile range.
(e) Use your graph to estimate the number of claims under £340.

3. Two maths. tests were trialled with 200 students. The results are shown below.

Mark range	1–10	11–20	21–30	31–40	41–50	51–60	61–70	71–80	81–90	91–100
Test A frequency	4	9	15	27	28	32	45	23	11	6
Test B frequency	7	10	24	29	34	38	31	18	7	2

(a) Copy and complete the cumulative frequency table.

Mark range	≤ 10	≤ 20	≤ 30	≤ 40	≤ 50	≤ 60	≤ 70	≤ 80	≤ 90	≤ 100
Test A frequency	4	13	28							
Test B frequency	7									

(b) Draw the cumulative frequency graphs for both tests on the same set of axes.
(c) Use the graphs to find the median, quartiles and interquartile range for each test.
(d) Write a few sentences comparing these tests.

Review   Delwyn was doing a project on school netball. As part of this project she compared the number of goals scored, in the games of one season, by two schools. The following frequency table shows this information.

Goals Scored	1–10	11–20	21–30	31–40	41–50	51–60
Number of Games: School A	0	2	5	9	4	0
Number of Games: School B	1	3	4	5	5	1

(a) The cumulative frequency graph for the goals scored by school B is shown below. Use this graph to find the median, lower quartile, upper quartile and interquartile range.

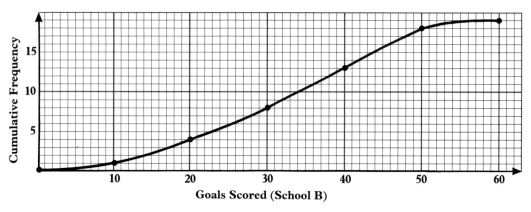

(b) Copy and complete the cumulative frequency table for school A.

Goals Scored	≤ 10	≤ 20	≤ 30	≤ 40	≤ 50
Cumulative frequency: School A					

(c) Draw the cumulative frequency graph for school A.
(d) Compare the goals scored by the two schools. In your comparison, use the medians, the quartiles and the interquartile ranges.

PRACTICAL EXERCISE 18:6

Gather some data. Some suggestions follow.

You could conduct a survey or an experiment or you could gather your data from reference books.

Draw graphs to display your data. Include cumulative frequency graphs.

Analyse your data. Include the median, quartiles and interquartile range as part of your analysis.

Suggestions: *Prices of cars advertised for sale.*
Wrist measurements of students.
Comparison of ages of male and female employees in a factory or office.
Comparison of time spent playing sport by the students in two different year groups.
Comparison of pulse rates of 10 year olds and 20 year olds.
Comparison of weekly wages earned by the workers in two industries.

If you wish, you could work as a group. If you do this, choose a theme such as sport. Gather, display and analyse data on many aspects of this theme.

Niccolo Tartaglia

Niccolo Tartaglia was born in 1499 at Brescia, Italy and died in 1557 at Venice. His real name was Niccolo Fontana. He adopted the name Tartaglia, which means "stammerer" after the lower part of his face was damaged with a sabre during the French sacking of Brescia in 1512. This damage left Niccolo with a permanent stammer in his speech.

Niccolo's parents were poor and could not afford tutors for their son. Niccolo educated himself. It is claimed that since his parents could not afford to buy slate for him to write on Niccolo used tombstones as slates.

Tartaglia was one of the most important mathematicians of the 16th century. He wrote books on mathematics and military science. In the military books, he used mathematics in the study of artillery fire; the first person to do this. He also tried to find laws to describe the motion of falling bodies. Tartaglia also published translations of the early Greek mathematician's, Euclid and Archimedes. He was not always truthful and, more than once, claimed to have invented some mathematics that had been invented by someone else. It is said that he claimed to have invented the "Arithmetic Triangle" (what we know as Pascal's Triangle) although this had already been published.

Tartaglia is famous for finding a method to solve cubic equations such as $x^3 + 6x^2 + 8x = 1000$, and for the quarrel between mathematicians that followed.

He was asked by another mathematician, Cardan, to publish his solution for these equations. Tartaglia refused to do this at this time as he hoped to make his reputation by writing a book on algebra which would include this discovery. Cardan was a man of influence and he persuaded Tartaglia to show him the solution. Some say Cardan promised to introduce him to a wealthy patron; others say Cardan promised to recommend that he be appointed as artillery adviser to the Spanish Army. Tartaglia showed Cardan the solution which Cardan published. This led to a dreadful quarrel which became a public quarrel. Although Cardan did acknowledge that the solution was not his own, the solution became known as Cardan's.

Of the quarrel, a biographer many years later wrote: "*The attempt to assert exclusive right to the secret possession of a piece of information, which was the next step in the advancement of a liberal science, the refusal to add it, inscribed with his own name, to the common heap, until he had hoarded it, in hope of some day, when he was at leisure, of turning it more largely to his own advantage, could be excused in him only by the fact that he was rudely bred and self-taught, and that he was not likely to know better. Any member of a liberal profession who is miserly of knowledge, forfeits the respect of his fraternity. The promise of secrecy which Cardan had no right to make, Tartaglia had no right to demand.*"

Tartaglia's best known work is a massive work of three volumes called "Treatise on Numbers and Measures." This was the best book on arithmetic that was written in Italy during the 16th century.

INDEPENDENT EVENTS

Event A and event B are **independent** if event A happening (or not happening) has no influence on whether event B happens. The probability of event B happening will be the same regardless of whether or not event A has happened.

Example   A coin is tossed twice. A head occurs on the first toss. This has no influence on whether or not a tail occurs on the second toss.
That is, the events "head on first toss", "tail on second toss" are independent.

Example   These counters are placed in a bag.
Two counters are drawn at random, one after the other.
The first counter is not replaced in the bag.
Suppose event A is "the first counter drawn is red" and event B is "the second counter drawn is red".
If event A happens, there will be 2 red counters left out of a total of 7 counters. Then $P(B) = \frac{2}{7}$.
If event A does not happen (i.e. the first counter drawn is black) there will be 3 red counters left out of a total of 7 counters. Then $P(B) = \frac{3}{7}$.
Events A and B are *not* independent.

DISCUSSION EXERCISE 19:1

- Suppose two counters are drawn with the first counter being replaced before the second one is drawn.
Are the events "the first counter is red", "the second counter is red" independent in this case? **Discuss.**

- **Discuss** whether or not the events A and B are independent in each of the following.

  Sue throws two backgammon dice, one grey and the other purple.
  Event A : Sue gets a 6 on the grey die.
  Event B : Sue gets a 6 on the purple die.

  Andrew uses the alarm on his clock-radio.
  Event A : There was a power failure last night.
  Event B : Andrew was late for school today.

Two babies are born on Saturday at Rochford Hospital.
  Event A : The first baby born is a girl.
  Event B : The second baby born is a boy.

Nicole and Ana are the finalists in the school tennis championship. In the final, they play a three-game match.
  Event A : Ana wins the first game of the final.
  Event B : Ana wins the second game of the final.

Femi and Oni are friends.
  Event A : Femi goes to the disco.
  Event B : Oni goes to the disco.

Jeremy and Jake sit beside each other in class.
  Event A : Jeremy catches a cold.
  Event B : Jake catches a cold.

Two cards are drawn, one after the other, from a pack of cards. The first card is not replaced before the second card is drawn.
  Event A : The first card drawn is a spade.
  Event B : The second card drawn is a spade.

Two cards are drawn, one after the other, from a pack of cards. The first card is replaced before the second card is drawn.
  Event A : The first card is the King of hearts.
  Event B : The second card is a heart.

- Event A is "it will rain on the first day of next month".
  Event B is "it will rain on the last day of next month".
  Are these events independent? **Discuss.**

  Suppose P(A) = 0·4 and P(B) = 0·4. Will the probability of it raining on both the first and last days of next month also be 0·4 or more than 0·4 or less than 0·4? **Discuss.**

- Write down some pairs of independent events and some pairs of events that are not independent. **Discuss.**

  For the pairs of independent events, **discuss** whether the probability of both events happening is less than, equal to, or more than the probability of one or other of these events happening.

- Daniel made the statement "The probability of two independent events happening is always less than the probability of one or other of these events happening". He gave an example to support this statement.
  Caitlin found a counter-example to show that Daniel's statement wasn't always correct. Think of a possible counter-example. **Discuss.**
  Daniel then amended his statement, so that it was always true. How might Daniel have amended his statement? **Discuss.**

The MULTIPLICATION PRINCIPLE

A black and a red die are tossed together.
Possible outcomes are

1, 1	1, 2	1, 3	1, 4	1, 5	1, 6
2, 1	2, 2	2, 3	2, 4	2, 5	2, 6
3, 1	3, 2	3, 3	3, 4	3, 5	3, 6
4, 1	4, 2	4, 3	4, 4	4, 5	4, 6
5, 1	5, 2	5, 3	5, 4	5, 5	5, 6
6, 1	6, 2	6, 3	6, 4	6, 5	6, 6

There are 36 possible outcomes.
The black number in each possible outcome is the number obtained on the black die, while the red number is the number obtained on the red die.

Suppose event A is "a number greater than four on the black die" and
       event B is "a five on the red die".

Favourable outcomes for event A are 5, 1 5, 2 5, 3 5, 4 5, 5 5, 6 6, 1 6, 2 6, 3
6, 4 6, 5 6, 6. There are 12 favourable outcomes. $P(A) = \frac{12}{36}$ or $\frac{1}{3}$

Favourable outcomes for event B are 1, 5 2, 5 3, 5 4, 5 5, 5 6, 5.
There are 6 favourable outcomes. $P(B) = \frac{6}{36}$ or $\frac{1}{6}$

The event (A *and* B) is "a number greater than four on the black die *and* a five on the red die". Favourable outcomes for event (A *and* B) are 5, 5 6, 5.
There are 2 favourable outcomes. $P(A \text{ } \textit{and} \text{ } B) = \frac{2}{36}$ or $\frac{1}{18}$

Notice that $P(A) \times P(B) = \frac{1}{3} \times \frac{1}{6}$
$$= \frac{1}{18}$$

Hence, $P(A \text{ } \textit{and} \text{ } B) = P(A) \times P(B)$.   Notice that the events A and B are independent.

The above example illustrates the multiplication principle for probability.

> The **multiplication principle** for probability is:
>
> for independent events, $P(A \text{ } \textit{and} \text{ } B) = P(A) \times P(B)$

Using the multiplication principle eliminates the need to list all the possible outcomes for two events. Using the multiplication principle, the above example can be done as follows:

P(Black $>$ 4 **and** Red 5) = P(Black $>$ 4) × P(Red 5) since events are independent

$$= \frac{2}{6} \times \frac{1}{6}$$

$$= \frac{1}{18}$$

Worked Example 1. Two cards are drawn from a pack, one after the other. The first card is replaced before the second card is drawn. What is the probability that both cards are Aces?

Answer We are asked to find P(both Aces). This is the same as P(Ace **and** Ace).

P(Ace **and** Ace) = P(Ace) × P(Ace) since events are independent

$$= \frac{4}{52} \times \frac{4}{52}$$

$$= \frac{1}{13} \times \frac{1}{13}$$

$$= \frac{1}{169}$$

Worked Example 2. **(i)** The arrow on this spinner is spun once. Find the probability of the arrow stopping in
   (a) a red section
   (b) a black section.

   (ii) The arrow is spun twice. What is the probability of spinning
   (a) black then red
   (b) black and red in any order?

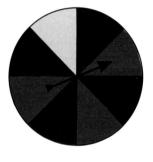

Answer **(i) (a)** $\frac{3}{8}$ **(b)** $\frac{4}{8}$ or $\frac{1}{2}$

(ii) (a) We want P(B **and** R) = P(B) × P(R) since events are independent

$$= \frac{1}{2} \times \frac{3}{8}$$

$$= \frac{3}{16}$$

(b) From (a), P(B **and** R) = $\frac{3}{16}$.   P(R **and** B) = P(R) × P(B)

$$= \frac{3}{8} \times \frac{1}{2}$$

$$= \frac{3}{16}$$

Hence, probability of spinning black and red in either order

is $\frac{3}{16} + \frac{3}{16} = \frac{3}{8}$.

Worked Example **3.** The probability that it will rain on any day in May is $\frac{1}{4}$.

Find the probability that
- **(a)** it will rain on both May 1st and May 21st
- **(b)** it will not rain on May 21st
- **(c)** it will rain on May 1st but not on May 21st.

(Assume that raining on May 1st and raining on May 21st are independent events.)

Answer   **(a)**   P(rain **and** rain) $= \frac{1}{4} \times \frac{1}{4}$

$= \frac{1}{16}$

(b)   P(not rain) $= 1 - $ P(rain)

$= 1 - \frac{1}{4}$

$= \frac{3}{4}$

(c)   P(rain **and** not rain) $= \frac{1}{4} \times \frac{3}{4}$

$= \frac{3}{16}$

DISCUSSION EXERCISE 19:2

- Another way of finding the answer to **Worked Example 1** is by listing all the equally likely outcomes. **Discuss** this method.

  In **Worked Example 2 (ii)**, one of the outcomes is "RR".
  What are the other outcomes? Are the outcomes equally likely?
  Could the answer to this example be found by listing all the outcomes? **Discuss.**

- In **Worked Example 2 (ii) b** we found the probability of spinning a black and a red in either order by finding P(B and R), then finding P(R and B), then adding these probabilities together.
  Discuss the following alternative ways of finding the probability of a black and a red in either order.

  - P(B and R in either order) = 2 P(B **and** R)
  $= 2 \times$ P(B) $\times$ P(R)

  - P(B and R in either order) = P(B **and** R **or** R **and** B)
  $=$ P(B) $\times$ P(R) $+$ P(R) $\times$ P(B)

EXERCISE 19:3

1. A coin is tossed twice.
   Find the probability of   (a)   a head on the first toss
                                (b)   heads on both tosses.

2. A coin and a die are tossed.
   Find the probability of   (a)   a multiple of 3 on the die
                                (b)   a head on the coin and a multiple of 3 on the die.

3. A die is thrown twice.
   Find the probability of a 4 and a 6 in either order.

4. A box contains 20 counters; 1 is red, 5 are blue, 10 are green and the rest are white. Two counters are chosen at random, the first being replaced before the second is chosen.
   Find the probability that   (a)   the first counter drawn is white
                                  (b)   the first counter is white and the second blue
                                  (c)   one of the counters is white and the other blue.

5. Once a month Kylie checks the oil and battery water in her car. The probability that the oil needs topping up is 0·3, the probability that the battery water needs topping up is 0·15. Find the probability that, the next time Kylie checks, both the oil and the battery water need topping up.

6. The probability that Irina is late for school is 0·3; the probability that Helena is late is 0·2. What is the probability that both girls are late for school? Assume these girls do not know each other. Why do you need to make this assumption?

7. In one Mercedes factory, 80% of the cars manufactured are left-hand drive and the rest are right-hand drive. The probability that a car needs its steering adjusted before it leaves the factory is 0·15.
   One car is chosen at random from this factory. Find the probability that this car
   (a)   is a right-hand drive
   (b)   is a right-hand drive which needs its steering adjusted
   (c)   is a left-hand drive which does not need its steering adjusted.

8. Of the 50 houses in Crane Close, there is always someone at home in 15 of them.
   (a)   What is the probability that a house, chosen at random in Crane Close, has someone at home?
   (b)   Alicia is conducting a survey. She chooses two houses at random, in Crane Close. What is the probability that Alicia finds someone at home in both of these houses?

9.

Brenda plays two games of patience. The probability that she gets all the cards out in any one game is $\frac{1}{5}$.

(a) Find the probability that Brenda gets all the cards out in both games.

(b) What is the probability that Brenda does not get all the cards out on the first game?

(c) Find the probability that Brenda does not get all the cards out on the first game but gets them all out on the second.

(d) Find the probability that Brenda gets all the cards out on just one of the games she plays.

Review 1   Jamie works in a car showroom which sells British, European and Japanese cars. 65% of the cars that Jamie sells are British and 20% are Japanese.

(a) What is the probability that Jamie sells a European car to his next customer?

(b) Find the probability that the next two customers both buy Japanese cars. (Assume these customers do not know each other.)

(c) Why do you need to make the assumption in **(b)**?

Review 2   This spinner is spun twice as part of a fairground game. Find the probability of spinning

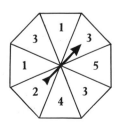

(a) a 1 on the first spin

(b) a 1 on both spins

(c) a 2 on the second spin

(d) a 3 on the first spin and a 2 on the second

(e) a 3 and a 2, in any order, on the two spins.

TREE DIAGRAMS

The possible outcomes of two events can be shown on a table.
A **tree diagram** is another way of showing the possible outcomes.

Example A die is tossed twice.
Let E be the outcome "an even number" and O the
outcome "an odd number".
This table shows all the possible outcomes when the die
is tossed twice. These outcomes are EE, EO, OE, OO.

		2nd toss	
		E	**O**
1st toss	**E**	**EE**	**EO**
	O	**OE**	**OO**

The tree diagram, below, also shows all the possible outcomes.
Level 1 shows the outcomes on the first toss, level 2 shows the outcomes on the second
toss.

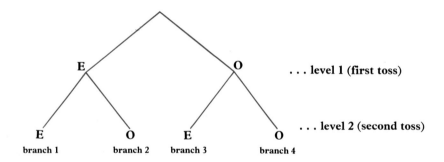

The two entries on the left-hand side of level 2 show that if the first toss
resulted in E, the second toss could result in either E or O. The two entries
on the right-hand side of level 2 show that if the first toss resulted in O, the
second toss could result in E or O.
Reading from top to bottom, down each "branch" of the tree diagram, we get
all the possible outcomes. Branch 1 gives the outcome EE, branch 2 gives the
outcome EO, branch 3 gives the outcome OE and branch 4 gives the outcome
OO.

Tree diagrams may be written horizontally instead of vertically. The information may be
written on the tree diagrams in different ways.

DISCUSSION EXERCISE 19:4

Discuss the possible outcomes shown on the following tree diagrams.

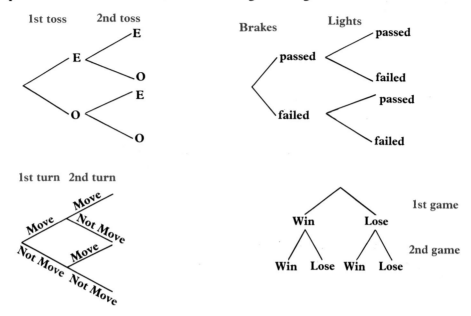

It is not necessary to have the same outcomes at each level of a tree diagram. Neither is it necessary to have the same number of outcomes at each level.

Example   A bank is going to sponsor either a sports programme (S) or quiz programme (Q) or a drama series (D) on TV. Each programme is given a rating; High (H) or Low (L). All the possible outcomes are shown on this tree diagram.

The possible outcomes are SH, SL, QH etc., where, for example, the outcome SH means the bank sponsored a sports programme and this sports programme was given a high rating.

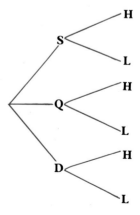

Probability

Tree diagrams for 2 events have 2 levels. Tree diagrams for 3 events have 3 levels.

Example A family has three children. The tree diagram below shows the possible sex of these children.

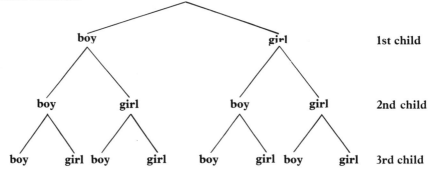

	1st child
	2nd child
	3rd child

EXERCISE 19:5

1. A die is tossed twice.
   Let S be the outcome "a six", NS be the outcome "not a six".
   Draw a tree diagram to illustrate. (On each level you will have S and NS.)

2. A coin is tossed three times.
   Draw a tree diagram to show all the possible outcomes.

3. Write down all the possible outcomes for the 3 events shown.

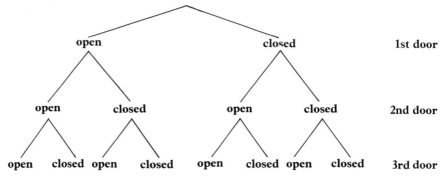

4. All the students at Deirdre's school will play sport this winter.
   They may choose from soccer, hockey or volleyball.
   They may or may not represent the school at the sport they play.
   Draw a tree diagram to illustrate.

   Review A football team may play either at home or away.
   They may win or draw or lose the game.
   Draw a tree diagram to illustrate.

344

USING TREE DIAGRAMS to FIND PROBABILITIES

Worked Example   On Rebecca's route to school there are two sets of traffic lights. The probability that Rebecca must stop at the first set is 0·7 and at the second set it is 0·4. Draw a tree diagram to illustrate.
Use the tree diagram to find the probability that Rebecca must stop at   (a)   both sets of these lights
　　　　　 (b)   just one of these sets of lights.

Answer   Firstly draw the tree diagram — *fig (i)*. Then enter the known probabilities — *fig (ii)*.

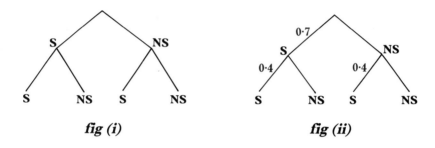

fig (i)　　　　　　　　　　　*fig (ii)*

On the above tree diagrams S is used for stop, NS for not stop. The first level shows what happens at the first set of lights. The second level shows what happens at the second set of lights.

The next step is to fill in all the missing probabilities on *fig (ii)*. Since the probability of stopping at the first set of lights is 0·7, the probability of not stopping is 0·3. Since the probability of stopping at the second set of lights is 0·4, the probability of not stopping is 0·6. *fig (iii)* shows the completed tree diagram.

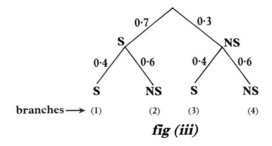

fig (iii)

We are now ready to answer the questions.
  (a) The event "Rebecca stops at both sets of lights" is given by branch 1.
      Probability of the outcomes on branch 1 occurring = 0·7 × 0·4
                                                        = 0·28
      [We multiply the probabilities written on branch 1 since
      P(S *and* S) = P(S) × P(S), using the multiplication principle.]

(b) The event "Rebecca stops at just one set of lights" is given by either branch 2 or branch 3.
Probability of the outcomes on branch 2 occurring = 0·7 × 0·6 or 0·42
Probability of the outcomes on branch 3 occurring = 0·3 × 0·4 or 0·12
Probability of the outcomes on branch 2 or branch 3 occurring = 0·42 + 0·12
$$= 0·54$$

[We add the probabilities given by these branches since
P(branch 2 **or** branch 3) = P(branch 2) + P(branch 3) using the addition principle.]

Worked Example On Rebecca's route to school there are three sets of traffic lights.
The probability that Rebecca must stop at the first set is 0·7, at the second set it is 0·4 and at the third set it is 0·8.
Draw a tree diagram to illustrate.
Use this tree diagram to find the probability that Rebecca must stop
at **(a)** all three sets of lights
     (b) just one of these sets of lights.

Answer There will be 3 levels in the tree diagram since there are 3 events. The first two levels are the same as in the previous worked example (shown again in ***fig (i)***.)
The completed tree diagram is shown in ***fig (ii)***.

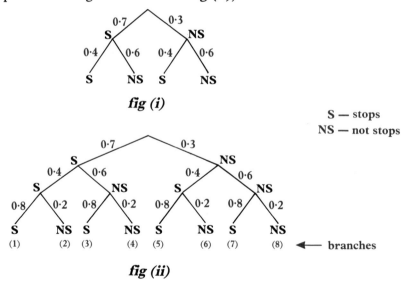

fig (i)

S — stops
NS — not stops

fig (ii)

(a) Branch 1 gives the probability that Rebecca stops at all three sets of lights.
P(stops at all three) = 0·7 × 0·4 × 0·8
$$= 0·224$$

(b) Branch 4 or branch 6 or branch 7 give the probability that Rebecca stops at just one set of lights.
P(stops at just one) = 0·7 × 0·6 × 0·2 + 0·3 × 0·4 × 0·2 + 0·3 × 0·6 × 0·8
$$= 0·252$$

The previous worked examples show the steps we must take to calculate probabilities using a tree diagram.

Step 1 Draw a tree diagram for the situation.

Step 2 Write on the given probabilities.

Step 3 Work out the other probabilities and write these on.

Step 4 Decide which branches answer the question.

Step 5 Do the calculation. We do this as follows:

To find the probability of the outcomes given by any branch, we multiply the probabilities written on that branch.

To find the probability of the outcomes given by more than one branch, we calculate the probabilities on each of the branches and then add these together.

EXERCISE 19:6

1. Apprentice chefs have two exams; a theory exam. and a practical exam. 7 out of 10 apprentice chefs pass the practical exam. but only 2 out of 3 pass the theory exam.

Copy and complete this tree diagram.

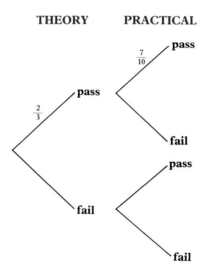

THEORY   PRACTICAL

Use the tree diagram to find the probability that an apprentice chef, chosen at random
   (a)   passes both the theory and practical exam.
   (b)   passes the theory exam, but not the practical
   (c)   passes just one of the exams.
   (d)   does not pass either exam.

2. In a multiple-choice test each question has 5 possible answers.
   Robin does not know the answers to two of these questions, so he guesses.
   Copy and complete this tree diagram. (C stands for correct, NC stands for not correct.)

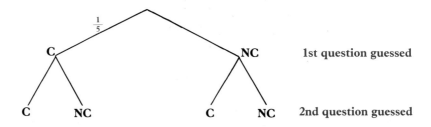

Use the tree diagram to find the probability that
   (a) Robin correctly guesses the answers to both questions
   (b) Robin correctly guesses the answer to just one of the questions
   (c) Robin correctly guesses the answer to at least one of the questions.

3. The probability that a letter posted at Shorfield Post Office is sent to a British destination is 0·9. Three letters posted at this post office are chosen at random.
   Copy and complete this tree diagram. (B is British destination, NB is not a British destination.)

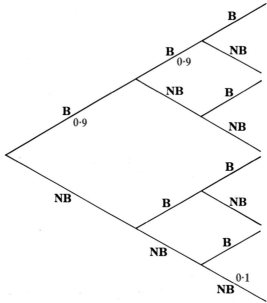

Use the tree diagram to find the probability that
   (a) all three of these letters are sent to a destination outside Britain
   (b) just two of these letters are sent to a British destination
   (c) at least one of these letters is sent to a destination in Britain.

4. **Draw tree diagrams to answer these questions.**
    (i) The probability that Kentucky Fried Chicken customers have chips with their meal is $\frac{9}{10}$; the probability of having salad with their meal is $\frac{2}{3}$.
    Find the probability that a customer will have
        (a) both chips and salad
        (b) neither chips nor salad
        (c) chips but not salad.

    (ii) One in every four calls received by a fire brigade is a false alarm.
    Find the probability that of the next two calls
        (a) both will be false alarms
        (b) neither will be a false alarm
        (c) one will be a false alarm.

    (iii) A cube has four red faces and two green faces. This cube is tossed twice.
    Find the probability that these tosses result in
        (a) both red faces
        (b) one green and one red face
        (c) at least one green face.

5. At the beginning of each netball game, the umpire tosses a coin. The captain of Yumiko's team always calls tails.
    Draw a tree diagram to show the outcome of the toss (Win or Lose) the next three times that Yumiko's captain calls.
    Use the tree diagram to find the probability that Yumiko's team
        (a) wins the toss each time   (b) wins the toss just once
        (c) wins the toss twice   (d) wins the toss at least twice.

6. The probability that everyone in Gillian's class is present on a Monday is $\frac{1}{2}$. On a Tuesday this probability is $\frac{3}{5}$ and on a Wednesday this probability is $\frac{2}{3}$.
    Draw a tree diagram to show these probabilities.
    Use the tree diagram to find the probability that during the first three days of the next school week
        (a) no one is absent from Gillian's class
        (b) all are present on two of the three days
        (c) someone is absent on each of the three days.

Probability

Review 1 A bag contains 100 discs, 70 of which are green and the rest red.
Half of the green discs and 10 of the red discs have numbers on them. A disc
is chosen at random from this bag.

Copy and complete the tree diagram.

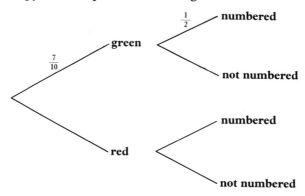

Use the tree diagram to find the probability that the disc chosen is
   (a)   a red disc with a number
   (b)   a disc with a number
   (c)   either a red disc with a number or a green disc without a number.

Review 2 A basketball team knows, from past experience, that it has a probability of $\frac{2}{5}$
of winning a game.
Draw a tree diagram to show the possible outcomes for the results of this
team during its next two games.
Use your tree diagram to find the probability that this team wins only one of
its next two games.

Review 3 Near the end of a maze there are three T junctions. (One of these is shown.)
The probability that a person turns left at each of
these is: probability 0·7 at the first, 0·2 at the
second and 0·4 at the third.
Use a tree diagram to find the probability that the
next person to go through this maze will
   (a)   turn left at all three junctions
   (b)   turn left at just one of these junctions
   (c)   turn right at all three junctions
   (d)   turn left at more than one of these
            junctions.

USING a TABLE OF PROBABILITIES

For independent events, we can use a table to find the probability of a combined event.

DISCUSSION EXERCISE 19:7

- The following example was done earlier on page 345, using a tree diagram.

  "On Rebecca's route to school there are two sets of traffic lights. The probability that Rebecca must stop at the first set is 0·7 and at the second set it is 0·4.

  Use a table to find the probability that Rebecca must stop at
  (a) both sets of these lights   (b) just one set of these lights."

  The steps taken to build up a table of probabilities (Table 3) are shown below. **Discuss** these steps.

Table 1

| | | 2nd set of lights | |
		S (0·4)	NS
1st set of lights	S (0·7)		
	NS		

Table 2

| | | 2nd set of lights | |
		S (0·4)	NS (0·6)
1st set of lights	S (0·7)		
	NS (0·3)		

Table 3

| | | 2nd set of lights | |
		S (0·4)	NS (0·6)
1st set of lights	S (0·7)	0·28	0·42
	NS (0·3)	0·12	0·18

Discuss how the answers to the questions can be found from Table 3.

- Table 3 illustrates the combined probabilities of two events. Could a similar table be used for the combined probabilities of more than two events? **Discuss.**

  Discuss the advantages and disadvantages of using a tree diagram or a table of probabilities.

  As part of your discussion, refer to some of the questions in Exercise 19:6.

INVESTIGATION 19:8

BIRTHDAYS

Would you think it unlikely that two students in a class of 20 have their birthday on the same day? You may be surprised. **Investigate.**

---

1. Daniel gathered data on the number of students in maths. classes in his school. Daniel's data is given below.

   20   18   22   19   23   22   25   23   18   20   21   26   24   24   21   20

   As part of Daniel's analysis of this data he found the median, the range, the lower quartile, the upper quartile and the interquartile range.

   What answers should Daniel get for these?

2. Are the following pairs of events independent?

   (a)   A die is tossed twice.

       Event A : a 4 on the first throw.

       Event B : a 4 on the second throw.

   (b)   An equal number of red and blue discs are placed in a bag. Cameron chooses two of these, at random, one after the other. If the first disc chosen is blue, it is replaced in the bag. If the first disc chosen is red, it is not replaced.

       Event P : the first disc chosen is red.

       Event Q : the second disc chosen is blue.

3. In a cottage garden collection of flowering plants, $\frac{2}{5}$ of the plants have mottled leaves and $\frac{3}{4}$ have white flowers.

   Copy and complete this tree diagram.

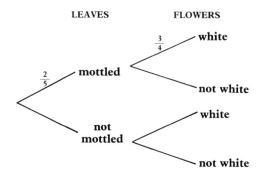

   One plant is chosen at random from this collection.

   Use your tree diagram to find the probability that this will

   (a)   be a white flowered plant with mottled leaves

   (b)   have neither white flowers nor mottled leaves.

4. Dina surveyed the students in her school to test the hypothesis "Left-handed pupils play more sport than right-handed pupils".

   Write down two questions (with possible responses) that Dina should have included in her questionnaire.

5. A restaurant offers 6 choices for the main course and 4 choices for dessert.
   Two of the main courses are pasta dishes; one of the desserts is cheesecake.
   Find the probability that the next customer who has both a main course and dessert
   chooses both a pasta dish and cheesecake. (Assume that all choices are equally popular.)

6. During one maths. lesson, students could choose to work on an investigation or on a
   practical activity. They could choose to work individually or as a group.
   Draw a tree diagram to illustrate.

7. **(i)** Copy these tables. Complete the cumulative frequency.

(a)

Time (min)	Frequency	Cumulative Frequency
$0 \leq t < 5$	3	3
$5 \leq t < 10$	4	7
$10 \leq t < 15$	16	23
$15 \leq t < 20$	24	
$20 \leq t < 25$	13	
$25 \leq t < 30$	7	

(b)

Mark for Test (%)	Frequency	Cumulative Frequency
1–20	2	
21–40	5	
41–60	9	
61–80	7	
81–100	4	27

(c)

Distance (km)	1·0–	1·5–	2·0–	2·5–	3·0–	3·5–	4·0–	4·5–5·0
Frequency	4	4	9	12	11	17	10	6
Cumulative Frequency								

(ii) Cumulative frequency graphs are to be drawn for the data in each of the tables.
What points should be plotted for each.

(iii) Draw the cumulative frequency graph for (c).
Use the graph to find the median and interquartile range.

8.

Two cards are selected at random from these cards. The first card is replaced before the
second card is chosen.   Find the probability that   **(a)**   the first card is a King
(b)   the first card is a King and the second is a Queen   **(c)**   both cards are red
(d)   a black and a red card are chosen, in either order.

9.

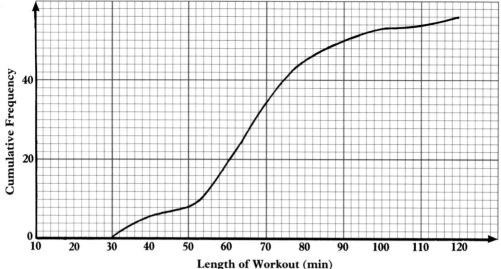

Length of Workout (min)

A gym. was analysing the time their members worked out for at different times of the day and on different days of the week.

The cumulative frequency graph shows the length of the workouts on a Monday of those members who arrived at the gym. before 9 a.m.

(a)   How many members arrived at the gym. before 9 a.m. on this Monday?

(b)   How many worked out for less than 1 hour?

(c)   How many worked out for less than 90 minutes?

(d)   How many worked out for between 1 hour and $1\frac{1}{2}$ hours?

(e)   What is the median workout time?

(f)   Find the lower and upper quartiles.

(g)   What is the interquartile range?

10. 70% of the people who use the Tunway Library are adults, 20% are school pupils and the rest are children under school age.

60% of the adults, 40% of the school pupils and 50% of the children under school age are male.

(a)   Copy and complete the tree diagram.

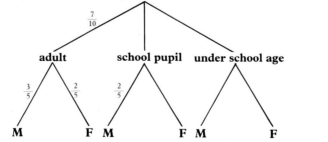

M – male
F – female

(b)   One person, who uses this library, is chosen at random to complete a questionnaire. Use the tree diagram to find the probability that an adult woman is chosen.

354

11. (i) Nathan did a survey on the prices of houses advertised for sale in his district. The data he collected is shown on this table.

   (a) Copy the table. Complete the cumulative frequencies.

   (b) Draw the cumulative frequency graph. Use this graph to find the median price and the interquartile range.

House Prices (£)			
Price Range at least	below	Number of Houses	Cumulative Frequency
20 000	40 000	5	5
40 000	60 000	8	13
60 000	80 000	15	
80 000	100 000	14	
100 000	120 000	24	
120 000	140 000	16	
140 000	160 000	9	
160 000	180 000	3	
180 000	200 000	2	

(ii) Nathan's cousin, David, lives in another district. David did a survey on the prices of houses advertised for sale in his district. David drew the cumulative frequency graph shown below, for his data.

Write a few sentences comparing the prices of houses in Nathan's and David's districts.

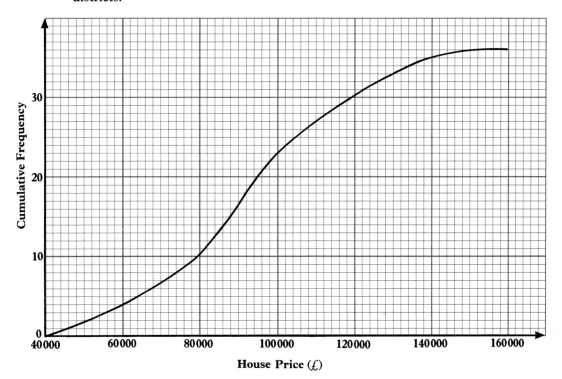

355

12.

Ranking \ Type	Horror	Drama	Comedy	Science Fiction
1	37	21	11	51
2	42	32	19	27
3	14	39	27	40
4	27	28	63	2

Amy asked the Year 11 students in her school to rank their preferences for types of films. Amy collated the data on the above table.

Make some conclusions from this data.

13. Two faults have been discovered in Mayota cars manufactured last year. All of these cars are recalled for a check.

The probability that one of these cars has faulty seatbelts is 0·1. The probability that the steering is faulty is 0·03.

Find the probability that one of these cars has **(a)**   both faults

(b)   neither fault

(c)   just one of the faults.

14. William's school is about to open a stationery "shop". William's class have been asked to survey pupil opinion about the likely use of this "shop".

Suggest questions that could be included in the questionnaire that William's class designs. Each question must include at least three possible responses.

15. In a fairground game of chance, the probability of winning a prize is $\frac{3}{10}$. Barbara plays this game three times.

Using a tree diagram, or otherwise, find the probability that Barbara
  (a)   wins 3 prizes
  (b)   wins just one prize
  (c)   wins at least one prize
  (d)   does not win a prize.

16. Jane wants to know if girls have better recall than boys. She designs an experiment to test whether this is true.

What sort of experiment might Jane design?

How might Jane go about collecting the data?

How might Jane analyse her data?

INDEX

ANSWERS

Number from Previous Levels

Page 18   **Revision Exercise**

1. **(a)** 100 times as large **(b)** 1000 times as large   2. Lucy pays 44p more.   3. b, c   4. **(a)** $\frac{2}{25}$
(b) $\frac{6}{25}$ **(c)** $\frac{1}{6}$ **(d)** $\frac{3}{10}$ **(e)** $\frac{7}{1000}$ 5. 8 hours 15 minutes   6. 1896, 2000, 2020   7. **(a)** mm
(b) g **(c)** t **(d)** m **(e)** km **(f)** mg **(g)** m*l*   8. **(a)** 32 **(b)** 13 **(c)** 8432 **(d)** 31 **(e)** 49
(f) 180 **(g)** 2000 **(h)** 45   9. **(a)** 8 m **(b)** 240 mm (24 cm)   10. **(a)** 1658 **(b)** about 829
11. **(a)** 20:9 **(b)** 1:3 **(c)** 3:8   12. **(a)** 38·4 **(b)** 2400 **(c)** 1740 **(d)** 0·194 **(e)** 700 **(f)** 2·825
13. **(a)** 153·6 km **(b)** 75 mph **(c)** £8·16   14. **(a)** 5°C **(b)** –4°C   15. **(a)** 95 marks
(b) £34·80   16. **(a)** 66·25 cm **(b)** 66·15 cm   17. **(a)** Natasha **(b)** One possible answer is
a = 15, b = 16   18. **(a)** 0·17 (2 d.p.) **(b)** 16·7% (3 s.f.)   19. 9·2% (1 d.p.)   20. **(a)** 21600 cm³
(b) 3 minutes 21. **(a)** 0·807 (3 s.f.) **(b)** 0·398 (3 s.f.)   22. 70   23. **(a)** 65·4% **(b)** France
(c) Ireland   24. **(a)** 2 × 2 × 3 × 7 **(b)** 1260 **(c)** 12   25. £150   26. **(i) (a)** £398 **(b)** £648
(c) £382 **(ii)** £938   27. 2·8 kg   28. Peter
29. **(a)** A possible answer is

3	7	4
2	5	3
1	4	6

(b) Not possible since 16 + 9 + 18 is not
equal to 15 + 17 + 14.
30. 10   31. A possible answer is 153.
32. 3

Chapter 1   Calculating with Fractions

Page 25   **Discussion Exercise 1:1**

1. £80   2. £1600

Page 26   **Exercise 1:3**

1. **(a)** $\frac{5}{7}$, $\frac{2}{5}$, $\frac{3}{4}$, $\frac{8}{9}$, $\frac{5}{6}$, $\frac{3}{10}$ **(b)** $\frac{7}{5}$, $\frac{4}{3}$, $\frac{17}{4}$, $\frac{6}{5}$, $\frac{9}{8}$, $\frac{10}{3}$ 2. **(a)** $2\frac{3}{5}$ **(b)** $4\frac{1}{4}$ **(c)** $1\frac{2}{3}$
(d) $4\frac{1}{2}$ **(e)** $2\frac{1}{5}$ **(f)** $3\frac{1}{6}$ **(g)** $12\frac{1}{2}$ **(h)** $8\frac{1}{3}$ **(i)** $5\frac{1}{7}$ **(j)** $1\frac{5}{9}$ 3. **(a)** $\frac{11}{4}$ **(b)** $\frac{7}{2}$ **(c)** $\frac{12}{5}$
(d) $\frac{13}{8}$ **(e)** $\frac{21}{4}$ **(f)** $\frac{17}{6}$ **(g)** $\frac{43}{8}$ **(h)** $\frac{43}{6}$ **(i)** $\frac{31}{9}$ **(j)** $\frac{53}{10}$ **Review (i) (a)** $5\frac{3}{5}$ **(b)** $2\frac{5}{7}$
(ii) (a) $\frac{13}{4}$ **(b)** $\frac{17}{3}$

Page 29   **Exercise 1:5**

1. **(a)** $\frac{4}{35}$ **(b)** $\frac{2}{5}$ **(c)** $\frac{10}{27}$ **(d)** $\frac{8}{15}$ **(e)** $\frac{15}{22}$ **(f)** $2\frac{2}{3}$ **(g)** $1\frac{1}{7}$ **(h)** $6\frac{2}{3}$ **(i)** $\frac{1}{2}$ **(j)** $2\frac{1}{4}$
2. **(a)** $7\frac{1}{2}$ **(b)** $4\frac{1}{3}$ **(c)** 6 **(d)** $4\frac{2}{3}$ **(e)** $11\frac{2}{3}$ **(f)** 10 **(g)** $3\frac{1}{4}$ **(h)** $13\frac{1}{3}$ 3. **(a)** $2\frac{1}{4}$ **(b)** $7\frac{1}{9}$ **(c)** 2
(d) $13\frac{1}{4}$ 4. Yes   5. $\frac{1}{10}$ 6. 216 miles   7. $11\frac{1}{3}$ square metres   8. **(b)** There are many answers.
Review 1 (a) $5\frac{1}{3}$ **(b)** $\frac{1}{6}$ **(c)** 16 **(d)** $5\frac{1}{5}$ **Review 2** $2\frac{7}{8}$ square metres

Answers

Page 31

Exercise 1:7

1. (a) $\frac{1}{4}$ (b) $\frac{1}{5}$ (c) $\frac{9}{50}$ (d) $\frac{5}{32}$ (e) $\frac{7}{30}$ (f) 4 (g) $2\frac{1}{2}$ (h) 30 (i) 12 (j) 20 (k) $1\frac{1}{3}$ (l) $\frac{7}{8}$
(m) $1\frac{1}{5}$ (n) $1\frac{1}{4}$ 2. (a) $1\frac{2}{5}$ (b) $2\frac{1}{5}$ (c) $\frac{5}{8}$ (d) $\frac{5}{9}$ (e) $1\frac{9}{10}$ (f) 6 (g) 3 (h) $1\frac{1}{2}$ (i) 6 (j) $11\frac{1}{3}$

3. 10   4. $1\frac{7}{9}$ 5. 8 hours   6. £1·20   7. 24   8. (b) There is more than one answer.

Review 1 (a) $\frac{2}{3}$ (b) 9 (c) $1\frac{7}{8}$ **Review 2** 8   **Review 3** 14

Page 34

Exercise 1:9

1. (a) $\frac{2}{3}$ (b) $\frac{2}{3}$ (c) $\frac{5}{9}$ (d) $\frac{1}{3}$ (e) 1 (f) $1\frac{1}{2}$ (g) $1\frac{1}{4}$ (h) $\frac{3}{8}$ 2. (a) $\frac{7}{10}$ (b) $\frac{5}{8}$ (c) $\frac{1}{12}$
(d) $\frac{7}{12}$ (e) $1\frac{7}{12}$ (f) $\frac{17}{24}$ (g) $\frac{37}{60}$ 3. (a) $1\frac{1}{2}$ (b) $1\frac{13}{24}$ (c) $\frac{8}{15}$ (d) $\frac{1}{4}$ 4. $\frac{1}{6}$

5. the glass   6. $\frac{1}{6}$ 7. $\frac{19}{40}$ 8. $1\frac{1}{6}$ **Review 1** (a) $\frac{8}{9}$ (b) $\frac{1}{6}$ (c) $1\frac{5}{12}$ (d) $\frac{1}{6}$

Review 2 $\frac{1}{30}$

Page 36

Exercise 1:11

1. (a) $4\frac{1}{4}$ (b) $4\frac{11}{12}$ (c) $1\frac{3}{10}$ (d) $6\frac{1}{5}$ (e) $1\frac{7}{8}$ (f) $1\frac{8}{15}$ (g) $\frac{5}{6}$ 2. $6\frac{1}{4}$ hours   3. $3\frac{3}{8}$ pages   4. 8

5. There are many possible answers.

6. (a)

$\frac{1}{2}$	$1\frac{1}{3}$	$1\frac{1}{6}$
$1\frac{2}{3}$	1	$\frac{1}{3}$
$\frac{5}{6}$	$\frac{2}{3}$	$1\frac{1}{2}$

(b)

$2\frac{4}{5}$	$1\frac{1}{20}$	$1\frac{2}{5}$
$\frac{7}{20}$	$1\frac{3}{4}$	$3\frac{3}{20}$
$2\frac{1}{10}$	$2\frac{9}{20}$	$\frac{7}{10}$

(c)

$1\frac{7}{12}$	$5\frac{13}{24}$	$4\frac{3}{4}$
$7\frac{1}{8}$	$3\frac{23}{24}$	$\frac{19}{24}$
$3\frac{1}{6}$	$2\frac{3}{8}$	$6\frac{1}{3}$

Review 1 (a) $4\frac{19}{20}$ (b) $1\frac{5}{12}$ (c) $\frac{17}{24}$ **Review 2** (a) $20\frac{1}{20}$ l (b) $\frac{9}{20}$ l

Page 37

Exercise 1:12

1. (a) ÷ (b) + (c) × (d) −   2. $10\frac{1}{2}$ 3. $\frac{1}{6}$ 4. 291km

5. (a)

$\frac{2}{5}$	×	$1\frac{7}{8}$	=	$\frac{3}{4}$
÷		÷		÷
$\frac{1}{2}$	×	$\frac{3}{4}$	=	$\frac{3}{8}$
=		=		=
$\frac{4}{5}$	×	$2\frac{1}{2}$	=	2

(b)

$1\frac{1}{2}$	+	$\frac{2}{3}$	=	$2\frac{1}{6}$
−				×
$\frac{3}{4}$	÷	$\frac{5}{16}$	=	$2\frac{2}{5}$
=				=
$\frac{3}{4}$	+	$4\frac{9}{20}$	=	$5\frac{1}{5}$

6. (a) $\frac{4}{15}$ (b) £5720   7. 16km   8. (a) 60mm (or 6cm) (b) $\frac{3}{4}$ 9. $\frac{3}{16}$ 10. 60l 11. 15

Review 1 (a) $\frac{5}{12}$ (b) I. M. Mahon (c) 1689   **Review 2** £50

Page 40

Exercise 1:14

1. 5   2. 5   3. 0   4. $3\frac{5}{14}$ 5. $1\frac{1}{2}$ 6. $1\frac{1}{6}$ 7. $1\frac{5}{6}$ 8. $1\frac{1}{8}$ 9. $4\frac{2}{3}$ 10. $1\frac{1}{2}$ **Review 1** $\frac{7}{16}$

Review 2 $5\frac{1}{10}$

Answers

Exercise 1:15

1. (a) $5\frac{1}{2}$ **(b)** 55 **2. (a)** 100 **(b)** $4\frac{1}{4}$ **3.** 240 **4.** Alison 49, Brenda $50\frac{2}{3}$, Ben $49\frac{1}{3}$

5. (a) Area = 3m², Perimeter = $7\frac{1}{6}$m **(b)** Area = $7\frac{1}{2}$m², Perimeter = $11\frac{1}{6}$m

6. (a) $3\frac{3}{5}$ **(b)** $3\frac{7}{12}$ **7. (a)** 14 **(b)** 20 **8. (a)** $17\frac{1}{2}$ **(b)** 187 **9. (a)** 2 minutes **(b)** $1\frac{1}{3}$ minutes

10. (a) 110 **(b)** 415 **(c)** $5\frac{3}{4}$ **11.** $3\frac{1}{3}$ **Review 1 (a)** £18 **(b)** £12 **Review 2** $52\frac{1}{2}$

Page 43

Puzzle 1:16

$\frac{1}{2} + \frac{1}{3} + \frac{1}{9}$ is not equal to 1.

Chapter 2 Estimating Answers to Calculations

Page 48

Exercise 2:2

1. Possible estimates are: **(a)** about 32 **(b)** about 7 **(c)** about 140 **(d)** a little more than 100 **(e)** about 150 **(f)** about 2 **(g)** about 20 **(h)** about 15 **(i)** about 30 **(j)** about $\frac{1}{2}$ **(k)** about 3200 **2.** Possible answers are: **(a)** 869 (3 s.f.) **(b)** 5·1 (1 d.p.) **(c)** 9·0 (2 s.f.) **(d)** 3·31 (3 s.f.) **(e)** 175 (3 s.f.) **(f)** 130 **(g)** 10·5 (3 s.f.) **(h)** 10·6 (3 s.f.) **(i)** 14 (2 s.f.) **(j)** 1280 (3 s.f.) **(k)** 0·63 (2 s.f.) **(l)** 24·4 (1 d.p.) **3.** about 400 **4.** about 20 **5. (a)** £79·44 (to the nearest penny) **(b)** 22·43m **(c)** £881·95 **(d)** £18·01 (to the nearest penny) **(e)** 233cm² (3 s.f.) **(f)** 2240cm² (3 s.f.) **(g)** 31200mm³ (3 s.f.) **(h)** 10 hours 50 minutes **(i)** 36 **Review 1** Possible answers are: **(a)** about 200 **(b)** about 60 **(c)** about 40 **(d)** about 5 **(e)** about 50 **Review 2** Possible answers are: **(a)** 384 (3 s.f.) **(b)** 4·8 (1 d.p.) **(c)** 5·66 (3 s.f.) **(d)** 19·4 (3 s.f.) **Review 3** 2400cm³ (2 s.f.)

Chapter 3 Calculating with Negative Numbers

Page 53

Exercise 3:2

1. (a) –3 **(b)** –7 **(c)** 7 **(d)** 3 **(e)** 7 **(f)** 3 **(g)** –3 **(h)** –7 **(i)** –7 **(j)** 8 **(k)** –6 **(l)** 1 **(m)** –10 **(n)** –12 **(o)** 4 **2. (a)** –6 **(b)** –3 **(c)** 12 **(d)** –6 **(e)** –2 **(f)** –7 **(g)** 14 **(h)** –3

3. (a)

+	-4	5	-2
4	0	9	2
-6	-10	-1	-8
2	-2	7	0

(b)

+	-2	6	2
-3	-5	3	-1
-2	-4	4	0
-8	-10	-2	-6

(c)

+	-5	4	0
3	-2	7	3
-1	-6	3	-1
-5	-10	-1	-5

4. (a) –2, 1 (b) –0·3, –2·3   5. 0·9° below normal   6. (i) (a) 60m (b) 1300m (ii) 1805m
7. £1245·65 overdrawn   8. (a) –1·6 (b) –9·1 (c) –1·8 (d) –4·2 (e) 3·4 (f) 6·6
(g) 2·1   Review 1 (a) –8 (b) 5 (c) –2·5 (d) 0·9 (e) –11   Review 2 (i) (a) 2 a.m.
(b) 2 p.m. (ii) (a) 7 p.m. (b) 2 p.m. (c) 6 p.m.   Review 3 6, 5, 4, 2, 1, –1, –2, –5, –8

Page 56   **Exercise 3:4**

1. (a) –21 (b) –10 (c) –16 (d) 20 (e) –15 (f) –4 (g) 6 (h) –4 (i) 3 (j) –4 (k) 4
(l) –6   2. (a) 24 (b) 60 (c) –30 (d) 6 (e) 9 (f) –10 (g) 4 (h) –2   3. (a) –3 (b) 8·8
(c) –7·5 (d) –1·6 (e) 4·1 (f) –2·1   4. (a) –4 (b) 6 (c) –24 (d) 24
Review 1 –20 in square 7, –4 in square 13.   Review 2 (a) –21 (b) 40 (c) –24 (d) –10
(e) –5 (f) 4

Page 58   **Exercise 3:5**

1. (a) –11 (b) 5 (c) –2 (d) 9 (e) 12 (f) –15 (g) 43 (h) 4 (i) –21   2. (a) 17 (b) –32
(c) 19 (d) 7 (e) 28 (f) 46 (g) 5 (h) –7 (i) –7   3. (a) –3 + 4 – (–1) = 2
(b) 2 × (–3) + (–4) = – 10   (c) 1 – (–4) + (–2) – 3 = 0   (d) –2 – (–6) ÷ (–3) + 5 = 1
(e) 6 [(–4) + 5] ÷ 3 = 2   5. A swan is drawn.   Review (a) –5 (b) –11 (c) 35 (d) 25
(e) –46 (f) –40 (g) –21

Page 61   **Exercise 3:7**

1. (a) –7 (b) 5 (c) 4 (d) –3½ (e) –1   2. (a) –22 (b) 12 (c) –6½ (d) –4½ (e) 12 (f) 4
(g) –15½ (h) –2 (i) –22 (j) 0   3. –1239   4. (4, 2) (–2, 5) (2½ , 2¾) (–3½ , 5¾) (9, –½)
5. (a) 212°F (b) 32°F (c) 14°F (d) 5°F (e) –40°F   6. (a) 52·5 (b) –2·25 (c) –1·25
(d) –7·75   Review 1 (a) –10°C (b) –20°C   Review 2 (a) –4 (b) –22 (c) 6 (d) 5
(e) $\frac{1}{4}$

Page 62   **Puzzles 3:8**

Possible answers are:

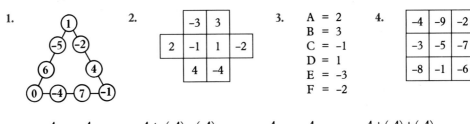

1.   2.

	–3	3	
2	–1	1	–2
	4	–4	

3. A = 2
    B = 3
    C = –1
    D = 1
    E = –3
    F = –2

4.

–4	–9	–2
–3	–5	–7
–8	–1	–6

5. $0 = \dfrac{-4}{-4} - \dfrac{-4}{-4},\quad 1 = \dfrac{-4 + (-4) - (-4)}{-4},\quad 2 = \dfrac{-4}{-4} + \dfrac{-4}{-4},\quad 3 = \dfrac{-4 + (-4) + (-4)}{-4},$

$4 = \dfrac{-4 - (-4)}{-4} - (-4),\quad 5 = \dfrac{-4 - (-4) \times (-4)}{-4},\quad 6 = \dfrac{-4 + (-4)}{-4} - (-4),\quad 7 = - [(-4) + (-4) + \dfrac{-4}{-4}],$

$8 = -4 \times (-4) + (-4) + (-4)$

Chapter 4   Indices. Standard Form

Page 65 **Exercise 4:2**

1. 5   **2.** 2   **3.** 5   **4.** 8   **5.** –7   **6.** –6   **7.** –4   **8.** –10   **9.** 4   **10** –9   **11.** 3   **12.** –3
Review 1 4   Review 2 –9

Page 67 **Exercise 4:4**

1. (a) $\frac{1}{2}$ **(b)** $\frac{1}{2}$ **(c)** $\frac{1}{2}$ **(d)** $\frac{1}{3}$ **(e)** $\frac{1}{3}$ **(f)** $\frac{1}{4}$ **(g)** $\frac{1}{7}$ **2. (a)** 2   **(b)** 4   **(c)** 3
(d) 8   **(e)** 10   **(f)** 2   **(g)** 3   **(h)** 5   **(i)** 2   **(j)** 3   **(k)** 2   Review 1 **(a)** $\frac{1}{2}$ **(b)** $\frac{1}{3}$
Review 2 **(a)** 5   **(b)** 6   **(c)** 4   **(d)** 2

Page 69 **Exercise 4:6**

1. a, d, g, i   **2. (a)** 340   **(b)** 8120   **(c)** 0·0625   **(d)** 0·008   **(e)** 70300   **(f)** 2·05   **(g)** 0·78
(h) 0·000101   **(i)** 370000   **(j)** 0·000037   **(k)** 15·2   **(l)** 3·4   **(m)** 0·00481   **(n)** 80
(o) 0·0000261   **(p)** 60000000000   **(q)** 0·0705   **(r)** 815·4   **(s)** 0·008154   **(t)** 94·07   **(u)** 0·9407
(v) 60000   **(w)** 0·0006   **3. (a)** 1   **(b)** 2   **(c)** 0   **(d)** 1   **(e)** 3   **(f)** –1   **(g)** –2   **(h)** –1   **(i)** –3
(j) 0   **(k)** 1   **(l)** –2   **(m)** –1   **(n)** 1   **(o)** –4   **4. (a)** $6·4 \times 10^{1}$ **(b)** $7·82 \times 10^{2}$ **(c)** $3·64 \times 10^{3}$
(d) $5·52 \times 10^{1}$ **(e)** $7·0 \times 10^{0}$ **(f)** $1·0 \times 10^{3}$ **(g)** $3·42 \times 10^{1}$ **(h)** $5·5561 \times 10^{2}$ **(i)** $7·24 \times 10^{1}$
(j) $8·0 \times 10^{-1}$ **(k)** $9·1 \times 10^{-1}$ **(l)** $4·3 \times 10^{-3}$ **(m)** $8·04 \times 10^{-1}$ **(n)** $4·0 \times 10^{-2}$
(o) $2·4 \times 10^{0}$ **(p)** $2·4 \times 10^{-1}$ **(q)** $2·4 \times 10^{1}$ **(r)** $2·4 \times 10^{-3}$ **(s)** $2·4 \times 10^{2}$ **(t)** $9·0 \times 10^{0}$
(u) $9·0 \times 10^{1}$ **(v)** $9·0 \times 10^{-2}$ **(w)** $9·0 \times 10^{-1}$ **5.** $6·12 \times 10^{7}$ **6.** 18000000   **7.** 1900000
8. $3·0 \times 10^{5}$ km/sec   **9.** 9460000000000 km   **10.** $1·5 \times 10^{10}$ light years   **11.** 0·0000003 sec
12. 0·00005 cm   **13.** $1·0 \times 10^{-10}$ mm   Review 1 **(a)** 23000   **(b)** 2·3   **(c)** 0·00023
(d) 0·30504   **(e)** 9010000   **(f)** 0·0064   **(g)** 346·5   Review 2 **(a)** $5·27 \times 10^{1}$ **(b)** $1·6005 \times 10^{4}$
(c) $6·0 \times 10^{0}$ **(d)** $8·3 \times 10^{-1}$ **(e)** $1·0 \times 10^{-1}$ **(f)** $2·0 \times 10^{-4}$ Review 3 2200000
Review 4 Sun: $1·6 \times 10^{-5}$ light years   Milky Way: $2·6 \times 10^{4}$ light years

Page 71 **Exercise 4:7**

1. (a) $7·4 \times 10^{9}$ **(b)** $8·5 \times 10^{9}$ **(c)** $7·28 \times 10^{7}$ **(d)** $4·8 \times 10^{3}$ **(e)** $8·24 \times 10^{-8}$ **(f)** $2·12 \times 10^{3}$
(g) $2·3 \times 10^{-3}$ **(h)** $2·1 \times 10^{8}$ **(i)** $1·5 \times 10^{2}$ **2. (a)** $1·44 \times 10^{13}$ **(b)** $3·0 \times 10^{2}$ **(c)** $7·0 \times 10^{5}$
(d) $1·28 \times 10^{-5}$ **(e)** $8·0 \times 10^{1}$ **(f)** $4·86 \times 10^{5}$ **(g)** $1·17384 \times 10^{11}$ **(h)** $9·1154 \times 10^{-1}$
(i) $1·2 \times 10^{-2}$ **(j)** $6·2548 \times 10^{-4}$ **(k)** $1·9 \times 10^{-5}$ **3.** $4·68 \times 10^{5}$mm²   **4.** $1·35 \times 10^{-19}$ grams
5. about $1·42 \times 10^{7}$ **6.** $2·04 \times 10^{2}$ kg   **7.** $2·5 \times 10^{-1}$ m³   **8.** 237   **9.** about 4·2 light-years
10. (a) Pluto   **(b)** Jupiter   **(c)** Saturn   **(d)** Pluto   **(e)** Neptune   **(f)** 5   **11.** $5·97 \times 10^{21}$ tonne
12. (a) $1·0 \times 10^{18}$ **(b)** $1·0 \times 10^{24}$ **13. (a)** 10^{3} **(b)** 10^{-4} Review 1 **(a)** $9·6 \times 10^{5}$
(b) $1·06 \times 10^{6}$ **(c)** $4·2 \times 10^{5}$ **(d)** $5·07 \times 10^{-3}$ **(e)** $5·0 \times 10^{-2}$ Review 2 $1·0 \times 10^{3}$ (1000 times
larger)   Review 3 **(a)** Paris   **(b)** Darwin   **(c)** Darwin   **(d)** Paris
Review 4 **(a)** $2·0 \times 10^{-1}$ km/sec   **(b)** about $1·08 \times 10^{9}$ km/h

Page 75 **Exercise 4:10**

1. (a) $6·95 \times 10^{3}$ **(b)** $1·88 \times 10^{5}$ **(c)** $6·104 \times 10^{2}$ **(d)** $4·15267 \times 10^{7}$ **(e)** $8·89719 \times 10^{2}$
(f) $7·6008541 \times 10^{2}$ **(g)** $7·34 \times 10^{-3}$ **(h)** $3·0662 \times 10^{-2}$ **(i)** $6·506 \times 10^{9}$ **2.** about £$1·1 \times 10^{11}$
3. about $1·528 \times 10^{5}$ **4.** about $6·717 \times 10^{5}$ tonne   **5.** about $7·963 \times 10^{5}$ **6.** about $8·514 \times 10^{9}$
7. about $1·238 \times 10^{5}$ **8.** $3·86 \times 10^{8}$ Review 1 **(a)** $6·601 \times 10^{-2}$ **(b)** $-8·73 \times 10^{0}$
Review 2 **(a)** about $8·28 \times 10^{7}$ km²   **(b)** about $2·47 \times 10^{8}$ km²

Page 77   **Exercise 4:12**

1. $9 \cdot 21 \times 10^{20}$ 2. $3 \cdot 7 \times 10^{22}$ 3. $6 \cdot 2 \times 10^{25}$ 4. $5 \cdot 830 \times 10^{23}$ 5. $1 \cdot 84$ 6. $89 \cdot 88$
7. $3 \cdot 0 \times 10^{-20}$ 8. $20 \cdot 3$ 9. $6 \cdot 1 \times 10^{-19}$ 10. $0 \cdot 444$ 11. $3 \cdot 57 \times 10^{14}$ 12. $1 \cdot 6 \times 10^{-6}$
Review 1 139   **Review 2** $2 \cdot 59 \times 10^{-16}$

Chapter 5   Number Review

Page 79

1. (a) $6 \cdot 78 \times 10^2$ (b) $2 \cdot 0 \times 10^0$ (c) $7 \cdot 04 \times 10^{-1}$ (d) $2 \cdot 0 \times 10^{-2}$ (e) $2 \cdot 83 \times 10^1$ 2. (a) $4\frac{1}{8}$

(b) $\frac{59}{8}$ 3. (a) about 20   (b) about 800

4.

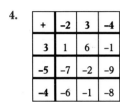

+	-2	3	-4
3	1	6	-1
-5	-7	-2	-9
-4	-6	-1	-8

×	7	-2	-3
-2	-14	4	6
-1	-7	2	3
2	14	-4	-6

5. (a) 47000   (b) $0 \cdot 06$ (c) $1 \cdot 8$
6. $5 \cdot 1 \times 10^6$ 7. $2465 \cdot 9$ km   8. (a) $\frac{1}{10}$
(b) 30   (c) $7\frac{1}{2}$ (d) $\frac{5}{6}$ (e) $1\frac{5}{7}$ (f) $\frac{7}{12}$
(g) $1\frac{13}{20}$ (h) $8\frac{4}{15}$ (i) $1\frac{5}{12}$ (j) $2\frac{9}{10}$ (k) $1\frac{3}{4}$

9. (a) 8   (b) -3   (c) $\frac{1}{2}$ (d) $\frac{1}{3}$ 10. $1 \cdot 14 \times 10^{-4}$ years   11. $\frac{7}{15}$ 12. (a) -9   (b) 9
(c) $-3 \cdot 9$ (d) 3   (e) -56   (f) 6   (g) -6   (h) -18   (i) 2   (j) -4   (k) -1   (l) -9   13. (a) 7
(b) 3   14. (a) 356 (3 s.f.)   (b) $11 \cdot 3$ (1 d.p.)   15. $-3\frac{3}{4}$ 16. (a) 69 B.C.   (b) 56   (c) 31 years
17. 8   18. $(4, -1), (-2, -4), (-1, -3\frac{1}{2}), (1\frac{1}{2}, -2\frac{1}{4}), (-1\frac{1}{2}, -3\frac{3}{4})$ 19. (a) $2 \cdot 34 \times 10^3$ (b) $4 \cdot 2 \times 10^3$
20. 20 hours   21. (a) $4 \cdot 0 \times 10^{-12}$ mm   (b) $4 \cdot 0 \times 10^{-15}$ m   22. 72 kg   23. $18 \cdot 6$ (1 d.p.)
24. (a) about 209 people per square kilometre   (b) about 99 people per square kilometre
25. (a) No   (b) about 3000 times   (c) Andromeda Galaxy   (d) $9 \cdot 5 \times 10^{12}$ km   (e) $4 \cdot 2$ (2 s.f.)
26. $10\frac{2}{3}$ m²   27. $\frac{9}{20}$ 28. (a) 33100 or $3 \cdot 31 \times 10^4$ (b) $2 \cdot 25 \times 10^{-3}$ or $0 \cdot 00225$
(c) $3 \cdot 56 \times 10^{17}$ (3 s.f.)   (d) $0 \cdot 0161$ (3 s.f.)   29. (a) $4 \cdot 05 \times 10^9$ (b) $3 \cdot 15 \times 10^8$ 30. $\frac{32}{41}$

Algebra from Previous Levels

Page 89   **Revision Exercise**

1. (a) 2, 3, 11, 19   (b) 8   (c) 4   (d) 4, 8, 16, 20   (e) 1, 2, 4, 20   2. (a) D   (b) C
3. (i) (a) x + 2   (b) 4x + 4   (c) x(x + 2)   (ii) $4 \cdot 5$m   4. (a) 7   (b) $0 \cdot 5$ (c) $-2 \cdot 5$ (d) -10
(e) 4   5. (a) 20 rods and 12 bolts in the 2nd size screen. 26 rods and 15 bolts in the 3rd size
screen.   (b) r = 2b - 4   6. (a) a = 5, b = -2   (b) m = 2, n = $0 \cdot 5$ 7. (i) (a) $\frac{1}{8}$ (b) $\frac{1}{3a}$
(c) $\frac{3}{x}$ (ii) (a) $0 \cdot 04$ (b) $0 \cdot 53$ (c) $2 \cdot 9$ (d) $0 \cdot 011$ 8. (a) 25, 36, 49   (b) 13, 21, 34
(c) 13, 18, 24   (d) 125, 216, 343   (e) 2, 1, $0 \cdot 5$ 9. (i) (a) $n \le 3$ (b) $n > -4$ (c) $1 < n \le 5$
(ii) (a) ———⊕——⊕———   (b) -2, -1, 0, 1   10. (a) 200 + 75d = 100d   (b) 8
                 -3   2

11. (a) $-2n - 3a$ **(b)** $12 - x$ **12. (a)** a is the price each adult paid; s is the price each student paid. **(b)** $5a + 44s = 184$ **(c)** Adults paid £6 each; students paid £3·50 each. **(d)** £84 assuming that each student would pay at the child's rate. **13. (a)** 4^5 **(b)** 4^{14} **(c)** 4^3 **14. (a)** 0810 **(b)** 100 km **(c)** 0835 **(d)** 50 km **(e)** once **(f)** 120 km/h **(g)** 100 km/h **15.** 21 **16.** The last digit of 7^{107} is 3. **17. (a)** Because 40 is between 16 and 54. **(b)** 2·7 **(c)** 2·71 **18. (a)** x^{a+b} **(b)** x^{a-b} **(c)** x^{a-b-c} **(d)** x^6 **(e)** $16x^6y^2$ **19. (a)** the sequence on the right; 7th term = 4374 **(b)** $t_n = 3n - 1$ **20. (a)** 5832, 5328, 8352 **(b)** 12 **21. (a)** 65 **(b)** 176 **22. (i) (a)**

x	0	3	6
y	8	4	0

(b)

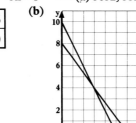

(ii) (a) $4f + 3s = 24$ **(b)** 3 marks for each question in the first section; 4 marks for each question in the second section. **(iii)** The solution for the equations in (b) can be found by finding where the graphs drawn in (a) meet.

23. (a) and **(c)** graphs

(b) $C = 2·5n$
(c) 10 games

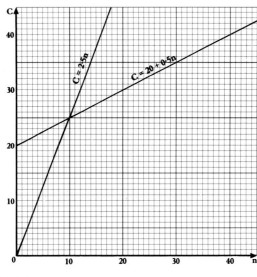

24. (a)

x	-3	-2	-1	0	1	2	3
y	6	1	-2	-3	-2	1	6

(b)

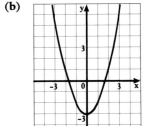

25. (a) 7 and 13 **(b)** 21 **26. (b)** 18·4 m **27. (a)** 240 m **(b)** 300 m **(c)** 1100 m or 1·1 km **28.** Sarah's **29. (i) (a)** $1 + 3 + 5 + 7 = 16$; $1 + 3 + 5 + 7 + 9 = 25$ **(b)** $Sn = n^2$ **(c)** 625 **(d)** 19 **(ii) (a)** Possible examples are $1 + 3 = 4$, $1 + 3 + 5 = 9$, $1 + 3 + 5 + 7 = 16$. **(b)** A possible example is $3 + 5 = 8$. **(c)** A possible correct statement is "if you add together two or more consecutive odd numbers, beginning with 1, you always get a square number".

Chapter 6 Formulae. Functions. Expressions

Exercise 6:2

1. (a) $h = \dfrac{2A}{b}$ (b) $h = \dfrac{2A}{a+b}$ (c) $h = \dfrac{V}{lb}$ (d) $h = \dfrac{3V}{A}$ 2. (a) $r = \dfrac{d}{2}$ (b) $r = \dfrac{c}{2\pi}$

3. (a) $l = \dfrac{A}{\pi r}$ (b) $l = \dfrac{P}{2} - w$ 4. (a) $m = \dfrac{y-c}{x}$ (b) $m = dv$ (c) $m = \dfrac{F}{a}$

5. (a) $I = \dfrac{V}{R}$ (b) $x = \dfrac{y-2}{m} - 3$ (c) $P = \dfrac{100I}{RT}$ (d) $r = \dfrac{D-5s}{\pi}$ (e) $s = \dfrac{v^2 - u^2}{2a}$

(f) $b = \dfrac{2A}{h} - a$ (g) $R = \dfrac{100A}{P} - 100$ (h) $h = \dfrac{A}{2\pi r} - r$ **Review** (a) $y = mx$ (b) $x = \dfrac{y}{m}$

(c) $t = \dfrac{v-u}{a}$ (d) $C = \dfrac{5(F-32)}{9}$

Exercise 6:4

1. (a) $r = \sqrt{\dfrac{A}{\pi}}$ (b) $r = \sqrt{\dfrac{3V}{\pi h}}$ 2. (a) $x = \pm\sqrt{a}$ (b) $x = \pm\sqrt{\dfrac{b}{5}}$ (c) $x = \pm\sqrt{\dfrac{2}{c}}$

(d) $x = \pm\sqrt{\dfrac{bd}{a}}$ 3. $l = \sqrt{\dfrac{3I}{m}}$ 4. $v = \pm\sqrt{\dfrac{2E}{m}}$ 5. $t = \sqrt{\dfrac{2s}{g}}$ 6. $y = \pm\sqrt{4ax}$

7. (a) $r = \sqrt[3]{V}$ (b) $r = \sqrt[3]{\dfrac{3V}{4\pi}}$ 8. (a) $l = n^2$ (b) $l = n^2 + 2$ (c) $l = \dfrac{a^2}{n^2}$ (d) $l = \dfrac{a}{n^2}$

9. $l = g\left(\dfrac{T}{2\pi}\right)^2$ **Review** (a) $d = \sqrt{\dfrac{c}{I}}$ (b) $r = \sqrt{\dfrac{A}{4\pi}}$ (c) $x = \pm\sqrt{a^2 y}$ (d) $n = \dfrac{a^2}{b^2} - 1$

Exercise 6:6

1. (a) 9 (b) 40 (c) 3·75 (d) –5 2. (a) 900° (b) 17 3. 1·56 cm 4. (a) 58·5 (b) 2·20
(c) 12·0 5. (a) 400 (b) 17 6. (a) $x = \sqrt[3]{V}$ (b) 4·31 mm 7. (a) 70·0 (b) 1·20
8. (a) 4·59 (b) 23·6, –23·6 (c) 4·0625 9. (a) 10·5 (b) 12 (c) 2·72 10. (a) 6·35 (b) 6·71
11. (a) 141 (b) 4·23 12. (a) 3·49 (b) 36 **Review 1** (a) 381·8 (b) 90 (c) 7 (d) 3
Review 2 (a) 1·6 (b) 6, –6 **Review 3** 37·5 cm²

Exercise 6:7

1. $A = \dfrac{P^2}{16}$ 2. $x = \dfrac{1}{y^2}$ 3. $s = \dfrac{v^2}{2a}$ 4. $y = 3x - 5$ **Review** $A = \dfrac{C^2}{4\pi}$

Exercise 6:9

1. $f(1) = 3$, $f(2) = 5$, $f(-2) = -3$, $f(-5) = -9$, $f(\frac{1}{2}) = 2$, $f(-\frac{3}{4}) = -\frac{1}{2}$ 2. $f(5) = 4$, $f(1) = 2$, $f(-3) = 0$,
$f(-7) = -2$, $f(0) = 1\frac{1}{2}$, $f(\frac{2}{3}) = 1\frac{5}{6}$, $f(1\frac{1}{2}) = 2\frac{1}{4}$ 3. $f(3) = 22$, $f(2) = 7$, $f(-1) = -2$, $f(-2) = 7$,
$f(\frac{1}{3}) = -4\frac{5}{9}$, $f(-\frac{1}{2}) = -4\frac{1}{4}$ 4. $g(4) = 2\frac{3}{4}$, $g(1) = 5$, $g(0)$ has no answer, $g(-2) = \frac{1}{2}$, $g(-\frac{1}{2}) = -4$
5. $h(1) = 0$, $h(5) = \frac{1}{2}$, $h(0) = -\frac{1}{3}$, $h(-1) = -1$, $h(-3)$ has no answer 6. –2 7. (a) 5 (b) 1
(c) $1\frac{1}{6}$ (d) $-\frac{1}{3}$ (e) $-\frac{1}{2}$ (f) 15 (g) $-\frac{1}{8}$ 8. (a) 2, –10 (b) 3, –1 (c) 1, –5 (d) –3, –7
(e) 4, 2 9. (a) –3·1 (b) $-\frac{3}{5}$ (c) 0·7 (d) $3\frac{1}{5}$ **Review 1** $g(2) = -9$, $g(-2) = -9$, $g(\frac{1}{2}) = 6$

Review 2 5, 1 **Review 3** $\frac{1}{8}$ **Review 4** –5

Page 113 **Exercise 6:11**

1. (a) $5x + 15$ (b) $3n - 12$ (c) $10 + 6n$ (d) $12 - 8a$ (e) $8x - 28$ (f) $15p + 5$ (g) $18 - 24n$
(h) $2 - 6n$ (i) $5n + 3n^2$ (j) $2x^2 + 3x$ (k) $3x - 2x^2$ (l) $a^2 - 5a$ (m) $6a - 2a^2$ (n) $8n^2 + 12n$
2. (a) $-3n - 6$ (b) $-6 - 8a$ (c) $-8n + 4$ (d) $-15 + 20x$ (e) $-18x - 30$ (f) $-20 + 25x$
(g) $-2p^2 - 4p$ (h) $-6a^2 - 15a$ (i) $-12x + 3x^2$ (j) $-6n + 2n^2$ (k) $-6q^2 + 15q$ 3. (a) $4x + 4b$
(b) $3x - 3a$ (c) $nx - ax$ (d) $4an + n^2$ (e) $12a - 15ax$ (f) $6n - 8an$ (g) $15an - 10n^2$
(h) $-6ax - 2x^2$ (i) $-4x^2 + 4ax$ (j) $-6an + 8ax$ (k) $p^2q + pq^2$ (l) $\pi r^2 + 2\pi rh$ (m) $abh - a^2b$
(n) $rs^2 - r^2s$ 4. (a) $13 + 6n$ (b) $1 - 3n$ (c) $5n^2 + 3n$ (d) $11n - 2n^2$ (e) $2x^2 + 4x$
(f) $14a - 2a^2 + 5$ (g) $5n + 9$ (h) $7x + 18$ (i) $16a - 8$ (j) $n^2 - 8n$ (k) $6x^2 - x$ (l) $4x + x^2 - 4$
(m) $10 + n + 2n^2$ (n) $4x^2 - 3x - 12$ Review 1 (a) $2l + 2w$ (b) $-3 + 6a$ (c) $x^2 + 4x$
(d) $2an - 10n^2$ (e) $-12n - 9n^2$ (f) $ab^2 - a^2b$ Review 2 (a) $-5 + 6n$ (b) $2 - 5a - 3a^2$
(c) $10n^2 - 3n$ (d) $16 - 9x$

Page 115 **Exercise 6:13**

1. (a) $3x + 6 = 3(x + 2)$ (b) $5a - 10 = 5(a - 2)$ (c) $14x + 4 = 2(7x + 2)$ (d) $16n - 12 = 4(4n - 3)$
(e) $4x + 4 = 4(x + 1)$ (f) $12n - 4 = 4(3n - 1)$ (g) $15d - 25 = 5(3d - 5)$ (h) $18 + 3n = 3(6 + n)$
(i) $6 - 3a = 3(2 - a)$ (j) $6 + 9x = 3(2 + 3x)$ (k) $15x - 10 = 5(3x - 2)$ 2. (a) $2(n + 1)$
(b) $3(1 - a)$ (c) $4(x + 3)$ (d) $6(1 + 2a)$ (e) $7(2y - 1)$ (f) $3(3x + 1)$ (g) $4(2 - 3y)$ (h) $5(2x + 5)$
(i) $4(2n + 1)$ (j) $11(1 - 2n)$ (k) $5(2 + 3n)$ (l) $3(3 - 7x)$ (m) $4(3n + 2)$ (n) $5(8 - 3n)$
(o) $2(x - 10)$ (p) $4(5n + 4)$ (q) $6(3 - a)$ (r) $4(3 + 4n)$ (s) $2(3x - 10)$ (t) $3(7 - 2n)$
(u) $8(4x - 3)$ (v) $6(3n + 4)$ (w) $8(2y - 3)$ (x) $12(2 - 3n)$ (y) $8(5 + 3a)$ (z) $9(2a - 5)$
3. (a) $2n^2 + n = n(2n + 1)$ (b) $ax - a = a(x - 1)$ (c) $4x + 3x^2 = x(4 + 3x)$ (d) $6x - x^2 = x(6 - x)$
(e) $10n^2 + 4 = 2(5n^2 + 2)$ (f) $30n + 12n^2 = 6n(5 + 2n)$ (g) $6p^2q + 3p = 3p(2pq + 1)$
(h) $\pi r - \pi h = \pi(r - h)$ 4. (a) $x(x + 5)$ (b) $a(a + 9)$ (c) $p(p - 3)$ (d) $y(5 - y)$ (e) $x(1 + x)$
(f) $y(2y - 5)$ (g) $a(1 + 2a)$ (h) $n(4n - 1)$ (i) $p(2 - 5p)$ (j) $a(5 + 6a)$ (k) $a(2 + a)$ (l) $a(5 - a)$
(m) $x(5x + 2)$ (n) $n(9n + 4)$ (o) $2(a^2 + 1)$ (p) $5(1 + n^2)$ (q) $4(2x^2 + 1)$ (r) $3(4 - y^2)$
5. (a) $2x(2x + 1)$ (b) $3a(3a - 1)$ (c) $3b(2 + b)$ (d) $4n(3 - n)$ (e) $8a(2 - a)$ (f) $8n(3n + 4)$
(g) $6x(5 - 2x)$ (h) $4a(2a - n^2)$ (i) $pq(p + q)$ (j) $ab(b - a)$ (k) $6q(p^2 + 2q)$ (l) $4pq(2p - q)$
(m) $3ab(a - 2b)$ (n) $n^2(n + 1)$ (o) $2a^2(3 - 4a)$ Review (a) $5(a - 3)$ (b) $4(3n - 8)$
(c) $a(3a + 5)$ (d) $5n(3 - 4n)$ (e) $\pi r(r + h)$ (f) $4ab(3b - 2a)$

Page 118 **Exercise 6:15**

1. (a) $6n^2 + 13n + 6$ (b) $6x^2 + 13x + 5$ (c) $12a^2 + 13a + 3$ (d) $12n^2 - 11n - 5$ (e) $2a^2 + 11a - 21$
(f) $2x^2 - 5x - 12$ (g) $10x^2 - 17x + 3$ (h) $n^2 - 3n - 28$ (i) $2x^2 + x - 15$ (j) $5n^2 - 21n + 4$
(k) $3x^2 + 14x - 5$ (l) $9a^2 + 3a - 2$ (m) $6x^2 + 13x + 6$ (n) $2n^2 - 9n + 9$ (o) $5y^2 + 8y - 4$
(p) $3x^2 + 4x - 4$ (q) $10a^2 + 29a + 10$ (r) $6 - 7d - 3d^2$ (s) $6 - 5x - 6x^2$ (t) $3 + 5n - 2n^2$
(u) $9x^2 - 4$ (v) $4 - n^2$ (w) $25x^2 - 16$ 2. (a) $a^2 + 5an + 6n^2$ (b) $3x^2 + 4ax + a^2$
(c) $6a^2 + 13an + 5n^2$ (d) $2c^2 - 5cx - 3x^2$ (e) $10x^2 - 3ax - a^2$ (f) $6x^2 - 5xy + y^2$
(g) $6a^2 + 19an + 10n^2$ (h) $6x^2 - nx - 2n^2$ (i) $15a^2 - 14an - 8n^2$ (j) $10n^2 - 17ny + 3y^2$
(k) $15a^2 + an - 6n^2$ (l) $12n^2 - 11nx + 2x^2$ (m) $4x^2 - n^2$ (n) $9n^2 - 4a^2$ (o) $25x^2 - 4y^2$
(p) $ax^2 + dx + acx + dc$ (q) $bn^2 + cn + abn + ac$ (r) $abn^2 + any - bnx - xy$
(s) $abx^2 - adx + bcx - cd$ (t) $qs - qx + psx - px^2$ (u) $ap + bp + aq + bq$ (v) $2ps + 6pt - as - 3at$
(w) $5ax - 15bx + 2an - 6bn$ 3. (a) $(3x - 1)(2x + 1)$ (b) $6x^2 + x - 1$ Review 1 (a) $x^2 + 7x + 10$
(b) $6n^2 - 11n + 3$ (c) $5 - 13a - 6a^2$ (d) $6y^2 - 5y - 6$ (e) $25x^2 - 4$
Review 2 (a) $2a^2 + 7ab + 3b^2$ (b) $12x^2 + 5nx - 2n^2$ (c) $rtx^2 - rux + stx - su$
(d) $3np - 6nq + ap - 2aq$

Chapter 7 Straight-Line Graphs: y = mx + c

Page 123   **Exercise 7:3**

1. (a) l_4, l_5, l_6, l_7, l_8 (b) l_1, l_2, l_3, l_9 (c) l_4 and l_8; l_3 and l_9

2. AB : 2, CD : $\frac{1}{4}$, EF : $\frac{1}{2}$, GH : 1, IJ : $\frac{3}{4}$, KL : 3, MN : 1   3. AB : –1,
CD : $-\frac{1}{5}$, EF : $-\frac{2}{3}$, GH : $-\frac{2}{5}$, IJ : –2, KL : –5, MN : –4   4. l_1 : $-\frac{1}{2}$, l_2 : –1, l_3 : $\frac{1}{4}$,
l_4 : 1, l_5 : –3, l_6 : 2, l_7 : $\frac{2}{5}$ 5. PQ : –2, QR : 1, PR : $-\frac{1}{5}$ 6. (a) $\frac{1}{5}$ (b) 20

7. AB : 20%, BC : 15%, CD : 20%, DE : 0%, EF : 35%   8. (a) $\frac{1}{12}$ (b) 4·6m

Review 1 l_1 : $-\frac{1}{5}$, l_2 : –1, l_3 : $\frac{1}{4}$, l_4 : 3, l_5 : $\frac{5}{2}$ l_6 : $-\frac{3}{2}$ **Review 2** 4

Review 3 $\frac{1}{5}$ and –3.

Page 129   **Exercise 7:5**

1. (a) 2 (b) $\frac{1}{3}$ (c) 1 (d) –3 (e) $-\frac{1}{2}$ (f) 3 (g) –1 (h) 5 (i) –5 (j) $\frac{2}{3}$ (k) $-\frac{3}{5}$

2. (a) 5 (b) 0 (c) –2 (d) 2 (e) 6 (f) 2 (g) 4 (h) 3 (i) 3 (j) –7 (k) 0

3.
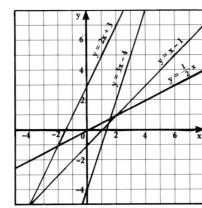

4.
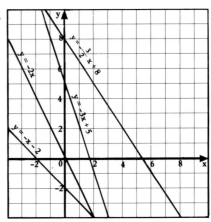

5.
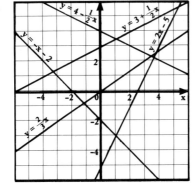

6. (a) (2, 3) (b) (3, 0) (c) (–2, 1)
(d) (–1, –3) (e) (0, –2) (f) ($\frac{1}{2}$, 2)
(g) (–2, $\frac{1}{2}$)   7. (3, 4), (6, 1), (1, –4),
(–2, –1)   **Review 1** (a) –2 (b) $\frac{2}{3}$ (c) 3
(d) –1   **Review 2** (a) 7 (b) 0 (c) –8
(d) 4   **Review 3** (a) (2, –2) (b) (–3, –1)
(c) (2, 2)

Page 132   **Exercise 7:7**

1. **(a)** $y = -x + 3$ **(b)** $y = -x + 6$ **(c)** $y = -x - 7$ **(d)** $y = \frac{2}{3}x + 2$ **(e)** $y = \frac{1}{2}x - 2$ **(f)** $y = \frac{3}{2}x + 2$

(g) $y = -\frac{1}{2}x + 1$ **(h)** $y = -\frac{1}{3}x - 1$ **(i)** $y = -x + \frac{1}{2}$ **(j)** $y = -\frac{3}{2}x - 2$ **(k)** $y = -\frac{1}{2}x + \frac{1}{2}$

(l) $y = -2x - 1$ 2. **(a)** $y = x - 4$ **(b)** $y = x + 1$ **(c)** $y = 3x - 6$ **(d)** $y = 2x + 2$ **(e)** $y = \frac{2}{3}x - 4$

(f) $y = \frac{3}{2}x + 3$ **(g)** $y = \frac{1}{4}x - 1$ **(h)** $y = \frac{2}{5}x - 2$ **(i)** $y = x - 6$ **(j)** $y = 2x + \frac{1}{2}$ **(k)** $y = \frac{3}{4}x - 3$

3.   4.

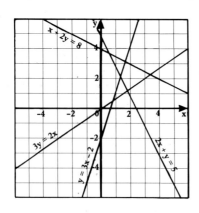   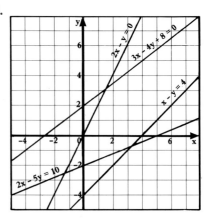

5. **(a)** $(-3, 2)$ **(b)** $(3, -2)$ **(c)** $(1, 1)$ **(d)** $(3, -5)$ **(e)** $(-2, 1)$ 6. $(-1, 3)$, $(6 -4)$, $(-3, -1)$

Review 1 (a) $y = -x - 2$ **(b)** $y = \frac{1}{3}x - 2$ **(c)** $y = -\frac{1}{2}x + 4$ **(d)** $y = -2x + \frac{2}{3}$ **(e)** $y = x - 7$

(f) $y = \frac{2}{3}x + 6$ **(g)** $y = -x + 4$

Review 2 (a)   **(b)** $(-2, -4)$

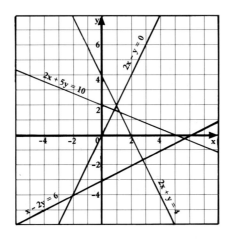

Page 136   **Exercise 7:10**

1. **(a)** $x + y = 0$ **(b)** $x + 2y = 3$ **(c)** $3x + y = 1$ **(d)** $y + 4 = 0$ **(e)** $x + 3 = 0$
(f) $x + 2y + 3 = 0$ **(g)** $2x + y + 3 = 0$ **(h)** $2y = x + 2$ **(i)** $2x + 3y = 12$ **(j)** $5y = 2x$
(k) $2y = 6x - 1$ **(l)** $5x + 5y = 2$ **(m)** $x + 2y = 6$ or $2y = 6 - x$
2. **(a)** l_1 : $y + 6 = 0$, l_2 : $2y = x - 4$, l_3 : $3y = x + 6$, l_4 : $2x + 3y = 12$,
l_5 : $3x + 4y = 24$ **(b)** l_1 : $2y = 3x + 10$, l_2 : $x + 2y + 6 = 0$, l_3 : $x + 4y = 12$,
l_4 : $4x + 3y = 0$, l_5 : $x + 2 = 0$ 3. AB : $x + 2y = 8$, BC : $2y = x$, CA : $x + 4y = 18$

372

4. (a) C   (b) y = 5x + 10   5. 5y = x + 30   **Review 1 (a)** 2x + 3y = 0
(b) 4y = 3x – 8   (c) x + 2y + 1 = 0   (d) x + 4 = 0   **Review 2** l_1: x + 5 = 0,
l_2: y = 2x + 5, l_3: x = 13, l_4: 3y = 2x – 6, l_5: 5y = 2x, l_6: y = 7,
l_7: x + 3y = 6, l_8: x + 2y = 6

Chapter 8   Inequalities

Page 143   **Exercise 8:4**

1. (a) x > 5   (b) n ≤ 2   (c) a ≥ –6   (d) n < 3   (e) n > 1·5   (f) n ≤ 6   (g) n < 5
(h) a < 3   (i) x ≥ –2   (j) a < 21   (k) n < –7   (l) n ≥ 5·5   2. (a) n > 2·5   (b) n ≥
–2·5   (c) n < –2·5   (d) n ≤ 2·5   (e) x ≥ –0·5   (f) x < 2   (g) a > –2·4   (h) a ≤ 2·5
(i) n < 0·8   (j) a ≥ 5·5   (k) n < –2   3. (a) 2   (b) –2   (c) –1   (d) –2   (e) –4
(f) 2   (g) 0   (h) 0   4. (a) –4 < x < 1   (b) 5 ≤ a ≤ 10   (c) –3 < n ≤ 2·5
(d) –1 ≤ n < 5   (e) –20 < n < 8   (f) –9 < x ≤ –3
5. (a) n must be less than or equal to –5.   (b) n must be between –1 and 10.
6. (a) 2, 3, 4, . . .   (b) 3, 4, 5, . . .   (c) . . . –1, 0, 1, 2   **Review 1 (a)** a ≥ 2
(b) a < –2   (c) x > –1·75   (d) n ≤ 7   (e) n > 1·5   (f) x ≤ –7·5
Review 2 (a) –3, –2, –1, 0, 1, 2, 3   (b) –3, –2, –1, 0, 1, . . .

Page 146   **Exercise 8:6**

1. (a) x ≥ 3 or x ≤ –3   (b) x > 2 or x < –2   (c) n > 6 or n < –6
(d) n ≥ 10 or n ≤ –10   (e) –5 < a < 5   (f) –10 < a < 10   (g) –7 ≤ x ≤ 7
(h) x > 8 or x < –8   (i) x > 9 or x < –9   (j) –2 ≤ n ≤ 2   2. (a) x ≥ 2 or x ≤ –2
(b) x ≥ 4 or x ≤ –4   (c) –2 < x < 2   (d) –7 < x < 7   (e) x > 5 or x < –5
(f) –8 ≤ x ≤ 8   (g) –3 < x < 3   (h) –6 ≤ x ≤ 6   (i) –5 < x < 5
(j) x > 1 or x < –1   3. (a) –5, –4, –3, –2, –1, 0, 1, 2, 3, 4, 5   (b) –2, –1, 0, 1, 2
(c) –3, –2, –1, 0, 1, 2, 3   (d) –1, 0, 1   (e) . . ., –4, –3, –2, 2, 3, 4, . . .
(f) . . ., –4, –3, –2, 2, 3, 4, . . .   4. (a) p is greater than 4 or less than –4.
(b) p is between –7 and 7.   **Review (a)** n > 5 or n < –5   (b) a ≥ 8 or a ≤ –8
(b) –2 ≤ x ≤ 2

Page 150   **Exercise 8:8**

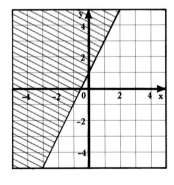

1. (a)

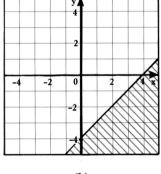

(b)

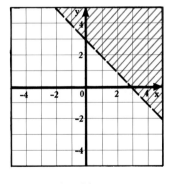

(c)

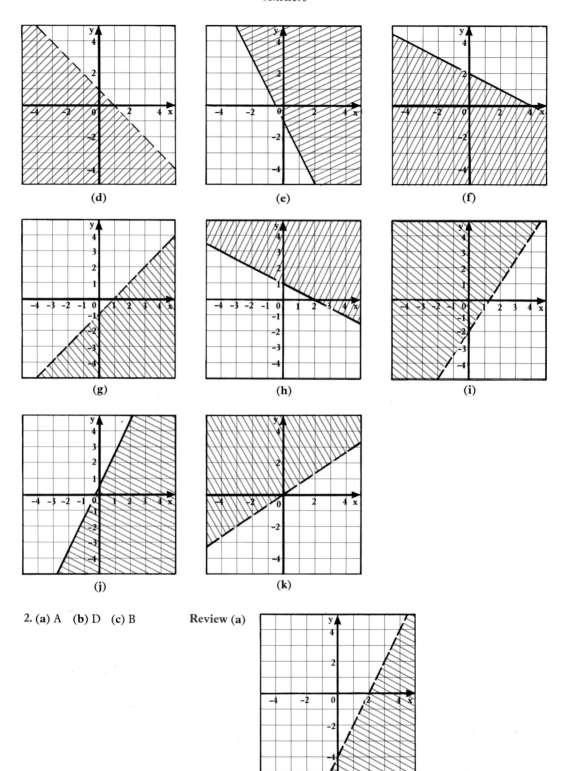

(d)

(e)

(f)

(g)

(h)

(i)

(j)

(k)

2. (a) A   (b) D   (c) B   Review (a)

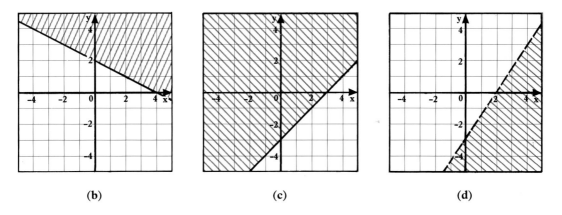

(b)   **(c)**   **(d)**

Page 152   **Exercise 8:10**

In these answers, just the required region is shown shaded.

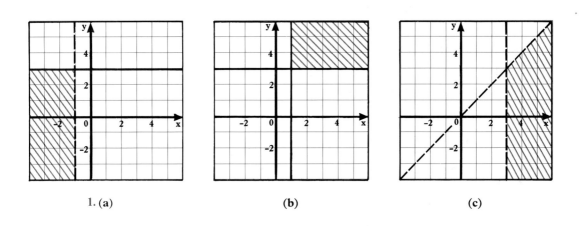

1. **(a)**   **(b)**   **(c)**

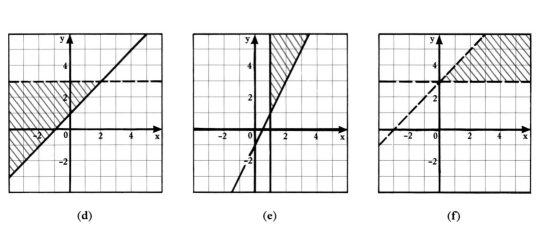

(d)   **(e)**   **(f)**

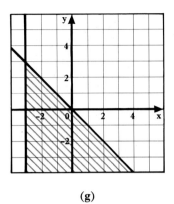

(g)

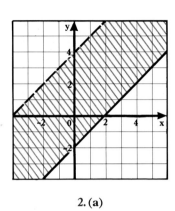

2. (a)

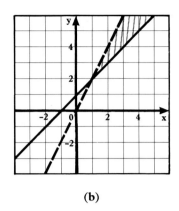

(b)

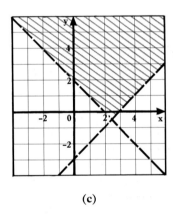

(c)

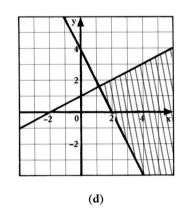

(d)

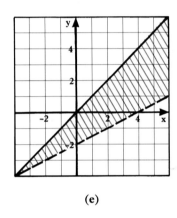

(e)

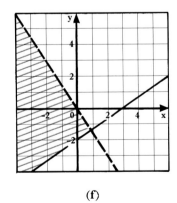

(f)

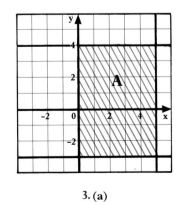

3. (a)

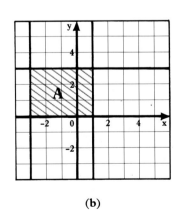

(b)

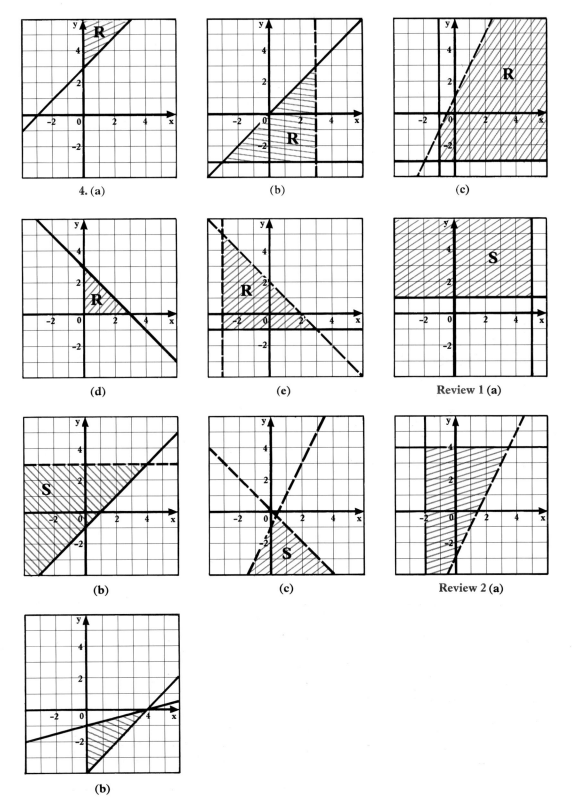

4. (a)

(b)

(c)

(d)

(e)

Review 1 (a)

(b)

(c)

Review 2 (a)

(b)

1. (a) x is the number of £5 cards; y is the number of £10 cards.
   (b) No
   (c)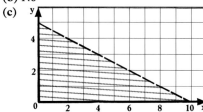

2. (a) x is the number of £2 books; y is the number of £1 books.
   (b) No
   (c)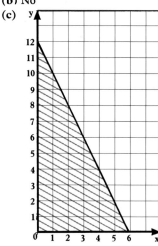

3. (a) No
   (b)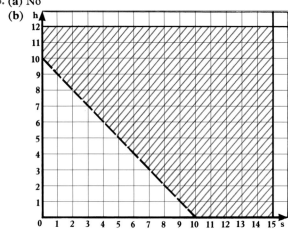

4. (a) No. $h \geq 0$, $s \geq 0$
   (b) $h \leq 3$, $s \leq 3$
   (c)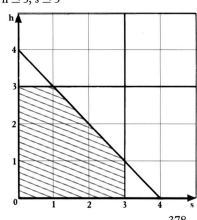

Review (a) No
   (b) $w \geq 0$, $m \geq 3$, $w \leq 6$
   (c)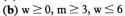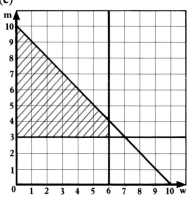

Exercise 8:12

1. **(a)** $y \le 3$, $y \ge x - 2$, $x + y \ge -2$, $y \le x$ **(b)** $y \le 3$, $y \ge 2x - 2$, $x \ge 0$, $y + 3x \ge 0$
2. $y \le 2$, $2y \ge x$, $x + 3y \ge 3$ 3. $y \ge 0$, $x \ge 0$, $y \le 2x + 1$, $y \le 3$, $x + 3y \le 12$, $x \le 6$
4. $x + y \ge 2$, $y \ge 1$, $2y \le x + 4$ 5. $x \ge 2$, $y \le 6$, $x + 2y \ge 6$
Review $y \ge 0$, $x + y \ge 0$, $3y \le x + 12$, $x \le 3$

Chapter 9   Graphs of some Special Functions and Real-Life Situations

Page 163   **Exercise 9:2**

1. **(a)** D   **(b)** B   **(c)** D   **(d)** A   **(e)** A

2. **(i)**   **(a)**
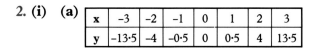

x	-3	-2	-1	0	1	2	3
y	-13·5	-4	-0·5	0	0·5	4	13·5

(b)
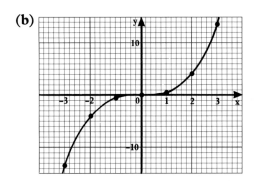

(ii)   **(a)**

x	-4	-3	-2	-1	0	1	2	3	4
y	11	4	-1	-4	-5	-4	-1	4	11

(b)
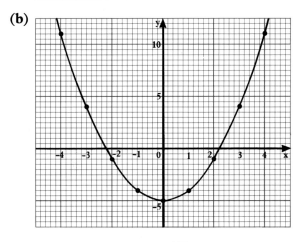

(iii) (a)

x	−3	−2	−1	0	1	2	3
y	−9	4	5	0	−5	−4	9

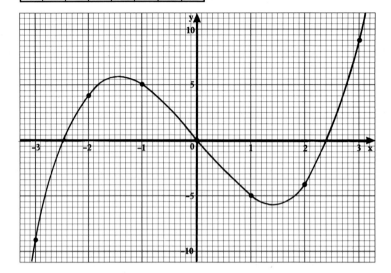

(iv) (a)

x	−5	−4	−3	−2	−1	−$\frac{1}{2}$	0	$\frac{1}{2}$	1	2	3	4	5
y	2	$2\frac{1}{2}$	$3\frac{1}{3}$	5	10	20	no value	−20	−10	−5	−$3\frac{1}{3}$	−$2\frac{1}{2}$	−2

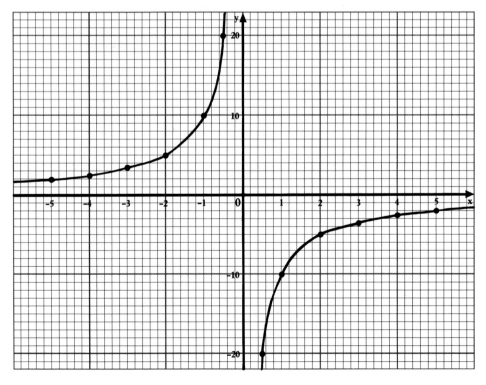

3. **(a)** A: 2, B: 1, C: 4, D: 3   **(b)** A: 4, B: 2, C: 3, D: 1   **(c)** A: 3, B: 4, C: 1, D: 2

4. **(b)**

x	5	10	15	20	25	30
y	12	6	4	3	2·4	2

(c)

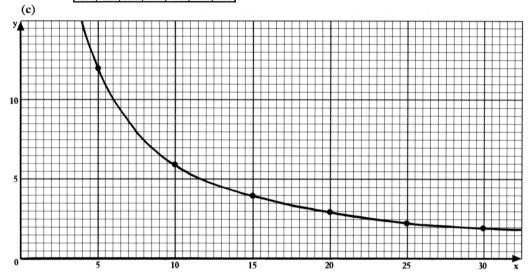

(d) 8cm

5. **(i)** **(b)**

x	5	10	15	20	25
V	250	2000	6750	16000	31250

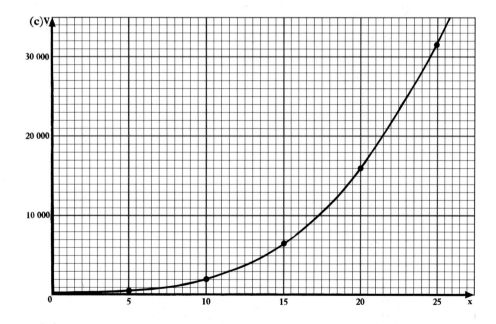

(d) about 21·5 cm

(ii) (b)

x	5	10	15	20	25
A	200	800	1800	3200	5000

(c)

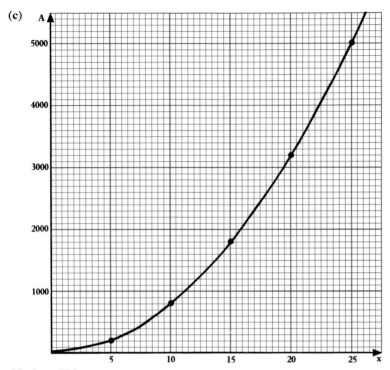

(d) about 17·7 cm

Review 1 D   **Review 2 (a)** B   **(b)** C   **(d)** A

Review 3 (b)

x	4	8	12	16	20
A	144	576	1296	2304	3600

(c)

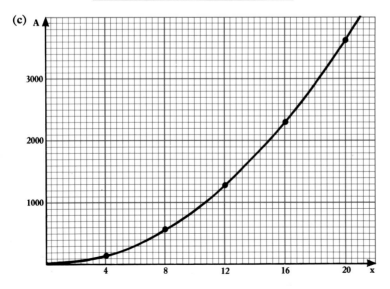

(d) about 2000 cm² (e) about 18 cm

Review 4 (a)

x	–3	–2	–1	0	1	2	3
y	$\frac{1}{8}$	$\frac{1}{4}$	$\frac{1}{2}$	1	2	4	8

(b)

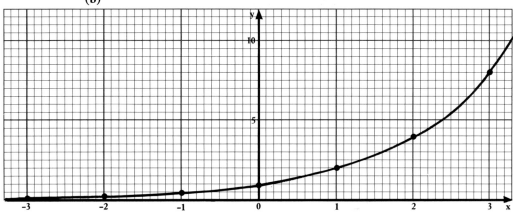

Page 172   **Exercise 9:6**

2. (a) At about 27 seconds and 54 seconds. (b) Karen finished before Susan. (c) Karen
(d) Susan was about 15 m ahead.   3. (a) The bookshop sold out of these books.
(b) The bookshop got in a new supply of these books. They sold more in this week than in
any other week.   (c) There may have been an advertising programme since sales increased rapidly.
5. C or D   6. (a) 25 mm   (b) none   7. A: 2, B: 3, C: 1, D: 4   8. A: 4, B: 3, C: 2, D: 1
Review 2 A: 3, B: 4, C: 2, D: 1

Chapter 10   Proportion

Page 181   **Exercise 10:2**

1. (a) If $C \propto N$, then $C = kN$. (b) k = 4·5 (c) C = 4·5 N (d) £85·50 (e) 34

2. (a) k = 6

x	3	5	9	20
y	18	30	54	120

(b) k = 3·5

x	2	10	16	35
y	7	35	56	122·5

(c) k = 0·4

x	1	3	5	7
y	0·4	1·2	2	2·8

3. (a) $m \propto g$ (b) m = 0·4 g (c) 4·8 mm
(d) 17·5 km   4. (a) s = kr   (b) s = 2·4 r   (c) 288 m
(d) 50   5. (a) e = 2·5 m   (b) 1·6 kg

6. (a) a = 0·12F   (b) 37·5 Newton   (c) 24 m/sec²   7. e, since this is the only straight-line graph
with equation y = mx.   8. If u = 0, v is proportional to t. The equation then becomes v = at,
where a is a constant.   **Review 1** (a) $s \propto t$ (b) s = kt   (c) s = 80t   (d) s = 180 km
(e) 3½ hours   **Review 2** (a) C = kW   (b) £16·20

Answers

Exercise 10:3

1. (a) $A = kl^2$ (b) $V = kr^3$ (c) $P = kn$ (d) $A = kl^2$ (e) $T = k\sqrt{l}$ (f) $r = kv^2$ 2. (a) $k = 0.5$
(b) $a = 0.5n^2$ (c)

n	2	4	5	8	20
a	2	8	12·5	32	200

3. 125 g   4. 14 m/sec (2 s.f.)   5. (a) $m = kl^3$ (b) $k = 3.2$ (c) 1600 g (2 s.f.)   6. (a) 32 m*l*
(b) 6 cm (1 s.f.)   7. (b) 30·4 (1 d.p.) (c) 4·9 (1 d.p.)   8. 3·2 seconds (1 d.p.)
Review 1 (a) $E = ke^2$ (b) 20 (c) 80 joules   Review 2 (a) 250 (b) 15   Review 3 4·2 amps

Exercise 10:7

1. (a) $m = \frac{k}{n}$ (b) $x = \frac{k}{y^2}$ (c) $b = \frac{k}{d^2}$ (d) $l = \frac{k}{P}$ (e) $t = \frac{k}{\sqrt{u}}$ (f) $a = \frac{k}{h^3}$ 2. (a) $h = \frac{k}{l}$

(b) 40 (c) 16 cm   3. 1·29 m (3 s.f.)   4. (a) $y = \frac{k}{x^2}$ (b) 2 (c) 0·5   5. 0·125 ohms
6. (a) 25·5 units (1 d.p.) (b) 18 mm (to the nearest mm)
7. (a) 7.84×10^5 cycles per second (3 s.f.) (b) 486 m (to the nearest metre)   8. 125 N/m²
Review 1

m	0·5	2	5	10	20
n	100	25	10	5	2·5

Review 2 8 units

Chapter 11   Algebra Review

1. (a) $3a - 3b$ (b) $2a^2 - 5a$ (c) $m^2n - mn^2$ 2. (a) $\frac{3}{20}$ (b) 30 metres   3. (a) $a < 2.6$
(b) $x \leq 1$ 4. (a) $P = \frac{k}{VT}$ (b) $h = \frac{A - \pi r^2}{2\pi r}$ (c) $b = 2S - a - c$

5. (b)

(c) 9·3 cm　　6. (a) 3 hours　(b) 60 km/h　7. (i) (a) $y = -5x + 7$　(b) $y = -\frac{1}{2}x + 3$

(c) $y = 3x - 1$　(ii) (a) -5　(b) $-\frac{1}{2}$　(c) 3　(iii) (a) 7　(b) 3　(c) -1

8. (a) 420 mm³ (2 s.f.)　(b) 2·7 cm (2 s.f.)　　9. $f = 2g - m + 0·13$　　10. 20 units

11. $-1, 0, 1, 2$　12. (a) $l_1 : -1, l_2 : -3, l_3 : \frac{3}{2}, l_4 : \frac{1}{3}$,　(b) $l_1 : x + y = 1$,

$l_2 : 3x + y + 6 = 0, l_3 : 2y = 3x - 6$ or $3x - 2y = 6, l_4 : 3y = x + 6$　　13. (a) $6 + x$

(b) $2a^2 - 2a - 2$　(c) $3n + 1$　(d) $4n - 15$　　14. (a) $-5 \leq p \leq 5$　(b) $p < -2$ or $p > 2$

15. (a) $2(3 - 4n)$　(b) $a(2 + 3a)$　(c) $2x(8 - 5x)$　(d) $\pi r(rh + 2)$　(e) $xy(x - y)$　　16. B since
it is the only parabola.

17.

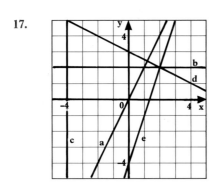

18. (a) $F = \frac{9}{5}C + 32$　(b) $r = \sqrt{\dfrac{V}{\pi h}}$

(c) $l = \dfrac{gT^2}{4\pi^2}$　　19. (i) 2n, 10

(ii) (a) $3n^2 + 17n + 10$　(b) $6n^2 - 19n + 10$

(c) $4x^2 - 7xy - 2y^2$　(d) $ac + bcx + adx + bdx^2$

20. A : 2, B : 3, C : 4, D : 1

21.

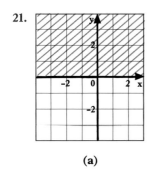

(a)

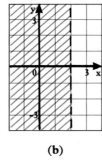

(b)

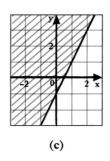

(c)

(d)

22. (a)

b	1	2	3	4	5	6	7	8
a	8	4	2·7	2	1·6	1·3	1·1	1

(b)

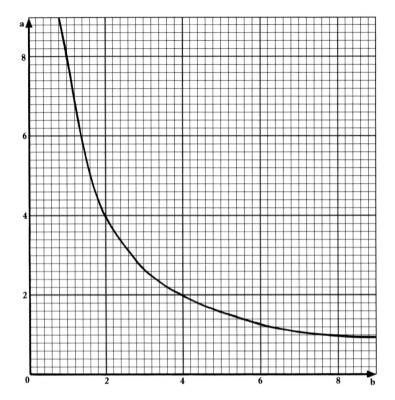

(c) 1·8   **23.** y = 7x + 4

24.

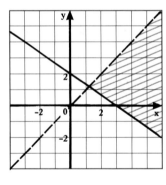

25. (a) The figures on the left of each column are in metres; those on the right are in feet.   **(c)** 30 metres
(e) 45 feet (to the nearest foot)

26. (a) x is the number of tapes, y is the number of CDs.
   (b) Neither x nor y can have a negative value.

(c)

27. AB   **28. (i) (a)** 5   **(b)** 21
(c) 21   **(d)** $3\frac{1}{2}$ **(ii) (a)** −1·2
(b) −1

386

30. (a) 8·2 cm (2 s.f.) **(b)** 65 cm³ (2 s.f.) **31. (a)** A : 3, B : 4, C : 1, D : 2
(b) A : 4, B : 3, C : 2, D : 1 **32.** $A = \dfrac{\pi d^2}{4}$ **33. (a)** 3·8 (2 s.f.) **(b)** 10·5 (3 s.f.)
34. $x \geq 0$, $y \leq x + 1$, $y \leq 3$, $x + 3y \leq 12$

Shape and Space from Previous Levels

Page 212   **Revision Exercise**

1. (a) regular hexagon **(b)** parallelogram **(c)** isosceles triangle **(d)** rhombus **(e)** trapezium
(f) pentagon   **2. (a)** prism **(b)** A, B, F, E, C, G, D, H **(c)** AB, CB, EF, GF, HG, DC,
HE, AD **(d)** ABCD and EFGH; ABFE and DCGH **(e)** 4 **(f)** No **(g)** ABFE and DCGH
3. (a) (–1, 0), (–4, –1), (–5, –1), (–4, –2), (–2, –3), (–1, –3) **(b)** (–1, 0), (2, 0), (2, 1), (1, 3),
(0, 4), (0, 3) **(c)** (–1, 0), (–1, –3), (0, –3), (2, –2), (3, –1), (2, –1) **(d)** A half-turn rotation,
about (–1, 0).   **4. (a)** 45·4 cm² (3 s.f.) **(b)** 500 m*l* **(d)** 6·2 cm   **5. (a)** 30·5 **(b)** 10
6. (a) 3·6 km (2 s.f.) **(b)** 56° **(c)** 326°   **7. (i) (a)** octagon **(b)** 135° **(c)** All the interior angles
of this octagon. **(d)** No. The sides are not equal. **(e)** 2 **(ii) (a)** 12 cm and 8 cm **(b)** 48 cm²
(c) 32 cm² **(iii)** Yes. One possible explanation is: corresponding sides are equal.   **8.** a = 98°,
b = 44°, c = 38°, d = 82°, e = 16°, f = 60° **9. (b)** 5·4 m **(d)** 4·3 m **10. (a)** scale factor = 2,
centre of enlargement is (7, 7) **(b)** (–1, 1), (–1, 4), (0, 4), (1, 3), (0, 3), (0, 1) **(c)** C
11. (b) 65590 m² **(c)** 6·56 ha **(d)** 16 acres **(e)** about 2 km   **12.** Shirdia could use C = $2\pi r$ to
find the radius, then A = πr^2 to find the surface area.   **13.** B (1, 8, 5), C (3, 8, 5), D (3, 2, 5),
E (1, 2, 0), F (1, 8, 0), H (3, 2, 0)   **14. (a)** x = 4·2 m, y = 2·8 m, z = 2·5 m **(b)** 13·4 m
(c) 5·75 m²   **15. (a)**   **(b)**

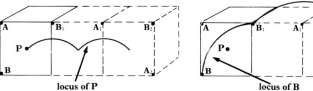

16. **(a)** 2 **(b)** It is possible to deliver the flowers without retracing steps but it is not possible to do
this and begin and finish at F. **(c)** 980 m **(d)** 900 m   **17. (a)**
(b) 12 cm² **(c)** 10 cm

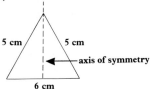

18. Possible answers are:

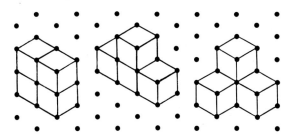

19. **(a)** Yes **(b)** Yes **(c)** No **(d)** A square cannot be used. An equilateral triangle could be.

Chapter 12 Dimensions

1. Dimension for volume must be L^3. Dimension for $\frac{7}{3}\pi r^2 l^2$ is L^4.   **2.** Dimension for area must be L^2. Dimension for $\frac{4}{3}\pi r^3$ is L^3.   **3. (a)** $2l + \pi d$ **(b)** $dl + \frac{1}{4}\pi d^2$

4. $V = \frac{26}{27}\pi r^2 h$ **5.** $V = \frac{1}{4}\pi d^2 l + \frac{1}{12}\pi d^2 h$ **6. (a)** $\frac{1}{4}\pi d(8d + 5h)$ **(b)** $\frac{7}{16}\pi d^2 h$

7. $V = \frac{1}{2}\,dl(2h - d) + \frac{1}{8}\pi d^2 l$; No   **8. (a)** $6ah + \frac{3}{2}\sqrt{3}\,a^2$ **(b)** $\frac{3}{2}\sqrt{3}\,a^2 h$

9. (a) $\pi r + \frac{1}{2}\,r$, $r(\pi + 3)$, $\frac{1}{3}\pi r$, $\pi r + 4l$ **(b)** πrl, $\frac{1}{4}\pi d^2$, $\pi r(r + l)$, $\frac{4}{3}\pi r^2$, $4\pi rl$, $\frac{1}{3}\,\pi rh$

(c) $4\pi r^2 h$, $\frac{1}{3}\pi r^2 h$, $\frac{4}{3}\pi r^3$, $4l^2 h$, $3lh^2$ **Review 1** Dimension for volume must be L^3. Dimension of $\frac{2}{3}\pi r^2$ is L^2.   **Review 2 (a)** $\frac{2}{3}\pi r^3 + \pi r^2 h$ **(b)** $2\pi r(h + r)$

Chapter 13 Similar Shapes

1. A and H, B and L, C and M, D and K, F and I, G and J
2. (a) the last two   **(b)** all three   **3. (a)** Q   **(b)** R   **4. (a)** PQ   **(b)** QR   **5. (a)** $\triangle$PRQ
(b) $\angle$PTS   **(c)** PQ   **6. (a)** $\triangle$ACB, $\triangle$ECD   **(b)** D   **(c)** $\angle$BCA   **(d)** ED   **(e)** AC
7. (a) Yes   **(b)** Yes   **8. (a)** always   **(b)** sometimes   **(c)** sometimes   **(d)** always   **(e)** always
(f) sometimes   **Review 1** Yes; the image on the left and the image third from the left are similar.   **Review 2 (a)** G   **(b)** A   **(c)** EH   **(d)** CB   **Review 3 (a)** No
(b) Yes

1. (a) 4 cm   **(b)** 3·6 m (1 d.p.)   **2.** 12·16 m (2 d.p.)   **3.** 1·8   **4.** 2·4 m   **5.** 40 cm
6. 24 cm   **7.** 15 cm   **8.** 4·8 cm   **10.** 2 m   **11.** 13·3 m (1 d.p.)
Review 1 8·19 m (2 d.p.)   **Review 2** 15·5 m   **Review 3** 9 cm

Chapter 14 Trigonometry

1. (a) AC   **(b)** QR   **(c)** EF   **(d)** GH   **2. (a)** BC   **(b)** PQ   **(c)** DE   **(d)** GI
3. (a) b   **(b)** r   **(c)** DE   **4. (a)** n   **(b)** m   **(c)** l **Review (a)** PR   **(b)** LM   **(c)** AB
(d) PQ   **(e)** a

1. (a) PQ   **(b)** QR   **(c)** PR   **(d)** PR   **(e)** PR   **(f)** QR   **2. (a)** $\frac{4}{5}$ **(b)** $\frac{12}{13}$ **(c)** $\frac{15}{17}$
(d) $\frac{7}{25}$ **3. (a)** $\frac{4}{3}$ **(b)** $\frac{12}{5}$ **(c)** $\frac{15}{8}$ **(d)** $\frac{7}{24}$ **4. (a)** $\frac{3}{5}$ **(b)** $\frac{5}{13}$ **(c)** $\frac{8}{17}$ **(d)** $\frac{24}{25}$

5. **(a)** sin B = 0·8, cos C = 0·8, tan B = 1·33 (2 d.p.), sin C = 0·6 **(b)** cos α = 0·28, tan α = 3·43 (2 d.p.), sin α = 0·96 **(c)** tan R = 0·75, sin P = 0·8, cos R = 0·8, tan P = 1·33 (2 d.p.) **Review (a)** MN **(b)** 16 **(c)** 0·47

Page 249   **Exercise 14:5**

1. 0·342 2. 0·225 3. 1·376 4. 0·325 5. 0·995 6. 0·872 7. 0·913 8. 0·127
9. 1·645 10. 1 11. 0·259 12. 0·574 13. 0·819 14. 0·966 15. 1 16. 0·985
17. 0·5 18. 0 19. 0·035 20. 572·957 Review 1 0·675 Review 2 0·951
Review 3 0·763

Page 252   **Exercise 14:7**

1. **(a)** cos **(b)** cos **(c)** tan **(d)** sin **(e)** tan **(f)** sin **(g)** tan **(h)** tan **(i)** cos **(j)** sin
2. **(a)** 51 cm (2 s.f.) **(b)** 1·4 km (2 s.f.) **(c)** 14 m (2 s.f.) **(d)** 72·1 mm (3 s.f.)
(e) 16 m (2 s.f.) **(f)** 17 km (2 s.f.) **(g)** 16·0 (3 s.f.) **(h)** 20 m (2 s.f.) **(i)** 4·4 km (2 s.f.)
(j) 19 cm (2 s.f.) 3. 1·8 m (2 s.f.) 4. 3·7 m (2 s.f.) 5. 5·74 m (2 d.p.)
6. **(a)** 8·9 m (2 s.f.) **(b)** 10·6 cm (1 d.p.) **(c)** 50·4 mm (1 d.p.) **(d)** 1·76 km (3 s.f.)
7. 2366 m (to the nearest metre) 8. **(a)** 28 mm (2 s.f.) **(b)** 4·35 m (3 s.f.)
(c) 3·1 cm (2 s.f.) **(d)** 8·2 cm (2 s.f.) Review 1 0·91 m (2 s.f.)
Review 2 **(a)** 18 m (2 s.f.) **(b)** 54 cm (2 s.f.) **(c)** 10 cm (2 s.f.) **(d)** 47·9 mm (3 s.f.)
(e) 50 m (2 s.f.) **(f)** 6·6 m (2 s.f.) **(g)** 11·5 km (3 s.f.)

Page 257   **Exercise 14:9**

1. **(a)** 56·1° **(b)** 62·5° **(c)** 43·4° **(d)** 86·1° **(e)** 20·2° **(f)** 34·6° **(g)** 89·0° **(h)** 82·8°
(i) 39·4° **(j)** 14·5° **(k)** 21·8° **(l)** 48·2° **(m)** 57·3° **(n)** 46·7° 2. **(a)** tan **(b)** sin
(c) cos **(d)** sin **(e)** cos **(f)** tan **(g)** sin **(h)** cos **(i)** tan **(j)** tan 3. **(a)** 42° **(b)** 28°
(c) 44° **(d)** 23° **(e)** 38° **(f)** 50° **(g)** 48° **(h)** 63° **(i)** 41° **(j)** 57° 4. 5·7° (1 d.p.)
5. 50·3° (1 d.p.) 6. 61·3° (1 d.p.) Review 1 **(a)** 47° **(b)** 70° **(c)** 53° **(d)** 17° **(e)** 70°
(f) 68° Review 2 15° (to the nearest degree)

Page 260   **Exercise 14:11**

1. **(a)** 51° (to the nearest degree) **(b)** 309° **(c)** 13 km (to the nearest km) 2. **(a)** P
(b) 32 km (to the nearest km) 3. **(a)** 34° **(b)** 128 km (to the nearest km)
(c) 190 km (to the nearest km) 4. **(a)** 40° **(b)** 19 km (to the nearest km) **(c)** 25 km (to the nearest km) 5. **(a)** 162 km (to the nearest km) **(b)** 32° (to the nearest degree); the bearing is 328° Review **(a)** 97 km (to the nearest km) **(b)** 60° (to the nearest degree) **(c)** 030°

Page 263   **Exercise 14:12**

1. 15 m (to the nearest metre) 2. 10 m 3. 36 m (to the nearest metre) 4. 47 m (to the nearest metre) 5. 13 m (to the nearest metre) 6. **(a)** 2702 m (to the nearest metre)
(b) 1588 m (to the nearest metre) **(c)** 20° (to the nearest degree) 7. **(a)** 131 m (to the nearest metre) **(b)** BC = 99 m (to the nearest metre); height of flagpole = 32 m 8. **(a) Step 1:** find angle WET. **Step 2:** find ET. **Step 3:** Use trigonometry to find WT. **(b)** 48 m (to the nearest metre) Review 1 7 metres (to the nearest metre) Review 2 **(a)** 5 m **(b)** 8 m (to the nearest metre) **(c)** HF needs to be calculated. TH and HF need to be added. **(d)** 10 m (to the nearest metre) Review 3 **(a)** 48·62 m (2 d.p.) **(b)** BC = 45 m (to the nearest metre). Distance between the houseboats = 99 m (to the nearest metre).

Chapter 15   Vectors

Page 271   **Exercise 15:2**

1.

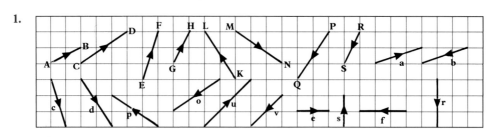

2. $\overrightarrow{PQ} = \binom{2}{1}$, $\overrightarrow{AB} = \binom{2}{2}$, $\overrightarrow{RS} = \binom{-2}{-3}$, $\overrightarrow{EF} = \binom{1}{-2}$, $\overrightarrow{GH} = \binom{-2}{3}$, $\overrightarrow{PQ} = \binom{3}{0}$,

$\overrightarrow{MN} = \binom{0}{-2}$, $\overrightarrow{VW} = \binom{4}{1}$, $\mathbf{a} = \binom{-1}{2}$, $\mathbf{b} = \binom{1}{2}$, $\mathbf{c} = \binom{2}{0}$, $\mathbf{d} = \binom{0}{3}$, $\mathbf{e} = \binom{-4}{-2}$, $\mathbf{f} = \binom{3}{-1}$,

$\mathbf{p} = \binom{6}{2}$, $\mathbf{q} = \binom{-5}{1}$ **3.** (a) $\mathbf{a} = \binom{7}{0}$ $\mathbf{b} = \binom{6}{-6}$ $\mathbf{c} = \binom{-2}{6}$ $\mathbf{d} = \binom{2}{1}$ $\mathbf{e} = \binom{2}{0}$ $\mathbf{f} = \binom{-4}{1}$

$\mathbf{g} = \binom{-1}{1}$ $\mathbf{h} = \binom{-1}{-1}$ $\mathbf{i} = \binom{-2}{-1}$ $\mathbf{j} = \binom{-3}{0}$ $\mathbf{k} = \binom{-2}{-1}$ $\mathbf{m} = \binom{1}{3}$ $\mathbf{n} = \binom{0}{2}$ $\mathbf{p} = \binom{0}{-1}$

(b) a rabbit   **4. (a)** twice   **5. (i) (a)** $\binom{-5}{0}$,   **(b)** $\binom{5}{0}$,   **(c)** $\binom{2}{-3}$,   **(d)** $\binom{0}{3}$,   **(e)** $\binom{4}{1}$,

(f) $\binom{0}{-6}$,   **(g)** $\binom{-5}{0}$,   **(h)** $\binom{-4}{4}$,   **(i)** $\binom{4}{-4}$ **(ii)** from B to T   **6. (a)** $\overrightarrow{PQ} = \binom{1}{2}$

(b) $\overrightarrow{PQ} = \binom{6}{1}$ **(c)** $\overrightarrow{PQ} = \binom{-3}{0}$ **(d)** $\overrightarrow{PQ} = \binom{2}{-3}$ **(e)** $\overrightarrow{PQ} = \binom{-2}{-4}$

Review (i) Simon's group and Bik's group   **(ii) (a)** $\binom{8}{-1}$,   **(b)** $\binom{5}{13}$,   **(c)** $\binom{-4}{-5}$,   **(d)** $\binom{6}{-5}$,

(e) $\binom{-6}{5}$

Page 276   **Exercise 15:4**

1. (a) c   **(b)** h   **(c)** f   **(d)** b   **(e)** q   **(f)** e   **(g)** b   **(h)** a   **(i)** h

3.

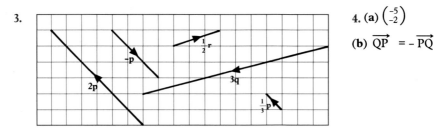

4. (a) $\binom{-5}{-2}$

(b) $\overrightarrow{QP} = -\overrightarrow{PQ}$

5. (a) $\overrightarrow{CK} = -\overrightarrow{KC}$ **(b)** $\overrightarrow{AB} = 2\,\overrightarrow{ED}$ **(c)** $\overrightarrow{AF} = 2\,\overrightarrow{IG}$ **(d)** $\overrightarrow{AB} = -2\,\overrightarrow{CK}$

(e) $\overrightarrow{LM} = \frac{1}{3}\,\overrightarrow{CK}$ **(f)** $\overrightarrow{DC} = -\frac{1}{2}\,\overrightarrow{AF}$ **(g)** $\overrightarrow{LM} = -\frac{1}{3}\,\overrightarrow{ED}$ **Review 1 (a)** g   **(b)** b

(c) c   **(d)** d   **(e)** h   **(f)** f   **(g)** f   **(h)** n

Review 2

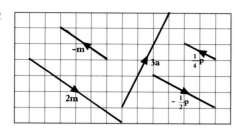

Page 279

1. (a) $\begin{pmatrix} 3 \\ -3 \end{pmatrix}$ (b) $\begin{pmatrix} 2 \\ 0 \end{pmatrix}$ (c) $\begin{pmatrix} 5 \\ 2 \end{pmatrix}$ (d) $\begin{pmatrix} 0 \\ 4 \end{pmatrix}$ (e) $\begin{pmatrix} -5 \\ -2 \end{pmatrix}$ (f) $\begin{pmatrix} 0 \\ -4 \end{pmatrix}$ (g) $\begin{pmatrix} -2 \\ 0 \end{pmatrix}$ (h) $\begin{pmatrix} -3 \\ 3 \end{pmatrix}$

2. (a) $\begin{pmatrix} -1 \\ -3 \end{pmatrix}$ (b) $\begin{pmatrix} -3 \\ 2 \end{pmatrix}$ (c) $\begin{pmatrix} -4 \\ -1 \end{pmatrix}$ 3. (a) $\begin{pmatrix} -3 \\ 3 \end{pmatrix}$ (b) $\begin{pmatrix} 0 \\ 7 \end{pmatrix}$ (c) $\begin{pmatrix} -1 \\ -5 \end{pmatrix}$ (d) $\begin{pmatrix} 5 \\ 0 \end{pmatrix}$ (e) $\begin{pmatrix} -2 \\ 2 \end{pmatrix}$

4. (a) A′(1, 4) (b) A′(0, 3) (c) A′(−1, −5) 5. (c) $\begin{pmatrix} -1 \\ 2 \end{pmatrix}$ (d) $\begin{pmatrix} -8 \\ -2 \end{pmatrix}$ 6. (c) A′(1, 4), B′(4, 1),

C′(2, −1), D′(−1, 2) (d) $\begin{pmatrix} 2 \\ -3 \end{pmatrix}$ **Review 1** $\begin{pmatrix} -1 \\ 3 \end{pmatrix}$ **Review 2** (a) $\begin{pmatrix} 5 \\ 1 \end{pmatrix}$ (b) $\begin{pmatrix} -3 \\ -4 \end{pmatrix}$ (c) $\begin{pmatrix} 2 \\ -3 \end{pmatrix}$

Review 3 (i) (a) $\begin{pmatrix} -2 \\ 3 \end{pmatrix}$ (b) $\begin{pmatrix} -5 \\ 6 \end{pmatrix}$ (c) $\begin{pmatrix} 2 \\ 3 \end{pmatrix}$ (d) $\begin{pmatrix} 6 \\ 3 \end{pmatrix}$ (ii) A **Review 4** (b) A′(−4, 1),

B′(−1, 3), C′(−3, 7) (c) $\begin{pmatrix} 4 \\ -3 \end{pmatrix}$

Chapter 16   Shape and Space Review

Page 284 1. (a) $\mathbf{a} = \begin{pmatrix} 5 \\ 2 \end{pmatrix}$ $\mathbf{b} = \begin{pmatrix} -3 \\ -3 \end{pmatrix}$ $\mathbf{c} = \begin{pmatrix} -6 \\ 0 \end{pmatrix}$ $\mathbf{d} = \begin{pmatrix} 0 \\ 4 \end{pmatrix}$ $\mathbf{e} = \begin{pmatrix} -2 \\ 4 \end{pmatrix}$ $\mathbf{f} = \begin{pmatrix} 2 \\ -4 \end{pmatrix}$ $\mathbf{g} = \begin{pmatrix} 5 \\ -3 \end{pmatrix}$

(h) $\mathbf{e} = -\mathbf{f}$ (or $\mathbf{f} = -\mathbf{e}$) 2. (i) (a) 0·92 (b) 0·42 (c) 0·92 (ii) (a) 74·9° (b) 78·7°

(c) 23·6° 3. The largest and smallest diagrams are similar. 4. (a) $\overrightarrow{CB} = \overrightarrow{DH}$

(b) $\overrightarrow{CF} = 2\overrightarrow{DE}$ (c) $\overrightarrow{EF} = \frac{1}{2}\overrightarrow{DA}$ (d) $\overrightarrow{AF} = -\overrightarrow{CD}$ 5. (a) B (b) A and C 6. 3·5 m (1 d.p.)

7. Dimension for area must be L^2. Dimension for $\frac{1}{3}\pi r^2 h$ is L^3. 8. 20 cm 9. (a) $\begin{pmatrix} 3 \\ 1 \end{pmatrix}$

(b) $\begin{pmatrix} 4 \\ 0 \end{pmatrix}$ (c) $\begin{pmatrix} 7 \\ 1 \end{pmatrix}$ 10. 0·5 cm 11. 5·5° (1 d.p.) 12. (a) $\begin{pmatrix} 2 \\ 1 \end{pmatrix}$ (b) $\begin{pmatrix} -2 \\ 2 \end{pmatrix}$ (c) $\begin{pmatrix} -2 \\ -3 \end{pmatrix}$

13. 32·7 m 14. D 15. 6·85 m (2 d.p.) 16. (a) 124 km (to the nearest kilometre)

(b) Angle PQR; 064° 17. (c) P′(2, −4), Q′(4, 0), R′(6, −3) (d) $\begin{pmatrix} -4 \\ 1 \end{pmatrix}$ 18. (a) 0·3 m

(b) 0·14 m (2 d.p.) (c) 76·8° (1 d.p.) 19. (a) $3r^2 l + \frac{1}{2}\pi r^2 l$ (b) $3r^2 + \frac{1}{2}\pi r^2$ (c) $6r + \pi r$

20. (a) 31° (b) 200 m (to the nearest metre) (c) 333 m (to the nearest metre) 21. 3·2 m

Data Handling from Previous Levels

Revision Exercise

1. (a) $\frac{353}{1000}$ (b) $\frac{643}{1000}$ 2. (a)

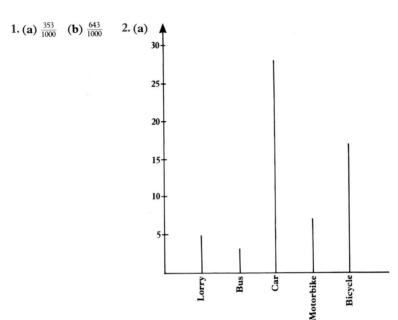

(b) Lorry: 30°, Bus: 18°, Car: 168°, Motorbike: 42°, Bicycle: 102°

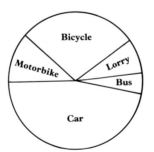

3. (a)   (b) $\frac{5}{18}$ (c) 7

Black \ Red	1	2	3	4	5	6
1	2	3	4	5	6	7
2	3	4	5	6	7	8
3	4	5	6	7	8	9
4	5	6	7	8	9	10
5	6	7	8	9	10	11
6	7	8	9	10	11	12

4. (a) Graph 3   **(b)** Graph 1   **(c)** Graph 2
5. Calais: mean midday temperature = 17·7°C (1 d.p.); range = 8°C;
Carlisle: mean midday temperature = 18·3°C (1 d.p.); range = 4°C
6. (a)

	Excellent	Good	Acceptable	Poor	Totals
Lights	52	34	9	5	100
Music	38	31	24	7	100
Decoration	24	18	43	15	100
Service	15	41	14	30	100
Totals	129	124	90	57	400

(b) 100   **(c)** 69   **(d)** No   **(e)** Possible graphs are: bar-line, pie chart
7. (a) The output is 3, 0, 0, 9, 0, 11. This flow diagram outputs the odd numbers unchanged and outputs 0 for each even number.
(b)

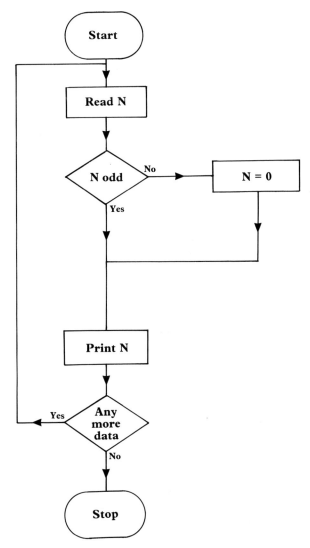

8. (a) HHH, HHT, HTH, THH, HTT, THT, TTH, TTT **(b)** $\frac{1}{2}$ **9.** b **10. (a)** $\frac{1}{3}$ **(b)** $\frac{5}{12}$ **(c)** $\frac{1}{6}$ **(d)** $\frac{3}{4}$ **(e)** 1 **(f)** 0 **(g)** $\frac{7}{12}$

11. (b)

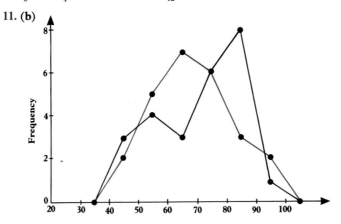

12. $\frac{3}{8}$ **13. (a)** positive correlation **(b)** negative correlation **(c)** positive correlation **(d)** no correlation **(e)** no correlation **14. (a)** 0·9 **(b)** Because some patients are both female and school pupils; that is, these are not mutually exclusive **(c)** 0·4 **(d)** 0·62 **(e)** 90
15. (a) (b)

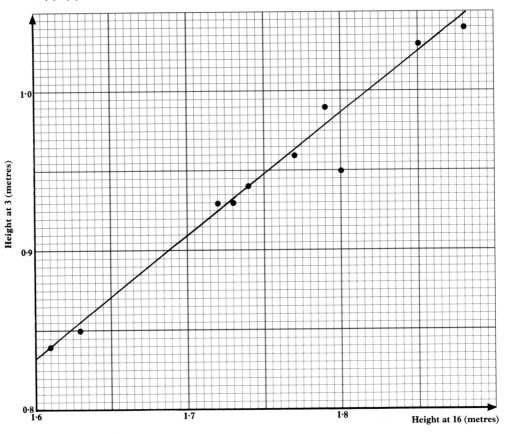

(c) about 0·89 m **(d)** about 1·83 m **16. (a)** 3 **(b)** 2 **(c)** 1

17. A possible flow diagram is

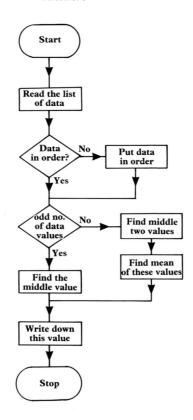

18. (a) A tally chart would be better.   **(b)** The data would not be very useful since it only applies to one quarter of an hour.   **19. (i) (a)** 11   **(b)** 210   **(c)** 19·1 trees (1 d.p.)   **(d)** 18 and 20 **(e)** 19 trees **(f)** 8 trees
(ii)

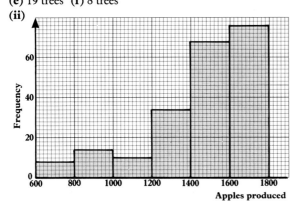

(iii) (a)

Class interval	1m –	2m –	3m –	4m –	5m – 6m
Mid-point	1·5m	2·5m	3·5m	4·5m	5·5m
Frequency	6	24	84	87	9

(b) 3·8 m (1 d.p.)   **(c)** 3m – 4m   **(d)** 4m – 5m
20. Both are correct. The events are exhaustive since one of them must happen. The events are mutually exclusive since they cannot happen together.

Chapter 18 Cumulative Frequency

Page 319   **Exercise 18:2**

1. (a) l.q. = 14, u.q. = 24   **(b)** l.q. = 6, u.q. = 19   **(c)** l.q. = 2, u.q. = 10   **(d)** l.q. = 16, u.q. = 27·5
(e) l.q. = 4, u.q. = 12   **(f)** l.q. = 2·5, u.q. = 7·5   **2. (a)** 10   **(b)** 13   **(c)** 8   **(d)** 11·5   **(e)** 8
(f) 5   **3.** Mr. Benzoni's class: range = 14, median = 13, l.q. = 9, u.q. = 17, interquartile range = 8;
Ms Patel's class: range = 8, median = 12, l.q. = 10, u.q. = 14, interquartile range = 4
4. median = 1, l.q. = 0, u.q. = 3, interquartile range = 3, range = 8   **Review 1 (a)** l.q. = 8·5,
u.q. = 15·5, interquartile range = 7   **(b)** l.q. = 3, u.q. = 5, interquartile range = 2   **Review 2**
Girls: l.q. = 0, u.q. = 5, interquartile range = 5, median = 2, range = 13; Boys: l.q. = 1, u.q. = 8,
interquartile range = 7, median = 2, range = 11

Page 323   **Exercise 18:3**

The answers read from the graphs are approximate answers.

1. (a) 30   **(b)** l.q. = 16, u.q. = 45   **(c)** 29   **(d)** 15 million   **(e)** 11 million   **(f)** 4 million
(g) 2 million   **2. (a)** (18, 23), (20, 32), (22, 48), (24, 57), (26, 60), (28, 61)
(b)   **(c)** median = 19·5°, l.q. = 17°,
                                                                  u.q. = 21·5°,
                                                                  interquartile range = 4·5°

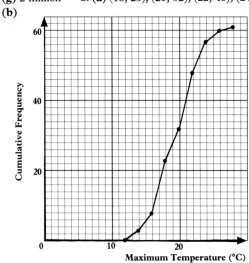

3. (a)

Height of Seedlings (cm)	Frequency	Cumulative Frequency
0 – 1	9	9
1 – 2	3	12
2 – 3	10	22
3 – 4	15	37
4 – 5	12	49
5 – 6	7	56
6 – 7	4	60

(b)

Time Spent on Leisure	Frequency	Cumulative Frequency
$10 \leq t < 15$	1	1
$15 \leq t < 20$	4	5
$20 \leq t < 25$	7	12
$25 \leq t < 30$	15	27
$30 \leq t < 35$	13	40
$35 \leq t < 40$	5	45
$40 \leq t < 45$	3	48
$45 \leq t < 50$	2	50

(c)

Weight of fruit (kg)	0·5 –	1·0 –	1·5 –	2·0 –	2·5 –	3·0 –	3·5 –	4·0 –
Frequency	6	5	8	7	14	18	27	12
Cumulative Frequency	6	11	19	26	40	58	85	97

(d)

Handspan (mm) at least	below	Frequency	Cumulative Frequency
160	170	2	2
170	180	0	2
180	190	4	6
190	200	10	16
200	210	7	23
210	220	3	26
220	230	1	27
230	240	1	28

4. (a)

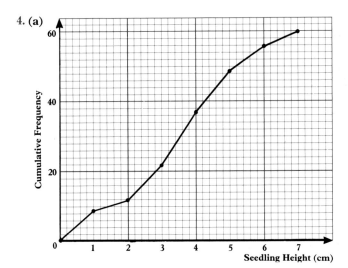

median = 3·5 cm
lower quartile = 2·3 cm
upper quartile = 4·7 cm
interquartile range = 2·4 cm

(b)

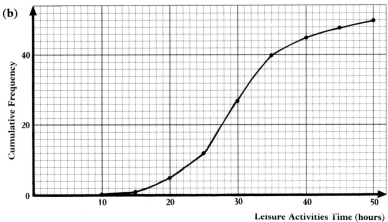

median = 29·5 hours   upper quartile = 33·5 hours
lower quartile = 25·5 hours   interquartile range = 8 hours

397

(c)

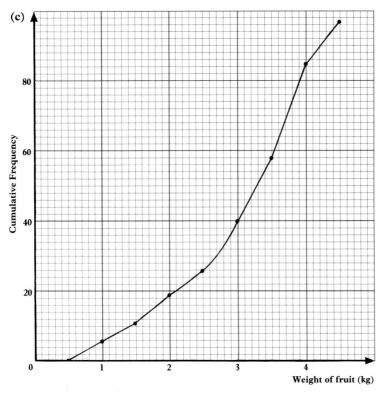

median = 3·25 kg
lower quartile = 2·4 kg
upper quartile = 3·8 kg
interquartile range = 1·4 kg

(d)

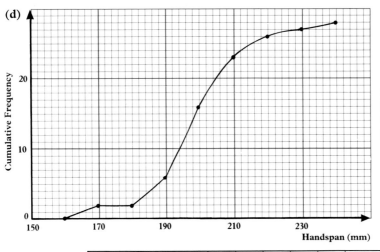

median = 198 mm
lower quartile = 191 mm
upper quartile = 206 mm
interquartile range = 15 mm

5. **(a)**

Length of Rhubarb on Unfertilized Plant (cm)	25 –	30 –	35 –	40 –	45 –	50 – 55
Frequency	2	5	8	7	5	3
Cumulative Frequency	2	7	15	22	27	30

Length of Rhubarb on Fertilized Plant (cm)	25 –	30 –	35 –	40 –	45 –	50 – 55
Frequency	4	2	6	6	9	1
Cumulative Frequency	4	6	12	18	27	28

(b)

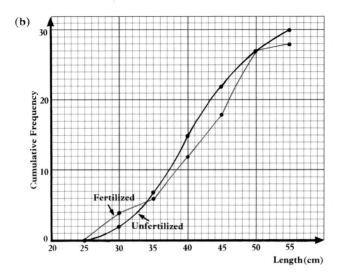

(c) Unfertilized: median = 40 cm; lower quartile = 35·5 cm, upper quartile = 45·5 cm, interquartile range = 10 cm. Fertilized: median = 41·5 cm, lower quartile = 36 cm, upper quartile = 46·5 cm, interquartile range = 10·5 cm   **6. (i) (a)** Since 98 have lifetimes less than 2000 hours then 2 are still working after 2000 hours of use.   **(b)** 1260 hours   **(c)** 300 hours

(ii) (a)

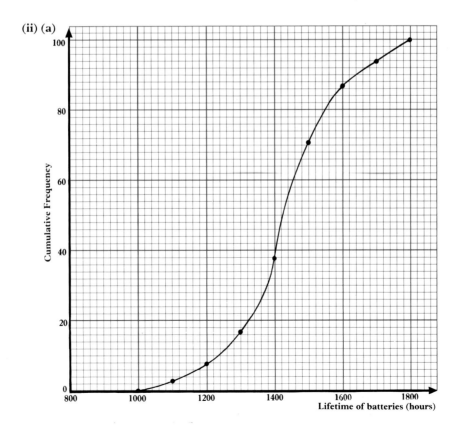

(b) median = 1430 hours, lower quartile = 1350 hours, upper quartile = 1520 hours, interquartile range = 170 hours

7. **(a)** (240, 10), (250, 22), (260, 31), (270, 38), (280, 40)

(b)

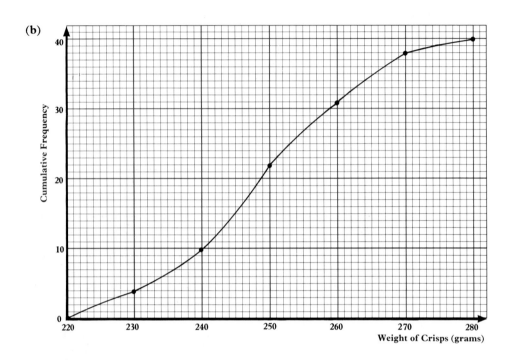

(c) 249 grams   **(d)** 19 grams

Review 1 (a)

Variety: Top Tom

Weight (grams)	Frequency	Cumulative Frequency
50–	4	4
70–	6	10
90–	10	20
110–	12	32
130–	24	56
150–	25	81
170–190	2	83

Variety: Goliath

Weight (grams)	Frequency	Cumulative Frequency
50–	4	4
70–	8	12
90–	13	25
110–	9	34
130–	24	58
150–	15	73
170–	11	84
190–210	4	88

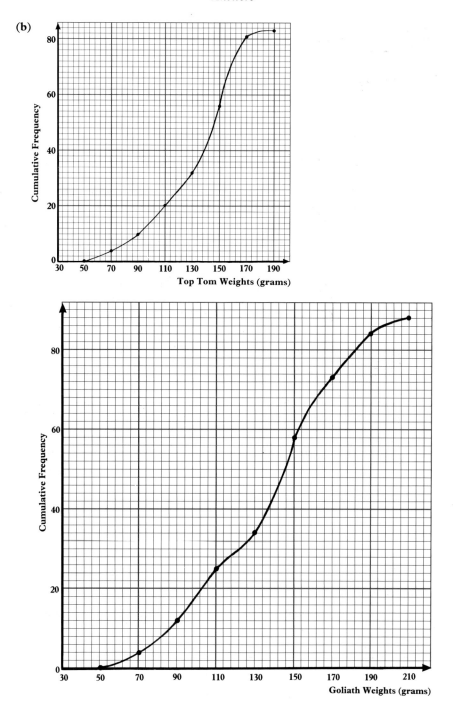

(b)

Top Tom Weights (grams)

Goliath Weights (grams)

(c) Top Tom: median = 140 g, lower quartile = 112 g, upper quartile =153 g, interquartile range = 41 g. Goliath: median = 140 g lower quartile = 106 g, upper quartile = 159 g, interquartile range = 53 g

Review 2 (a) 10   **(b)** 21   **(c)** 11   **(d)** 60   **(e)** 15 years   **(f)** lower quartile = 7·5 years, upper quartile = 26·5 years   **(g)** 19 years

Exercise 18:5

1. (a)

Price (£)	≤ 200	≤ 400	≤ 600	≤ 800	≤ 1000	≤ 1200	≤ 1400	≤ 1600
Cumulative Frequency	1	3	9	17	24	28	33	35

(b)

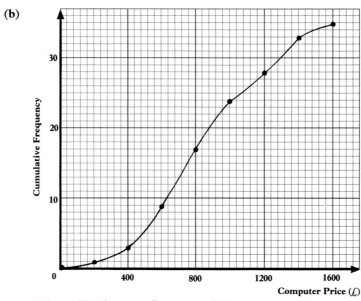

(c) median = £820, interquartile range = £530

2. (a)

Claim (£) at least	below	Number of claims	Cumulative Frequency
0	100	15	15
100	200	62	77
200	300	89	166
300	400	54	220
400	500	28	248

(b)

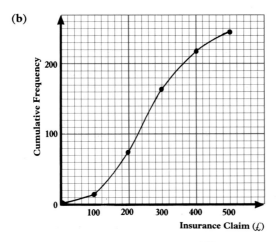

(c) median = £250   (d) £150   (e) 190

3. (a)

Mark range	≤ 10	≤ 20	≤ 30	≤ 40	≤ 50	≤ 60	≤ 70	≤ 80	≤ 90	≤ 100
Test A frequency	4	13	28	55	83	115	160	183	194	200
Test B frequency	7	17	41	70	104	142	173	191	198	200

(b)

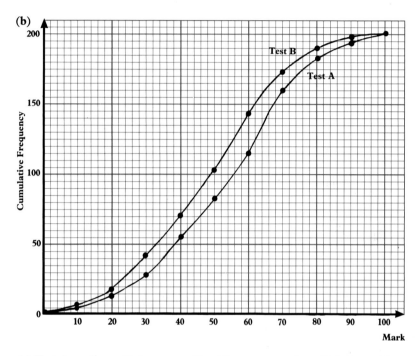

(c) Test A: median = 56, lower quartile = 39, upper quartile = 67, interquartile range = 28.
Test B: median = 49, lower quartile = 33, upper quartile = 62, interquartile range = 29
Review (a) median = 33, lower quartile = 22, upper quartile = 42, interquartile range = 20
(b)

Goals Scored	≤ 10	≤ 20	≤ 30	≤ 40	≤ 50
Cumulative frequency: School A	0	2	7	16	20

(c)

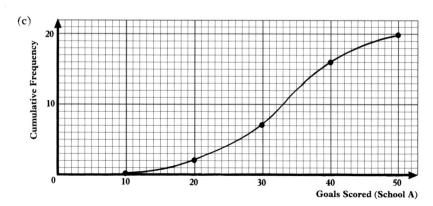

Chapter 19   Probability

Page 340   **Exercise 19:3**

1. (a) $\frac{1}{2}$ (b) $\frac{1}{4}$ 2. (a) $\frac{1}{3}$ (b) $\frac{1}{6}$ 3. $\frac{1}{18}$ 4. (a) $\frac{1}{5}$ (b) $\frac{1}{20}$ (c) $\frac{1}{10}$ 5. 0·045   6. 0·06

If they know each other the events are not independent and the probabilities cannot be multiplied.

7. (a) 0·2 (b) 0·03 (c) 0·68   8. (a) $\frac{3}{10}$ (b) $\frac{9}{100}$ 9. (a) $\frac{1}{25}$ (b) $\frac{4}{5}$ (c) $\frac{4}{25}$ (d) $\frac{8}{25}$

Review 1 (a) 0·15 (b) 0·04   If they know each other the events are not independent and the

probabilities cannot be multiplied.   Review 2 (a) $\frac{1}{4}$ (b) $\frac{1}{16}$ (c) $\frac{1}{8}$ (d) $\frac{3}{64}$ (e) $\frac{3}{32}$

Page 344   **Exercise 19:5**

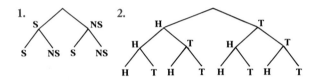

3. If O stands for open, C stands for closed, the possible outcomes are: OOO, OOC, OCO, OCC, COO, COC, CCO, CCC.

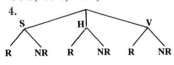   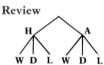

S – soccer H – hockey
V – volleyball R – represents school
NR – doesn't represent school

H – home A – away
W – win D – draw
L – lose

Page 347   **Exercise 19:6**

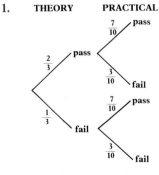

(a) $\frac{7}{15}$ (b) $\frac{1}{5}$ (c) $\frac{13}{30}$ (d) $\frac{1}{10}$

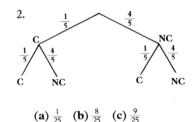

(a) $\frac{1}{25}$ (b) $\frac{8}{25}$ (c) $\frac{9}{25}$

3.

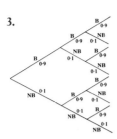

(a) 0·001 (b) 0·243 (c) 0·999

4. (i)

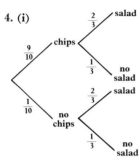

(a) $\frac{3}{5}$ (b) $\frac{1}{30}$ (c) $\frac{3}{10}$

(ii)

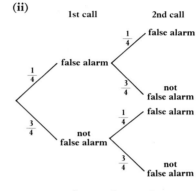

(a) $\frac{1}{16}$ (b) $\frac{9}{16}$ (c) $\frac{3}{8}$

(iii)

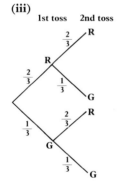

R - red   G - green

(a) $\frac{4}{9}$ (b) $\frac{4}{9}$ (c) $\frac{5}{9}$

5.

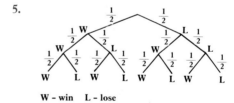

W - win   L - lose

(a) $\frac{1}{8}$ (b) $\frac{3}{8}$ (c) $\frac{3}{8}$ (d) $\frac{1}{2}$

6.

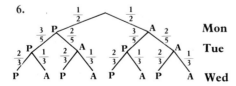

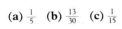

P - all present   A - someone absent

(a) $\frac{1}{5}$ (b) $\frac{13}{30}$ (c) $\frac{1}{15}$

Review 1

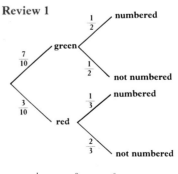

(a) $\frac{1}{10}$ (b) $\frac{9}{20}$ (c) $\frac{9}{20}$

Review 2

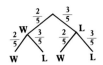

W – win   L – lose

P(wins only 1 game) = $\frac{12}{25}$

Review 3

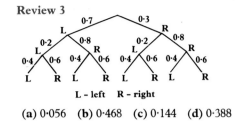

L – left   R – right

(**a**) 0·056   (**b**) 0·468   (**c**) 0·144   (**d**) 0·388

Chapter 20   Data Handling Review

Page 352

1. median = 21·5, range = 8, lower quartile = 20, upper quartile = 23·5, interquartile range = 3·5

2. (**a**) Yes   (**b**) No

3. 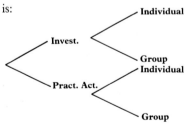   (**a**) $\frac{3}{10}$ (**b**) $\frac{3}{20}$

4. Possible questions and responses are:

   Are you left-handed?   Yes ☐   No ☐

   For how many hours did you play sport last week?

   less than 1 ☐   between 1 and 2 ☐   between 2 and 3 ☐   between 3 and 4 ☐   more than 4 ☐

5. $\frac{1}{12}$

6. a possible tree diagram is:

```
                          ┌─── Individual
              ┌── Invest.─┤
              │           └─── Group
    ──────────┤               Individual
              │           ┌───
              └── Pract. Act.┤
                          └─── Group
```

7. (**i**) (**a**)

Time (min)	Frequency	Cumulative Frequency
$0 \leq t < 5$	3	3
$5 \leq t < 10$	4	7
$10 \leq t < 15$	16	23
$15 \leq t < 20$	24	47
$20 \leq t < 25$	13	60
$25 \leq t < 30$	7	67

(**b**)

Mark for Test (%)	Frequency	Cumulative Frequency
1–20	2	2
21–40	5	7
41–60	9	16
61–80	7	23
81–100	4	27

(c)

Distance (km)	1·0–	1·5–	2·0–	2·5–	3·0–	3·5–	4·0–	4·5–5·0
Frequency	4	4	9	12	11	17	10	6
Cumulative Frequency	4	8	17	29	40	57	67	73

(ii) (a) (0, 0), (5, 3), (10, 7), (15, 23), (20, 47), (25, 60), (30, 67) **(b)** (0, 0), (20, 2), (40, 7), (60, 16), (80, 23), (100, 27) **(c)** (1·0, 0), (1·5, 4), (2·0, 8), (2·5, 17), (3·0, 29), (3·5, 40), (4·0, 57), (4·5, 67), (5·0, 73)

(iii)

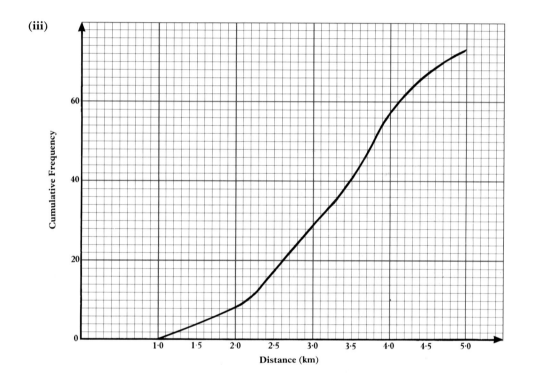

median = 3·35 m, interquartile range = 1·4 m

8. (a) $\frac{1}{5}$ **(b)** $\frac{2}{25}$ **(c)** $\frac{9}{25}$ **(d)** $\frac{12}{25}$

9. (a) 56 **(b)** 19 **(c)** 50 **(d)** 31 **(e)** 66 minutes **(f)** l.q. = 57 minutes, u.q. = 77 minutes **(g)** 20 minutes

10. (a)

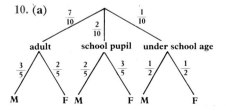

(b) $\frac{7}{25}$

11. (i) (a)

House Prices (£)			
Price Range		**Number of Houses**	**Cumulative Frequency**
at least	**below**		
20 000	40 000	5	5
40 000	60 000	8	13
60 000	80 000	15	28
80 000	100 000	14	42
100 000	120 000	24	66
120 000	140 000	16	82
140 000	160 000	9	91
160 000	180 000	3	94
180 000	200 000	2	96

(b)

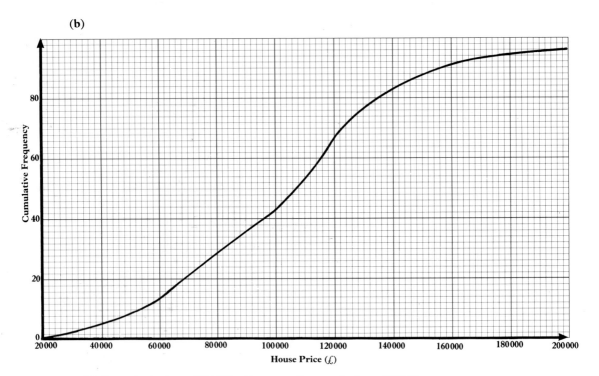

Median price is about £106 000   Interquartile range is about £50 000

(b) In David's district, median is about £92 000, l.q. is about £77 000, u.q. is about £110 000 interquartile range is about £33 000. These figures should be included in the comparison.

12. Conclusions such as the following could be made: There were 120 Year 11 students;

Comedy films were the least popular since only $\frac{30}{120}$ or 25% ranked these as the 1st or 2nd choice; etc.

13. (a) 0·003   **(b)** 0·873   **(c)** 0·124

14. Possible questions and responses are:

Which is your school year group? Year ☐   Year 8 ☐   Year 9 ☐   Year 10 ☐   Year 11 ☐

Which of the following do you think the shop should sell? (You may tick more than one.)

Pencils ☐   Pens ☐   Tipp-Ex ☐   Paper Clips ☐   Sellotape ☐   Drawing Pins ☐

Do you think you would buy from the shop? Yes ☐   No ☐   Not sure ☐

15. (a) $\frac{27}{1000}$ **(b)** $\frac{441}{1000}$ **(c)** $\frac{657}{1000}$ **(d)** $\frac{343}{1000}$